About the Author

AMY LICENCE is a late medieval and early Tudor historian focusing on women's lives. Her other books include *In Bed With the Tudors* ('A fascinating book examining the sex lives of the Tudors in unprecedented detail' *THE DAILY EXPRESS*), *Elizabeth of York: Forgotten Tudor Queen* and *Cecily Neville: Mother of Kings* ('This insight is so rare and so valuable' PHILIPPA GREGORY, 'Vivid, very readable, and wonderfully detailed' SARAH GRISTWOOD). She is currently writing a major new biography of Anne Boleyn, also for Amberley. She lives in Canterbury.

The Six Wives
&Many Mistresses of

Henry VIII

the
Women's
Stories

The Six Wives & Many Mistresses of Henry VIII

the Women's Stories

AMY LICENCE

AMBERLEY

for Tom, Robin and Rufus

This edition first published 2015

Amberley Publishing
The Hill, Stroud
Gloucestershire, GL5 4EP

www.amberley-books.com

British Library Cataloguing in Publication Data.
A catalogue record for this book is available from the British Library.

ISBN 978 1 4456 5052 4 (paperback)
ISBN 978 1 4456 3379 4 (ebook)

Typesetting and Origination by Amberley Publishing.
Printed in the UK.

Contents

The Six Wives and Many Mistresses?

Whoso na knoweth the strength, power, and might,
Of Venus and me her little son Cupid;
Thou Manhood shalt a mirrour been aright,
By us subdued for all thy great pride,
My fiery dart pierceth thy tender side.
Now thou who erst dispisedst children small
Shall wax a child again and be my thrall.[1]

This is not a biography of Henry VIII. The narrative of his life is already well known. It is the story of the women who shared his bed, as his legal wives or his mistresses, and explores their relationships in the context of the sexual and cultural mores of the day. Specifically, it focuses on what is known about the circumstances under which the king wooed them: the promises he made, the gifts he gave, the sweet nothings he whispered and how their lives changed as a result. It charts their status as fiancées, wives, queens and mothers, set against wider sixteenth-century notions of duty, religion, gender and class, and the places where their behaviour conformed to, and transgressed from, the definitions of these concepts.

In that sense, this is a collective biography overlapping a number of individual lives with that of the king. Yet while the focus is not always on Henry, he is the unavoidable common thread. His character, both as a king and a man, raises questions of power and its exercise, at the interface of his private and public roles. His relationships range from those that were opportunistic and temporary, conducted in the homes of his friends or during his absence from court; to his established mistresses, well known to his intimate circle; to the brides he led to the altar, whom he elevated to the status of queen and whose role was also a national and political one.

Henry VIII remains a controversial figure. He was also unique. Of course, he operated within the context of his times but, to state an obvious if often overlooked point, his personality was his own. Therefore it is not helpful to compare him to modern figures, or to apply modern psychological concepts or labels, or even to draw conclusions based on comparisons with his contemporary monarchs. Henry was a complex man, one of the most enigmatic and challenging to a historian, in spite of the wealth of contemporary sources documenting his life that survive. There is a mass of primary material about Henry, so much so that the question for the biographer becomes what to leave out, as well as what to include. However, this book is also composed with recognition of the multitude of crucial evidence that has been lost. And some of those silences are significant. Even when appearing at his most decisive, his most exuberant, extroverted and triumphant, Henry is also at his most elusive to the modern world, as demonstrated by the vast range of interpretations writers have placed upon his actions. Little wonder, then, that his private life continues to elude us. As always, then and now, like the inimitable signature image created by Holbein in 1537, Henry must stand alone.

This book challenges the long-standing view of the king as a lover. It is a frequently repeated statement that Henry VIII only had two mistresses – Elizabeth Blount and Mary Boleyn – and, indeed, beside his French peer, the sybaritic and syphilitic Francis I, his track record with women makes him appear demure, even restrained. He certainly had no official mistress in the way of the Valois king, although he did offer Anne Boleyn the role, which she refused. This widely held view persists because of the paucity of material that relates to his extra-marital affairs, but it may be an incorrect conclusion. While Francis paraded his conquests with pride, Henry was a deeply private man and preferred to keep his amours known only to a small, loyal core of companions: his closest friend, his chief minister, the attendants on his bodily needs and the guards who ensured his safety.

The popular image we have of Henry VIII, the private man, was created by default. We only know about his affair with Elizabeth Blount because she happened to become pregnant. Equally, the name of Mary Boleyn would have little significance had Henry not decided to marry her sister. As it is, the theory that Mary was Henry's mistress was not widely accepted until the nineteenth century, and even then it was challenged and dismissed as an attempt to slur the king's character. Without those two related facts, the image we would have of Henry today would be as an anachronistic shining example of marital fidelity, and we know this was not the case.

There is no question that Henry was very good at covering his tracks. So good, in fact, that he continues to throw us off the scent five centuries later. What happened late at night when the king was a guest in the properties of friends, or on royal progress, or abroad, would not necessarily have become general knowledge. The modern argument that something would have been whispered at the time if Henry had slept with more women runs counter to the many occasions of Tudor scandal known to scholars today for which no contemporary rumours survived. It underestimates the nature of surviving source material. It also underestimates the king and the world he inhabited. An early scandal at his court gave Henry a dislike for having his personal linen aired in public and his subsequent encounters were conducted in privacy. Carrying his own personal lock from palace to palace and restyling his privy chamber, as well as staying at the properties of sympathetic friends, he achieved a degree of privacy that ensured information about his amours was kept to a minimum. He was not able to eradicate it all, though.

Henry was a complex and multidimensional man, and there are many aspects of his reign and personality that do not feature in this story, except for where they have significance for a particular woman. It is beyond the scope of this book to follow him into Parliament, trace the impact of the Reformation, examine his relationships with his children or observe him as a diplomat. Consequently a one-sided account of Henry emerges, but this is a deliberate prioritisation in order to facilitate greater exploration of the man as a lover. The spotlight falls on his bedchamber, his bedclothes, on courtiers dressed in masks, on the keyholes, shadows and hidden corners of his palaces of pleasure. It exposes an unfamiliar figure lying behind the oft-repeated image of the prudish, restrained king, shedding light on an earthy, hungry, sexually voracious man who had ample resources to achieve his desires. This study also rejects the unrealistic notion that Henry abstained from sex while wooing Anne, from 1525 to the autumn of 1532. The notion of a delicate, prim and strait-laced king is belied by the cumulative weight of direct and indirect evidence about his sexual exploits. This is not an attempt to sensationalise this aspect of his life, but rather to study his wives and mistresses in the context of sixteenth-century sexuality and kingship. Henry was not quite 'of such slight morals that he slips readily into the gardens of others and drinks from the waters of many fountains', as Francis I was described, but he was no prude either. Perhaps the most telling comment about his extramarital activity comes from his own pen, when he offered to take Anne Boleyn as his only mistress, 'casting off all others besides you out of my thoughts and affections, and serve you only'. Who were all these others?

The power was almost always in Henry's hands. As an absolute king, he could dictate the terms of his sexual affairs and the nature of his marital relations. And he dictated all of them, even the ones where he allowed his lovers the illusion of control. That control was always his gift to them. This does not preclude a romantic reading of Henry's character, or the fact that he was capable of falling deeply in love; nor does it blame him for his actions or choices, or attempt to justify them. Henry could be tender, devoted and passionate, an ideal lover of the time, but ultimately he remained king, and that created an uneasy blend of mastery and obligation in and out of bed. Those who failed to facilitate his wishes when it came to his intimate relationships and politics were swiftly removed. Henry's greatest personal difficulties arose when his needs came into conflict with circumstances beyond his control, such as fertility, age or mortality. He was not a king who liked to be denied. He was prepared to change the centuries-old religious practices and identity of his country, reject the Pope, challenge canon law and risk his immortal soul by excommunication in order to achieve his aims. There is no question of Henry doing anything by halves.

In recent years, there has been much scholarly focus on the perceived changes in the king's character. The year 1536 has been identified as a significant turning point in the transformation of the most accomplished and beautiful young monarch in Christendom into the obese despot who sent friends and enemies alike to their deaths. Some historians have sought different catalysts, comparing pivotal moments in the king's life to find the origins of change. This provides too simple a solution to Henry's complex and evolving character, to his reluctance to face his own mortal limitations, which not even the resources of his entire court, his entire country, could alter. The seeds of the paranoid, defensive figure of his later years were already present in the young man. In fact, it was his gradual realisation that he was no longer that golden figure that allowed his petulant, despotic self to emerge. Yet the old man could still be as tender hearted and passionate as the youth, even if his health and corpulence would not allow him to play the nimble lover. His character is decisively revealed through a study of his sexual relationships as an evolving whole, rather than as a series of steps. His amours present a more gradual change, a fluctuating juxtaposition between his true nature and his reactions to circumstances when he felt out of control, but essentially a continuity, although exaggerated, of the same elements of his character.

Inevitably, the experience of being the wife or mistress of Henry VIII varied over time. In 1543, the husband Catherine Parr married against her better judgement and the wishes of her heart was hardly recognisable as the ardent young man who had jumped into bed with the curvaceous, auburn-haired Catherine of Aragon. At seventeen, Henry was tall, dazzlingly handsome, athletic, learned and fearless; he danced all night following long days of jousting, disguisings and banquets, capturing the attention of every woman in the room. He was used to getting what he wanted, and with age came the painful realisation that he commanded young women's attention because of his status rather than his person. This book presents a number of Henrys, just as it looks at a series of relationships. Even when these overlapped, the king was a different lover with each woman, according to the context and nature of the encounter. It is this book's aim to delineate the differences and highlight the similarities.

To this end, I have identified three key phases of Henry's intimate relationships, to better analyse the experience of his women.

Firstly, between 1509 and 1525, we see a youthful Henry, engaged in the quest for pleasure, jousting, dancing, feasting and indulging in a number of short-term flirtations and liaisons, some of which became sexual. The young king was a dazzling figure, believing himself the embodiment of the courtly love tradition, yet he was also very much a man of his times and his chivalric romanticism did not prevent him from sowing his wild oats. This period is commensurate with his first marriage to Catherine of Aragon, whose tenure as his wife was longer than those of all his other wives put together. They were well matched. Yet it is also the story of the disintegration of their relationship, which began passionately and cooled over time, although until 1525 Catherine was still secure in her position as queen and wife. These were Henry's 'green years'.

The second period, 1526 to 1537, is dominated by the king's desire for a son. Once Catherine had gone through the menopause Henry needed to look elsewhere for a legitimate heir, placing him under increasing pressure, an escalating desperation, to achieve dynastic security and prove his manhood. This is essentially a reactionary time for the king, as he struggled to control the unforeseen circumstances that not even his immense temporal power could alter. As the years passed and the legal separation from Catherine eluded him, he did not put his sexuality on hold. Until he married Anne Boleyn late in 1532 he continued his pursuit for physical satisfaction, although the extent to which this involved Anne is another question. Henry ultimately achieved his aim with the birth of his son by Jane Seymour in 1537, but he had turned his world upside-down in the process. These are the years of turmoil on almost every plane: religious, political and personal.

Finally, this work presents the years 1537 to 1547 as Henry's attempt to recreate the stability and happiness of a loving marriage, similar to that he had experienced with Catherine of Aragon in the early years. In his old age, he wanted a woman to share his bed and be at his side on public occasions; one who combined the breeding, looks and intelligence that would make her a suitable queen. However, as Henry discovered, you can't repeat the past. By 1537, he was no longer the man he had been and the reputation he had acquired as a 'dangerous' lover preceded him on the international stage. Frustratingly, the women he wanted didn't always want him, although some were still unable to refuse the proposals of the king. It might be accurate to consider this section the years of self-deception.

It has been essential to this work to allow Henry's women to occupy a percentage of the book that accurately reflects the duration and result of their connection with him. Therefore, the woman who features most frequently is Catherine of Aragon, his wife of over twenty years. Her life and Henry's were entwined long before their wedding day and well after their eventual separation. From 1488, when Catherine was first proposed as a bride for an English prince, to her death in 1536, she occupied a position in relation to Henry that was rarely simple in terms of their domestic life and her impact upon English history. Following her, Anne Boleyn's term of eleven years as the king's love was of equal importance on the national stage.

This triangle of Henry, Catherine and Anne has fascinated readers for centuries and will, no doubt, continue to do so. However, his other wives and mistresses have often been glossed over in traditional narratives as having less of an impact upon English history. This book rejects that approach. Instead, it seeks to understand the experiences of all the women wooed and won by Henry – or, rather, by a number of different Henrys – over the course of the years. They may have left less of a mark on national politics and shared his bed for less time but Henry was no less important to them as a result. The king may be the factor they have in common but the focus is firmly on them.

The question of evidence is also central to this book. No chronicler or ambassador followed Henry into his bedchamber and modern knowledge of his two known mistresses hangs upon accidents. The large amount of material relating to his wives reflects their public position; it should be unsurprising, then, that there is a veil of silence drawn over those whom Henry kept behind closed doors.

This secrecy was a personal and dynastic shield and was cultivated by the king in the same way that he manufactured his image in portraits and pageants. Early in his reign Henry learned of the need to choose his confidants carefully, and the extent to which Thomas Wolsey, a cardinal and papal legate, facilitated the arrival of Henry's illegitimate son shows how well the king was served. Also, by the late 1530s he had executed the majority of the rakish young men known as his 'minions', who were his early secret confidants, closing off another potential avenue of memoirs, letters and records. However, the amount of direct and suggestive evidence about his extramarital adventures – the anecdotes, scattered records and comments of his contemporaries – build a picture of a libidinous monarch whose personal sensitivity helped conceal much of his private behaviour. It would seem, after much research and reflection, that the title *The Six Wives and Many Mistresses* is an accurate representative of the king's love life. This is a reassessment of Henry the lover through the eyes of the women who shared his bed.

Yet with this blood of ours the blood of kings
Shall be co-mixed, and with their fame our fame
Shall be eternis'd in the mouths of men
        The Famous History of the Life and
        Death of Captain Thomas Stukeley

PART ONE
Catherine of Aragon

1

A Maid from Spain, 1485–1500

Not of adventure, but of free election
Ye toke this name, Kateryn, for very love and trust
Which name is regestered in the high court above
And, as I holpe you to Criste, your first mate,
So have I purveyd a second spouse trewe
But ye for him the first shalnot forsake[1]

On 15 December 1485, a baby girl was born in the Palace of Alcalá de Henares, just over twenty miles north of Madrid, in central Spain. It was the thirteenth-century seat of the local archbishop, fortified against the infidels, with thick walls of yellow stone and red brick fusing the best of Renaissance and Moorish design. Little of the building now survives, but it is likely to have been decorated in the ornate Mudéjar style of elegant white filigree carving, tile work and ornamental metals set around gracious courtyards. The air would have been thick with the scents of pine groves and olives, oranges, spices and incense. Long summers saw temperatures soar across that parched landscape, while winters could prove desperately cold.

Amid one such winter, with the palace fires blazing, the little girl arrived. Her mother, the thirty-four-year-old Isabella, Queen of Castile, was no stranger to the rigours and dangers of childbirth. She had already borne six children, four of whom had survived the process, but this daughter would be her last. Contemporary accounts portray the queen as paradoxically sweet and ruthless. Austrian humanist Jerónimo Münzer wrote that she was 'tall, somewhat chubby and of agreeable countenance'. She was devout, wise and 'constantly at the side of her husband', although her 'sweet disposition' was coupled with a warlike ferocity that underpinned her conflicts with the Portuguese, Jews and Moors. Her secretary, Hernando del Pulgar, described her as 'intelligent and discreet' and 'disposed to doing justice', pursuing the 'path of sternness rather than that of mercy'.[2] She had blue eyes and while Münzer described her hair as reddish, Juan de Mariana called it golden and commented that she 'wore no make-up', 'demonstrating a singular gravity, modesty and moderation'.[3]

Isabella had been married since the age of eighteen to her second cousin Ferdinand II of Aragon in a match which unified much of Spain. Yet she had been no mild, blushing bride. Before the ceremony, in 1469, the groom had agreed to a series of eight concessions initiated by his future wife, promising to maintain native customs in her kingdoms and respect her male relatives. Another clause related to their future offspring, whom he vowed to never remove from her or take out of their lands without her permission.[4] In 1492, Ferdinand was described as 'darkened through the labour of war', with 'long brown hair and his bread trimmed in the style of the time, with broad eyebrows, balding, with a small mouth, red lips, small and thin teeth, broad shoulders, a straight neck, a clear voice, quick of tongue, a clear mind, of grave and proper judgement, with a gentle and courteous manner and merciful towards those with whom he negotiated'.[5] He would play a key role, albeit a distant one, in his daughter's future career.

Isabella's labour progressed through the day and night of 16 December. Herbs and wine, prayers and religious icons would have been offered to help relieve her pain. She was stoical in suffering, though, one visitor to her court later reporting that 'neither when in pain through illness nor during the pains of childbirth ... did [her ladies] ever see her complain'.[6] The child was healthy. She was checked by the midwives and washed in a little brass basin before being handed to her mother. Isabella's treasurer, Gonzalo de Baeza, kept detailed records of the baby's early days, from the name of her first nurse, Elena de Carmona, to her christening by the Bishop of Palencia, when she wore a gown of white brocade lined with green velvet and edged in gold lace.[7] She may have been named after her English great-grandmother, Catherine of Lancaster, or Catalina in her native tongue. It was an early indication of the destiny they had in mind for her.

Just over a thousand miles to the north, Catherine's future homeland had recently undergone some dramatic changes. She had been conceived in mid-March 1485 but very soon after this, before Isabella may have even suspected her condition, England's brief stability began to unravel. News came of scandalous rumours at Richard III's court, followed by the death of Queen Anne and the threat of invasion to the realm. It was still a distant reality, though, for the pregnant Isabella. Throughout that summer she was preoccupied by her own war with Granada, travelling from Cordoba to Baena and Jaén in the south. It is likely that she stayed in the castle of Santa Catalina, originally an eighth-century Moorish palace, rebuilt with five towers and a chapel to the saint. It would have been around this time that she first felt her baby move, or quicken, and she may have given thanks at the altar there, suggesting an alternative source for the child's name. St Catherine, or Catalina in Spanish, had been a princess, a scholar and martyr to her faith, considered beautiful, dignified and intelligent. It was certainly a legacy that her namesake would live up to. Before Isabella left for Alcalá de Henares that September, news came from England of a major battle which had seen the defeat of the ruling House of York.

England's history over the last three decades had been turbulent. Tales of conflict and the betrayal of anointed kings would have been familiar to Isabella as a child, as ambassadors, merchants and visitors crossed the Channel and travelled south. In 1455, when she was only four, long-standing political tensions had erupted into bloodshed while England swung between the rule of the Yorkists and Lancastrians. Then, fighting between rival claimants had given way to treachery and treason between brothers. The last medieval king, Richard III, had declared his own nephews to be illegitimate and had taken the crown for himself in 1483. Yet his reign had been brief. That summer of 1485, an invasion force led by Henry Tudor, the half-nephew of the last Lancastrian king, had defeated and killed Richard at the Battle of Bosworth Field. A new regime had begun.

By the time Isabella had arrived at her lying-in place, Tudor had been crowned as Henry VII in Westminster Abbey. As a newcomer on the international stage, though, Henry's position was not yet secure and the recent rapid changes led the Spanish monarchs to display a degree of uncertainty, perhaps even scepticism. That November, when explorer Christopher Columbus captured four Venetian boats full of Spanish merchandise, Ferdinand and Isabella wrote from Alcalá de Henares requesting his arrest if he landed at an English port, but the name of the English king was omitted from the document in case things had changed again.[8] Henry VII, however, was not going anywhere. When baby Catherine was a month old he married Elizabeth of York, the daughter of Edward IV and descendant of the York Plantagenet line, and only eight months later she delivered a son, whom they named Arthur. This was Ferdinand and Isabella's chance. As early as March 1487, when Arthur was six months old, they approached Henry with the suggestion of marrying their youngest daughter to the new Tudor prince.

The man entrusted with the task was Dr Roderigo De Puebla, the first Spanish resident ambassador in England. On 30 April 1488 he received instructions to conclude a treaty between Catherine and Prince Arthur, then aged two and a half and eighteen months

respectively.[9] Henry VII responded from Windsor that July, congratulating the Spanish on their success against the Moors and hoping
'the friendship already existing between them will soon be rendered
stronger by the ties of blood'. The same day, De Puebla confirmed
that Catherine's marriage portion was expected to be 200,000 gold
scudos, with the value of one scudo being 4s 2d.[10] This made one
Spanish scudo slightly more than the average weekly wage for an
English labourer in the mid-fifteenth century, or the cost of eighty
eggs or six gallons of wine.[11] The contract was set out in the Treaty of
Medina del Campo, signed by Ferdinand and Isabella in March 1489
and ratified by Henry VII the following year.

With the initial arrangements made, the young pair settled down
to wait until they were old enough to live together as man and wife.
Certainly Arthur was too young to be aware of the situation, and
although young Catherine may have been informed, and was perhaps
even pleased to be a source of success to her parents, both families
were aware that many dynastic matches were made young and
broken before they were consummated. Arthur was invested as Prince
of Wales in 1490 and established in his own household at Ludlow,
where he embarked on his education under the supervision of three
successive tutors. In training for his future reign, the boy followed a
syllabus including history, poetry, classics, rhetoric, ethics, archery
and dancing. The years passed.

In the meantime, Catherine was being prepared for her role.
She was not only taught the traditional feminine accomplishments
of embroidery and dancing, but studied similar topics to Arthur,
including religion, canon and civic law. Her future mother-in-law,
Queen Elizabeth, advised her to take every opportunity to speak
French 'in order to learn the language and be able to converse in
it when she comes to England'. Additionally, she should learn to
drink wine, as 'the water of England is not drinkable, and even if it
were, the climate would not allow the drinking of it'.[12] As Catherine
reached a suitable marriageable age, her departure was delayed over
concerns about her mother's health, an outbreak of the plague and
fears over the influence of Yorkist pretenders challenging the Tudor
regime. The English urged Ferdinand and Isabella not to delay
sending their daughter, so that she could accustom herself to life in the
country she would one day rule over and they could begin the process
of moulding her according to English habits. The Spanish ambassador
to Scotland, Don Pedro de Ayala, had experience of the climate and
customs of the English court and wrote to confirm that Catherine
would suffer 'grave inconveniences' on account of the 'manner and

way of life of the people in this island' and it was better to send her at once, 'before she had learnt to appreciate our [Spanish] habits'.[13]

Technically, Catherine became Arthur's wife without leaving Spanish soil at all. On 12 March, the thirteen-year-old princess wrote to De Puebla in Latin, empowering him to 'repeat and re-enact, in her name, all he has concluded and done in respect to the said marriage'.[14] Her parents echoed her desire, stating that it was time to conclude the union as the papal dispensation had arrived from Rome.[15] The paperwork was required because both parties were still below the minimum legal age for marriage. At nine o'clock in the morning on 19 May 1499, after first Mass, a proxy ceremony was held in the chapel at Bewdley Palace in Worcestershire. Situated about twenty miles east of Ludlow, it had become a royal palace under the Yorkist king Edward IV, Arthur's maternal grandfather, and was used by the young prince when presiding over the Council of the Marches. Standing in for Catherine, De Puebla was well placed to record the details.

John Arundel, Bishop of Coventry and Lichfield, officiated at the ceremony. He explained to the groom that the process of declaration would make the union 'henceforth indissoluble'. The short, dark-haired boy, only twelve years old, replied 'in a loud and clear voice' that he 'was very much rejoiced to contract with Catherine, Princess of Wales ... from his deep and sincere love' for her.[16] De Puebla spoke Catherine's part, before joining hands with the prince on behalf of his 'lawful and undoubted wife'.[17] A second proxy ceremony was enacted at Ludlow that October, with De Puebla again taking the role of blushing bride at the Prince's side and then at the banquet that followed, where he was afforded more respect 'than he had ever before received in his life'.[18] After the ceremony, Arthur wrote to Catherine that he 'felt an earnest desire to see her' and begged that her departure might be hastened, as 'the delay respecting her coming is very grievous'. He entreated that he 'may often and speedily hear from her' and signed himself 'her loving spouse'.[19] It was a strange situation; a marriage with the bride and groom in separate countries, never having met. All that remained now was for Catherine to travel to England.

2

A Royal Welcome, 1501

Now fayre, fayrest of every fayre,
Princes most plesant and preclare,
The lustyest one alyve that byne,
Welcum of England to be Quene![1]

The arrangements had been made but still the princess lingered in Spain. A string of family losses, including her brother, sister and infant nephew, may have inclined Catherine's mother to retain her longer than was strictly necessary. Grieving for her losses, Isabella was loath to depart with her youngest daughter, in the knowledge that she faced a long and arduous journey, with no guarantees of any future reunion. Ultimately, though, she was committed to Catherine's role as future Queen of England. She wrote instructing De Puebla that she was honoured to hear of the preparations Henry had made for Catherine's arrival, but that she 'should not be the cause of any loss to England' and that 'the substantial part of the festival should be his love'.[2] Henry, however, misleadingly characterised by later historians as something of a miser, did not take her advice; that March he spent a glorious £14,000 on nuptial jewels, proving that could part with his money when the situation required it. When Catherine finally set foot on English soil, she found he had spared little expense on celebrations.

The journey was not easy. It took a long time for Catherine to reach the coast, pausing first to pray at the famous pilgrimage shrine of St James at Santiago de Compostela. Her fleet was delayed, then beaten back completely, by the inclement weather. Henry had sent a skilled pilot, Stephen Brett, to guide the Spanish fleet through the Bay of Biscay and around the tip of Brittany.[3] Even he could do little to prevent the terrible storms they encountered and, having been blown off course to Southampton, which was considered the safest port, Catherine arrived at Portsmouth on Saturday 2 October 1501. The unsuspecting citizens turned out in an impromptu welcome to see the young princess and her exotic entourage disembark to the clamour of church bells. Among them were a number of Africans, or 'moors', who excited much attention as the first recorded in England since the Roman period. On her long journey to London through the wet English autumn, Catherine had her first taste of her adoptive country, with its rolling fields, woodlands and villages clustered around perpendicular churches.

There was a brief, bashful meeting with her young husband-to-be when she reached Dogmersfield in Hampshire. At first Catherine resisted, citing protocol, even taking to her bed, but Henry insisted and she had little choice but to capitulate. Until that point she had known Arthur only through his letters, a set of fairly formal Latin missives deploying the usual conventions of anticipation and an artificial sort of intimacy. His father ushered him in from the rain to meet her; a real boy of flesh and blood instead of a mere signature at the end of a piece of paper. She was shy but he was gentle, a dark-haired, thin youth, half a head shorter than her, with the hooded eyes and beaked nose of his father. With the help of the bishops they conversed in a sort of Latin, renewing the vows they had previously made in separate countries. Catherine summoned her minstrels and watched as he danced 'right pleasant and honourably',[4] wondering what her life would be like with this slender, serious young man who was due to inherit the Tudor throne.

Waiting for Catherine at Kingston-on-Thames, about thirteen miles south-west of Westminster, was her guide for the final leg of the journey. This was her first meeting with the future Henry VIII. Arthur's younger brother was Duke of York, a sturdy and golden-haired boy of ten, reputedly as gregarious and energetic as his brother was serious and reflective. He conducted Catherine along the south bank of the Thames, conversing with her in Latin,[5] before their arrival at London Bridge, where the spectacle began. The author of the *Receyt of the Ladie Kateryne* recorded her arrival in considerable detail, including verses stating how she had adopted an English name in honour of her new country. Catalina had become Catherine.[6] Twelve pageants with special effects depicted astrological, historical and natural images; in one, the moon and sun passed through their spheres by the efforts of men on treadmills behind the scenes. St Catherine in her wheel and St Ursula smiled down on her from temporary scaffolds, although the infanta's English was not good enough for her to understand their words of welcome. They were framed by blue and red tissue curtains, walls painted with flowers and pillars topped with the three-feather motif of the Prince of Wales, Lancastrian red roses and Beaufort portcullises.[7] There were virgins, angels and saints; bulls, greyhounds and lions; dragons and centaurs, serpents and mermaids. The conduits ran with free wine. Trumpets, shawms and sackbuts made 'heavenly noise', children sang and officials greeted her, dressed in 'rich jewels and massy chains' and riding horses that sparkled with gold bells.[8]

The welcome lasted all the way from London Bridge to Gracechurch Street, through Cornhill, Cheapside, the Standard at Chepe, on to her lodgings in the Bishop's Palace, near St Paul's. King Henry observed her arrival from the home of a merchant named Whiting, 'not in very opyn sight',[9] along with his mother, queen and eldest son. His presence was meant to be a secret but the many Yeomen of the Guard positioned at the windows, leads and gutters and in the street below indicated his choice. The Privy Accounts list that Whiting received £6 13s and 4d for the occupation of his house. Catherine rode past 'upon a great mule, richly trapped after the manner of Spain' with Henry, Duke of York, on her right and the papal legate of Spain on her left. Her 'fair auburn' hair hung down past her shoulders, loose under the cap she wore, held in place by a gold ribbon.[10] According to the Tudor chronicler Edward Hall, the streets were hung with velvet, satin, silk and tapestries, the roads themselves gravelled and railed off. Watching the procession was a twenty-three-year-old student of Lincoln's Inn named Sir Thomas More, who wrote that Catherine 'possessed all the qualities that make for beauty in a very charming young girl', and hoped that the 'highly publicised union [would] prove a happy omen for England'.[11] Her young guide conducted her safely to St Paul's, where she made an offering to St Erkenwald, then on to her lodgings in the Bishop's Palace.

There was no doubt in anyone's mind about the attractiveness of the diminutive princess. Concepts of beauty vary across location and time but, for the late medieval mind, they were particularly associated with the outward manifestation of health and fertility. In the summer of 1505, when Henry VII asked his ambassadors to report on the appearance of Queen Joan of Naples, his detailed instructions give a good picture of what was considered desirable among Catherine's contemporaries. Joan's face was considered pleasing, as it was unpainted, 'amiable, round and fat', her skin was reported as clear and her complexion was 'fair, sanguine and clean'. Her teeth were described as 'fair, clean and well set', her brows were 'like a wire of brown hair' and her lips 'somewhat round and full', with no discernible hair growing on them. In attempting to get close to her person, they 'never felt any savour of spices, and believe her to be of a sweet savour'. Critical for the creation of heirs, her figure was assessed at 'somewhat round' and 'not of high stature', with her breasts 'somewhat great and full and trussed somewhat high'. Her limbs were in good proportion, arms round and large, her neck 'full and comely', her hands 'full and soft' and her fingers 'right fair and small, and of a meetly length and breadth'.[12] The teenaged Catherine, with her petite, plump figure and regal colouring, did not disappoint the English.

The afternoon before her wedding Catherine made the short trip to Baynard's Castle, a huge, fortified royal palace on the riverbank practically next to St Paul's. Waiting for her there was her future mother-in-law, Elizabeth of York, the beautiful Plantagenet princess Henry VII had taken as his queen after defeating her uncle at the Battle of Bosworth. Now the mother of six children, Elizabeth welcomed the young woman, called for musicians and spent the afternoon with her in 'pleasure and goodly communication, dancing and disports'. Perhaps, on the eve of her wedding day, the queen imparted some motherly advice to Catherine regarding what she might expect. As the youngest daughter of a large family, with married elder sisters, Catherine was probably not naïve about the duties of a wife. The physical proximity suggested by royal architecture, the nature of the lying-in process, behavioural manuals and references in popular culture suggest that the sixteenth century was less squeamish about sex than a modern reader might expect. It also seems likely that Isabella would have seen this as her remit before her daughter departed Spanish shores. It may be that Catherine was fully aware of what lay ahead in the marital bedroom. Or, rather, what was supposed to lie ahead.

3

Marrying Arthur, 1501

When we shall make our wedding feast,
There shall be cheer for man and beast;
I mun be married a Sunday.[1]

The following morning, Sunday 14 November 1501, Catherine rose and said her prayers. No doubt she gave thanks that the match her parents had been planning since she was three years old was about to take place. As a devout Catholic and dutiful daughter, she would have remembered Ferdinand and Isabella and those she had recently left behind in the parched lands of sunny Spain. It was also the day of St Erkenwald, the Anglo-Saxon Bishop of London, at whose Westminster shrine she had left offerings only days before. Perhaps she also prayed for the health of the prince of this foreign land, whose language and customs seemed so strange to her, along with her new

English family and homeland. Her welcome had been rapturous, the people enthused by her regal bearing, her beauty and Plantagenet descent. It was a good start: one day she would be their queen.

Catherine's retinue of Spanish ladies bustled about her that morning, led by the formidable Dona Elvira Manuel, 'first Lady of Honour and first Lady of the Bedchamber', to whose care her mother had specifically trusted her. She laced Catherine into a wide Spanish petticoat stiffened with young, pliable green wood, which fell in a huge sweeping circle about her ankles. This would be the first time that Catherine's future subjects saw a woman dressed in a 'vertu-gardo', which would later come to be known as a farthingale. In the cathedral it would cause a sensation. However, for a decade or so the reaction was more bemusement than emulation among the conservative English, with their rigorous sumptuary laws. Over the top of the petticoat the Spanish ladies pulled a white silk dress, decorated on the bodice and sleeves with large pleats. Catherine's head was covered with a silk veil, hanging down as low as her waist, weighed down by the inch-and-a-half-wide strip of pearls, gems and gold that decorated its borders. The *Receyt*'s author considered it to be most like 'unto menys clothing'.[2]

When Catherine emerged in her bejewelled finery, Prince Henry was waiting. His role was to conduct her into St Paul's Cathedral and give her away, in place of her absent father. Like his elder brother, Henry wore a suit of spotless white velvet and gold that must have dazzled onlookers. Perhaps in later years some would remember the younger boy's clothing, making an unusual visual trio of bride, groom and brother. The occasion had been designed as nothing less than a deliberate piece of theatre to establish the young couple as dynastic heirs and future monarchs in the minds of the congregation. The traditional royal wedding location of Westminster had been rejected in favour of St Paul's, in order to maximise the size of the congregation witnessing this historic event. Henry VII, along with his wife and mother, had retreated to watch the ceremony from behind a screen so as not to overshadow the pair in terms of status. Everything proclaimed that England's future lay with these young people. His job done, for the time being, Prince Henry stepped back.

Hand in hand, Catherine and Arthur mounted a specially built platform. Over a metre and a half from the ground and twelve feet wide, it allowed them to parade along its red worsted surface at eye level, ensuring maximum impact. The *Receyt* refers to it as a levy, or timber bridge, resting on wooden pillars, stretching for the entire length of the cathedral (around 600 feet long), with steps to ascend and descend. It also included a round stage where the ceremony was conducted.[3] One chronicler commented that they made a 'lusty and amorous' couple. They turned to face the crowds, to the north and south, displaying themselves to the sound of cheering. Resplendent in their nuptial whiteness, on a level with the statues and icons of the cathedral, and full of youth, they must have seemed the embodiment of the infant sixteenth century.

After the ceremony Arthur stood aside in order to conduct the formal business of paperwork, allowing Henry to take his sister-in-law by the arm. He escorted Catherine back along the platform to the wedding feast in the Bishop's Palace, where trumpeters greeted their arrival and the walls were hung with expensive cloth of arras. She was served with four courses of 'the moost delecat deynties and curious mets' from 'the hool realm of Englond'.[4] The 1501 wedding menu does not survive but those dishes served to Archbishop William Warham at his enthronement at Canterbury in 1503 may give some idea of the kind of luxury fare enjoyed by the young couple. Warham's ceremony fell on a fish day, when he was presented with sturgeon and whelks in foil, roast eels and carp in a sharp sauce. Sweet dishes included florentine cream, honey tart, baked quince and orange, apple fritters and royal custard followed by comfits, sugar plate and hippocras to drink.[5]

The food and its service were designed to display the royal wealth to the full. Arthur and Catherine would have been honoured by the creation of subtleties, sculptured in marzipan, of allegorical, historical and religious figures. Warham's table had been graced by one design featuring a king seated on a throne, surrounded by kneeling knights and flanked by two gentlemen on horseback. A second design centred on St Eustace kneeling in a park under a great tree of roses, with a white hart bearing a crucifix between its horns. Another featured King Ethelred being taught about Christianity by St Augustine, all the figures being made of marzipan.[6] The subtleties for Arthur and Catherine's wedding would have featured symbols of their dynasties and relevant saints. In 1501, observer Walter Ogilvie noticed the 'jewel-encrusted goblets' and 'dishes of purest gold' on display in the cupboards to dazzle the guests. After the feast, young Henry danced with his elder sister, Margaret, casting off his jacket in a gesture of impulsive confidence. There were disguisings and interludes, one featuring an arbour with a gate that was rotated before the king, another made in the shape of a large circle, covered in fine lawn and lit from the inside by over a hundred lights. Ladies danced inside, showing up as shadows within.[7]

The celebrations lasted five hours, after which the party shifted to Baynard's Castle. There the marital bed chamber was ceremonially prepared according to custom and scattered with drops of holy water. The bed itself had been carefully chosen, with rich hangings and furnishings fit for a future king and queen. Typically they might have been made from velvet and silk, in strong colours like red, black, green and blue, with panels of cloth of gold and silver. These were often fringed with taffeta and ribbon and heavily embroidered with floral and dynastic motifs, or coats of arms. When Arthur's grandmother, Cecily Neville, died in 1495, she had bequeathed him a set of bed hangings decorated with the image of the wheel of fortune; perhaps these were used on this occasion, with their poignant reminder about the brevity of life. In readiness, the sheets were smoothed and pillows plumped. The Lord Chamberlain, John de Vere, Earl of Oxford, had the job of testing the bed, lying on both sides to ensure there was no weapon or spike secreted among the bedclothes.

Undressed by her ladies, Catherine was 'reverently laid and reposed' as Arthur's gentlemen led him to her side.[8] The consummation of a match was the final stage of the process, essential in religious and legal eyes to validate the union and prevent later annulment; in 1469, Isabella's bloodstained bedsheets had been displayed after her first night with Ferdinand as proof that intercourse had taken place. Although the English did not go this far, some act of intimacy was required to satisfy and dispel the onlookers who accompanied the newlyweds into the chamber, with their advice and blessings, bawdy jokes and music. First the bride and groom partook of the wine and spices designed to fortify them through the night, warm the constitution and sweeten the breath. Then, as in the case of Arthur's sister Mary thirteen years later, they may have been required to touch skin as a symbol of the act to come. This was usually a quick, shy contact of bare legs, before the chamber doors were closed and the young couple were left alone. Writing in the 1540s, when it was politic to believe in the consummation of the match, Edward Hall wrote that 'this lusty prince and his beautifull bride were brought and ioyned together in one bed naked, and there dyd that acte, whiche to the performaunce and full consummacion of matrimony was moost requisite and expedient'.[9] However, only two people knew what really happened on that night.

Presumably the young couple knew what was expected of them. Lying between their perfumed sheets, listening to the roar of the fire and the receding footsteps of the court, it was the first time they had been alone together. Arthur had just turned fifteen, and Catherine was nine months older. Neither had any intimate experience with the opposite sex and Arthur's diminutive height might indicate he had not yet experienced the growth spurt of puberty that led his grandfather, father and brother to be above average height. Communication was difficult, as Catherine's English would remain poor for years and they had already discovered that their common language, Latin, sounded almost unrecognisable when pronounced in a foreign tongue. Equally, neither of them would have realised that any urgency was required. Hindsight informs us that the clock was ticking but, at the time, the two would have considered themselves at the start of a lifelong partnership. There was no hurry. Perhaps, exhausted after the days of ceremony, they simply fell into a welcome sleep. It may even be that, 14 November falling on a Sunday (also a major Saint's day), the Catholic pair bowed to strict canonical teaching regarding abstinence on the Sabbath. It is possible that Catherine may have been disappointed, or equally she may have felt relieved. Arthur's boast to his gentlemen the next morning, about being in the midst of Spain, may have owed more to bravado than experience.

Ten days of disguisings, dancing and other entertainments followed. A few days later, as part of the jousting, the pageant of a 'goodly ship' appeared outside Westminster Palace, full of sailors firing serpentines and other guns.[10] On another occasion, a chariot of cloth of gold was pulled by four marvellous 'beasts': a red lion, a white lion, a white hart with gilt horns and an ibex, although the author of the Receyt noticed that the legs of two men operating each creature were visible below.[11] Later, a pageant of mountains was created in Westminster Hall. The first was green and planted with 'fresh' olive, laurel, orange and fir trees, as well as herbs, flowers and fruit, so it was a 'great delite ... to behold'. The second mountain was like a dark rock, scorched and burned in the sun, studded with 'ors of sundry metals', including gold, silver, lead, copper, with crystal and amber 'subtly pictured and painted', all drawn along on gold chains. Both disgorged people in costume, who danced to the tabor, harp and recorder.[12]

Eventually the party relocated to the king's new palace at Richmond, a fantasia of fruit-filled gardens, octagonal turrets and fountains in marble-lined courtyards.[13] The days were given over to pleasure, with tennis courts, archery butts and a bowling alley and games of chess, cards and dice. A Spanish tightrope walker juggled with swords and hung by his toes and teeth, while a 'man-mermaid' adorned a two-storied pageant. Henry led a great hunt in Richmond Park, where the 'th'Erl of Hispayne strake a dere with his crossbow' and the slaughtered creatures were given to the Spanish guests to eat.[14] When the time came for Catherine's retinue to depart, on 29 November, Henry alleviated her sorrow by offering her a choice from a display of rich gems, although he was privately fuming that the second half of her dowry remained unpaid.[15] The next day, Arthur wrote to Ferdinand and Isabella from the palace that he 'had never felt so much joy in his life as when he beheld the sweet face of his bride. No woman in the world could be more agreeable to him.' He promised to be a good husband.[16] King Henry also wrote that their 'beloved daughter' had found a 'second father who will ever watch over her happiness and never permit her to want anything'.[17] As it turned out, neither Tudor would keep their promise.

4

Ludlow, 1502

The harbinger of death
To me I see him ride
The cough, the cold, the gasping breath,
Doth bid me provide
A pickaxe and a spade
And eke a shrouding sheet
A house of clay for to be made
For such a guest so meet.[1]

Whatever had happened on their wedding night, Catherine and Arthur were now man and wife, yet Henry had doubts about whether they should live together at once. The initial plan, reported to Ferdinand and Isabella by Gutierre Gómez de Fuensalida, was for consummation to take place to seal the match, followed by two or three years of separation.[2] This was confirmed by Pedro de Ayala, who was summoned by Henry at the end of November in order to discuss the matter. According to the Spaniard, the king was reluctant to act 'except in accordance with her wishes', a phrase that Catherine shrewdly echoed back when asked for her opinion. Henry's councillors were divided over the consummation, with some saying 'it would be good for the princess to go to Wales, and others saying no'.[3] It seems that the pair were considered too young, and that Catherine would have been too isolated in Ludlow given that Arthur's administrative commitments would require him to travel and leave her for long periods of time. Henry asked 'the prince to use his influence with the princess' to make her declare she would rather depart with him. Catherine stuck to her guns, though, with the single-mindedness and politic use of formality that would later characterise her dealings with Henry VIII, and insisted that she had no other will than Henry's and would be content with whatever he decided.[4]

Sixteenth-century medical opinion was divided over the merits of teenage sex. While many aristocratic marriages were forged before the children came of age, and required consummation in order to be legal, paradoxically, the pair was often permitted to spend the wedding night together then abstain for several years for the sake of their health. Sex was generally thought to be beneficial in physical and emotional terms, and the denial of natural urges was believed to foster wasting illnesses or lead to suffocation in accumulated reproductive fluids, but the timing was crucial. Too much too soon was considered highly dangerous. The love match of Catherine's brother John, Prince of Asturias, and Margaret of Austria had lasted only six months in 1497, with contemporaries citing their overenthusiastic lovemaking as the cause of his decline. Two months into the marriage, observer Martire wrote that John was 'consumed with passion' and was looking pale. His doctors urged him to 'seek a respite in the incessant acts of love' and warned that his increasing weakness was compromising his health.[5] He died at the age of nineteen. Perhaps with this in mind, Ayala agreed it would be better to retain Catherine in London while Arthur returned to Ludlow, 'especially because the prince and the princess would more easily bear being separated and [their abstinence from] intercourse if she remained with him and the queen, who could alleviate her sorrow for being separated from the prince, a thing which it would be much more difficult to bear if she were to live in his house in Wales, adding many other reasons which the king himself had given me only a few days before for retaining the Princess during the next two years near his person'.[6] In the end, though, he was overruled and the opposite decision was taken. Later, these concerns would come back to haunt the king.

The days dragged on and the young pair remained at court through December. They celebrated the feasts of St Andrew and St Nicholas, then that of St John the Evangelist, with prayer, offerings and feasting. Perhaps they amused themselves with cards, chess and dice, of which the king was fond but not too good, frequently losing, according to his accounts, although Prince Henry's gambling expenses were greater. The records also contain payments for dancing, players and the 'setting' of the royal clavichord. Henry paid the £2 wages of

Catherine's 'stryngmynstrels' at Westminster on 4 December, as well as making other payments to members of her entourage. The 'mores', or Morris or Mooresque, dancers that were given £1 13s in payment may have arrived in England with Catherine; she certainly brought her own African musician, John Blak or Blanke, who remained in England for at least a decade and is depicted wearing a turban in the Westminster Tournament Roll. Her exotic attendants, so different in appearance to their English hosts, would have excited attention at a court where those of unusual physical appearance were retained by way of curiosities. Another visitor at court that season was the Scottish poet William Dunbar, who received a payment of £2 from Henry.[7] His poem 'Of a Black Moor', or 'My ladye with the mekle [large] lips' may well have been inspired by a member in Catherine's entourage.

Catherine's sixteenth birthday came and went. Then, the decision having been made by Henry, with 'show of great sorrow', the prince and princess left London together on 21 December. Catherine caught her first glimpse of Ludlow Castle, on the Welsh borders, just before the year came to a close. It was a solid eleventh-century edifice, built adjoining the town on a high point overlooking the River Teme, a defensive and administrative position on the border between England and Wales. In the inner bailey stood a round chapel dedicated to Mary Magdalene and fifteenth-century renovations had added new floor levels and larger windows in the keep. It had been home to Arthur's lost Yorkist uncle, the elder of the Princes in the Tower, during his youth in the 1470s and 1480s. There, the future Edward V had been trained in the arts of kingship, much as Arthur had been.

They had arrived at the bleakest time of year. The household would have been prepared for their arrival, with clean rushes on the floor and fires lit against the inclement weather. Sitting upon a rocky promontory overlooking the surrounding countryside, the castle had little shelter from the extremes of the winter. Catherine may even have arrived before her belongings. On 18 February, a man named John Wint was paid 10s for transporting the 'Princesse stuff' from Plymouth to Ludlow, although payments typically showed up weeks or months after the recipient had petitioned for them.[8] After the crowds and luxury of the Westminster Court and the dazzling modern beauty of Richmond, Catherine must have found Ludlow life fairly basic, even lonely.

Although the majority of her Spanish retinue had been dismissed back in November, Catherine retained a core of ladies about her from her home. She must have derived the most comfort from the presence of her compatriot women, including the teenaged Maria de Rojas, daughter of the Count de Salinas, who is not to be confused with Maria de Salinas, who took her place in 1503/04. Also among her entourage were Inez or Agnes Venegas, Kateryn Montoya or Mountoria, Maria and Kateryn de Gavara, Katerina Fortes and the wife of John de Quero. Still struggling with English, Catherine must have sought refuge among these familiar faces.

It was during this time that Catherine's lifelong friendship with Margaret Pole began. The daughter of George, Duke of Clarence, and sister of the Earl of Warwick, executed for treason in 1499, Margaret was a reminder of the old Yorkist regime. Aged twenty-eight and already the mother of three children, she became one of Catherine's ladies-in-waiting, while her husband was Arthur's chamberlain. Religious, intelligent and educated, she would later be a patron of Erasmus and was a suitable motherly figure to support the new princess in her role as a future English queen, in a way that her Spanish Dona Elvira could not. Also present in her household were members of the Blount family, with the young couple Sir John and the 'remarkable and forthright' Lady Catherine, of nearby Kinlet, being frequent visitors. The pair were probably in their early twenties[9] and had been married at the Yorkist manor of Bewdley, or Tickenhill, now in Arthur's possession and a frequent destination for his role in administering local justice. With Kinlet lying fifteen miles to the east of Ludlow, and just five miles north-west of Bewdley, it is likely that the Blounts were the closest aristocratic neighbours to be suitable companions to the princess. Catherine may have met their infant daughter, the golden-haired and blue-eyed Bessie; perhaps she imagined herself soon becoming the mother of a young family.

Catherine probably spent most of her time with her ladies. Her young husband was frequently engaged in the administrative duties that had accumulated during his absence; a diminutive boy-man, thin, frail and standing less than five feet tall, riding off to preside over the Council of the Marches. Typical of royal households, Catherine and Arthur had distinct spheres within the house, physically separated by occupying the different suites of rooms befitting their status. This created a gender division among their staff. Arthur's establishment was headed by Richard Pole, with John Arundel as chancellor and Richard Crofte as steward, while their female relations formed Catherine's circle. The one figure who united them may have been John Nele, the dean of their chapel. Not all meals were taken together, with some households eating in separate chambers and only coming together for the celebration of key calendar dates. Catherine later reported that they kept to their separate bedrooms, only sharing a bed on seven nights in the entirety of their marriage.[10]

There was little opportunity for the marriage to get established before it was over. By many accounts the weather remained terrible and, based on the letters sent by Catherine and Dona Elvira Manuel, Isabella christened it 'that unhealthy place'.[11] In spite of this, according to the *Receyt*, Arthur continued 'upholdyng and defendyng the pore ... repressing malice and unlawful disposicion, amplifying and increasing the laws, and the service of Almighti God'.[12] His tenure was brief, 'from the Fest of the Natyvite of Criste ... unto the solempne Fest of the Resurrection'.[13]

Less than five months after their wedding, at the end of March 1502, Arthur and Catherine both fell ill. The sweating sickness had been raging in the local area, causing fever, burning thirst and rapid death. While she recovered, he worsened. The epidemic may have been the catalyst that complicated an underlying weakness in Arthur, perhaps pulmonary or testicular tuberculosis. Catherine's doctor diagnosed his condition as 'tisis', or 'phthisis', a general term for a wasting condition, which could include many possible diseases. This 'lamentable and ... moost pettiful ... sikeness'[14] claimed his life on 2 April 1502. Having believed herself destined to be Queen of England since she was three years old, Catherine found herself a widow.

5

The Young Widow, 1502–03

Brittle beauty, that Nature made so frail,
Whereof the gift is small, and short the season;
Flowering to-day, to-morrow apt to fail.[1]

Spring arrived at Ludlow, but it did not bring the usual joy associated with it by medieval poets. It took several weeks for Catherine to recover from her illness, breathing out 'bad humours' and pained by the terrible news brought to her on her sickbed. She was isolated in her Ludlow chamber with just her immediate household for company, dependent on her women and servants for news of the outside world. Her French-born apothecary, John de Soda, or Soto, who had accompanied her from Spain, would have prepared various medicines and treatments to aid her recovery.

Catherine's young husband was interred in Worcester Cathedral during her illness, with the members of his household lining up to symbolically break their white staves of office and cast the pieces into his tomb. The under-treasurer was reimbursed £566 by the king, but Catherine would have been unaware of the splendid carvings and ceremony that had been made in his honour. Even if she had been well, it was not customary for spouses to attend funerals and she was honourably represented by two Spanish gentlemen, perhaps including her chamberlain, Dona Elvira's husband. There was another dynastic reason for her seclusion, too.

The eyes of the court were turned in Catherine's direction in expectation. It was customary, on the death of a married prince, to wait and see whether or not his wife was pregnant, regardless of the nature of their intimate relationship. The arrival of a posthumous heir, as Catherine's family knew all too well, could significantly change the line of succession. Only five years previously, when her elder brother John, Prince of Asturias, died at the age of eighteen, his wife Margaret was pregnant, although her child was stillborn in December 1497. If Catherine had conceived, she would be carrying the next heir to the throne and her future would be secure. No doubt her Spanish ladies blushed as they were asked questions about her health and laundry, but they could not conjure up a baby out of thin air. Nor could Catherine.

Mistakes could easily be made when it came to women's bodies in the sixteenth century. The diagnosis of pregnancy was an imprecise science and the symptoms of other common illnesses could easily be mistaken for the usual indications that conception had taken place. In some cases, even experienced women were not certain of their condition until the first foetal movements took place, in the middle of the second trimester. Catherine's doctors would have needed to be especially careful as her recent illness, with its accompanying sweats and dizziness, may have masked any signs that she was carrying a child. The delay in granting Henry the role of Prince of Wales was to ensure that there would be no male offspring of Arthur's to claim the title. It was finally conferred on him on 22 June, almost three months after Arthur's death, although his formal investiture would not take place until 1503. By that time, there was no question of an infant prince.

But Catherine already knew that. Such a custom rested on the assumption that she and Arthur had consummated their marriage. With such private information remaining behind closed doors, the observation of the princess was a sensible political precaution, based on the balance of possibilities. However, only the princess herself would have known without question whether there was any likelihood that she may have conceived a child. In spite of the adolescent Arthur's boast on the morning after his wedding that he was thirsty as he had been 'in the midst of Spain' all night, Catherine's women reported how she had been subdued the following morning. It was later claimed by one of Arthur's officials, Maurice St John, that relations between the prince and princess had led to a decline in Arthur's health. Stating that they had lain together at Shrovetide, St John said the prince 'began to decay and was never so lusty in body and courage until his death',[2] directly relating this to the consummation of the marriage. However, Catherine would later describe how, in all their four and a half months of marriage, the pair had only shared a bed on seven occasions, and at no time had Arthur 'known her'. In fact, she remained 'as intact and incorrupt as when she emerged from her mother's womb'.[3]

However, the question arises of just how well informed Catherine was about sex and the nature of consummation. Her later misreading of her own body in 1510 demonstrates a surprising naivety about the reproductive process, and even though she may have understood the concept in theory, the practice may have been a very different matter. Incredible as it may seem to a modern reader, it is possible that an inexperienced Catherine was herself unsure of exactly what had happened. Assuming Arthur had attempted to consummate the marriage, his teenage fumblings may have met with limited success. He may have not yet reached puberty or, as some historians speculate, he may have been suffering from testicular tuberculosis, or a similar condition that hindered his performance, but this does not mean he did not try. Nor is it clear exactly what constitutes consummation. Arthur's comment suggested it did occur, while Catherine refuted it completely. It is possible that they were both correct.

To address a sensitive situation directly, just how far was penetration required in order to constitute a successful consummation? If the pair indulged in some sort of foreplay, it is not inconceivable, given their youth, that both reached separate conclusions about their degree of success. Arthur may have achieved some shallow degree of penetration which was not sufficient to rupture Catherine's hymen, leaving her still technically a virgin. Both were inexperienced, and lacked a common language as well as, presumably, a detailed knowledge of the anatomy of the opposite sex. Under such circumstances, their attempts at intimacy may not have gone smoothly. Catherine's reported quietness the following morning might indicate the embarrassment and discomfort after a bungled effort rather than complete non-consummation. In later years, when she was forced to defend her virginity, she had the comparison of Arthur's efforts with the wedding night she spent with the robust seventeen-year-old Henry. It is perfectly possible that Arthur thought consummation had taken place while his wife thought it had not. While Catherine kept her counsel in 1502, many at court made the assumption that the union had been consummated and the official waiting period prevailed.

Swiftly, Ferdinand and Isabella tried to secure their daughter's position. However, far away in Spain, it was not clear exactly how they could achieve this for the best. As early as 10 May they instructed the Duke of Estrada to conclude, in their names, 'a marriage between their daughter Catharine and [the king's] son Henry, Prince of Wales'.[4] They also requested the return of 100,000 scudos, the half of her marriage portion that had been paid so far, and the settlement of her dowry lands. Yet Estrada was also issued with the conflicting charge to bring Catherine home to her parents as soon as possible. Two days later, the Spanish sovereigns had 'heard that the Princess of Wales is suffering' and asked that she 'be removed, without loss of time, from the unhealthy place where she is now', meaning Ludlow.[5] They expected 'confidently' that King Henry would 'lose no time in fulfilling all his obligations' to her. Having heard reports of his lack of support, they declared they could not 'believe him capable of exposing the princess, in this her time of grief, to want and privation'.[6] It was not to be supposed that the 'King of England would break his word at any time, and much less at present, while the princess is overwhelmed with grief'.[7] Sadly, Ferdinand and Isabella were to be proved wrong.

6

Betrothal Games, 1503–05

The vows you've broken, like my heart,
O why did you so enrapture me?
Now I remain in a world apart
But my heart remains in captivity.[1]

Catherine was initially installed at Durham House on the Strand, the London home of the bishops of Durham. Henry VII's queen, Elizabeth of York, sent a litter of black velvet fringed with black valance and ribbon to carry her the 150 miles across the middle of England back to the capital.[2] Durham House was considered a palace worthy of royalty, with its private apartments overlooking the river, large chapel and hall with marble pillars. It was mostly built on two storeys around a sizeable courtyard, with tall towers, a walled garden leading down to the river and a landing stage for Catherine to access court. In 1540, according to Stow's *Survey of London*, it hosted the feast of the May Day revels, easily accommodating the king, queen and her ladies, the entire court, six challengers dressed in white velvet and forty-six defendants, the knights and burgesses of the House of Commons, the mayor and aldermen and their wives.[3] That November, Henry paid Catherine's monthly expenses, which amounted to £83 6s 8d. It was the equivalent to about ten suits of armour, or a similar number of good-quality riding horses according to late fifteenth-century prices. She would also have attended the court at Westminster, perhaps witnessing the disguisings and singing, music and costumes, tumblers and misrule that appear in the Privy Purse accounts. Perhaps, in January 1503, she visited the Tower to see the leopard presented to Henry VII for the royal menagerie.

As a child in Spain, Catherine had witnessed the extravagant mourning of young widows. Her eldest sister, Isabel, had been widowed at the age of twenty, when her husband was killed in a riding accident. Her response had been to immerse herself in mourning and the comfort of religion, hacking off her long hair and fasting until she was 'thinner than a dried-out tree'. At the age of eleven, she would also have heard of the grief of her sister-in-law, Margaret of Austria, following her short and passionate match to Catherine's brother, John. Margaret remarried but her second husband died in 1504, leading her to vow she would remain a widow and earning her the name 'Lady of Mourning'. Catherine, though, had other ideas. There was little more she wanted than to become a wife and queen.

It was at this point that Henry VII came up with a shocking plan. Upon Arthur's death, his own wife, Elizabeth, had consoled him with the idea that they would have more children. Although she was thirty-six, and considered old in terms of childbearing, she conceived quickly and was brought to bed early of a daughter in the Tower of London. Tragically, though, neither mother nor child survived. Protocol suggests it is unlikely that Catherine attended the solemn funeral, where Elizabeth's full-length effigy lay upon a coffin draped with black velvet and topped by a white gold cross. The loss of Arthur was a considerable blow, but, miles from her parents, her main source of comfort may well have been the bereaved queen. With Elizabeth's death Catherine would have lost an ally, an alternative mother figure, and witnessed the effects of grief upon the king and his son. Now the whole court was in mourning again.

In April 1503, only two months after Elizabeth's death, Henry suggested that he might take Catherine as his new bride. At this point he was forty-six and, although 'still remarkably attractive', with a 'cheerful' face, his 'teeth were few, poor and blackish, his hair was thin and white, his complexion sallow'.[4] Catherine was seventeen. The proposition, if she was aware of it, must have been a shock. It was not the reason she had been sent to England and the contrast between Henry VII and his new heir was considerable. Isabella wrote back to the Duke d'Estrada in horror, describing the match as a 'very evil thing, one never before seen and the mere mention of which offends the ears ... we would not for anything in the world that it should take place'. To Dona Elvira, she repeated her wish for Catherine's immediate return to Spain and made arrangements for her to join the returning merchants' fleet, then in Flanders.[5] 'In this way the king will be deprived of the hope of marrying her.' Whether or not Henry was truly set upon this 'barbarous and dishonest'[6] course of action, the question of his remarriage was soon set aside in favour of his son.

In June 1503, to her great relief, Catherine's betrothal to Prince Henry was finalised by the Bishop of Salisbury. Her marriage portion would comprise the remaining half of the original 200,000 scudos, to be made up of 'coined gold', plate and vessels of gold and silver, jewels, pearls and ornaments, 'according to the valuation of silversmiths in London'.[7] Both sides acknowledged that Catherine's previous marriage placed her and Henry within the prohibited degrees of affinity, so a papal dispensation was necessary. However, the Spaniards were taking no chances. They did not trust Henry not to find some legal loophole, so they stipulated that the dispensation must cover the eventuality that the union with Arthur 'had been consummated'.[8] Ferdinand was in little doubt about his daughter's inexperience. Either Catherine or her ladies must have communicated fairly directly with him regarding the intimate details of her married life. He clarified that 'although they were wedded, Prince Arthur and Princess Catherine never consummated their marriage. It is well known that the princess is still a virgin. But as the English are much disposed to cavil, it has seemed to be more prudent to provide for the case as though the marriage had been consummated.'[9] Thus Ferdinand hoped to prevent any problems arising in the future regarding Catherine's marriage and status. With just one small twist of fate, the topic may never have arisen again.

With the political hot potato of Catherine's virginal status in abeyance, arrangements went ahead for her to marry again. The ceremony was to take place 'as soon as Prince Henry shall have completed the fourteenth year of his age', which would be in June 1505, and Catherine was to 'enjoy, during the lifetime of her royal husband, all the privileges and revenues that other queens of England have enjoyed before her'.[10] Finally, it appeared that Catherine's future would unfold as she had hoped. She was now a frequent visitor at the Tudor court, participating in feasts and hunts, travelling to Windsor, Richmond and Westminster. There would have been occasions for her to observe the boy who would become her next husband. Both had found their futures altered considerably since the day they and Arthur had made such a striking trio in white silk for the wedding celebrations of autumn 1501. At the least, a degree of familiarity or sympathy would have sprung up between them, if not a friendship; perhaps even more.

Catherine would have witnessed the arrangements being made for the marriage of Princess Margaret to King James IV of Scotland. Margaret was four years younger than Catherine, a possible friend and comfort, but the pair would have only had a brief window to become friends before Margaret left England. Hearing about the proxy marriage at Richmond, with the Scottish ambassador draped in cloth of gold, and seeing the preparations for Margaret's departure, with her crimson Italian bed hangings embroidered with red roses, Catherine would have been reminded of her own marital journey. Amid the jousting and feasting that followed, did she reflect on how soon the excitement of her arrival and celebrations of her wedding had turned to grief? When Margaret left Richmond, accompanied by the king, on 27 June 1503, they left behind the newly betrothed couple of Catherine and Henry. Perhaps the pair drew closer together during this time, as a result of their recent losses. It is not difficult to imagine the young widow and the teenage prince dining together or riding in Richmond Park, reminiscing about departed loved ones.

Widowhood in the early sixteenth century could sometimes confer status and independence. Under English common law, the position of a *femme sole*, a woman without a man, was one of greater financial freedom and control, allowing her to own property, make contracts and manage the affairs of her unmarried children. However, this would not prove to be the case for Catherine. She had little power over her future and was instructed by her parents to be submissive while the game of diplomatic relations played out over her head. After the death of Elizabeth of York, she lacked an English mother figure at court to fight her cause and she continued to struggle with the language.[11] Then, in November 1504, she received news of the death of her mother, Isabella of Castile, who had passed away at Medino del Campo at the age of fifty-three. Less than four months later, while she was still in deepest mourning, she was shocked by the news that her father had remarried. His new wife was Germaine de Foix, niece of Louis XII of France and his own great-niece, who, at seventeen, was three years younger than Catherine herself.

Apart from any personal dislike Catherine may have felt for her father's new marriage, it was to prove an unexpected political setback for her cause. Her wedding to Prince Henry should have been imminent, after Pope Julius II had finally issued a dispensation for the pair to wed in November 1504. As Henry approached his fourteenth birthday the following summer, preparations should have been made for pageants and feasts, lengths of material ordered, jewels chosen and seamstresses kept busy, plying their needles with gold and silver thread. But this new Spanish–French match had annoyed the English king. For centuries, Spain and England had been traditional allies in the 'auld alliance' against their common enemy of France. After all the overtures of friendship in recent years and the treaties confirming their position, Henry VII considered the Aragon–Foix marriage to be an act of betrayal. He stated that Ferdinand had been 'ensnared' by the French and repaid the love of the English 'with ingratitude'.[12]

Isabella's death created a further financial barrier to Catherine's marriage. Traditionally a separate kingdom from Aragon, Castile now passed intact to her eldest surviving daughter, Joanna. It had always been a larger, more influential region than Aragon, so Catherine was now the daughter of Aragon only, instead of the joint kingdoms, decreasing her marital value. Also, Joanna, or rather her controlling husband Philip, now held the purse strings when it came to the payment of the second half of Catherine's dowry. Isabella's will allowed for Ferdinand to rule in the event of Isabella's incapacity or absence, but Philip was determined to claim the Castilian throne.

For Henry VII, the loss of Castile and Ferdinand's new union proved to be a huge financial disappointment. He now considered the possibility of cancelling Catherine's match altogether so that he might make a more lucrative European alliance for his son, perhaps with the French princess, Margaret of Angoulême, later known as Margaret of Navarre. Born in 1492, Margaret was closer to Henry in age than Catherine, and was already renowned as a beautiful, educated and intelligent young woman. She would later become an author and the patroness of humanists and reformers. However, the king was reluctant to let Catherine leave England, which would necessitate the return of that part of her dowry which had already been paid. His desire to pursue a French match, retain Catherine's money and punish Ferdinand underpinned the events of June 1505.

All at court were aware that Prince Henry was approaching the significant age of fourteen. At the end of the month he would be able to legally marry, or to repudiate the arrangements made for him by his father. Catherine was anticipating becoming the wife of the young man to whom she had grown closer over the past three years, having more time to get to know him than she had with Arthur. On 22 June 1505, Ferdinand wrote to advise his daughter to 'revere and be very obedient to the king, as is her duty, and as being a means of making him love her more, and of doing more for her'.[13] Henry VII's secretary, Thomas Ruthal, drew up clauses for an 'intimate treaty' between England and Spain, and Henry was considering taking Catherine's cousin Joan of Naples as his queen.

Then, on the day before Prince Henry's birthday, the very eve of the proposed match, these hopes were suddenly dashed. At Richmond Palace, before the Bishop of Winchester and other assembled dignitaries, the boy made a public declaration absolving him from any obligation to Catherine. Stating that 'as he is [*sic*] now near the age of puberty … he will not ratify the said marriage contract, but, on the contrary, denounces it as null and void'.[14] The move was probably prompted by King Henry's frustration with Ferdinand's refusal to pay the second half of Catherine's dowry. The timing, coming a day before the betrothal would have become legally valid, was designed to humiliate the Spanish.

7

The Other Spanish Princess, 1506–07

One there is, and euer one shalbe,
For whose sake my hart is sore dyseasyd;
For whose loue, welcom dysease to me!
I am content so all partys be pleasyd:
Yet, and God wold, I wold my payne were easyd![1]

It is not clear exactly when, or if, Catherine found out about Prince Henry's repudiation of her. Perhaps she was shrewd enough to understand that it was part of the complex Anglo-Spanish dynamic, more a political reaction by the king to her father's French alliance than a rejection of her person. Perhaps, after years of waiting, she did feel it as a betrayal. It is very unlikely that her feelings were taken into account by any of the men involved. Her long-cherished hopes, so nearly attained, had been dashed again, for reasons beyond her control. She was approaching her twenty-first birthday. By the same age, her mother and sisters Isabella, Joanna and Maria had already been married and all, save for the widowed Isabella, had borne at least one child. That September, Henry wrote to Ferdinand to assure him the wedding would still go ahead. If Catherine had been informed at all about her fiancé's repudiation of her that June, she now learned that the interminable waiting game had begun again.

Catherine may have believed that the broken engagement was her fault. In fact, it may have suited Henry VII and his son to make her believe so, as a lesson about her behaviour. Writing to the Pope in the preceding months, Prince Henry had complained that his intended wife had 'threatened to make a vow dedicating herself to a life of vigorous contemplation and physical abstinence'.[2] This sounds quite plausible, as religious devotion was the only protest within Catherine's control, given the crippling financial and emotional restraints under which the princess found herself. Julius II responded that Catherine's body was not her own property, that she was subject to Prince Henry as her future spouse: 'A wife does not have complete authority over her own body apart from [separate from] her husband.'[3] Thus Catherine's perceived wilfulness became a valid justification for punishing her further, for passing the blame on to her for what was, in essence, a political decision.

In spite of the recent uncertainties over her own future marriage, Catherine was still willing to intercede in the case of another potential bride. On 8 September she wrote to her father on behalf of Maria de Salazar, who had been in service to Queen Elizabeth and then to herself, and who now hoped to be married in Flanders. Catherine asked for the woman's marriage portion to be clarified, as well as the pension that Ferdinand had bestowed on her father, a Captain Salazar. She urged speed, in order that Maria 'may not lose this marriage, which is most good and honourable' and so that 'justice may be observed towards her' for having served Catherine well 'as a worthy woman'.[4] She requested that the bearer of her letter should be rewarded with a captainship for his brother, and pleaded the case of her other waiting women, as they should marry, but she had 'nothing to bestow upon them'.[5] The following year she wrote again, this time on behalf of her doctor, who had nursed her through great illness, hoping that his son might be rewarded with an ecclesiastical benefice in Naples.[6] Although her powers were limited in her current position of stasis, Catherine used what influence she had to further the causes of those who had served her well.

Regardless of the uncertainty over her future, Catherine was still not living in conditions to which her past entitled her. Little financial provision had been made for her as, in his will, Arthur had left everything he owned to his sister Margaret, an unusual step that has never been satisfactorily explained. In 1502 Henry VII had awarded her an annual income of £83 6s 8d, which was roughly the equivalent of the revenue of a nobleman of the day. Under the supervision of William Holybrand, appointed by the king to keep a close eye on her purse strings, she was unable to support her staff of fifty servants. Although her household had been scaled down since her widowhood and a few of her ladies had found husbands of their own, her staff were living in penury, 'ready to ask for alms' and were 'all but naked' for lack of funds to buy clothes. She had been forced to sell some bracelets in order to buy a dress of black velvet and claimed that, since her arrival in England, she had only purchased two new dresses.[7] Caught in the crossfire of international relations, she was dependent on the king and in the difficult position of having to maintain her submissive position in spite of her belief that her destitution reflected 'dishonour on his character'.[8] The daughter of the King of Spain, raised to become Queen of England, who should have been decked in gold and silver finery, was forced into wearing rags.

Although she had fully recovered from the illness that laid her low at Ludlow, Catherine's health continued to be poor. In December 1505, she feared that she had 'lost her health' entirely. Suffering from various 'agues', hot and cold sweats, fever, stomach complaints and the loss of appetite, she pleaded for support from her father-in-law and her father. Her exhausted and malnourished body refused to cooperate when her surgeons attempted to bleed her, which was the usual cure-all of the time. She considered their help immaterial anyway, as the 'moral afflictions' of her position were 'beyond the reach of the physician'.[9] That month she was moved from Durham House to cramped lodgings on the 'edge' of the large complex of Westminster, so although she was technically closer to the court when it was in residence, this represented a marginalisation.[10] Although her health improved through 1506, her spirits remained depressed by the continuing conditions of poverty in which she was forced to live. By 1507, she was defying express orders not to sell off her gold and silver plate as she and her household were 'obliged to live in rags' and described her life as 'martyrdom'.[11] Yet, in spite of the 'great ... contempt' shown to her, Catherine wrote to her father that, 'though submissive, she cannot forget that she is the daughter of the King of Spain'.[12] If nothing else, amid the greatest adversity, she remained regal.

Then an unexpected chain of events altered the political scene. Since the death of Isabella, the purse strings of Castile, including funds for Catherine's dowry, had been in the hands of her sister Joanna. Or, more specifically, since Ferdinand renounced his hold over his daughter in the 1505 Treaty of Salamanca, they were in the hands of Joanna's husband, Philip the Handsome. Although she had only been ten at the time, Catherine would have recalled her elder sister's departure from Spain and heard stories of the wedding in the Low Countries and the six healthy children she had subsequently borne. The marriage had started passionately enough, with Philip summoning a priest as soon as Joanna arrived, in order to legally consummate the union at once.

Joanna fell deeply in love. As the years passed, though, her husband's controlling behaviour, his infidelity and manipulation of her legal rights eroded the match and Joanna descended into depression and mental illness. Early in 1506, she and Philip defied advice not to travel in the middle of winter and sailed from Flanders to Castile to claim the throne, but they soon encountered terrible storms. The wind was so severe that, in London, the brass eagle weathervane was blown off the top of St Paul's Cathedral.[13] Having been tossed about for thirty-six hours, scattering their forty ships with great loss of life and the loss of the royal treasure ship, the royal galleon limped into the Dorset harbour of Melcombe Regis on 16 January. Although accidental, it was a wonderful opportunity for Catherine to see her sister again after nine years. It was also a chance for Henry VII to persuade Philip to release the remaining dowry and undermine the new Spanish–French alliance. Fate had landed them in his lap. He did not intend to let them go.

Dressed in crimson and scarlet, Prince Henry was dispatched to meet Philip and Joanna at Winchester and conduct them to Windsor. It was not until 10 February, almost a month after their arrival, that Catherine was summoned to the castle to be reunited with her sister. This in itself was ominous. The sixteen-year-old to whom she had bid farewell as a child was now twenty-six, scarred by her tumultuous marriage and the rigours of childbearing, as well as whatever mental health problems she may have been experiencing. Catherine must have longed to share her disappointments and privations with her sister, as well as their grief over the loss of their mother, and perhaps their feelings over their father's remarriage. Finally Catherine would have an ally of her own blood, with whom she could converse in her native tongue. Perhaps she hoped Joanna might even champion her cause with Henry, on seeing the terrible living conditions to which her sister was reduced. Yet she was to be disappointed. The sisters scarcely had the opportunity to share any secrets, let alone speak in private. They spent a short time together during which they were closely supervised, before Joanna drew the meeting to a close for reasons which are unclear. Disappointed, Catherine was sent back to Richmond while Joanna headed to Falmouth to await her husband. The princess wrote to her sister of the 'great pleasure it gave me to see you and the great distress which filled my soul, a few hours afterwards, on account of your hasty and sudden departure'.[14]

It had been a successful visit for Henry, though, whose month-long entertainment of Philip had paid off. A treaty of commerce was signed, on favourable terms to the English cloth merchants, and in exchange for recognising Philip as King of Castile Henry received the assurance that the Yorkist Earl of Suffolk, Richard de la Pole, would be surrendered to him from his foreign exile. It was also a success for Prince Henry, who had been impressed by Philip's regal behaviour and handsome appearance, modelling himself after the 'talented, generous and gentlemanly' figure and sharing his passions for chivalry and sports.[15] In later life, he would hang Philip's portrait in Greenwich Palace, in a room named after the archduke.[16] While in England, Philip invested the young prince with the Order of the Golden Fleece. Perhaps Catherine was permitted to attend, or else heard about the occasion, while away at Richmond.

The king managed to detain Philip with questions of trade and policy until the end of March. On 9 April Prince Henry wrote to him in Spanish, in the first letter that survives in his hand, expressing his 'heart's desire' to hear occasional news of Philip's 'good health and prosperity' and referring to Catherine as his 'most dear and well-beloved consort, the princess my wife'.[17] The archduke was still on English soil at this point, as further bad weather delayed his departure until 22 April. It was the last they would see of Philip. Five months later, news arrived at the English Court that he had died as the result of an infection at the age of twenty-eight. The pregnant Joanna was distraught. The news had been enough to tip her fragile mental state over the edge.

Worrying reports followed concerning Joanna's behaviour.

Apparently she refused to part with her husband's body and was travelling about the country with it at night so she, or he, would not be seen. Heavily pregnant, she was reputed to open the coffin and kiss him, as well as eating from the floor and failing to pay attention to her appearance, which became unkempt.[18] She delivered her final child, a girl named Catherine, the following January. None of this was sufficient to prevent Henry VII from deciding she would make him a suitable wife.

The king turned to Catherine for help. Somehow he managed to persuade her that he would make a suitable husband for her sister, or else she was convinced by her own desire to have Joanna close at hand, even as her own mother-in-law. It was the princess herself who wrote to Ferdinand, in March 1507, proposing the match. Their father replied, 'It is not yet known if Queen Juana be inclined to marry again,' but if she were, 'it shall be with no other person than the King of England.' Joanna herself was not to know of the suggestion, as 'she would most probably do something quite to the contrary'.[19] De Puebla reported that 'no king in the world would make so good a husband to the Queen of Castile as the King of England, whether she be sane or insane'. Her mental health was not considered a barrier – 'the English seem little to mind ... the derangement of her mind' – as it would not interfere in her producing children.[20] In return for her living in England, Ferdinand was to retain the Castilian crown. Henry's efforts to woo her did not yield results, mostly because Joanna herself was resolved never to remarry. She would remain a widow until her death almost fifty years later.

Catherine's loneliness did not abate. She wrote to Joanna from Eltham that she had suffered more attacks of fever, but was now in better spirits.[21] Henry also expressed concerns about her health and offered her the use of a house at Fulham that had been set aside for the use of the Castilian ambassadors, if 'it would improve her health to be so near him'.[22] This might have been Fulham Palace, one residence of the Bishop of London, which had been recently renovated, with a new timber roof to the great hall installed in 1495. Catherine may well have accepted this offer, as it would have placed her only five miles to the east of the king and prince's favourite residence of Richmond Palace, where she appears to have been a regular visitor during 1507. One question still preyed on her mind, though.

Although they were now geographically closer, Catherine believed she and Prince Henry were being kept apart. She reported to Ferdinand in mid- April 1507 that, although they were under the same roof, she had not been permitted to see Henry for four months.

Having previously been companions at court, the pretty Princess and the sixteen-year-old Henry may well have formed an attachment or even reached some personal understanding about their joint futures. The Spanish Ambassador de Puebla reported that there was 'no finer youth than the Prince of Wales. He is already taller than his father and his limbs are of a gigantic size. He is as prudent as to be expected from a son of Henry VII.'[23] The king's response to her plight was again to deny any special relationship between the two young people – 'he no longer regards himself and the Prince of Wales, as bound by the marriage treaty, because the marriage portion has not been paid' – adding ominously that 'other princesses have been offered in marriage to the Prince of Wales, with much greater marriage portions'.[24] Having watched him develop into an impressive young man, Catherine felt the loss of Henry's company keenly.

Widows in the sixteenth century were the recipients of very mixed messages. On one hand, the church prized virginity as the highest of all states of womanhood, closely followed by the chaste life of widowhood. On the other, contemporary medical understanding dictated that such conditions could be injurious to women's health and advocated a return to the marital state in order for the impulses of women's sexually ravenous bodies to be properly satisfied. According to the theory of the four humours governing the body, it was believed that the womb was of a cold, damp nature, which craved the corresponding hot, dry seed of a man. Frequent references to Catherine suffering from fevers and being purged and bled, as well as her daily swings between 'cold and heat', would have been diagnosed in this light. Using her astrological sign of Sagittarius to suggest treatment, Catherine's warm, dry and choleric nature would have been balanced with foods that were believed to possess qualities of coldness and wetness such as lettuce, melons and cucumbers. Abstaining from sex could lead to illness, melancholy and misbehaviour in women; effectively, the patriarchal medical system advocated sex as a means of control within marriage, to keep wives happy and in line. Distanced from her father and sister, having lost her mother, and now kept apart from Henry, whom she had anticipated marrying years ago, Catherine was about to cause a scandal by stepping out of line.

8

Princess of Scandal, 1507–09

Ye be an apte man as ony can be founde
To dwell with vs & serue my ladyes grace
Ye be to her yea worth a thousande pounde[1]

At this difficult point, Catherine turned to her faith. She had always been a devout Catholic, observing the rituals of prayer, Mass and fasting; her journey to England in 1501 had begun with a visit to the shrine of St James at Santiago de Compostela and concluded with offerings to St Erkenwald at St Paul's Cathedral. Lonely and uncertain about her future, Catherine was now twenty-two, well past the age at which most of her peers were married, and uncertain whether her ambitions would ever reach fulfilment. The one certainty in her life was religion, and it is little surprise that she may have immersed herself in its practices.

Prayer and fasting formed a central part of the Catholic faith, with the devout eschewing certain foods or abstaining entirely, rising before dawn to pray for hours on their knees. The prime occasion in the calendar was Lent, when forty days of fasting, meaning limited food, in imitation of his Jesus' suffering, was believed to prepare a Catholic spiritually for the celebration of the resurrection. Likewise, on Wednesdays, Fridays and Saturdays the eating of meat was prohibited, offering an opportunity to individuals to contemplate their faith and draw closer to God. Recent studies into the lives of female medieval saints reveal the extent to which severe ascetic religious practices were common among women at the time, with a sort of 'holy anorexia' or non-eating to the point of starvation acting as a demonstrable sign of devotion.[2] Many medieval women were denied any sense of autonomy in their own lives, in managing their marital states, fertility and property, so may have found an outlet in strict religious observation and control. The Venetian ambassador commented in 1513 that English women carried long rosaries, attended Mass every day and were generally very devout.[3]

Catherine's excessive devotions had already caused concern. Back in 1505, Pope Julius II wrote to Henry VII in an attempt to curb her habits in case they damaged her health.[4] Later in her life, her devotion would reach a pitch of intensity that saw her rise for Matins at midnight and wear the shift of St Francis under her clothes as she knelt on the stone flags in prayer. The same year she had written to her father requesting that a 'friar of the order of San Francesco de Obsservancya' be sent to her, as she did 'not understand the English language, nor how to speak it' and it was a great inconvenience to not have a Spanish friar, 'especially now to me, who, for six month has been near to death'.[5] Her request took a while to be fulfilled. By 1507, Catholicism offered the degree of consolation and comfort she needed at a difficult time. It arrived specifically in the form of a young man who appeared in her household that spring.

Fray Diego Fernandez was a young Observant Franciscan from Castile. He appears to have had humble origins, although he had somehow acquired a university education and worked his way up through the ranks. Little more is known about his origins and no portrait survives, but the new Spanish ambassador Fuensalida, who arrived in England in 1508, stated that he was young, 'light, haughty and licentious' and had succeeded in gaining the 'confidence and affection' of the princess.[6] Fuensalida could find no personal charms in Diego, outlining his lack of learning, appearance, manners, competency and credit.[7] Catherine, on the other hand, considered him to be 'very competent', giving 'good advice and a good example'; in fact, she believed Fray Diego was 'the best that ever [a] woman of my position had'.[8]

Despite her poverty, she spent what little money she had on 'buying books and other things for him', causing more outrage among her unpaid servants. As Fuensalida explained, she had been forbidden to sell her jewels and plate, which formed part of her dowry, but 'in spite of these injunctions she sold some plate, and would have sold more had she not been prevented by her servants, in order to satisfy the follies of the friar'.[9] Her domestic situation was continuing to cause her great distress, following the reduction of allowances for her servants and the complete cessation of payments to her physician and Diego. Fuensalida reported that Catherine was so ill she could barely speak and was threatening to go on hunger strike, unless better provision was made for them; the ambassador reported that his own retinue ate better food than she did. That July, he considered that she was 'seriously ill'.[10]

The confessor was able to exploit a vacuum at the heart of Catherine's own household in order to become closer to her. Since the departure of Dona Elvira, dismissed in 'horrible hour' for having conspired against Ferdinand, Catherine had relied more on Francesca de Carceres, the 'most vivacious and spirited of her maids'.[11] Francesca now incurred Diego's wrath by meeting secretly with Fuensalida and talking with him about the confessor's hold over the princess. When Catherine found out and was furious, Francesca accepted a marriage proposal from the Genovese banker Francesco Grimaldi, then living in London, and left her mistress's employment.

Diego's influence began to alienate Catherine from the Tudor court. On one occasion, as she was preparing to attend a summons to Richmond, he counselled her to defy the king's orders and feign illness. Catherine was placed in a difficult situation, as Princess Mary was waiting for her, having seen her in perfect health earlier in the day. When Catherine explained that she was quite well, and able to attend, Diego stated that it would be a mortal sin for her to go, ensuring her compliance. This episode resulted in a breach of three weeks between Catherine and the king and, when summoned to hear Henry's response, she attended but ignored his reprimand.[12] Even when Diego's advice conflicted with her courtly role, she placed her spiritual over her temporal welfare. Her adoption of this course would later have massive implications for English history.

The reasons for Catherine's attachment are obvious. Far away from home, grieving for her mother and alienated from the English court, she saw Diego as an ally, a protector and a conduit to the divine. Uncertain whether her marriage would ever go ahead, she was kept apart from Prince Henry and had been denied the affection and generosity the king had promised her parents he would extend to her. It is not surprising that she was drawn to an alternative male figure, especially one with the authority of the Church behind him, whose talk of eternal rewards acted as a panacea in the light of her continued suffering.

Diego's motives, however, are far more sinister. Likened by more than one historian to Rasputin for his emotional manipulation of Catherine, he certainly received what few resources she had to offer and may have anticipated serving her once she became queen, with all the rewards that could bring. Exploiting her loneliness and piety, he established an emotional connection based in their shared faith and its rituals, quickly becoming Catherine's 'greatest consolation'. When her favouritism provoked a response among other members of her household, Catherine defended Diego, feeling 'quite desperate' at the possibility of losing him.[13] Was the princess in love? Perhaps unconsciously. She had certainly fallen under the spell of her charismatic confessor as a representative of Catholicism, perhaps as a father figure or as a friend. There may have been a degree of 'romance' about her desire for his company and enslavement to his word, but it was a relationship based on inequality and exploitation. Episodes such as the one where he forbade her from attending court raise the question of how far she was a willing victim.

Given their social disparity and Catherine's status and purpose,

Diego would have been insane to initiate any sort of sexual relationship between them even if he had desired to do so. He would later prove himself capable of immoral liaisons, sleeping with a woman of her household and losing his position as a result. Did he have feelings for Catherine? In 1510, he described her as 'the most beautiful creature in the world with the greatest gaiety and contentment' but those may well have been the platitudes of a servant to a newly crowned queen. The most implacable obstacle was Catherine herself, deeply imbued with a sense of her position and the correct conduct it required. There is no possibility that she engaged in any sort of physical affair with Diego, and his continuance at her side implies he was not fool enough to attempt one. No doubt he was aware that she had developed an unhealthy attachment to him and derived satisfaction from the power he exercised over her.

This did not go unnoticed. At court, scandal quickly spread about the nature of the pair's intense relationship. Fuensalida believed Diego to be immoral, exploiting Catherine's vulnerable state and faith in order to control her: 'The most effectual weapon in the hands of a priest is the belief of others that he is the dispenser of rewards and punishments in the future life. Of this, Fray Diego made a most unscrupulous use, declaring everything to be a mortal sin which displeased him, however innocent it might be.'[14] Fuensalida described the confessor as 'infamar', a Spanish word that translates as 'something more infamous than slander'.[15] He saw Catherine was in danger of tarnishing her delicate reputation but his attempts to intervene led to a breach between him and the princess.

Eventually, Fuensalida wrote to Ferdinand. It was a 'delicate' and 'dangerous' task but he could not allow the situation to continue unchecked. On 20 March 1509, he explained that Catherine was 'so submissive to a friar ... that he makes her do a great many things which it would be better not to do'.[16] He added that Diego's activities were bringing the princess and her household into disrepute, being 'injurious to her reputation' and leading her to behave 'imprudently'.[17] There was a 'very great need to remedy these things of this friar, and to remove him from here as a pestiferous person, for that he certainly is'.[18] Diego remained with Catherine 'against the will of all the English, and especially against the will of the king and his highness', referring to Prince Henry.[19]

In response, the friar visited the ambassador and demanded an explanation, complaining of the 'evil tongues' and 'slanderous imputations', with all their connotations of an illicit affair.[20] More powerfully for the princess, he threatened to leave her. Catherine urged her father not to credit 'anything ... written to him respecting her household, and especially her confessor', who, she swore by her salvation, 'serves her very loyally'.[21] Writing on 20 March, she added,

> I would rather die than see what I have suffered and suffer every day from this ambassador and all my servants. I shall not believe that your Highness looks upon me as your daughter if you do not punish it, and order the ambassador to confine himself to the affairs of his embassy, and to abstain from meddling in the affairs of my household. May your Highness give me satisfaction before I die, for I fear my life will be short, owing to my troubles.[22]

She begged her father to allow her to keep Diego, who was regularly threatening to leave her, in terms that speak of the extent of her emotional attachment, her 'only consolation' in her otherwise miserable life. She would 'perish' otherwise. Ferdinand must write to King Henry, she pleaded, asking for Diego to remain and be 'well treated and humoured'. From Richmond, she wrote dramatically in code, hoping he would see her letter 'before her life is sacrificed, as she fears it will be soon, owing to the trials she has to endure'.[23] Finally, she threatened 'to do something in her despair that neither the King of England nor her father would be able to prevent'.[24] It sounded very much as if Catherine was in love and, confronted with the possibility of losing her beloved, intimated she was considering suicide. Heinous threats indeed for a Catholic princess.

It is unclear how this desperate situation would have played out if not for the timely death of Henry VII. The king's health had deteriorated since the spring of 1507, when he suffered from a 'quinsy', a complication of tonsillitis, which left him unable to eat or drink for six days. The following February he was again seriously ill with a fever or 'disease of the joints' that left him debilitated for three months, but again he recovered. As the scandal of Catherine's relationship with her friar broke, in the spring of 1509, Henry was already in the grip of his final illness. Eleven days after the flurry of letters to Ferdinand, the king signed his will at Richmond Palace. He had already been shut away in his private apartments for a week, with his son at his side. Although there were reports as early as the end of March that Henry was in his death throes,[25] the end did not come until 21 April. Suddenly, Catherine's world was transformed. The young man to whom she had been betrothed, on and off, for six years had become the tall, handsome, seventeen-year old Henry VIII.

9

In Henry's Bed, June 1509

This yonge king, which peised al
Hire beaute and hir wit withal
As he that was with love hent
Anon thereto yaf his assent[1]

At first, it seemed that the succession of Henry VIII marked an end to Catherine's hopes. Since hearing the news Ferdinand had been attempting to secure the marriage, even finally raising the remaining 100,000 scudos from Spanish bankers. Fuensalida did not believe that it would take place, advising the princess to resign herself to the loss, and had even begun shipping her possessions to Bruges in anticipation of leaving England. The new king could have the choice of any young princess in Christendom. Perhaps the ambassador also feared that her reputation had been damaged by the Fray Diego scandal. Three weeks of doubt followed for Catherine. Then, on 3 May, Fuensalida was summoned to a meeting with Henry's secretary, Thomas Ruthal, and his Lord Privy Seal, Richard Fox.[2] He was astonished by what they told him.

Tradition dictated that Henry was lodged in the Tower during this time, but his council had met without him at Richmond. There they had debated the merits of the Spanish alliance and the need for the new king to father heirs. Apparently Henry had agreed with them, having been urged by his dying father to make Catherine his wife, yet the evidence suggests it was also by his own inclination. The princess was dignified, mature and gracious, a beautiful older woman whose sufferings Henry had observed and could now alleviate with one romantic gesture. She was more than a match for him in character, learning and lineage and Henry clearly recognised this. Objections were raised by the Archbishop of Canterbury, William Warham, who believed that Catherine's marriage to Arthur prohibited her from becoming Henry's wife and that the original papal dispensation was flawed, but he was overruled. In the end, Warham obliged the council by issuing a marriage licence on 8 June, which permitted the wedding to take place after only one reading of the banns, instead of the usual three.[3]

Once they had permission, Catherine and Henry did not waste time. On 11 June, at Greenwich Palace, the twenty-three-year-old princess finally became a wife again, only this time she was to be a wife in more than name. Her auburn-haired husband towered over her at the altar, standing six feet and two inches tall beside her diminutive form of less than five feet. Contemporaries left little doubt regarding the attractiveness of the new young king in their accounts. Henry was a 'perfect model of manly beauty'[4] and 'moost coomly of his parsonage',[5] 'very fair and his whole frame admirably proportioned', 'affable and gracious', 'prudent, sage and free from every vice'.[6] The French ambassador simply described him as 'magnificent', while his Venetian counterpart predicted, accurately, that 'for the future, the whole world will talk of him'. Eight years after their first meeting in November 1501, when he had accompanied her on her entry into London, Catherine of Aragon and Henry VIII were finally pronounced man and wife. As he took her hand, bright with its wedding ring, a glittering future was unveiled before them. Young, beautiful, royal and rich, they were the most glamorous couple in Europe.

It was significant that the couple rejected the gloomy confines of Richmond Palace, closely associated with Henry VII's life and death, in favour of the privacy of Greenwich. A new reign and new wife required a new location. They gathered for the ceremony in the oratory of the Friar's Observant church. As the candles burned before the icons of the saints, Archbishop Warham joined them as man and wife before witnesses George Talbot, Earl of Shrewsbury, and William Thomas, Groom of the Privy Chamber. It was small, private and low-key. This was quite deliberate.

Eight years earlier, Catherine's wedding to Arthur had been celebrated with wonderful pageants and poems, tournaments and feasts, public and international spectacle, stretching for weeks. Coupled with the use of legend, allegory and dynastic symbols, this was considered an important marker of the legitimacy of a regime, an 'external sign of princely power'[7] and an authenticator of its marriages. The Tudor poet William Forrest summed it alliteratively as 'hys power, peereles, without peere must appeere'.[8] Henry VII had employed spectacle at every public ceremony of his reign, from his coronation and marriage to the unions he planned for his children. Therefore, his son's choice, in 1509, represented a significant departure. The scale and secrecy adopted by the new king for his marriage could not help but draw comparison in the eyes of his bride. No doubt this was due, in part, to the speed at which the wedding took place, in order to allow Henry and Catherine to enjoy a joint coronation, but it was also an act of assertion. Henry had chosen Catherine for personal reasons, for her beauty, nobility and the affection that had sprung up between them; ever the romantic, he may have been drawn by her years of suffering, throwing off the repressive mantle of his father to save the damsel in distress. He may have written to Margaret of Savoy that he was fulfilling his parent's deathbed wish, but in a letter to Ferdinand he explained that he would have chosen Catherine above all other women. The king was making the point that his choice of wife was his business.

The news quickly spread. By nightfall, Henry's gentlemen and Catherine's ladies were busily preparing their bedchamber in the royal apartment block. Standing five storeys high, overlooking the river and gardens with their ornamented walkways, heraldic beasts and fruit trees, the royal apartments had been improved according to plans designed by Elizabeth of York. The king's suite of rooms adjoined those of his new wife, forming a right angle of interconnecting chambers. The bed had been made following an elaborate ritual, the mattress checked by the Yeomen, then spread with a bed of down, followed by a fustian, with no man allowed to touch it by hand until the first sheet was laid on top of that. More sheets followed, along with 'such pyllows as shall please the kyng', upon a bolster. This was flattened down by Yeomen lying upon it, although they were to make the sign of the cross and kiss the bed where their fingers came into contact with it. The curtains at the sides were let down and a squire set the king's sword at the head of the bed. A secret groom had 'the kepynge of the sayde bedde with a light unto the tyme the kynge be disposed to goo to yt'. Then, each man was to be rewarded with a loaf of bread and pot of ale or wine, but must take care not to set any dish on the counterpane nor wipe their hands on the curtains.[9]

Catherine would have been dressed modestly in a nightshift, a fairly simple garment, usually white, almost identical in design to those worn under the clothing during the day. As queen, hers might have been embroidered, or lined, or laced. She would also have worn a white linen biggin, or night-coif, to cover her hair. Increasingly, it was less common to sleep naked, for both men and women, but Catherine would have worn nothing underneath her shift, which would probably have been discarded in the act of love. In his chambers, Henry's gentlemen undressed him to his shift, removed his hose and wrapped him in a gown for the walk between his room and that of his new wife. It was common for bawdy wedding night jokes and anecdotes to be exchanged on such occasions among the experienced men of the court and Henry may have taken wine and spices, which were thought to engender heat and encourage the libido.

As she lay between the perfumed sheets awaiting the arrival of her lusty young husband, Catherine probably had a better idea of what to expect than she had in 1501. No doubt she was excited, and probably nervous. Arthur had been just fifteen, half a head smaller than her and thin, and his father's concerns suggest he may already have been delicate in health. Now, striding into her bedchamber was the athletic Henry, strong, tall and long-limbed, in rude health and beautiful as a young god with his gold-red hair combed in the French fashion. He may well have been as inexperienced as her, but there is little doubt that the match was fully and enthusiastically consummated. For Catherine, the long years of virginity were over.

We might be forgiven for assuming that sex in the past was the same as sex today, that the actual physical act does not differ. This is true only to an extent. Approaching sex with a completely different attitude, the Tudor man and woman would have been following a complex code of rules that gave their encounters a different significance. A number of sexual practices were considered sinful, in religious terms and also in the folklore that described the conception and appearance of children, which was Catherine and Henry's ultimate aim and, as the king and queen, their morals and practices would need to have been exemplary. With gentlemen of Henry's bedchamber on the other side of the door and Catherine's maids or ladies in antechambers close by, there were always prying eyes or sensitive ears to consider: privacy is a modern luxury. Intercourse in the missionary position between husband and wife was considered the least of many potential evils, necessary for purposes of procreation and to prevent men from seeking satisfaction elsewhere. Other forms of sexual gratification – oral or anal sex, foreplay or masturbation, 'carnal thoughts' – were seen as sinful, as they did not result in pregnancy and could result in birth defects. Sin, of course, may have been a powerful aphrodisiac for some, and court records prove that these Church laws were frequently broken. Likewise, having sex on certain days of the Church calendar, or during menstruation, was supposed to produce small, unhealthy children.

An Italian visitor to England in 1500 remarked that the nation was of a 'licentious' disposition but that he had not observed anyone to be 'in love'. He concluded that English men were either 'the most discreet lovers in the world, or that they are incapable of love'. On the other hand, he believed that the women were 'very violent in their passions'.[10] Of course, the court changed significantly with Henry's succession, with greater emphasis on romance and chivalric displays of devotion and love; the royal marriage was echoed by a number of weddings among Catherine's ladies and Henry's gentlemen, which set a new 'romantic' tone.

The Italian's view of English women was in accordance with the cultural and medical beliefs regarding their sexual desire and activity.

Contemporary beliefs stated that a woman's 'crooked instrument' was designed to help satisfy her 'foul lust' and fuelled such stories of couples becoming locked together 'fast like a dogge and a biche together', such as that of Pers Lenard, related by Geoffrey de la Tour Landry, who suffered this humiliation after having sex on an altar. This required a public, naked penance.[11] Physically, women were believed to be imperfect versions of masculinity, with the male genitalia inverted to create the womb and ovaries. According to Tudor thinking, which proposed that all of nature was in 'sympathy' and craved its counterpart, this meant their imperfection was always demanding to be completed, through sexual union with men. As previously explained, wombs were considered to be cold and wet, with the corresponding male seed being hot and dry, and this created a picture of women in a perpetual state of desire. The Galenic theory of the four humours could also determine levels of libido. Born in the winter, Catherine was considered to be of a phlegmatic, or cold and wet temperament, calm and unemotional. By contrast, Henry's summer birth made him choleric, volatile and quick to lose his temper, but the hot, moist qualities of this humour would have made him Catherine's exact opposite and complement. Once again, the newlyweds were perfectly matched by the standards of their day.

Henry approached the marriage bed as an innocent. Given his status and the careful upbringing of his father, he is unlikely to have had a mistress before 1509, or to have had sex at all. The claim made by one historian[12] that his first lover had been Elizabeth Denton, *née* Jerningham, the woman who had been appointed mistress of his nursery in 1496, finds little support in other non-fiction works. It rests entirely upon grants made to Elizabeth for her service in 1509, and then in 1515, although this latter payment is clearly made 'for service to the late king and queen'. In the same month, comparable payments were made to Elizabeth Saxby and Elizabeth Wolvedon, who had served members of the royal family without suggestion of impropriety. The succession of a new monarch typically saw rewards being given to those who had loyally served the previous regime or other family members, and Denton's role in the household of Elizabeth of York and her children is consistent with this. She would later govern the future households of two of Henry VIII's children, further suggesting her speciality and suitability in such a position of care and the unlikeliness that she would abuse this parental trust.

There is also the question of Henry VII's control over his growing son. Given the terrible loss and grief he had suffered with the death of Arthur, Henry VII was not prepared to take any chances with the health of his second heir. The prince was closely monitored until 1509, being forbidden from taking part in potentially dangerous activities such as jousting and having his apartments accessible through those of his father. The fears Henry VII had entertained regarding the overenthusiastic sexual behaviour of teenagers, causing him to doubt the wisdom of Arthur and Catherine cohabiting, would have redoubled after Arthur's premature death seemed to confirm them. Not a single rumour regarding Prince Henry's private life survives prior to his marriage. He was scarcely in a position to indulge in affairs or brief encounters, and in the interval between his succession and marriage his attitude towards Catherine was one of romantic chivalry, of eager anticipation of his wedding night with her. It seems almost incontrovertible that Henry was a virgin on his wedding day.

Contemporary literature furnishes us with many examples of men equalling women in their sexual drive and performance. The bawdy boasts of bridegrooms seemed to have been a longstanding convention of early sixteenth-century wedding celebrations. A verse of Dunbar's Middle Scots poem 'In a Secret Place' is sufficient to give a flavour of the sort of wooing humour in this tradition, even with only minimal translation:

> My bonny babe with the rich brylyoun
> My tendir gyrle, my pretty flower
> My tyrlie myrlie, my crowdie mowdie,
> When that oure mouthes do meet at one
> My stang does stiffen with your towdie[13]

In 1501 Arthur had called for a drink, being thirsty after his 'hot work' in the 'middle of Spain all night', oblivious to the future significance of his words. Now, his brother bragged about finding Catherine a virgin before a number of witnesses, scarcely imagining that his words would come back to haunt him over twenty years later. When confronted with his comments by Imperial ambassador Eustace Chapuys, in April 1533, he claimed 'it was spoken in jest, as a man, jesting and feasting, says many things which are not true'.[14] There was no suggestion in 1509 that Henry was anything less than satisfied with his new wife.

By contrast, brides were celebrated in elaborate and beautiful poetic metaphors. Dunbar's descriptions of Margaret Tudor in 1502 as being serenaded by birds, more bright than beryl, more precious than diamonds, emeralds, rubies and pearls, follow a more traditional literary convention. Symbolised by the Tudor union rose, Margaret was 'the fresche ros of cullour reid and quythe', more dainty than all other flowers, a 'bloom of joy' to temper the harsh spikes of the Scottish thistle, when she married James IV. Catherine, the Spanish pomegranate, with her much-admired complexion, long red-gold hair and curvy figure, fitted the ideal of early sixteenth-century beauty, and Henry's ideal as well. In their bed, politics and passion were well married.

10

Coronation, 24 June 1509

Then he brought the king's son out and put the crown on him and gave him the testimony; and they made him king and anointed him, and they clapped their hands and said, 'Long live the king!'[1]

Catherine and Henry's wedding was probably concluded quickly to allow for a joint coronation, but the bride was not about to complain. When it came to this ceremony, though, no expense was spared and all the correct protocol was followed, in line with the *Ryalle Book*, produced in the reign of Henry's grandfather. Two weeks of preparations followed, in which Catherine's ladies were fitted with scarlet, fur-lined costumes,[2] feasts were planned, speeches written and London braced itself for the sort of pageantry and display it had not witnessed since her arrival in 1501. Secluded away with Henry in their Greenwich idyll, absorbed in each other's company and the glow of their newfound passion, Catherine must have been ecstatic. In many ways she and Henry made an ideal pair; both being conscious of their royal dignity, devout and learned, with a taste for the finer things in life, they could as happily dispute points of theology and Latin texts as take part in the hunt in Greenwich Park or dance late into the night. Together, through those heady summer days, a bond was forged of trust and intimacy that married duty and desire, personal and dynastic. As Catherine wrote to her father, she was 'well married'.

On Saturday 23 June, at about 4 p.m., a procession set out from the Tower of London. Henry went first, beneath a golden canopy, resplendent in a robe of crimson velvet furred with ermine, a jacket of raised gold and placard studded with gems. Around his neck was hung a collar of rose-red Afghanistan rubies. His horse was draped with damask gold and ermine, flanked with knights in red velvet and followed by nine children of honour, dressed in blue powdered with gold fleurs-de-lys. Catherine followed, carried in a litter drawn by

white palfreys draped in white cloth of gold. She wore white embroidered satin, with her hair hanging long and loose, topped with a
coronet 'set with many rich orient stones'. Her ladies followed, either
riding on palfreys or drawn in chariots, in embroidered cloth of gold
or silver, tinsel or velvet, according to their status.[3]

Also listed among her retinue were her controversial confessor Fray
Diego, the newly knighted Thomas Boleyn, and the close companions
of Henry VIII, Charles Brandon and the Duke of Buckingham,
resplendent in gold and diamonds. The streets of London were
sanded and railed to keep back the expectant crowds and houses
were hung with rich tapestries and cloths of arras and gold, all along
the route to Westminster Abbey. Yet not even the king could control
the weather. As they rode through Cornhill, approaching a tavern
called the Cardinal's Hat, a sudden shower drenched Catherine and
almost destroyed her silken canopy. Bedraggled, she was forced to
shelter 'under the hovel of a draper's stall' until the weather cleared.[4]
No doubt, in the minds of superstitious onlookers, such rainfall on
Midsummer's Day was a grave omen indeed for their new queen.
And so, as chronicler Hall recorded, 'with much joy and honour',
they reached the safety of Westminster Palace, where the royal couple
dined before passing the night in the Painted Chamber.

The following morning Catherine and Henry processed from the
palace into the abbey, where two empty thrones sat waiting on a
platform before the altar. A contemporary woodcut shows them seated
level with each other, looking into each other's eyes and smiling as the
crowns are lowered on to their heads. It is a potent image of the occasion,
intimate in spite of the crowds behind them, suggesting a relationship
of two people equal in sovereignty, respect and love. In reality, the
positioning of Henry's throne above hers, and her shortened ceremonial,
without an oath, indicates the actual discrepancy between them. He had
inherited the throne as a result of his birth; she was his queen because
he had chosen to marry her. Above his head the woodcut depicted a
huge Tudor rose, a reminder of his great lineage and England's recent
conflicts; Henry's role was to guide and rule his subjects. Over Catherine
sits her chosen device of the pomegranate, symbolic of the expectations
of all Tudor wives and queens: fertility and childbirth. In Christian
iconography, it also stood for resurrection. In a way, Catherine was
experiencing her own rebirth, through this new marriage and the chance
it offered her as queen, after the long years of privation and doubt.

Westminster Abbey was a riot of colour. Quite in contrast with
the sombre, bare-stone interiors of medieval churches today, these
pre-Reformation years made worship a tactile and sensual experience,

with wealth and ornament acting as tributes and measures of devotion. Inside the abbey, statues and images were gilded and decorated with jewels, walls and capitals were picked out in bright colours and walls were hung with rich arras. All was conducted according to the advice of the 200-year-old *Liber Regalis*, the *Royal Book*, which dictated coronation ritual. The couple were wafted with sweet incense while thousands of candles flickered, mingling with the light streaming down through the stained-glass windows. Archbishop Warham was again at the helm, administering the coronation oaths and anointing the pair with oil. Beside her new husband, Catherine was crowned and given a ring to wear on the fourth finger of her right hand, a sort of inversion of the marital ring, symbolising her marriage to her country. She would take this vow very seriously.

The coronation proved popular. Henry wrote to the Pope explaining that he had 'espoused and made' Catherine 'his wife and thereupon had her crowned amid the applause of the people and the incredible demonstrations of joy and enthusiasm'.[5] To Ferdinand, he added that 'the multitude of people who assisted was immense, and their joy and applause most enthusiastic'.[6] There seems little reason to see this just as diplomatic hyperbole. According to Hall, 'it was demaunded of the people, wether they would receive, obey and take the same moste noble Prince, for their Kyng, who with great reuerance, love and desire, saied and cryed, ye-ye'.[7] Lord Mountjoy employed more poetic rhetoric in his letter to Erasmus, which stated that 'Heaven and Earth rejoices, everything is full of milk and honey and nectar. Our king is not after gold, or gems, or precious metals, but virtue, glory, immortality.' In his coronation verses Thomas More agreed with the general mood, explaining that wherever Henry went 'the dense crowd in their desire to look upon him leaves hardly a narrow lane for his passage'. They 'delight to see him' and shout their good will, changing their vantage points to see him again and again. Such a king would free them from slavery, 'wipe the tears from every eye and put joy in place of our long distress'.[8]

> Now the people, freed, run before their king with bright faces. Their joy is almost beyond their own comprehension.
>
> They rejoice, they exult, they leap for joy and celebrate their having such a king. 'The King' is all that any mouth can say.
>
> The nobility, long since at the mercy of the dregs of the

population, the nobility, whose title has too long
been without meaning, now lifts its head, now rejoices
in such a king, and has proper reason for rejoicing.

The merchant, heretofore deterred by numerous taxes,
now once again plows seas grown unfamiliar.
All are equally happy. All weigh their earlier losses
against the advantages to come.

Now each man happily does not hesitate to show the
possessions which in the past his fear kept hidden in
dark seclusion.[9]

There was clearly a mood of exhilaration in the air in 1509, the very real sense of a new age dawning. No doubt Catherine shared it. After the final, difficult years of the widowed Henry VII's reign, this young and attractive couple must have literally seemed like a godsend.

The feasting continued. In Westminster Hall, the new king and queen sat down to a three-course feast, 'whiche was sumpteous, with many subtelties, strange devices … and many deintie dishes'. The order of service was 'admirable', with 'cleane handelynge and breakyng of meates' and 'plentifull abundance'.[10] It was all accompanied by the usual court rituals: the Duke of Buckingham riding into hall to announce the arrival of the food, followed by the defence of the new king by his champion, Sir Richard Dimmock, who then called for drink, to signal his shift from defence to enjoyment. After all the proclamations and oaths, Henry was served with wafers and hippocras, a drink of wine mixed with sugar and spices, in a gold cup.

Two days after her coronation, Catherine was not too bound up in her own celebrations to forget the needs of others. On 26 June, she wrote to her father from Greenwich regarding their servant Calderon, who had borne a letter to her. As he had proved his worth and was no longer 'at a fit age to serve as a quarter-master', she asked that he be given 'an office which he may hold as long as he lives, since he deserves it so well, in order that he may have a rest'.

A few days later, the coronation jousts began at Greenwich. Catherine and Henry sat inside a wooden stand, which was fashioned into a castle overspread with Tudor imagery. Hall's account gives a sense of the complexity of the design:

a Castle, on the toppe thereof, a greate croune Emperiall, all the imbattelyng with Roses and Pomegranate gilded, and under and about thesaid Castle, a curious vine, the leaves and grapes thereof, gilded with fine Golde, the walls of the same Castle, coloured white and green lozenges. And in every lozenge, either a rose or a pomegranate, or a sheaf of arrows, or else H and K gilded with fine Gold.[11]

Out of the mouths of 'certain beasts' and gargoyles, ran red and white wine, as the 'fresh young gallants ... gorgeously apparelled' entered the field. Thomas Howard, Duke of Norfolk, and his retinue echoed the castle's design, wearing the Tudor colours of green and white, with beaten roses and pomegranates of gold, fringed with damask. Representing the 'home team', they were presented to the king and queen by Pallas Athene, Greek goddess of wisdom. The challengers, dressed in blue velvet, gold and silver, represented love. The mock battle, or tourney, that followed was concluded by the intervention of the king, as night was 'commyng on'.[12]

The following day, 28 June, was Henry's eighteenth birthday. More celebrations followed, with the same knights joined by men dressed all in green, from cap to hose, blowing on horns amid a pageant of a park, where fallow deer and 'curious Trees made by crafte' were enclosed by a white-and-green fence. When the deer were released and killed by greyhounds, their carcasses were offered to the queen. The knights fought again, with love and wisdom unable to defeat each other, and prizes were distributed by the king 'to every man after his deserts', drawing the event to a close. The following day, Henry's grandmother Margaret Beaufort died in the Deanery of Westminster Abbey. Having been an imposing figure at court since 1485, the final link with Henry's childhood was broken.

11

Catherine's Court, 1509

Manhood I am, therefore I me delight
To hunt and hawk, to nourish-up and feed,
The greyhound to the course, the hawk to the flight,
And to bestride a good and lusty steed—
These things become a very man indeed[1]

In 1510, Thomas More wrote a poem which he called 'The Twelve Properties or Conditions of a Lover'. With the happiness of the newly wed royal couple evident to all, More explored the contemporary ideals of amatory behaviour, which included fidelity and devotion as well as the more specific examples of dressing, or adorning, oneself for the pleasure of the spouse, being frequently in their company and coveting the lover's praise. It was also essential to 'believe of his love all things excellent, and to desire that all folks should think the same' and 'to serve his love, nothing thinking of any reward or profit'.[2] This accorded with the advice given to Henry in 1501, by his tutor John Skelton, to 'choose a wife for yourself and always love her only'.[3] With Henry soon to adopt the title of 'Sir Loyal Heart', his devotion to Catherine was beyond doubt.

Henry had certainly grown into an impressive young man. According to Thomas More's coronation verses, he had 'strength worthy of his regal person' and stood taller than his companions. There was 'fiery power' in his eyes, Venus in his face and 'such colour in his cheeks as is typical of twin roses'. Yet he possessed other skills, too. He was skilled in the physical arts of war, with 'his hand ... as skilled as his heart is brave' with 'the naked sword, or an eager charge with levelled lances, or an arrow aimed to strike a target'. More also described how Henry's virtue 'shone forth from his face' and his countenance bore 'the open message of a good heart'. Wisdom dwelled in his judicious mind and his breast was untroubled; he bore his lot with modest chastity, his gentle heart was warmed by clemency and his mind far from arrogant. He deserved to rule for restoring laws to their 'ancient form and dignity' and his natural gifts had been enhanced by a 'liberal education', with his father's wisdom and his mother's 'kindly strength'. Henry was also Catherine's intellectual equal, having studied the Classics, French, Latin, Italian, theology, modern sciences and composing music, as well as playing upon the flute, virginals and recorder. His devotion was also commendable; the king usually heard Mass three times daily – and sometimes as often as five times a day – and it was common for him to hear vespers and compline with the queen in her chambers.[4] This was the man with whom Catherine fell in love. In all things, he seemed to be her perfect match just as she was his.

More's praise for the new queen extolled her birth and qualities as qualifiers that made her Henry's true equal:

> This lady, prince, vowed to you for many years, through
> a long time of waiting remained alone for love of you.
> Neither her own sister nor her native land could win her
> from her way; neither her mother nor her father
> could dissuade her.

In her you have as wife one whom your people have
been happy to see sharing your power,
one for whom the powers above care so much that they
distinguish her and honor her by marriage with you.

In her expression, in her countenance, there is a remarkable beauty uniquely appropriate for one so great and
good.

It was you, none other, whom she preferred to her
mother, sister, native land, and beloved father.

This blessed lady has joined in lasting alliance two
nations, each of them powerful.

She is descended from great kings, to be sure; and she
will be the mother of kings as great as her ancestors.

Until now one anchor has protected your ship of state –
a strong one, yet only one.
But your queen, fruitful in male offspring, will render it
on all sides stable and everlasting.

Great advantage is yours because of her, and similarly is
hers because of you.

There has been no other woman, surely, worthy to have
you as husband, nor any other man worthy to have
her as wife.[5]

The summer days passed happily. That July, Henry wrote to
Ferdinand from Greenwich that he was diverting himself with
'jousts, birding, hunting and other innocent and honest pastimes,
also in visiting different parts of his kingdom, but does not on that
account neglect affairs of state'.[6] Catherine also wrote to her father
that month, describing her happiness and that the 'time is ever
passed in continual feasts'. She explained that 'among the reasons
that oblige me to love him [Henry] much more than myself, the one
most strong, although he is my husband, is his being the so true son
of your highness'. She asked her father to send Henry three horses –
a jennet, a Sicilian and one from Naples – 'because he desires them
so much'.[7] The King of Aragon was 'exceedingly glad to hear that

she and the king her husband are well and prosperous, and that they love one another so much'. He hoped 'their happiness will last as long as they live. To be well married is the greatest blessing in the world. A good marriage is not only an excellent thing in itself, but also the source of all other kinds of happiness. God shows favour to good husbands and wives.'[8] Catherine and Henry do genuinely seem to have been in love. An early poem or 'ballet' attributed to Henry includes the line, 'I love true where I did marry.'[9] Even Fray Diego could see it, writing to Ferdinand that 'the king my Lord adores her'.[10]

Judging by the rapidity of Catherine's conceptions in the early years of the marriage, their physical relationship was close. A surviving manuscript from 1440, *Jacob's Well*, outlines contemporary expectations for moderate, appropriate sex within marriage: 'For wedlock truly knit, truly kept and used in order, is of such virtue that it keepeth their flesh from deadly sin. If you use your wife or husband as your sweetheart in intent, only for lust ... not for love, nor the fruit of wedlock, nor to be honest, but as an unreasonable beast ... beware of the fiend.' The text also reminded married couples that foreplay could lead to impurity and sin: 'When you feeleth or toucheth with mouth in kissing, with hand in groping, and with any member of thy body ... that stirs you to lust and sin, then you enter into ... wickedness.' This was echoed in the *Book of Vices and Virtues*, which advised against any 'use of one's wife' that went against 'the order of wedlock'.[11]

Even during these early days of pure enjoyment, Catherine would have been hoping to fall pregnant. The literature of the day suggests a fairly pragmatic and direct approach to sex, with an emphasis on the need for female enjoyment – within the correct religious lines – and far less prudish than might initially be supposed. It was considered imperative for a woman to 'emit seed' in order to conceive, so her husband was instructed to 'smoothly stroke his lady, breasts and belly and excite her'.[12] Another fourteenth-century text, written by Edward II's doctor of physic, advised a man to 'arouse a woman to intercourse' by speaking, kissing and embracing her, 'to caress her breasts and touch [her] between the perineum and vulva and to strike her buttocks with the purpose that the woman desires ... and when the woman begins to speak with a stammer, then they ought to copulate'.[13] Another technique suggested by a medieval advice manual was 'froting' or rubbing, 'when a man hath great liking between him and his wife in bed'.[14] With the imperative to conceive an heir, Catherine and Henry need have felt little guilt in attempting to achieve the Church's primary concern of wedlock, whatever foreplay Henry decided to employ.

With their physical relationship blooming, the years of austerity were also quickly being forgotten. Catherine's household and properties marked her new status as Henry's queen and bedfellow, with 160 ladies and two palaces at her disposal, in addition to all the other royal residences. Baynard's Castle, on the Thames, had particular associations for Catherine, having been the location of her wedding night with Arthur, but added to this was Havering Palace, also known as Havering-atte-Bower, a Saxon hunting lodge situated where the modern city of London spills into the west of Essex. Havering had been part of the queen's dower since 1267 and sat in 16,000 acres of land, with views across the Essex marshes and good hunting, part of which now forms Havering Country Park. The palace no longer survives, having fallen into ruin by the seventeenth century, but floor plans surviving from 1578 cover an area of one hundred metres square. The main buildings included a great hall, presence chamber, two chapels and royal apartments overlooking the gardens and courtyard. The majority of Catherine's time was divided between the royal residences of Westminster and Windsor, Greenwich and Whitehall, with Eltham, Richmond and Woodstock. There were also a number of other castles and houses in possession of the Crown, at which she would have stayed from time to time.

The Tudor court was a huge, complex and peripatetic institution. Its nucleus was the king, supported by a number of departments above and below stairs, and it travelled wherever he went, occupying his properties and ensuring the wheels of royalty continued to turn smoothly, from the making of the king's bed and preparation of his clothes, to those charged with the intimate tasks of dressing, shaving and washing him. There were those who supplied, stored, prepared, tested and served food and drink, those who swept, cleaned and lit fires, those in the exchequer who counted out the money and others who tended for the king's horses, dogs and falcons. Others were employed to ensure Henry's safety, or to enact his wishes, tend to his mortal soul, dispense his alms, or generally to ensure the smooth running of an establishment that could run to thousands.

As queen, Catherine's household was a separate body under the umbrella of the court. Assigned specific ladies and servants, it would sometimes operate separately in the interests of the queen and sometimes in conjunction with the main court, when Henry and Catherine were jointly in residence at one of the royal properties. The hub would have been Catherine's set of royal apartments, preserved for her in each palace, usually comprising a bedroom, presence chamber and one or more other retiring rooms. She might dine there quietly, or entertain guests, or watch jugglers or musicians perform, or emerge into the main court; the architecture of Tudor palaces, with their clusters of rooms connected according to protocol, echoed and enabled the existence of separate cogs in the wider court machinery. It allowed a degree of privacy for the newly wed couple as well as providing the opportunity for them to retreat into their own spaces. Although they were assigned separate bedrooms, it was customary for the king to visit the queen, accompanied by his grooms of his chamber, who would light his way and announce his approach to Catherine's ladies, whose task was then to ready her for his attentions. Thus, the bedroom doors might be closed and secured, with the ornate golden lock Henry carried from palace to palace, but the couple's closeness in these early days would have been no secret. In fact, the exact timings and durations of their encounters could be measured as the grooms were required to wait outside the room until it was time to escort Henry back to his own bed.

Among her household, Catherine retained a number of her loyal Spanish ladies, who had remained loyal throughout the past seven years. If Catherine was going to confide in anyone about her martial happiness it would have been Maria de Salinas, then aged around twenty, who had come from the royal court of Castile in 1503 to replace her cousin. The princess was reputed to love Maria 'more than any mortal'.[15] Maria's sister Inez Albernos, then married to Juan Guevara, a Spaniard resident in London, may also have been among the queen's retinue in these early years. There were also the sisters Isabel and Blanche Vargas, as well as Inez, or Agnes, de Venegas, the daughter of Catherine's governess in Spain, then in her mid-thirties, who was also married in the summer of 1509, to William Blount. Blount's young daughter from his first marriage, Gertrude, also became one of Catherine's maids of honour, as did Anne Luke, Henry's wet nurse back in 1491, and Jane Popincourt, who had been a French tutor to Henry's sisters Margaret and Mary, later being attached to Mary's household. She would also have derived comfort from the loyal service of her apothecary John de Soto, who would remain with her all her life, and the presence of her Spanish doctor Ferdinand de Victoria.

Eight English women were selected as Catherine's ladies-in-waiting. Their role was more permanent and intimate than that of the thirty-odd maids of honour that also served the queen, attending to her personal needs and witnessing her daily life as Henry's wife. Two of them, Elizabeth and Anne, were the sisters of Edward Stafford, Duke of Buckingham, and daughters of Katherine Wydeville, Henry's great-aunt. Elizabeth Stafford, Lady Fitzwalter, was then aged around thirty and had been married for around five years to the Earl of Sussex. Her younger sister, Anne, had already been widowed once, when she married George Hastings, Earl of Huntingdon, in December 1509. Catherine was also served by Agnes Tylney, Countess of Surrey, Anne Hastings, Countess of Shrewsbury, and Anne, Countess of Derby, as well as Elizabeth Scrope, Countess of Oxford, Mary Say, Countess of Essex and Margaret Scrope, Countess of Suffolk. They were the wives, sisters and daughters of the men in Henry's household, with many bearing royal blood from three or four generations back; the new Tudor court was truly a family affair.

The male names of some of Catherine's household from 1509 give a sense of the different divisions within the establishment and its range. Above stairs she had two secretaries, the English Richard Decons and John de Scutea, her 'secretary for the Spanish tongue', and her almoner was Dr Bekensall. The Irish Thomas Butler, Earl of Ormond, became her chamberlain, with Sir Robert Poyntz as his deputy and, along with her confessor Fray Diego, six further chaplains tended to her soul. Those responsible for serving her at table included her carvers Alexander Frognall and Edward Knevett, her cup-bearer Edward Jernynygham, servers John Verney and George Bekonsall plus two more specifically for her chamber, Anthony Polen and John Morton. Her ushers William Bulstrode, Roger Ratclyff and Edward Benestede were supported by six squires attendant, sixteen Yeomen Ushers and a host of other grooms and pages of the chamber.

Beyond her suite of rooms, in various offices in the bowels of the Tudor palace were John Adams, who ran her bakehouse; Richard Brampton and Nicholas Clyff, who had charge of her pantry; Thomas Astley, who ran her larder; and John Case, her master cook. The cellar, buttery and ewery were overseen by a total of eight men. The surviving Tudor kitchens at Hampton Court give a good idea of the scale of this below-stairs operation, being extended by Henry in 1529 to include fifty-five separate rooms devoted to the different processes of storage and preparation. From the huge main kitchens with their walk-in fireplaces where meat turned on spits, to the slaughter rooms, bread ovens and high ceilings stained with smoke, the kitchens were constantly alive with noise and activity. The nose would have been met by a mixture of smells, typically with the favoured Tudor mixture of sweet and spicy. Among them were the flesh, wet and dry larders, boiling rooms, spicery, confectionery and pastry house. Catherine's stable was overseen by Sir Thomas Tirrell, her master of the horses, along with a number of grooms, clerks, saddlers, Yeomen of the chair, pages, fourteen palfreymen, men assigned to the bottles, the beds, the robes and the closet and a master of the aviary.

The long party gave no signs of abating as the court moved between royal palaces that August and September. It must have been an idyllic time for her, in love with and beloved of this young and attractive paragon of royalty, at the heart of a new court, with all the privilege that could bring and the promise of happy years lying ahead. There was, inevitably, excitement at the start of a new reign, when the character of the king dictated the nature of his court and rule, and, as More's verses testify, Henry's ascent signified a splendid new era for a world on the cusp of the Renaissance. The honeymoon continued for months, ending in October when the pair returned to Greenwich. For Catherine, only one thing could have improved upon her current joy and, as the summer wore on, she began to suspect that her happiness was to be complete. She was pregnant.

12

Pregnancy, 1509–10

The same time that a man
Knoweth fleshly a woman
That seed in her root take[1]

Catherine's pregnancy was announced at court on 1 November. It seemed to validate the match and the dynasty, confirming that Henry had chosen the correct queen in the eyes of God. Henry wrote to inform Ferdinand that 'the child in the womb was alive', placing Catherine's quickening around mid-November. Diagnosing pregnancy was not an exact science and the physical symptoms suggested by contemporary texts such as *Hali Meidenhad* could easily be mistaken for illness or overlooked altogether. The erratic nature of Catherine's recent health, coupled with her fasting, may well have conspired to interrupt her menstrual cycle and, as Ambassador Caroz would later confide to Ferdinand, the queen's periods were so irregular that it was difficult to know for certain whether or not she was pregnant. Even if her periods had been regular and then stopped, indicating that conception had taken place, pregnancy could not be diagnosed with any certainty until the child's first movements in the womb, which usually took place between the fourth and fifth months for a first-time mother. This would have placed the moment of conception in July, just weeks after the wedding.

One medical manual of the day, penned by a French doctor, contained the belief that the moment of conception could be easily identified by a pair of lovers. His explicit detail echoes the image of the hungry womb drawing in the seed it craved, then closing around it. A man should feel an 'extraordinary contentment' and a 'sucking or drawing at the end of his yard', which should not be 'over moist' once withdrawn. A woman should experience a sensation of 'yawning or stretching' in the womb, or a shaking and quivering not dissimilar to passing water, followed by a chill in the shoulders and back and a rumbling in the belly as the womb contracted.[2]

Another medieval instructional text, *Sidrak and Bokkus*, gives advice about how quickly conception may occur:

> May a man get a child, by thy life,
> Everytime that he toucheth his wife?
> Man there is in this world non
> That might get his wife upon
> A child at every time and ay
> When he fleshly by her lay.[3]

The author explained that pregnancy did not always occur and, of course, such failures were attributed to women, as they were 'cold of seed' and 'cold to seed is no nurture'. They believed that male 'kind', or sperm, was gathered from every limb of the potential father and that the act of intercourse created a certain physical response in him that diverted the sperm from his body into his member:

> That he hath his deed to fulfill
> Maketh his body to sweat therewith
> Blood inward from every lith [bodypart]
> And that blood cometh full swiftly
> And to the ballocks goeth full hastily
> And from thence it issueth so
> When it cometh the pintil [penis] unto.[4]

Exactly when Catherine became aware that she might be pregnant is unclear, especially because her menstruation had been erratic in the past. Contrary to contemporary medical texts, she probably did not notice the moment of conception, although she probably was hoping to fall pregnant fairly soon as a sign of divine blessing on her marriage.

Secure in her position and Henry's love, she would have confided her suspicions to him sometime in the early autumn. No doubt he was delighted and they enjoyed some form of private celebration.

However, in spite of these physical details, exact conception dates were notoriously difficult to determine. This made it difficult to predict when the child would arrive. Catherine was surrounded by experienced doctors who would have been alert to possible symptoms, all eager to be the first to announce to the king that he was soon to be a father. They might have employed a range of pregnancy tests, including examining Catherine's urine, or floating a needle in it to see whether rusting occurred. Other superstitious methods included waving a chicken wing across a woman's belly or making her drink rainwater at night.

Antenatal care was considered important, particularly an expectant mother's behaviour. Catherine's doctors would have been full of advice regarding her behaviour and diet. It was recommended that she eat bland food and avoid certain dishes. All meat from 'animals that could beget' was prohibited, along with old pork, fatty food, fish, salty and sweet flavours, certain fruits and vegetables. Likewise, old roebuck and venison were off limits as they led to melancholy, and peacock and crane created bad blood. Younger beasts were preferred, including milk-fed lamb, piglets and roast hare, although that was thought to cause a woman to urinate excessively. Rich women were advised to treat themselves to fat young turtledoves or pigeons. The recommended drinks were wine and beer. Ferdinand had his own advice to add:

> Her pregnancy is a great blessing, since she, her husband, and the English people have wished it so much. May God give her a good delivery. Will continually pray the Almighty to grant his prayers till he is informed that she has given birth to her child. Begs her to be careful of her health. During her pregnancy she must avoid all exertion, and especially not write with her own hand. With the first child it is requisite for women to take more care of themselves than is necessary in subsequent pregnancies.[5]

While Catherine awaited her confinement, the long party continued. The royal couple spent their first Christmas together at Richmond, blending the feasting and jousting with the religious services and devotions of the season. Henry was in high spirits. Along with his gentlemen, he dressed up as one of his favourite folklore figures, Robin Hood, in a short coat of Kentish green complete with bow and arrows and, with his men's faces hidden by hoods, burst into the queen's chamber and insisted that she and her 'abashed' ladies join them in a dance. It was typical of the disguises, role play and identity games that he would enjoy throughout his life, although the timing was possibly a little thoughtless, given Catherine's advanced stage of pregnancy and the advice of doctors that women in her condition should avoid shocks. Henry's actions were in the tradition of misrule, which encouraged the subversion of social roles, tricks and revels and to which end William Wynesbury was appointed as the Lord of Misrule for the duration of the festivities, from Christmas until Twelfth Night. It all fitted with the air of exuberance and revelry that set the tone at the start of the new reign.

One of the verses of the song 'Greensleeves', traditionally ascribed to Henry, adds further weight to the theory that this, and similar disguises, were used by the king to woo women:

> My men were clothed all in green,
> And they did ever wait on thee;
> All this was gallant to be seen,
> And yet thou wouldst not love me.

The festivities continued into January, with jousting being held before the palace gates, on the present location of Richmond Green. It was the first time that the king had participated in public and all eyes were on him. Along with his close companion William Compton, he came to the field disguised, broke many staves and won many accolades, although his ability and physique made him unmistakeable and a cry of 'long live the king' exposed his identity. Compton, who had been Henry's companion since his youth, fared less well, being 'hurte ... sore, and was likely to die'. Compton recovered, though, and was soon to play a significant role in the royal marriage.

Henry and Catherine were excited about her approaching confinement. In accordance with ordinances set out by Margaret Beaufort, they made preparations by ordering a birthing or groaning chair. This was a sturdy chair with the central part of the seat missing and was commonly used at the time for seated deliveries. There was also a copper gilt bowl to catch the blood and placenta, and also sent was the silver font from Canterbury Cathedral, which was shipped up to Greenwich, where a suite of rooms was being equipped with heavy arras and carpets, cradles, bed of state, altar with relics and mountains of linen. The royal surgeon, Jehan Veyrier, was on standby, although traditionally the delivery room would be attended by women, except in the event that surgical intervention was deemed necessary. Veyrier was a native of Nimes, in southern France and had been part of Henry VII's household, so would have been known and trusted by the king and queen. In December, the Great Wardrobe was instructed to deliver the surgeon some black chamlet for a gown. In mid-January, Henry was occupied with the opening of his first parliament, allowing Catherine to patiently await the arrival of her child.

On the night of 30 January, when she was around seven months pregnant, Catherine experienced a little pain in one knee. It seemed innocuous enough but, the following night, her labour started prematurely and she miscarried a daughter. The pain was so intense that she made a vow to send a rich headdress of hers to St Peter the Martyr and entrusted it to a niece of the Spanish treasurer. According to Fray Diego, the secret was kept from the court, known only to himself, the king, two Spanish women and a surgeon, probably Jehan Veyrier. It was one of the sad ironies of contemporary medicine that the treatment used to help expel an unsuccessful pregnancy and the afterbirth contained pomegranate rind, the very fruit Catherine had chosen as a symbol of her fertility.

However, over the next few days, the queen's belly remained rounded and gave no signs of returning to its pre-pregnancy shape. This was enough to convince her surgeon that she was actually still pregnant and had only miscarried one of a pair of twins. It is little surprise that Catherine allowed herself to be convinced by those whose job was to read the signs of her body. The weight of her own hopes, coupled with those of Henry, disposed her to believe that she still carried a viable foetus, the fleshly embodiment of their marital and dynastic success, a sign that the long years of penury had been worth it. Thus she waited, expectant of delivering a second child in March. The court was none the wiser.

On Shrove Sunday, which fell on 20 February, Henry hosted a great banquet at Westminster that Catherine and her ladies attended. After leading her to her seat and 'making chere', Henry and his friends disappeared, to return in a series of disguises: as Turks in 'bawdkin', powdered with gold and wearing red velvet hats and swords; as Russians in grey fur hats and boots, carrying hatchets; as Prussians in crimson satin and feathered caps, accompanied by torchbearers with faces blackened to represent Moors. This was followed by a group of mummers, who usually performed comical or allegorical plays, and then the banquet ended. The tables were cleared away and 'the quene with the ladies toke their places with their degrees'. Dancing followed and, while everyone 'toke much hede to them', Henry slipped away again and returned in a procession that followed a drummer and flautist, where all the men were dressed in multi-coloured costumes bearing the devices of golden castles and sheaves of arrows. Led by Henry's sister Mary, the ladies wore kirtles of purple and crimson, embroidered with Catherine's device of the pomegranate, their faces covered with fine black material, again in the semblance of Moors. More dancing followed and after 'a certayne tyme they departed every one to his lodging'.[6]

Soon after this, on 28 February, Catherine entered confinement. The process was a formal, ceremonial one, timed to take place around three to four weeks before the expected date of delivery, to allow for miscalculation. After taking Mass, formally attended by lords and ladies of the court, she was accompanied into her great chamber, where she was served with wine and spices. Henry was absent from this ceremony, as his status would have outstripped hers, thus allowing Catherine to be the sole centre of attention. The party progressed to the inner chamber, where prayers were said before the beds, and the men were then formally asked to leave. Male physicians would have been on hand but only in the eventuality of emergency, and otherwise it was an exclusively female zone. Her ladies would have taken over the male roles in her household, collecting the necessary supplies, which were left outside the door.

Margaret Beaufort's ordinances were followed again, with their specifications for the exact number, design and colour of the cushions, linen and bedding. The chamber was hung with heavy arras to keep out the draughts and light, although one window was left uncovered to allow the patient mother a glimpse of the world outside. Paintings and tapestries depicting alarming or violent images were removed, as they were thought to imprint themselves upon the character of the unborn child. A huge ceremonial bed, measuring eight feet by ten, was covered in crimson satin and used for the lying-in process, while the actual birth itself was intended to take place on a pallet bed. Likewise two cradles were prepared; one, of five-foot length and decorated with silver buckles and the royal arms, was for public display, while a smaller one of wood was intended for sleeping.

Catherine would have prayed before she entered her confinement and every day and night through it. Women did die in labour, even queens, as Elizabeth of York had proved. No doubt as a first-time mother Catherine was anxious about the degree of pain and danger she may experience, but, as a queen fulfilling her duty, this would have been balanced by the pride of the moment. Her religious comforts would have been close to hand: the rosary and prayerbook, icons and relics, including the famous girdle of the Virgin Mary, on loan from Westminster Abbey. Otherwise, the days of waiting would have passed slowly enough, in gentle pursuits like reading, listening to music, needlework and watching her ladies dance. Catherine knew that the outcome of her bodily changes were important dynastic news, awaited eagerly within her realm and further afield.

March became April but the queen's labour pains did not arrive. She would have grown impatient and confused, praying for the onset of delivery and perhaps trying some of the herbal or dietary remedies thought to help, such as eating spinach and butter, drinking wine mixed with leek, rue and savin, or walking in her chamber in the hope that the motion would trigger her contractions. April became May. Her inflamed womb, probably the result of an infection, began to go down and her menstrual cycle recommenced in April. During that month, Catherine was forced to accept that the child she had miscarried in January had not come from a multiple pregnancy. There was no twin, no royal heir.

Catherine must have been crushed by the confusion arising over her pregnancy and the humiliation of the weeks of waiting. She finally confessed to her father that she had miscarried a daughter and explained the delay by informing him it was the result of English belief that this was bad luck. According to her letter, she and Henry remained cheerful and she thanked God 'for such a husband'.[7] Fray Diego wrote to Ferdinand with the truth, saying that he had been forced to keep the secret from him for fear of annoying Catherine and that 'all the physicians deceived themselves until time was the judge of truth'. Ironically, the headdress she had vowed to St Peter the Martyr in January, in the hopes of delivering a healthy child, had never reached its destination. The Spanish treasurer had kept it for himself, an act which a superstitious Catherine must have deplored.

However, it seemed that Catherine and Henry had broken one of the fundamental cultural and religious rules of the lying-in process. During the spring months of her confinement, when the queen was supposed to be sequestered away, Henry had visited her on at least one occasion. Convention dictated that pregnant women, especially those in an advanced state of pregnancy, should refrain from sex, as it could harm the unborn child and was for purposes of fornication rather than reproduction. Often a blind eye was turned when a husband sought solace elsewhere during this time but it is clear that Henry desired Catherine and, in spite of her religious convictions, she either desired him also or was persuaded to sleep with him. During this controversial encounter in the lying-in chamber, surrounded by the paraphernalia of imminent birth, she actually did conceive. By the time she emerged in public, late in May 1510, she was several weeks pregnant. Catherine could entertain hope again, but she was also fighting against a scandal that signified the end to the long honeymoon between her and Henry.

PART TWO
The Queen's Rivals

13

Anne, Lady Hastings, 1510

The first point is to love but one alone,
And for that one, all other to forsake
For whose loveth many, loveth none[1]

With his wife in confinement, Henry threw himself into sport as a distraction from temptation. He would 'exercise himselfe dailie in shooting, singing, dancing, wrestling, casting of the barre, playing at the recorders, flute, virginals, in setting of songs, and making of ballads ... in hunting, hawking and shooting'.[2] On 20 May, it was acknowledged that the early summer months were a particularly quiet time that could breed the idleness that led to vice and it was said that 'disportes' should be practised 'to eschew idleness, the ground of all vice, and give honourable and healthy exercise'.[3] At Greenwich, an artificial green tree was set up bearing a white shield on which those who accepted the challenge should write their names. Then, every Thursday and Monday for a month, gentlemen would 'meet all comers' at the barriers, 'casting spear and target and with bastard sword from 6 a.m. till 6 p.m.'. If these games were intended to keep Henry out of mischief, they did not work.

Among Catherine's ladies were two sisters of the Duke of Buckingham, Elizabeth and Anne. The elder, Elizabeth, then aged around thirty, was the wife of Robert Radcliffe, Earl of Sussex, and the mother of at least two young children by 1510. As such, she would have been well placed to share in Catherine's excitement about her pregnancy and offer advice about the process to an inexperienced queen. Radcliffe had also been in the household of Prince Arthur and attended Catherine's first marriage so, after his marriage in 1505, his wife was probably known to Catherine. The childless younger sister Anne, in her late twenties, had been married for a second time, on 2 December 1509, to George Hastings, Earl of Huntingdon. Henry and Catherine probably attended the ceremony, with the king making the standard offering of 6s 8d. Perhaps the bride also caught his eye.

The siblings had a controversial descent. Their mother had been sister to Queen Elizabeth Wydeville, whom Henry's grandfather Edward IV had married in secret, after falling for her renowned blonde beauty. This meant that the sisters were first cousins of Henry's own mother, Elizabeth of York. Their father, Henry, Duke of Buckingham, also had his own claim to the throne via his descent from John of Gaunt, a claim he believed was equal to, if not stronger than, that of the king. He had been the close friend of Henry's great-uncle Richard III before leading a rebellion against him and losing his head as a consequence. Anne had been born the year of her father's execution, making her eight years older than Henry. Her first husband had been an illegitimate son of Walter Herbert, who had been the guardian of Henry VII as a boy. Her second husband, Hastings, was the grandson of one of Edward IV's close friends who had been executed by Richard in the days leading up to his succession. Their histories were closely bound up with those of Henry and, although no portraits of them survive, there is a good chance they had inherited some of the legendary Wydeville beauty. Anne's attractiveness created a scandal in Catherine's household when she was wooed by an influential man. His identity, though, remains in question.

One account of what happened in May 1510 is given by the Spanish ambassador Luis Caroz. He stated that Anne was 'much liked by the king, who went after her' while Catherine was in confinement. With medical teaching presenting regular sexual activity for men as essential to health, it was almost a convention that married men would seek a physical outlet while their wives were off limits. Under these circumstances extramarital sex was not considered to be a threat to the marriage, especially as many matches were arranged, but was viewed more as a bodily function that fulfilled a need, like eating or sleeping. Women's bodies were demarcated according to class and function. Noblemen might frequent brothels or have casual encounters with women of lower classes, as their 'base' nature was considered more conducive to sexual satisfaction while the duty of a wife was procreation. This neat divide allowed a compartmentalisation of love and sex, but it was a disconnection that speaks volumes about the interaction of the classes and genders. It was also not so cut and dried in many cases. When it came to marriages like Henry's, in which husband and wife clearly gave the appearances of being in love and deliberately employed the language, devices and behaviours of the courtly tradition, it was bound to cause heartbreak. Poems such as More's 'The Twelve Properties of a Lover' advocated exclusivity. Some monarchs were quite open about their affairs, like Francis I of France, but perhaps it was Henry's desire to maintain this persona of the devoted lover while taking a mistress that led him to keep his affairs as secret as possible and explains his reactions to their exposure.

There is no doubt that Henry would have made the first move. The cult of courtly love would allow him to act within the chivalrous tradition towards ladies of the court, paying compliments, being attentive and making gifts. But it was a discreet game. No woman could refuse the attention of a king; a direct rejection or coldness would be a slur to the king, a mark of disrespect and probably the end of a career. Thus it was a game of subtle flirtation, body language and inference. Anne was not inexperienced, having been married once before, and she may have caught Henry's eye as early as the day of her second wedding, perhaps even before. It would have been an unthinkable and dangerous breach of etiquette for Anne, given Henry's status and his marriage to her mistress, to have initiated an affair by making advances to Henry. However, as she danced with him, or sang, she would have made her willingness apparent by smiling, flattering and showing her appreciation of his attentions and person. With significantly more experience than Henry, Anne may well have noticed his attraction to her and decided to exploit it, taking the role of the older woman and encouraging her young suitor. It would have then been up to the king to find some discreet way of showing he was interested in taking the connection further, perhaps through gifts, whispered words, a caress, or the message of an inter-mediary like Compton.

Yet Anne's behaviour did not go unnoticed at court. Whether the incident involved some harmless flirting or developed into a full-blown physical affair, Elizabeth Radcliffe was sufficiently concerned by her sister's behaviour to take action. According to Caroz, a 'very anxious' Elizabeth called a meeting in her private chambers, summoning her brother, her husband and Hastings, to decide upon the best course of action. Then, while Buckingham was in Anne's chamber, Sir William Compton arrived to speak with her, or, as Caroz says, the two 'met Conton [sic] in her chambers',[4] suggesting he had interrupted a tryst. As Henry's Groom of the Stool, Compton was probably closer to him than anyone, a fact recognised by the French ambassador, who suggested that no one had more influence with the king. After his father's early death in 1493 he had become a ward of Henry VII, when he was eleven and Prince Henry was still a toddler, serving him as a page and developing a bond of trust. It is symbolic that the pair often shared the same disguise, causing confusion over their identities in the jousting of 1510 and subsequent pageants and games. Years later, a courtier named Elizabeth Amadas, who was arrested for treason and witchcraft, claimed that Compton and Sir John Dauncey would find willing women to introduce to Henry at his house in Thames Street. Although this evidence was given under duress and cannot be proven either way, it is certainly plausible in terms of the secrecy and arrangements such liaisons would have necessitated.

In the poetry of Henry's day, Thames Street already had associations with wanton women. During the king's youth, his tutor John Skelton had penned some verses dedicated to a woman named 'Anne' who lived at the Key in Thames Street. These were probably composed before 1504, but were published in 1527 and their tetrameter form suggests they were set to music like Skelton's other poems, so were probably performed during the intervening years. The poem exploits the genre of courtly love and the convention of the available, sexually gratifying, lower-class woman. It takes the form of a dialogue, probably for one male and one female voice, with the man alternately praising his 'praty piggesny' (pretty sweetheart) and accusing her of having a sharp tongue and being promiscuous. She assures him he will not have to pay for her favours but criticises him for his pride. Her comment that her lover has need of her and others, coupled with the extended metaphor of his key being loose in any lock, implies that she was a prostitute operating from an inn, the Key, located in Upper Thames Street.

A map of Tudor London made in 1520 shows a number of inns accessible directly from this street, including Chequer Inn, Berkeley's Inn and New Inn, but no Key Inn. This may be as easily explained as a change of name, or the reversion of the property to a private dwelling or other business. It may have stood on the south side of Thames Street, close to the many keys, or quays, that gave access to the river. Perhaps it was located near Stew Key, close by the Tower, reminiscent of the stews, or brothels, of Southwark. A block to the east, the aptly named Love Lane had been home to a 'stuehous' as early as 1428.[5] Equally, the Key might have been the euphemistic name for a brothel, just as the poem puns on the use of the key in the lock. If so, it was considerably more subtle than some of the previous establishments in London, which could be found in Slut's Hole, Codpiece Alley and Gropecuntlane.

Thames Street was well connected. It gave access to the Manor of the Rose, the London residence of the Duke of Buckingham in parallel Candlewick Street. This might have provided Henry with a venue for pursuing his amour with the duke's sister and was served by many quays that led to the south bank. When night had fallen, trusted oarsmen may have carried the king across the river for the evening, just as they did when Henry installed Jane Seymour downriver and visited her under cover of darkness in 1536. From 1510, Charles Brandon's 'large and sumptuous' mansion of Suffolk Place, surrounded by gardens, also provided the king with a safe, secret place to woo women.[6] It was also conveniently close to the most famous stews of the city, overseen by the Bishop of Winchester, where the prostitutes referred to as 'Winchester Geese' may have been brought into the seclusion of properties connected with the king. Just as Henry was an ardent devotee of the saints' shrines he would destroy in the 1530s, he may also have enjoyed the attentions of women from the very stews he later attempted to close down in an attempt to redress divine wrath incurred by his youthful antics.

There were clearly some grounds for concern about Anne's behaviour. Buckingham confronted Compton in his sister's chamber, perhaps questioning him about his intentions and purpose for being there. Compton repeated the quarrel to the king. Henry then 'spoke angrily to the Duke', offending Buckingham to the extent that he left the court the same night 'and did not return for some days'. The immediacy of Henry's response suggests he was waiting for Compton to return with a message about a tryst. It is easier to understand Henry's anger if the accusations were directed towards him, rather than one of his courtiers. Hastings also left, taking Anne with him and installing her in a convent sixty miles away. Was this an example of Buckingham's well-known pride in action, taking umbrage at having been chastised by the king? It seems unlikely that he would have needed to leave court over the affair of a courtier in any other circumstances. It is also interesting that Buckingham acted to protect his sister's reputation, rather than that of her husband, which supports the notion that he was compliant in the affair. If Henry had been above suspicion and devoted to the marital fidelity he appeared to be practising, he may even have welcomed the actions of Buckingham to expose an illicit liaison that posed a threat to a marriage he had personally approved.

However, Henry then went on to dismiss Elizabeth and her husband from his wife's household and would have sent away more 'tale-bearers', who were 'insidiously spying out every unwatched moment',[7] except that he feared a 'great scandal'. It had become a matter of gossip at court and the king had acted too late to try to contain the spread of it. Again, this makes it seem unlikely that this was simply a matter of one courtier's wife having an affair with another courtier. Henry was clearly angry about his private business being made public, which also suggests that his concept of his marriage was less ideal and romantic in reality than the image he had projected, or that Catherine had not necessarily expected him to follow the contemporary practice of pursuing sexual gratification elsewhere. This was a fundamental misunderstanding but, until this point, Henry still might have got away with it. The dismissal of her lady, Elizabeth Radcliffe, caused the queen to ask questions. Soon she found out what had been going on and could not conceal her feelings.

According to Caroz, 'all the court knew that the queen was vexed with the king and he with her'. It was their first big quarrel and, although they probably exchanged their heated words in strict privacy, there is no doubt that the fallout would have been felt by their respective households and that gossip was rife through the whole establishment. Caroz added that the queen showed 'ill-will' towards Compton and Henry was annoyed with her as a result. It is understandable that Catherine would be upset by the dismissal of one of her closest female companions and ladies-in-waiting, but in that eventuality the target of her annoyance would have been Henry, not Compton. Her antipathy towards Compton suggests there was more to it. At this point, Caroz went too far. When he attempted to advise his source, Fray Diego, about the correct behaviour for a queen finding herself in Catherine's situation, the friar rounded on him, claiming he had 'got it all wrong'.

Perhaps Caroz had over-interpreted the issue, but there was certainly something amiss that caused the first serious quarrel between the king and queen. For Catherine, the last twelve months had been blissful. The possibility of Henry's adultery fractured their previous closeness and shattered the proudly displayed imagery of romance that had been a feature of their public façade since their dual coronation. No doubt the queen felt not only personally betrayed, but publicly humiliated. The behaviour of her ladies and the scandal attached to the event reflected badly on her household. It was a harsh lesson to learn about her young husband. Through the month of May 1510, into the early summer, a 'storm went on between them'. The honeymoon period was over.

Further grounds for the theory that Anne Hastings did become Henry's lover at some point during these early years comes from the New Year's gift he bestowed upon her in 1513. Featuring in the records for that year, Anne received thirty ounces of silver gilt, the third largest of all the presents in the king's bequest, marking her out with a degree of preference which otherwise is unexplained. By comparison, Elizabeth Boleyn, wife of the rising diplomat Sir Thomas, was the recipient of a cup with a gilt cover weighing sixteen and a half ounces.[8] It does not seem unreasonable to speculate that

Henry's initial desire for Anne may have been thwarted in 1510 but that he may have discreetly continued to woo her following her return to court. The New Year's gift of 1513 may indicate that he met with some success. Around this time Anne fell pregnant, bearing her first son, Francis, in Leicestershire at some unspecified point in 1514. The relationship of this birth to the gift is an intriguing one, although there were no contemporary suggestions that the child might have been fathered by Henry and the king never sought to acknowledge him as his son. However, at the time, it would have been considered ungentlemanly for any man to claim the child of a married woman as his own; the only illegitimate child Henry would own would be that of an unmarried mother. According to the law, any baby born within wedlock was automatically accepted by the husband, unless under very unusual circumstances. Francis Hastings would find favour at court in the future, becoming a Knight of the Bath in 1533. On balance, given Henry's later desperation for a son, it seems unlikely that Francis Hastings was his child, although it remains a tantalising possibility.

What is known for certain, though, is that William Compton did go on to have an affair with Anne, starting around 1519, while she was still married to Hastings. He left money in his will of 8 March 1522 for prayers to be said for her soul, which was unusual outside the family unit: 'two chantries to be founded in his name at Compton, to do daily service for the souls of the king, the Queen, my Lady Anne Hastings, [myself], my wife and ancestors'.[9] When the affair took place is unclear, but in 1527 Compton was summoned to the Court of Arches by Cardinal Wolsey to swear an oath that he had never slept with Anne during his wife's lifetime. Given that he did not marry until 1512 and his first wife, Werburga Brereton, died sometime before 1522, when he wed Elizabeth Stonor, this wording does not rule out Compton and Anne having had an affair. The Hastings marriage survived the events of 1510 and 1527, with George writing affectionate letters to Anne during his absence and naming her as executor of his will. They had eight children together. Anne remains an enigmatic figure, the older, experienced woman who possibly introduced Henry to the illicit passions of extramarital affairs, a sophisticated player at the heart of the young man's romantic and lavish court.

14

The Baby Prince, 1510–11

The child that hath full the shape
In the mother, by what hap
Is it sometime brought to nought
And may not alive forth be brought?[1]

Humiliated and hurt as Catherine was, she had her new pregnancy to focus on. When she rode with Henry to the King's Head in Cheape, London, on the night of St Paul's Day, 29 June, her condition had not yet begun to show. Within weeks, though, she would have felt the child quicken. That September, eight yards of purple velvet were ordered for the nursery and Henry embarked on a royal progress to a number of religious sites, giving thanks for his wife's conception. Certain saints had particular associations with fertility and childbirth. In pre-Reformation England, the cult of the Virgin Mary was the most popular, attracting the prayers, offerings and visits of expectant parents. It had also been a favourite of Henry's mother. In 1510, he knelt before the Virgin's statue at Walsingham, the East Anglian centre of her following, before embarking on a longer trip to give thanks to St Thomas at Canterbury, St Bridget at Syon Abbey, the Black Cross at Waltham Abbey and other places.

Catherine did not go with him. She was probably being more cautious after her experience earlier that year and remained at Eltham for the duration of his absence. The palace had been Henry's childhood home and had been extensively remodelled along Burgundian lines by his grandfather, Edward IV. The old great hall had been replaced, new kitchens created and an impressive entrance and courtyard were added. Catherine would have occupied the queen's lodgings, which Edward had designed, with its brick range of five bay windows alternated with chimney breasts and a recreational gallery, the first of its kind. It also had a conduit system, allowing for a constant supply of fresh water.[2] Yet Catherine did not intend to give birth at Eltham. During those weeks, her rooms at Richmond were being transformed into the lying-in suite, worked on by carpenters, cleaners and painters and equipped to receive the expectant queen and her child. The *Ryalle Book* lists the quantities, details and colours of the equipment required to furnish her two beds and the cradles, with cloth of gold, crimson satin, blue velvet and the royal arms and symbols acting as reminders of the queen's position and power. On Henry's return that October, they travelled to Greenwich before proceeding to London to attend a banquet at the Fishmongers' Hall in Thames Street. By 8 November they were at Richmond, where Henry tilted with William Compton and Charles Brandon. Catherine may have watched this entertainment, but she did not attend the following supper and nor did the ambassadors from Spain nor her cousin Emperor Maximilian, as Henry urged them to go and pay a late-night visit to his queen in her chamber.

Meanwhile, arrangements were proceeding for the daily care of the imminent arrival. A lady mistress was appointed to oversee the royal nursery, which would have comprised wet and dry nurses, rockers and other servants including those responsible for cleaning, washing and preparing the baby's clothes, linen and bedding and those liaising with the kitchens to ensure a suitable diet for those who would be breastfeeding. Queens did not suckle their own babies, allowing them to return to royal duties sooner and enabling their menstruation to return more quickly, increasing the chance of conceiving again. Wet nurses were chosen for their healthy looks and their good character, as it was believed their thoughts and the food they consumed could be imprinted on the developing child.

Catherine would have had a say in the appointments, selecting from within her own household when she chose Henry's nurse, Elizabeth Denton, as her lady mistress. Some confusion has arisen, though, when it comes to identifying his wet nurse, who is listed as Elizabeth Poyntz. Two people named Elizabeth Poyntz had connections with Catherine's household but their comparative status makes one the more likely candidate than the other. One lady of that name was the daughter of the queen's vice-chamberlain and chancellor, Sir Robert of Iron Acton. Her royal connections went back to the reign of Edward IV, as her mother, Margaret, was the illegitimate daughter of Anthony Wydeville, brother-in-law to the king. This gave her and Henry VIII mutual great-grandparents. Elizabeth's exact age is not known, although the date of her parent's marriage has been suggested as 1479. She was not the eldest child, her brother having arrived in around 1480, so she was likely to have been of an age with the queen, born in the mid-1480s. However, it seems that Elizabeth was unmarried at this point, later becoming the wife of Nicholas Wykes. It would be unusual for an unmarried woman to have received this appointment so there is a good chance that, in fact, the Elizabeth Poyntz referred to in the nursery accounts was Sir Robert's daughter-in-law, the wife of his eldest son, Anthony. Elizabeth Huddesfield had married Anthony Poyntz in 1499 and her son Nicholas was born in 1510. In order to have a regular supply of milk, a wet nurse would have recently borne a child of her own, suggesting that Elizabeth was employed in that capacity; this is confirmed by a grant made to her in August 1511, referring to her as the prince's nurse.

Catherine entered confinement early in December. The act of a queen bearing a child was a symbolic event of international significance. While it was a very personal occurrence, racking Catherine's body with contractions and threatening her life as she laboured to expel her infant, she was acutely aware of the political and dynastic importance of the moment. The memories of her recent experience would also have been fresh, as she prayed and waited. Women were advised to walk up and down their chambers to induce labour, and other superstitious practices included firing arrows and loosening all the ties, laces and fastenings in the chamber, as these were thought to act in sympathy to impede the child. Even sitting with crossed legs or folding the arms was frowned upon. Catherine did not have long to wait, though. Christmas passed, with Henry remaining at Richmond to observe the festivities. Then, on the last day of the year, she went into labour, either braced on the pallet bed or seated in a groaning chair or the crimson velvet chair ordered specially.[3] She would have held relics such as the girdle of Westminster, or similar talismans like cowrie shells or precious stones, as well as the inevitable prayers. Her child arrived in the early hours of January 1511. It was a boy.

The joy of the new parents was complete: this male child seemed to herald a secure future and indicate divine approval of the dynasty, the new king's reign and marriage. Pre-written messages announcing his birth were hastily dispatched across Europe. Through the parishes of England, the church bells rang and prayers were said giving thanks for his safe arrival. In London, the cannon at the Tower were fired, bonfires burned and the streets ran with wine, to celebrate, as chronicler Edward Hall described, 'the great gladness of the realm'.

But Catherine only knew about this second-hand. Following the custom of the time, she remained in her lying-in chamber for the next few weeks, including the ceremony of baptism on 5 January, when her son was given the name Henry. The godparents were William Warham, Archbishop of Canterbury, Henry's aunt Catherine, Countess of Devonshire, and Thomas Howard, Duke of Norfolk and Earl of Surrey – the latter two deputised for Louis XII and Archduchess Margaret of the Netherlands, Catherine's former sister-in-law. The baby was suckled by a wet nurse and sent off to sleep by rockers while his mother recovered. The following day, a banquet was held in the hall at Richmond, followed by a pageant depicting a mountain, glistening as if it were set with gold and precious stones, on top of which stood a golden tree hung with roses and pomegranates. The mountain opened to reveal a lady dressed in cloth of gold and costumed children who performed a Morris dance.

Catherine's lying-in process would have lasted around a month. Her body needed time to recover but she was also considered impure until the service of churching, or purification, had cleansed her from the physicality of birth. After she had undergone the ritual of sitting up, assisted by high-status women, she would have been dressed in fine clothes and walked the short distance to her great chamber, where the bed of state was set up. There, the nobility and chapel royal[4] witnessed her two duchesses drawing back the curtains and Catherine being raised from the bed by two dukes, in a symbolic return to public duty. She was offered a lighted candle, which she carried in procession to the church door, for a short service of blessing. It was symbolic that Catherine's purification was timed to coincide with Candlemas, on 2 February, the traditional ceremony of cleansing of the Virgin Mary, when queens usually took the role of Mary in that day's procession.[5] It associated her with the delivery and purity of the Virgin, whose cult was at its height in pre-Reformation England. It was also a joyful affirmation of her survival. In turn, Henry set out on another pilgrimage to Walsingham, where he left an offering and commissioned the royal glazier, Bernard Flower, to make a stained-glass window for the Lady chapel.

Henry and Catherine relocated to Westminster to celebrate their son's safe arrival and the queen's return to court. Having re-emerged in public, she was the guest of honour at a joust on 13 February, where Henry first took the name Sir Loyal Heart. Seated with her ladies in a stand draped with cloth of gold and arras, she looked out across a pageant of a gold castle surrounded by a forest, led by a lion and an antelope. Foresters in green blew their horns and the pageant opened to reveal four knights on horseback, carrying spears, with their names embroidered on their horses' trappers and their costumes covered with the letters H and K, embroidered in gold. With Henry, as Sir Loyal Heart, were Sir Thomas Knyvet as Good Hope, Sir Edward Neville as Valiant Desire and William, Earl of Devonshire, as Good Valour.[6] The address of those answering the challenge acknowledged Catherine and the 'good and gracious fortune of the birth of the young prince that it hath pleased God to send to her and her husband'. The following day the jousts continued, with knights dressed in gold and russet velvet and gentlemen and Yeomen dressed in similar colours, with yellow caps and scarlet hose. Catherine and her ladies looked on as Henry approached under a pavilion of gold, decorated with their initials, topped by an imperial crown, trembling spangles and a 'goodly plume'. In contrast, Sir Charles Brandon, in a russet satin gown 'like a recluse or religious figure', offered his services to Catherine, which she accepted. He was followed by Sir Henry Guildford, the Marquis of Dorset, Sir Thomas Boleyn, then Henry Stafford, Buckingham's younger brother, and many other knights. Their feats of strength and bravery, dedicated to Catherine, continued to surprise and delight the entire day. It was the most elaborate display of affection and respect for the queen, an extended public affirmation of Henry's love for his wife. For Catherine, it must have gone a long way to repairing the damage done by the Anne Stafford incident and strengthening the marital bond. Henry was proud of her and wanted to show the world the extent of his love.

After the jousts, Catherine accompanied her husband to hear evensong and, after supper, repaired to the smaller White Hall. Not to be confused with the palace that later went by the same name, Westminster's White or Lesser Hall adjoined the Painted Chamber and, at about a quarter of the size of the surviving Great Hall, it was a more intimate venue. A banquet was held, followed by dancing, minstrels playing and a second pageant. Lords and ladies in cloth of gold, white and purple satin, threw the golden H and Ks sewn on to their garments to the people watching. This provoked such a dash for the gold that some attempted to pull off the king's clothes and would have 'foughten and drawn blood' had they not been restrained by guards, as Holinshed relates: 'Suddenlie the rude people ran to the pageant and rent, tare and spoiled the pageant.' It was a terrifying moment, as the good-humoured celebration turned ugly, but Henry and Catherine retired to the king's private apartments, where the feasting continued and 'this triumph ended with mirth and gladness'.

Nine days later, terrible news came from Richmond. The little prince had died. Coming in such contrast to their celebrations and happiness, Catherine's grief was extreme. She 'made much lamentation', 'like a natural woman'. Henry made little outward show of grief, and 'like a wise prince took this dolorous chance wondrous wiselie, and the more to comfort the quene he dissembled the matter'.[7] According to Holinshed, by Henry's 'good persuasion and behaviour', Catherine's sorrow was 'mitigated, but not shortlie'.[8] Briefly, she had glimpsed the happiness she had longed for: a devoted husband and a healthy son. With little understanding of the factors influencing infant mortality, deaths of this nature could only be explained as the will of God. For some reason, Catherine believed, as she knelt in long hours of prayer, this was part of the divine plan. Either that or she and Henry had done something to anger God.

Catherine may have even thought it was all her fault. Certain sexual practices were stigmatised by canon law, such as intercourse during menstruation, on Sundays, the vigils of saints' feasts, fast days or processional days, before taking the Eucharist, when performing penance and on the days before Ascension. It has been calculated by Debra Hassig that, taking all these prohibited dates into account, couples were only left with forty-four days in the year when sex was considered acceptable, or just under once a week.[9]

Catherine and Henry had transgressed a boundary by sleeping together while she was still technically in confinement, in April or May 1510. Having experienced her first miscarriage before entering the lying-in chamber in anticipation of delivering that infant's twin, she had not been purified by the churching process but had entertained her husband within the all-female sanctuary of the birth chamber. Perhaps it was an act borne out of desperation, or desire for mutual comfort, as the days passed and she had realised she was not about to give birth. To Catherine's Catholic mind, though, and also perhaps Henry's, this loss may well have been an indictment of the act of conception. If so, this would have a terrible burden. According to protocol, neither parent was present when their young son was brought to Westminster and buried in the abbey.

15

Regent, 1511–13

The greatest honour that can be.[1]

In 1511, perhaps to distract themselves from their loss, Henry and Catherine turned their focus towards Europe. With the model of her warlike parents in mind, the queen would have relished the chance to become part of a military partnership, demonstrating the continuing greatness of the English Crown in a way that also supported her father's policies. Caroz and Fray Diego were instructed to persuade Catherine to convince Henry to declare war on France. Ferdinand's next tactic was to appeal directly to his sense of chivalry, pointing out that this was an opportunity to engage in a real battle instead of the mock tournaments and combats he staged for courtly entertainment. It was a challenge issued directly to his manhood. The twenty-year-old king could not resist.

That November, Henry joined Ferdinand, Emperor Maximilian and the Pope in the Holy League, which had been established as part of the Italian Wars raging between France, Venice and the Pope since 1508. This established a further family connection for Catherine, as Maximilian was the father of Philip the Handsome, her former brother-in-law. Henry and Ferdinand followed this by signing the Treaty of Westminster, to pledge their support against the 'infidel' of France. In exchange for invading and defeating the ambitious Louis XII, Pope Julius offered to reward Henry with the French crown. Henry was keen to begin, to gain this illustrious prize as well as the Pope's good will. In spring 1512, he chose Sir Edward Howard to lead a successful fleet against the French at the Battle of Saint-Mathieu and rewarded him with the position of Lord Admiral. It was a good start, with England's forces in a safe pair of hands. However, Howard died in March 1513 during a failed attack on a French fleet.

The campaign on land had not fared any better. In 1512, the first invasion only served to cast shame upon England thanks to a disastrous expedition to Guienne led by the Marquess of Dorset, at which Ferdinand's promised support did not appear and the unpaid, unfed English soldiers rebelled. This was the point when Catherine stepped in. Acting as the intermediary between the Spanish envoy, Martin de Muxica, and Henry, Catherine upheld her father's complaint that the English force had been unreliable, rather than blaming him for his abandonment. She stated that Henry was aware 'how shamefully the English had behaved and was very angry with them'.[2] There is no doubt, though, that she was fully supportive of her husband's authority, stating that it was not proper for her to meet the envoys before their formal reception with the king. Catherine was at Henry's side when the ambassadors were received a week later, after which the Spaniards witnessed an interrogation of the captains in a sort of mock trial. Liaising with her father, the queen advised Henry and his commons to finance another French invasion and championed the view of the injured Spanish. That month she also made enquiries of the Venetian ambassador about the cost of hiring ships, although she ultimately decided the price they demanded was too high.

Catherine's role in this was a significant one. It was a fine line to walk, trying to support her husband's ambition and reputation but also defend Ferdinand despite his betrayal in signing a treaty with the

French. She embraced the role of negotiator, comfortable at the heart of politics on an international scale, mediating with ambassadors, influencing decisions and shaping interpretations of events. No doubt her nationality and her comparative maturity also played a part beside the inexperienced twenty-year-old king. Henry took her advice and overlooked Ferdinand's failure to support him; that autumn, it was agreed in Parliament that he would lead the expedition in person, 'with fire and sword'. Just how far was Catherine aware of her father's real intentions? He had used Henry's involvement for his own ends, to engage the French while he gained Navarre, and cited English unreliability for his own French alliance. His daughter may have believed his protestations, making her and Henry his dupes and marking a significant act of betrayal and manipulation on his part. If she did suspect, she persisted with her martial policy anyway, perhaps hoping that it would bring England a comparable glory with that which her mother had achieved in Spain.

That Christmas at Greenwich, the king was keen to remember his Plantagenet roots and how they associated him with the warlike Henry V and Edward IV, who had been successful against the French in both battle and diplomacy. He sat atop a pageant made in the shape of a mountain decorated with broom flowers made from green silk and gold, which was wheeled into the hall and presented to Catherine to celebrate Epiphany. As one of six Lords of the Mount, dressed in crimson velvet set with gold spangles, he descended and danced before taking his place at Catherine's side for the banquet. They were partners in every sense – on the throne, in the royal bed and, hopefully, on the international stage. And Catherine was soon to be in charge of the country.

On 11 June, Henry appointed his wife 'Regent and Governess of England, Wales and Ireland during the king's absence in his expedition against France, for the preservation of the Catholic religion and recovery of his rights'. She was given 'power to issue commissions of muster', to give assent to Church elections, to 'appoint sheriffs, to issue warrants under her sign manual'. John Heron, Treasurer of the Chamber, was instructed to pay 'any sums of money ordered by the queen ... to whatever persons she may appoint, for defence of the kingdom'.[3]

Catherine left Greenwich with Henry four days later, at the head of 600 guards dressed in new costumes of green and white, with silver spangles and embroidery. They made a leisurely progress through Kent, arriving at Canterbury on 20 June, where they went to the cathedral to pray and make offerings to St Thomas. The minutes of the Chamber of Canterbury recorded that they stayed in the tent, or pavilion, at Blean, the royal forest overlooking the city, which was the final stopping point on the pilgrims' route. It was Catherine's first visit and she was presented with a cup of silver and gilt, weighing over thirty-one ounces and engraved with the city's arms. A local man, John Alcocke, was paid for the cup, at 4s 10d per ounce. Coins to the value of £13 6s 8d filled the cup, as an additional gift. The king's trumpeters, herald at arms, henchmen and footmen each received 6s 8d and Catherine's footmen were rewarded with 5s each. Additionally, 10d was given 'to a person going to Ashford, to provide two great oxen to be presented to the king'.[4] On 28 June, Henry and Catherine arrived at Dover Castle, where Henry tarried 'only for a wind to cross' to Calais. They spent the night there before Henry set sail, arriving at 7 p.m. the same day. Catherine was now in charge of England. She was also pregnant again.

Despite her condition, it was Henry's health and welfare that concerned Catherine. Without an heir, his loss would be catastrophic for the country and she wrote to her sister-in-law Margaret of Savoy, on 1 August, asking her to send a physician to her husband, to be with him in case of need. She also wrote to Henry's trusted almoner and Privy Councillor, Thomas Wolsey, hoping he would put her mind 'at rest', by relaying news of the king's welfare. Wolsey did write to Catherine 'so often', for which 'payne' she thanked him in her replies. In the meantime she continued to run the country to the best of her ability, with the assistance of Archbishop Warham. News soon came of an initial victory at the Battle of the Spurs, which Catherine described as the greatest victory: 'none such hath been seen before'.[5] She was also 'very glad to hear [of] the meeting' between Henry and the Emperor on 11 August, which took place in a tent of cloth of gold, with Henry dressed in gold, with golden bells hanging from his horse, in contrast with the Emperor's mourning attire.[6] Soon after this, Henry achieved another success by taking Therouanne, then moved on to lay siege to Tournai.

Henry had been in France for a month or so when rumours reached Catherine that the Scots were planning to take advantage of his absence and invade England. King James IV was Catherine's brother-in-law; she had been a young widow when he had been married by proxy to Henry's sister Margaret, at Richmond in January 1503. Now James was compromised by Henry's entry into the Holy League, being bound by treaties to both England and France. In the end, James drew up his will naming Margaret as regent for their infant son and marched south to invade. His first troops crossed the border on 13 August. Catherine ordered that the property of all Scotsmen in England was to be seized. Then she summoned Sir Thomas Lovell and the Earl of Surrey, with his sons Edmund and Thomas Howard, to muster armies and ordered the standard to be raised on 3 September. As regent and queen, her role was one that required her to adopt a traditional female role, being 'horribly busy making standards, banners and badges' while at the same time taking on Henry's job as king, locked away in talks with the royal council, preparing to defend the country. She was certainly determined to look the part, as the royal goldsmith, Robert Amadas, was paid for 'garnishing a headpiece with a gold crown'.[7]

Catherine headed north, perhaps with the intention of speaking to her men herself, as the Venetian ambassador recorded, but she did not get that far. Heavily pregnant, it seems unlikely that she would have risked her unborn child by riding onto the field of battle when she had the competent Surrey and his sons to rely on. If she did make a 'splendid oration to the captains ... in imitation of her mother', as her old tutor, Peter Martyr, related, she must have done it in London before they departed, not anywhere near the location in Northumberland, where the armies were about to clash. When the Battle of Flodden Field took place, on 9 September, at Branxton, she was three hundred miles away at Woburn Abbey, waiting to hear the outcome. Eventually news came and Catherine forwarded Surrey's letter to Tournai. As Henry later described to the Duke of Milan, 'the fight was long and sharply contested on both sides, but at length the Almighty, avenging the broken treaty, gave victory to the English'.[8] Among the dead was James IV, his body 'having been found and recognised and taken to the nearest church. He thus paid a heavier penalty for his perfidy than we [Henry and Catherine] could have wished.'[9]

For Catherine, though, it was a triumph, and she described it to 'my Henry', as 'the most happy that can be remembered'.[10] She had wanted to send Henry the battered body of the dead king as a trophy of war, but, recognising that this was offensive to English sensibilities, she opted instead to dispatch his bloodstained coat, to be put to use as a banner. The cross which James had been wearing, enclosing a fragment of the true cross, was kept in the royal treasury. In turn, 'as a present'[11] Henry sent his wife a French prisoner, the Duc de Longueville, Charles d'Orleans, cousin to Louis XII. He was lodged in the Tower during her absence, with an entourage of six, at a cost of £13 6s and 8d.[12] From Woburn Abbey, she set out to Walsingham on 16 September to give thanks for the victory and her pregnancy.

16

Etiennette de la Baume, 1513

From Dover to Calais, with willing mind
Lo! How desire is both sprung and spent
And he may see, that whilom was so blind.[1]

Across the Channel, Henry was amusing himself with more than just martial feats. On 10 September, he arrived in Lille, at the court of Margaret of Savoy, riding in pomp and triumphantly displaying the fleur-de-lys badge of France. In spite of the pressing campaign, he managed to stay overnight in the city, lodged in 'the palace of the Prince', which is likely to have been the Palais Rihour. This palace had been completed in 1477 by the Emperor's father-in-law, Charles the Bold, and was a huge quadrangle of a building, of which only a section remains. The part that still stands, though, is an impressive fifteenth-century staircase, giving a flavour of the palace stairs where Margaret of Savoy is recorded as meeting Henry, making 'deep reverence'.

The English king was lodged in four rooms hung with Margaret's tapestries, all worked with gold, and slept on a bed of gold, decorated with the arms of Spain. It is not impossible that he had some company between those golden sheets. At dinner, both host and guest began eating in their separate chambers, but Margaret rose 'from the banquet in her quarter, took her plate with her and went to sup with the king, accompanied by some of her principal damsels, notably Madame the Bastard. Madame clearly captivated Henry as he danced with her from the time the banquet finished until nearly day, in his shirt and without shoes.'[2] That night, he presented 'them', which suggests the ladies collectively, with a 'beautiful diamond in a setting of great value'.[3]

Who was this mysterious Madame the Bastard, who kept Henry dancing, half-undressed, until almost dawn? The chances are that she was descended from one of Margaret's two great-uncles, making her of dubious but royal blood. The illegitimate Anthony and Corneille, known as the Bastards of Burgundy, both fathered children, with Corneille's son Jean siring two daughters before his death in 1479. These were probably too old to qualify for the Madame who captured Henry's attention, but they may have borne children of their own.

However, some research has suggested that Margaret's great-grand-father, Philip III, fathered at least eighteen children outside marriage and had over twenty mistresses. The lady who kept Henry up all night may well have been one of their line. The siege of Tournai began the next day and, after enjoying archery, jousting and more music making, Henry eventually visited the town on 13 September. It fell to the English ten days later.

The good news delighted Queen Catherine. She had reached Walsingham on 23 September, from where she made her way back to London to await the return of her husband and the arrival of her child. Exactly what happened in the following weeks is unclear, but on 8 October the Imperial agent James Bannisius reported that 'the Queen of England had given birth to a son'.[4] According to this version of events and that of Venetian ambassador, de Favri, the child was born alive but died soon afterwards. Some accounts date his arrival earlier, to 17 September, but this is unlikely given Catherine's pilgrimage to Walsingham a week later – she would still have been in the traditional period of confinement and recovery, even if the child was lost. If she had experienced a miscarriage, her doctors would have advised her against travelling again so soon. Given her movements, it would appear that the child was premature, as she had not yet entered confinement, and that he was born and died early in October, probably on the same day. Catherine must have felt this third loss keenly. A veil of silence descended at court. The lack of reports of her loss has led some to speculate that she was not even pregnant at all. Indeed, the last seven or eight months must have seemed strangely unreal for her as, once again, she had no healthy baby to show for her efforts.

Henry was still in Tournai on 12 October, with Margaret of Savoy, Charles of Castile and 'divers' other nobles as his guests, when he wrote to the Pope stating that he 'must return to England' and had summoned a parliament for 1 November.[5] The following day, the beleaguered town received notice of his departure. They were probably pleased to see him go but Henry had a final parting gift. Before he departed, he passed an order forbidding the defeated people to 'make, sing or utter libels in the form of songs, ballads or otherwise against kings or princes'. With that, he left the battlefield again in pursuit of pleasure. The party had reached Lille again by 16 October, where Wolsey settled payments to stewards, cooks, clerks and others including £20 to 'the gentlewomen called watchers of my lady's chamber' and £40 to Sir Thomas Boleyn, the king's future father-in-law. That summer, Margaret had acquired a new maid of honour who may have been present in her retinue when she met Henry. The maid was a dark-haired English girl of twelve years named Anne Boleyn. If she was there, Anne would have seen the tone of the festivities turn flirtatious, with Henry's close friend Charles Brandon conducting an ardent game to woo the widowed Margaret and stealing a ring from her finger under the pretence of an engagement. Unsurprisingly, his proposal came to nothing, but the English court had victories to celebrate and the lavish parties would have provided them with plenty of young and attractive women with whom to play the games of courtly love.

On Sunday 16 October, Henry heard divine service with Margaret of Savoy and his teenaged nephew Charles, the Prince of Castile, who was betrothed to his sister Mary.[6] Two days later, he took part in the jousts for which the knights were dressed in purple velvet and a tent of cloth of gold was erected; there were 'many speres broken and many a good buffet given', after which the jousters unmasked and rode about the tilt yard 'and did great reverence to the ladies'.[7] The following day, Henry hosted a 'sumptuous' banquet of a hundred dishes for Charles and Margaret after which the ladies danced with men masked in 'bonnets' of gold and 'passed the time at their pleasure'. Perhaps Henry danced again with Madame the Bastard, or it may be that this was the moment that another woman caught his eye.[8]

During his stay at Lille, either on this occasion or previously, the king came into contact with a Flemish maid of honour in Margaret's household called Etiennette de la Baume. The daughter of Marc de la Baume, Comte de Montrevel and Lord of Chateauvillain, her connection with Henry rests on the survival of a single letter, written in intimate terms and referring to a promise the king had made her 'when we parted'. The wording, content and timing of the letter suggests that she had been his mistress at some point during this visit to France. If Henry had previously contemplated, or indulged in, a relationship with Anne Hastings, with the subsequent scandal it had caused at court in 1510, he would have had fewer reservations about having a brief affair while separated from Catherine by the English Channel.

Etiennette's parents had been married on 10 July 1488 and, with at least one elder brother, she is likely to have been born around 1490, making her a similar age to Henry. The letter, which survives in the State papers for 17 August 1514, was written two months before Etiennette's marriage to Ferdinand de Neufchatel, Seigneur de Marnay and Montaigu, which took place that October. It opens with the writer making Henry the gifts of a bird and some 'roots of great value, belonging to this country',[9] which were likely to have been medicinal rather than designed for the king's table. Then Etiennette proceeded to remind the king that he had called her his 'page' and 'told me many beautiful things ... when Madame went to see the Emperor, her father, and you at Lille'.[10] This use of sweet talk and nicknames, possibly with role play as part of their affair, indicates an informality and flirtation at the very least, if not a full-blown sexual encounter. It gives an intimate glimpse into the nature of Henry's lovemaking, wooing his lady with promise and fine words, with Henry perhaps disguising Etiennette as his page in order to smuggle her into his room, or continuing his love of play and dressing up in order to entice her into bed. She may well have been an attractive diversion for a few nights between the gold sheets but Henry had been mindful of her reputation and appears to have offered her a considerable reward, or perhaps compensation for the loss of her virtue.

A year later, Etiennette wrote to Henry from what she describes as his house at Marnay. He might have installed her in a property there but Marnay is over 500 kilometres from Lille and no record remains of Henry owning a house there. Yet, this does not mean that he did not. Perhaps he contributed towards her rent or made her a gift that went unrecorded. By 1514, the situation had changed for Etiennette and, with her father now urging her to marry, she reminded Henry that 'when we parted at Tournay you told me, when I married, to let you know and it should be worth to me 10,000 crowns or rather angels'.[11] The tone of the letter and the promise of the dowry strongly suggest that Henry and Etiennette were lovers briefly during the campaign of 1513, which the lady now used to secure her financial future. She, or her father, may have intended the letter to suggest that they had a secret to tell, but any possible intention to blackmail the English king was not overt.

That November, according to the Venetian ambassador, Henry had 'clad himself and his court in mourning for love of a lady', which may have been Etiennette, on the occasion of her marriage.[12] It is not clear whether or not the king did send her a dowry when she married later that year. Maybe he disliked having the reminder of his infidelity, especially as the letter arrived during a time when Catherine was pregnant again. Maybe he recalled her fondly and sent her a suitable gift. His generosity may be suggested by the fact that Etiennette's marriage did go ahead on 18 October 1514, but no other contact is recorded between them. She died around 1521.

By 20 October, Henry was at Calais, staying at the Exchequer, awaiting a favourable tide. It came two days later. Arriving safely at Dover, he headed to Richmond for his reunion with Catherine, which was 'so loving' that the bystanders 'rejoiced' to see it. The royal couple then repaired to the queen's property of Havering-atte-Bower in Essex, where they feasted and were entertained by pageantry and dancing. Given that the ambassadors had known of Catherine's lost child early in October, the news would have reached Henry before his return. He had already digested and accepted it before he saw his wife again. Like his response to the death of Prince Henry in 1511, he was probably pragmatic and 'manly', reassuring Catherine they were still young and that she would fall pregnant again soon. She did, in fact, conceive six months later, but by then a new threat to her happiness had emerged that would drive a further wedge between her and her husband.

17

Jane Popincourt, 1514

I count women lost, if we love them not well,
For ye see God loveth them never a deal
Mistress, ye can not speak with the God.[17]

Henry's sister Mary was getting married. The date had been fixed for May 1514 and the location was to be Calais; her bridegroom would be the young man to whom she had been betrothed since December 1507, Catherine's nephew Prince Charles of Castile, the son of her sister Joanna. It was a match that promised to cement the alliance of England, Spain and the Holy Roman Empire. Young and beautiful, described as a 'paradise' by the Venetian ambassador, Mary anticipated finally coming face to face with her fiancé as preparations began for their wedding.

Within a few weeks of the date, though, Henry had completely changed his mind and the best-laid plans of a decade were rejected in favour of a hasty new match that suited the recent changes in international affairs. Furious with Ferdinand's pursuit of his own self-interest, he instructed Wolsey to open negotiations for Mary to wed the recently widowed Louis XII instead, breaking the engagement with Charles on the pretext that the boy had failed to ratify it when reaching the age of fourteen. Instead of the teenaged bridegroom she had been expecting, Mary's new husband was to be the fifty-two-year-old widowed king, 'an old man ... and gouty'.[2] The crown of France offered Mary a degree of compensation when the proxy marriage took place at Greenwich on 13 August. The Duke de Longueville spoke the French king's vows in his place, presenting the princess with a gold ring before the assembled crowd. Catherine was a witness, pregnant again, and dressed in ash-coloured satin, with gold chains and a cap of gold. The ambassadors from Spain and the Emperor were not invited, which might have 'caused much comment universally',[3] but not as much as the mésalliance of the nubile young Tudor with the ageing Valois.

In public, Mary accepted the last-minute switch of bridegroom. Obediently, she wrote to her new husband that she would 'love him as cordially as she can' and claimed to have heard the vows repeated on his behalf 'with great pleasure'. A formal consummation took place, with Mary taking to her bed in a state of undress 'in the presence of many witnesses'. The Duke de Longueville acted as proxy for Louis: dressed in a doublet and red hose, 'but with one leg naked from the middle of the thigh downward, he went into bed and touched the Princess with his naked leg. The marriage was then declared consummated.'[4] There was no escape for Mary now, but she did manage to extract a promise from her brother that if she should wed again, her second husband would be of her own choosing. Catherine and Henry accompanied the bride to Dover and waved her off across to France. On 9 October, Louis and Mary were married in person at Abbeville. Among her retinue of eighty damsels and English lords were Ambassador Thomas Boleyn's young daughters Mary and, soon, Anne. Another lady from Catherine's household had expected to be present also, but found herself excluded at the last minute.

Jane Popincourt was probably French-born and her family may have originated from the area of Dancourt-Popincourt, an hour's drive south of Lille. She might have been a descendant of the premier president of the Paris *parlement*, Jean de Popincourt, who died around 1403. His grandson was ambassador to England from the 1450s, so Jane may have travelled to England with him, or as a result of his influence. Before this, Jane appears to have gained experience in service at the French court, perhaps beginning her career under Charles VIII, in the household of his wife, Anne of Brittany. Charles' death in 1498, followed by Anne's remarriage to his successor, Louis XII, may have been the catalyst that prompted Jane to leave France and head for England the same year. Louis' later actions would certainly suggest he had reason to personally dislike Jane, or that something about her religious beliefs or behaviour had offended him. When Louis took the throne, Jane may have realised it was wiser to be away from court, perhaps away from France altogether. By 1498, she was teaching French to princesses Margaret and Mary at Eltham, through 'daily conversation', and probably acting as a companion and maid. The minimum age she might have been for this role was in her mid-teens, placing her date of birth in the late 1470s, or 1480 at the very latest, although it is more likely that such a responsibility would have been given to someone a little older.

Jane appeared to do well at the English court. By 1502, she had become one of Mary's maids of honour and in this capacity would have been known to both Henry, as Prince of Wales, and Catherine, who was then a widowed princess. Jane's name appears in the records when a Robert Ragdale was paid to mend the clothes of the princesses, with 7d 'for the mending of two gowns for Johanne Popyncourt'. Jane clearly established herself to be of good enough character to become part of the new queen's household on Henry's accession in 1509, when she was paid 50s for court expenses.[5] With her history and fluency, it was reasonable to expect that she would be chosen to accompany Mary to France in the autumn of 1514.

However, Jane's reputation preceded her. After the Duke de Longueville, Louis d'Orleans, was captured at the Battle of the Spurs and sent to England, she had become his acknowledged lover. The duke was initially imprisoned in the Tower before taking a more central role at the English court and being treated as an honoured guest and something of an informal ambassador. Longueville was still a young man, in his early thirties, married with four children, the last of whom was born in the year of his capture. The extent of his involvement with Jane is uncertain, although the presence of both of them at court during 1514 and at the celebrations for the marriage of Princess Mary might suggest an opportunity. Perhaps after the pretence of consummating Mary's marriage by proxy, Longueville shed his red hose and hopped into bed with Jane instead. After all, it was his last night at court.

When the duke returned to France the next day Jane had anticipated following in the retinue of Mary Tudor, but she was to be disappointed. Direct intervention from Louis himself meant that she was the only woman who was personally rejected from the party. Perusing the list of his future wife's attendants, he had struck off Jane's name, reputedly commenting that she should be burned. Taken literally, this fate was usually reserved for heretics, and sometimes female murderers, but it may also suggest a dislike of a more personal nature. Some historians have inferred that this objection, coupled with a payment of £100 later made by Henry to Jane, suggests that they were lovers and that Louis objected to her immorality. It is quite likely that the French king disliked her on those grounds, but the identity of the lover, or lovers, to which he objected, is less certain. Louis may have been acting to protect Longueville's wife, Joan of Hachberg, a cousin of Louis by virtue of their shared great-grandparents. Equally, he might have rejected Jane on grounds of personal dislike, a conviction about Jane's religious views or perhaps her conduct in the household of his former wife, Anne, Queen of France.

Another interesting detail is included in Hall's account of Longueville's English stay as part of his chronicle for the year 1514. He confirms that the duke was treated well in his pseudo-captivity, being 'highly enterteyned in England of many noble men and had great cheer'. When he returned to France with Mary, though, his royal reception was decidedly frostier, as Louis 'would scarce know them'.[6] This suggests that it was disapproval of the duke's relationship with Jane that lay at the root of the king's animosity, although Hall was writing at some remove from the events he described.

Frustrated in her desire, Jane remained in Queen Catherine's household during the autumn of 1514, and it is at this point, between October and the following January, that she is reputed to have consoled the English king. She partnered Henry in a masque at Eltham Palace to mark the festivities for Twelfth Night, but at this point news had already arrived of the death of Louis and Jane would have been anticipating her return. Henry granted her permission to leave for France and awarded her the £100, which is the main evidence on which the theory of their intimacy rests. If nothing else, Henry did not think any less of Jane for having been Longueville's mistress. By dancing with her in public, he was condoning her relationship with a married man, although it is interesting that this performance may not have taken place before the queen. Given Jane's possible age, her history at the English court and role, a one-off payment of this kind is consistent with other rewards given to courtiers for loyal service to the Tudor family over the years.

Although it cannot be ruled out that Jane Popincourt entered the royal bed following the departure of her French lover, no direct evidence places her there. There is no flirtatious letter surviving to indicate an intimate tone between her and the English king, as in the cases of Elizabeth Carew and Etiennette de la Baume. Perhaps it is most suggestive that Jane did not return to France immediately. Something kept her in England. Perhaps it was Henry himself, which means her affair with him might post-date Louis' disapproval. In the end, a whole year elapsed before she left England, to be reunited with

Longueville, in the spring of 1516. He died a few months later. Jane's movements after this are not known.

Henry's switch in foreign policy, from Spain to France, did not just have an effect on Princess Mary. Queen Catherine suffered, too. As the visible symbol of the old alliance in English eyes, after relations between the two countries had deteriorated significantly her Spanish accent and blood provoked memories of Ferdinand's perfidy. It was not an easy time to be a Spaniard in England. Italian visitors reported that the French and Spanish ambassadors were not on speaking terms and Ferdinand's representatives stayed at home, feeling 'quite dispirited', as 'the English abuse Spain excessively for her bad faith in making truce with France'.[7] Although Catherine had tried her best to walk the delicate path between remaining loyal to both her father and her husband, she might have borne the brunt of Henry's new hostility. Italian gossip reported rumours that Henry was intending to divorce her and Fray Diego advised her to 'forget Spain and everything Spanish, in order to gain the love of the King of England and the English'. Later he reported that the king had 'badly used' Catherine.[8] It seems unlikely that Henry was considering divorce, given that Catherine was again pregnant, and no other reports support this claim. If such a report ever reached the queen's ears, it must have been an unpleasant reminder of the international breach and her own track record when it came to bearing children.

18

Elizabeth Carew, 1514

> Your key is meet for every lock
> Your key is common and hangeth out
> Your key is ready, we need not knock
> Not stand long resting there about
> Of your doorgate we have no doubt[1]

It may have been around this time that Henry's attention was diverted away from Catherine again. That October, materials to equip her chamber and nursery had been ordered, including a cradle lined with scarlet – which was a cloth, not just a colour – and other lengths of blue material. She was due to enter confinement in November and, as her pregnancy advanced during the autumn, she would have been aware of the arrangements that were also being made for the marriage of another young lady in her household. Elizabeth Byran was then aged around fourteen, the daughter of the queen's vice-chamberlain, Sir Thomas Bryan of Marsworth and Cheddington, and Margaret Bourchier, a lady-in-waiting. Through her mother's descent from Edward III, Elizabeth had royal blood and a connection with one of the most powerful men at court, Sir Thomas Howard, who was her step-grandfather. This made her a cousin of three of Henry's future wives.

Elizabeth's intended husband was Nicholas Carew, one of the king's closest friends. The son of the Captain of Calais, Carew was one of the young men of the Privy Chamber who became Henry's intimate companions, sharing his love of sport and pleasure, as opposed to his core of older councillors, to whom the king delegated most of his business matters. Five years younger than the king, Carew had been raised in the royal household at Eltham from the age of six, receiving his lessons beside Henry in the schoolroom. Carew was a fearless jouster, Master of the Horse, a knight, ambassador and a reprobate,[2] considered by Wolsey, along with his fast crowd, to be a bad influence on the king. In 1519, the cardinal and other senior figures at court would attempt to break the hold Carew and his circle had over Henry.

This group of boisterous, rakish young men came to be known as the king's minions. Among their number was Elizabeth's brother, Sir Francis Bryan, later named by Thomas Cromwell as 'the vicar from hell' for his role in the downfall of his cousin Anne Boleyn. Bryan has been described by later historians as a rake and a hellraiser, the accomplice to Henry's affairs, who reputedly once called for a 'soft bed then a hard harlot'.[3] He sported a patch after losing an eye in the jousts and was not averse to throwing stones and eggs at the local population when on embassy abroad. Bryan's other brother-in-law, Sir Henry Guildford, became Henry's Master of the Horse in 1515 and was also a regular participant in court revels, designing pageants, dancing and enjoying the king's confidence and favour. In 1513 he had composed an interlude, a symbolic drama part way between the medieval morality style and the more modern form of the play, to celebrate the victory in France. In it, Guildford had played the part of the king himself. Henry's early friendships with these young men and their sisters and wives often blurred the lines of propriety and role, in disguise and reality.

Late in 1514, Elizabeth and another young woman were linked in a letter written to Henry by Charles Brandon, newly created Duke of Suffolk, which suggests that the duke had been indulging in flirtatious behaviour with one or both of them. At this stage, though, it was someone else's flirtation and deviated little from the conventions of courtly love. Brandon was still in France, in the retinue of Princess Mary, soon to become Louis XII's queen. He was clearly missing the attractions of the English court, though, writing to Henry, 'I beseech your Grace to [tell] unto Mistress Blount and Mistress Carew the next time that I write unto them or send them tokens they shall either write to me or send me tokens again.' The implication of these words is a dual flirtation between the two women, the handsome young widower Brandon and the king. Brandon's letter invites Henry to get involved, to almost take his part during his absence, to be the bearer of a flirtatious message, to enter the game.

Close to the king since their shared childhood, Brandon's track record with women had been little less than scandalous, played out before the eyes of the young Henry. In his early twenties, Brandon had fathered a child outside wedlock with Anne Browne, to whom he was betrothed. However, he deserted Anne in order to marry her aunt, Margaret Neville, the niece of Warwick the 'Kingmaker', cousin of Henry's Yorkist grandfather. The new bride was almost twenty years older than her young groom and Anne's advancing pregnancy caused her family to take action. Later that year, the match was declared void in the archdeacon's court and soon afterwards, early in 1508, Brandon married Anne Browne, who went on to bear him a second child, before dying in 1511. Henry's biographer, John Matusiak, suggests that 'every juicy detail of the whole sordid business was no doubt imparted to the eager prince, who then went on, it seems, to draw his own merry conclusions about the proper place of marriage in the affairs of young men of vigour'.[4] The opportunistic widower then entered another betrothal, to Elizabeth Grey, another lady who appears in the records of courtly entertainment, but extricated himself around this time while seeking a more highborn bride and engaging in flirtation with more of Catherine's waiting women. His marital history would become even more complicated in the coming years.

On 7 November, Henry made a grant of £500 to Elizabeth's mother, Lady Bryan, 'to her marriage, which by God's grace shall be espoused and wedded to Nicholas Carewe, son and heir apparent to Sir Richard Carewe, knight, before the feast of the Purification of Our Blessed Lady the Virgin'.[5] Elizabeth and her mother both signed it. In fact, Elizabeth and Nicholas did not wait until Candlemas, the February date of the Purification; they married in December 1514, soon after receiving the grant, around the time Catherine entered her confinement. Henry attended the wedding and subsequently made the pair a number of expensive gifts, beyond what was expected for his wife's ladies-in-waiting. Elizabeth received 'many diamonds and pearls and innumerable jewels' as well as lengths of velvet, cloth of silver and damask; in 1515, Nicholas Carew was given his own tilt yard at Greenwich, perhaps as a reward for turning a blind eye. Elizabeth remained a favourite as late as 1529, when the Privy Purse accounts show that she was given an emerald by the king and she would become a favourite with some of Henry's later wives, predeceasing the king by a year.

There is no concrete evidence that Henry and Elizabeth had an affair, but this pattern of gifts is reminiscent of similar items given by the king to Queen Catherine and later to Anne Boleyn, while he was wooing her. It is also significant that the second lady mentioned in Brandon's letter, Elizabeth, or 'Bessie', Blount, is known to have become Henry's lover, although this information only survives because she bore his illegitimate son. If Bessie Blount had never become pregnant, her story would have remained just as speculative as that of her friend. It is entirely likely that Elizabeth Carew ended up in the king's bed, sometime before or after her marriage, as the situation is reminiscent of William Compton's wooing of Anne Hastings on the king's behalf, back in 1510. Perhaps Carew was now fulfilling the same role.

Henry had learned from the scandal of 1510 and the reactions of Catherine and his courtiers. As was the case with his Yorkist grandfather Edward IV, he followed contemporary codes of courtly love, which favoured liaisons with married women instead of deflowering one who was yet unwed, thus affecting her chances of making a respectable match. A compliant husband could facilitate meetings, either in the couple's home or one of Henry's many hunting lodges. He would not attract shame or stigma, but would enjoy the protection Henry's status could offer as well as the commensurate financial rewards. A husband would also provide a veneer of legitimacy if Elizabeth were to fall pregnant, as any child born to a married woman was automatically considered to be the offspring of the husband, unless he objected and stated otherwise. To do so would be a challenge to the king, a slur on his reputation, and required legal proof, so it was convenient for Henry that Anne Stafford, Elizabeth Bryan and later Mary Boleyn were married to men he could trust. As king, Henry could always bend the rules, as he would do with Bessie Blount in 1518, but navigating through the complex territory of public reputations and private desire could prove a difficult game.

Bessie was also provided with a suitable husband once the king had tired of her.

Henry's reputation as a prudish king is something of a misnomer, having arisen from the secrecy he employed when it came to his affairs and his character later in life. The manipulative and ruthless figure of later years, relentless in his pursuit of his desires when it came to politics and women, did not suddenly appear overnight. He was just as wilful and determined in his youth when it came to pursuing women for pleasure, although his actions were less visible. The slenderness of the early evidence, often surviving only by accident, is the result of his need for secrecy, to maintain the youthful, chivalric ideal of Sir Loyal Heart and the mask of public dignity. Henry's youthful reading, of French romances and stories about the Knights of the Round Table, filled him with the ideals of courtship, pursuit and surrender and, far from being prudish, the culture at the secret heart of his court was reflected in the marital scandals and liaisons of his companions, who were less well placed to conceal their antics, of which many stories survive.

A neat cultural divide categorised women at Henry's court; the wife, the dynastic equal and producer of heirs, was separate from the mistresses and casual flirtations. Virginity was less of a stumbling block, too. Young women might be flirted with, partnered in a dance under the cover of disguise, even seduced, before they became wives and retired into a life of loyal domesticity. A promise was sufficient to make a seduction legitimate, if the rakish minions required such a thing as legitimacy. Equally, men could and did love their wives but it was with a different kind of love; for Henry and the young bloods of his court these were the years to sow their wild oats, to gain experience, to pursue pleasure and excess. Henry was restless in his youth. He wanted it all. According to the Venetian ambassador, he was 'never still or quiet' but wanted to 'have his feet in a thousand shoes'. Wolsey, who perhaps knew Henry the best during this time, commented that not even an angel descending from Heaven could change the king's mind once it was made up.[6] Henry was an absolute king, believing himself godlike in his egotism and birthright; the vows of matrimony were not about to compromise his desires.

In later life, the king's attitude towards women would change but his stubbornness and sense of entitlement would not. The big difference was that, before the mid-1520s, Henry was still hoping that Catherine would deliver a live son who would survive. As a result, nothing must be allowed to challenge his marriage or the status of the children born to his wife. The excessive secrecy, sometimes described as prudery, of his affairs, was partly the chivalric identity he had constructed and partly a conscious policy to separate short-term physical pleasure from what his marriage represented. This was not a simple case of love *versus* duty; Henry was still in love with Catherine in 1514. He was simply conforming to the standards of his times, just as his grandfather had done, seeking the physical release which contemporary doctors advised, at a time when his wife was unavailable. In later years, the quest for a legitimate son meant that these amours moved into the public arena. Women who would previously have only been his mistress were considered for the role of wife, with the result that, from around 1527, his private life became public and is far better known.

The weight of rumours, the comments made by those who knew Henry and the suggestive evidence all indicate that Henry did, in fact, enjoy a significant number of casual encounters and short-term sexual liaisons in these early 'green' years. In 1515, the French ambassador wrote that Henry cared 'for nothing but girls and hunting' and the king's doctor, John Chambers, described him as 'overly fond of women' and frequently experiencing 'lustful dreams'. William Thomas, writing shortly after Henry's death, stated that 'he was a very fleshly man ... he fell into all riot and overmuch love of women', while those hostile to Wolsey accused him of procuring women for the king, which is not implausible, given that he would organise arrangements for the arrival of Henry's illegitimate son, as well as the christening, where he stood as godfather. In 1533, an anonymous writer in Rome stated that Henry's forthcoming child would be weak 'owning to [its] father's complexion and habits of life'.[7] Even considering the negative context in which some of these descriptions arose, they cannot all be dismissed as attempts to blacken the king's character. The words of his own doctor must be considered persuasive.

Then there is the account of Henry's casual encounter with a 'wench' near Eltham. This story, lodged in the Privy Papers for September 1537, described the king installing an unknown woman, the lover of a William Webbe, in a property, in order to live with her in 'avowrty', or adultery.[8] This was the only occasion when a slighted man 'cried vengeance' and openly accused Henry of adultery, but it was given no serious consideration and Webbe disappears from history soon after. It was a brave act, or perhaps a foolish one, and may be typical of other encounters where those involved felt unable to speak out. In the same year, another subject stated that 'as for the king, an apple and a fair wench to dally withal would please him very well'.[9] Henry certainly had the resources to keep his love life secret.

The separation of the royal apartments into the king's and queen's suites, the use of country properties and those of the minions, coupled with Catherine's retreat into confinement, would have facilitated discretion. In his youth, Henry went to considerable lengths, behind closed doors, to ensure that the heavily pregnant Catherine would not be upset again. The king was living a double life.

19

Labour and Loss, 1514–15

It is most fair to men mortal to suffer labours and pain for glory and fame immortal.[1]

If Henry had practised discretion to avoid upsetting Catherine with his amours, he may have been unable to conceal his annoyance when it came to the behaviour of her father. If certain accounts are to be believed, her 'grief' over the hostility directed towards Spain, and Spaniards in England, was directly responsible for her next loss. The queen's pregnancy had progressed as expected but, in the winter of 1514, it resulted in the birth of a short-lived son, named Henry, like the child born three years earlier.

Some confusion has arisen over the dating of this fourth loss, with various historians locating it as early as November 1514 and as late as February 1515, although a date in the earlier part of this timeframe looks most likely. This is confirmed by Wolsey's letter to Louis XII on 15 November, stating that the queen 'looks to lie in shortly' and was pleased to hear that if she 'bears a son, Louis will gladly be godfather'.[2] Hall related that 'in November the queen was delivered of a prince which lived not long after'.[3] On 31 December, Peter Martyr wrote that 'the Queen of England has given birth to a premature child' and was in no doubt about the cause: 'through grief, as it is said, for the misunderstanding between her father and husband. He reproached her with her father's lack of faith.'[4] There seems to be little ambiguity in this statement, which claims that Catherine miscarried through grief after being harshly treated by Henry, although Martyr was relying on gossip, as he was not on the scene to witness whether this actually took place or not.

This confusion is complicated by a letter Catherine wrote to Ferdinand from Greenwich on 31 October 1515. In it, she describes how she gave birth to a child after Candlemas, which falls on 2 February. Assuming the translation and dating of this letter are correct, this discrepancy is difficult to explain, unless Catherine was again not being strictly accurate with her father. Ferdinand had been suffering from ill health, so it is possible that she was choosing the right time to impart the information. If she had miscarried late in December, it is too soon for her to have lost another child by early February, although it is not impossible that the Italian Peter Martyr, then resident in Spain, was the recipient of incorrect information. If she had miscarried in early November and conceived again almost immediately afterwards, it is just possible that this letter refers to a foetus which can only have been two months old. This seems barely long enough for her to have realised her condition given the imperfect diagnoses of the time, but it cannot be entirely ruled out.

Pregnancy customs also suggest the child was lost in the winter of 1514 and not later. Catherine was recorded as being present at an entertainment and banquet held at Greenwich on Twelfth Night, 6 January 1515.[5] As part of the festivities, a 'fierce fight' was conducted, to the sound of trumpets, when eight wildmen jumped out of a mock castle, 'all apparelled in green moss ... with ugly weapons and terrible visages', and fought with knights. As it was widely believed that expectant mothers should avoid sudden shocks, loud noises and ugly scenes, which could imprint themselves on the character of the foetus and cause miscarriage, it does seem unlikely that such a display would have taken place before the queen if Catherine had still been pregnant at that point. At any rate, during the winter of 1514/15 Catherine lost her fourth child in five years. This cast into doubt her primary function as a queen: her ability to bear a healthy child.

Catherine had proven that she could conceive. The problems lay in her ability to carry a child to term and with infant mortality. Clearly there was something wrong, but no one at the time understood what. It wasn't unusual for women to lose children at birth or soon after, as Catherine knew from the experiences of her own family; modern estimates have given a sixteenth-century pregnancy a 50 per cent chance of success, followed by a 2–5 per cent risk of the newborn dying. Superstition laid the blame firmly at the feet of the woman, for failing to observe the proper rituals or having lewd or inappropriate thoughts or being physically deficient. In religious terms, such a pattern of losses would be interpreted as a divine comment on the nature of her marriage or on Catherine and Henry as individuals or rulers. Medical opinion of the day viewed pregnancy and delivery as an entirely female issue, with a man's role ending after the moment of conception: there was no understanding of the way in which male genes could affect the development and survival of the foetus and cause premature death or miscarriage months after intercourse had taken place. There is one plausible medical explanation though, developed in recent years, that might have identified the root of the problem.

According to research undertaken by medical anthropologist Kyra Kramer, it was all in the blood.[6] Henry VIII may have had a Kell positive blood type, an unusual occurrence which would lead to complications if his wife was of the more widespread negative type. In such a case, a first pregnancy usually resulted in the birth of a live child but, following this, the mother would develop a reaction to subsequent Kell positive foetuses and attempt to expel them by miscarriage. Henry's children Elizabeth, Edward and Henry Fitzroy were all their mothers' eldest children, and while Catherine may have lost her first child in 1510 for other reasons, her son Henry, born in 1511, may have been Kell negative and died from some other infantile illness. Likewise, her only child to survive, Mary, is likely to have been Kell negative also. The theory gains greater credence when compared with the gynaecological record of Henry's sister Margaret Tudor, whose first marriage produced six pregnancies and only one surviving child. Henry's Kell positive status may also have led him to develop McLeod syndrome later in life, causing the personality changes and mood swings some historians have identified as dominating his final years.

Other theories offer syphilis and diabetes as answers for Henry's reproductive difficulties. Syphilis can be ruled out conclusively, as it was easy to diagnose and Henry was never treated by any of the common methods, such as mercury powders and guaiacum wood from the Caribbean, which appear frequently in the accounts of other kings known to have the disease. Diabetes is a more viable possibility, as both kinds can affect the development of healthy sperm and the damage to blood vessels and the nervous system can result in erectile problems, although this would have been more of a problem for the king later in life.

Interestingly, one late medieval poem offers a lone voice about the role of the father in the debate about fertility. Phrased as a dialogue, the questioner asks:

> Why may not young men also get
> Strong children as old men do?[7]

The answer given is that young men's seed is green, or underdeveloped, and the passage of it through their body was difficult:

> And the passage in the body
> When that the nature shall pass by
> Is too strait, therefore the kind [sperm]
> No kindly issue may it find.
> And if that they any children get
> They shall never be strong nor great
> For it falleth in every thing
> Feeble seed, feeble all the spring [offspring].[8]

The poem also covers what Catherine's contemporaries would have taken as an explanation of the loss of a full-term foetus. Firstly there was the 'suffrance of God's will', but there were also a number of things a pregnant woman was blamed for having done, including 'feeble nourishing' and 'the fellness of wicked nurture', that which denied her child a chance to grow in the womb. Another reason given was the inability of some women to bear childbirth, being insufficiently strong and not able to 'suffer the pain of childing' in the correct manner. This would cause her to 'stireth her and turneth about, so that the child falleth out'. Either way it was considered to be Catherine's fault, through her inability to nurture an heir or bear the pain of birth, or as punishment for offence she had given to God.[9]

In the spring of 1515 Henry was only twenty-three, yet he had begun his attempt to father a child relatively young, at just eighteen. Five years on, he was still young enough to hope for success and consider that, by now, his seed would have been strong enough, according to the ideas of the poem. It was quite another matter for Catherine. She was approaching thirty and must have felt her gynaecological failure deeply, surrounded as she was by a household full of attractive, accomplished young women who were getting married and bearing children. Soon, one of them would find her way into Henry's bed.

PART THREE
Bessie Blount

20

Catching the King's Eye, 1514–15

The inflammate desire / of your good intent
Newes to compile / eschewing idleness
Cometh of grace / and of wisdom excellent
To occupy such / as haue no business
Whiche unto of doing / much harm doth oppress
For surely idleness / is portresse of all synne
Every vice / ready to let in[1]

Bessie Blount is the first woman who is known, with any certainty, to have been Henry's mistress. As a young and beautiful teenager in the queen's household, she would have been dazzled by the authority and appearance of the king, as a member of a court that was geared towards the continual celebration, even exaggeration, of Henry's talents and person. While directly answerable to Catherine, Bessie's role was complementary to the king: to adore, revere, flatter and serve, to participate in his masques and dances, to collude in his disguises and secrets. In short, one of her roles was to flatter his ego, for whatever rewards it may bring her.

It is sometimes easy to overlook just how exceptional Henry was in his early years, as his reputation has been shaped more by the large, despotic 'mouldwarp' figure he became in later life. In his youth, Henry was the early sixteenth century's embodiment of the ideal man – beautiful, learned, talented and rich, with his boisterous, gorgeous court a series of long parties and excess consumption. He was a fantasy figure made flesh, whose word was law, whose displeasure was a secular equivalent of excommunication. For his courtiers of both gender, his favour fell on them like the sun's rays and its withdrawal was like its eclipse. It is small wonder that Bessie yielded to his advances.

Bessie already had a connection to Catherine of Aragon from the days of the queen's first marriage. Her family came from Kinlet, in Shropshire, a property associated with Arthur, Prince of Wales, which the young couple may have visited. Bessie's grandfather was Sir Thomas Blount of Kinlet, whose wife, Anne Croft, came from a family with longstanding associations with Ludlow Castle and service to its inhabitants. Bessie had been born at Kinlet in around 1500, and Catherine may even have seen the little girl in Shropshire while she was still an infant. The Blount family already had a powerful advocate in their relation Lord Mountjoy, Henry VIII's Master of the Mint, who was married to Catherine's lady-in-waiting and fellow Spaniard Agnes de Venegas. Perhaps it was his intervention that brought his young relative to the notice of the Tudors again.

It was common practice for young men and women of high rank to be placed in an aristocratic household around the age of twelve, and Bessie's relatives placed her in the most lucrative of positions in autumn 1512, under the protection of the queen herself. She was not the only young woman there, as a Mrs Stonor had been designated the 'mother of the maids', overseeing their conduct and training. Bessie was linked with Elizabeth Carew in Brandon's letter of 1514, suggesting that the pair were friends and of a similar age. It also proves that both women had come to the king's attention, with Bessie showing up again in official records that Christmas. By the age of fourteen, she had spent enough time at Henry's court to acclimatise to its atmosphere and rules; she had witnessed the game of courtly love being played out, taken part in dances and masques, joined Catherine in pretending to be amazed when Henry removed his disguise at the end of the evening and witnessed the queen's recent losses. She would have added to her existing accomplishments, learning languages, playing and composing music, reading, gambling and acquiring a veneer of the polish she observed in her elders. In contemporary terms, her looks matched the early Renaissance ideal of fair skin, blue eyes and golden hair. She was young, noble, accomplished and attractive. Henry's court was a heady place in the early years, the most exciting place to be for any young woman with social ambitions.

During the New Year celebrations of 1515, shortly after the time Catherine lost her fourth child, Elizabeth took part in a masque in the queen's apartments. On 1 January, eight revellers danced in costumes of cloth of silver and blue velvet, embroidered with the letters H and K, which 'straunge apparel pleased muche every person, and in especial the queen', who invited them to perform in her chambers.[2] The four ladies who danced in the roles of women of Savoy were Elizabeth Carew, Bessie Blount, Lady Guildford and Lady Fellinger (*sic*).[3] They were partnered by four men disguised in Portuguese attire, who were Nicholas Carew, Henry himself, Charles Brandon and Lord Fellinger. Henry had been partnered with Bessie. Catherine 'hartely thanked the kynges grace for her goodly pastyme and kissed hym'.[4] Yet the queen's warm response might have been masking her true feelings. She had learned to turn a blind eye to Henry's amours, in the interests of harmony and pleasing her husband. It may be telling that, when the dance was repeated on Twelfth Night, Bessie's place at Henry's side had been taken by Jane Popincourt.

A significant amount of time and preparation went into the many elaborate entertainments hosted at Henry's court. Following an Italian tradition, he was the first king to use them as a permanent part of his court celebrations, rather than attached to specific dates in the Catholic calendar. The liberating qualities of masks had long been recognised and no doubt the king enjoyed the thrill of dancing incognito, but the carefully choreographed moves and use of moveable staging must have necessitated many rehearsals and costume fittings. These would have been conducted in secrecy, in order to preserve the concealed identities of the players. Perhaps these performances also provided the opportunity for flirtation, right at the heart of the court. It was an opportunity for the king to show favouritism by selecting those he wished to participate, with whom he would be sharing the secret preparations, a legitimate opportunity to get closer to certain women without supervision. The account books and expenses of some of these more elaborate events show that the planning process, of sewing, building, painting and rehearsing, was begun as early as a month in advance, with a string of performances or events drawn out over the intervening days. No doubt Henry enjoyed the process for its own sake, but it was also a useful tool for breaching the structure of the separate royal households and blurring the lines of intimacy. Did Catherine notice that some of her ladies had gone missing?

The 1524 book *The Education of a Christian Woman*, written by Spanish Humanist Juan Luis Vives and dedicated to Catherine of Aragon, advises against young women participating in masked dances, for the immorality and licence involved: 'Like little children, [they] take great pleasure in covering their face' and running about where they 'see and know everyone but are not recognised by anyone'. Vives cautioned that this was the first step towards a moral decline: 'Under that mask, many shameful things are concealed ... a woman who would be ashamed to come out and dance if she were known is not afraid to do so when she is masked, and consequently there is no respect for age, social status, fortune or reputation ... not only to they hear obscenities and things unworthy of them but they say fearlessly what they would not dare to think if they were recognised.' At Henry's court, the masks were always removed at the end of the evening and identities revealed, but the confidence that disguise gave facilitated illicit romance – 'a mask levels everything in the eyes of the beholder ... thus little by little they become used to shamelessness so that the harm that modesty suffered under the mask is now flaunted and displayed'. In Vives' eyes, masks related directly to the themes of carnival and social inversion; they offered all women the ability to escape their roles and encouraged immorality. He concluded that 'it is to be feared that these amusements may be the occasion of great misconduct'.[5] Perhaps his patroness shared his concerns.

Vives was also critical of the disruptive influence of dancing on young women at court, quoting St Ambrose's letter to his sister:

> Is there anything more conducive to carnal lust than to reveal with crude movements those hidden regions of the body with either nature or moral discipline has concealed, to cavort with the eyes, to roll the head around, to toss back the hair? As a natural consequence this will lead to an offense against the divinity. What sense of shame can exist where there is dancing, confusion, loud noise?

After observing such a dance, Vives related that 'the king, delighted with the spectacle, told the girl she could ask of him what she wished'.[6] Vives' direct correlation between dancing and sex strikes a note which is far more worthy of the accusation of prudery than the English king who loved to dance in his youth, yet the message is still pertinent: dancing and masques formed part of the courtly rituals of flirtation and courtship and provided an opportunity for greater familiarity between the sexes than when they were confined to the separate households of Henry and Catherine.

The fact that Henry drew his lovers, including three of his later queens, from within his wives' establishments, made for an especially difficult atmosphere for any woman married to him at the time. A queen's position required her to educate and steer such young women in their acquisition of accomplishments and in the direction of a suitable husband. A later play composed by John Heywood during the 1530s, *The Play of the Weather*, represented the gentlewoman's household as the breeding place of vice, through dancing, singing and display; all the elements that contributed towards the magnificence of Henry's court in its early years. The bawdiness of some of these plays suggests they were conducive to flirtation and innuendo that could readily spill over into the real lives of the courtly players:

> Why have ye always kissed her behind?
> In faith good enough if it be your mind.
> And if your appetite serve you so to do,
> By our Lady, I would have kissed mine arse too...

> But by conjecture this guess I have,
> That I do speak to an old bawdy knave.
> I saw you dally with your simper de cocker;
> I rede you beware she pick not your pocket.
> Such idle housewives do now and then
> Think all well won that they pick from a man.[7]

The character of 'Merry Report' goes on to ask the laundress who speaks these lines whether he can 'meddle' with her and the Devil both together. His speech raises the question of airing dirty linen; literally in this sense, but also as a thinly veiled reference to immoral behaviour:

> Thy face were sun burned and thy clothes the sweeter
> Then that the sun from shining should be smitten
> To keep thy face fair and thy smock beshitten.[8]

Later referred to by William Thomas as a man of 'fleshly' appetites, Henry used masques and disguises to conduct his dalliances under the very nose of the court.

While the king was planning his courtly entertainments and his illicit amours, Catherine was dealing with another kind of dishonour in her household. Having served her for eight years, her confessor, Fray Diego, was convicted of fornication by an ecclesiastical court and dismissed in disgrace. According to one historian, his amours came to light when members of the court complained about his behaviour, leading Diego to comment that if he was 'badly used, the queen is still more badly used'. Later that year, after he had returned to Spain, Catherine added a postscript in a letter to her father, begging him to show the friar favour as he 'has served her very faithfully all the time he was in England, and much better than certain persons pretend'.[9] His loss would have been felt by the queen but, perhaps considering the bad advice he had given her, Diego's departure represented a significant break with Catherine's past. She remained loyal to him in spite of it, losing an important confidant and defender to whom she had been very close.

Henry was also dealing with a scandal of his own, involving his family and one of his closest friends. On 28 December, King Louis of France had written to Henry that 'his satisfaction with the queen his wife was such that Henry might be sure of his treating her to her own and his satisfaction'.[10] Four days later Louis died in Paris, leaving the eighteen-year-old Mary a widow. When the news arrived in England,

Wolsey had drafted a letter to advise her that 'during her heaviness ... among strangers', she should not forget that Henry 'would not forsake her' and that she should 'do nothing without the advice of his grace'.[11] In the confinement of her mourning, while the French court waited to see whether she was pregnant, Mary had been the target of attention from the new king, Francis I. Wolsey urged her that 'if any motions of marriage or other offers ... be made unto you, in no wise give hearing to them'.[12] On 14 January, Henry sent Charles Brandon to bring his sister home to England but, six weeks later, Mary capitalised on the promise she had extracted from her brother and she and Brandon were married. Henry was furious but eventually allowed the pair to return, providing they paid a large fine.

At home, the festivities continued. Catherine and her ladies were present at the jousts that began on 3 February, where Henry was 'highlie to be praised' for exceeding all others in having broken twenty-three spears. On May Day, she took rode out from Greenwich with Henry to 'take the open aire' at Shooter's Hill and, 'as they passed by the waie', spotted a company of two hundred men in green livery, led by one figure who called himself Robin Hood. This was another staged encounter, with roles played by members of the king's guard, who led the royal couple into the woods to see how the outlaws lived. Further role play followed, with Henry asking Catherine if she dared 'adventure to go into the woods', to which she replied that 'if it pleased him, she was content'.[13] In bowers of flowers, carolled by singing birds, they dined on venison, game birds and wine, while musicians played on flutes and singers sang. Followed by a crowd of thousands, they were accompanied home by the figure of Lady May herself, personification of the day itself, and her retinue of ladies given such seasonal names as Flora, 'pleasance', 'sweet odour,' 'humidity' and 'green'.[14] Bessie Blount was one of twenty-five ladies who accompanied Catherine, riding white palfreys, dressed in clothes 'slashed with gold lama and very costly trim'.[15] If her affair with Henry had not already begun, it may have started that July, indicated by the unexplained advance made to her father of two years' worth of his salary. This strongly indicates Henry's fondness for Bessie and either her compliance or his anticipation of it.

An Italian observer at Greenwich, Nicolas Sagudino, was more than impressed with Henry's appearance and skill, writing that he was 'very expert in arms, most excellent in his personal endowments, so adorned with mental accomplishments of every sort, he has few equals in the world. He speaks English, French and Latin; understands Italian; plays almost every instrument; sings and composes;

and is free from all vice.' Along with the king's guards, Sagudino had never seen 'finer fellows', and he was full of praise for the ladies-in-waiting, whom he considered 'very handsome'. Even the fool, 'Jack Madcap', had proved himself 'an excellent boon companion'. It was only Catherine for whom the Italian reserved his private criticism, stating that she was 'rather ugly than otherwise and thought to be pregnant'.[16] In fact, it was around this time that Catherine conceived her fifth child, so her condition would not yet have been visible but her gynaecological history may well have taken its toll on her once-youthful appearance.

It cannot have been easy for the queen, entering another cycle of hope with the memories of her recent disappointments. In a few short years she had lost her youthful curvaceous beauty, which had had been so praised upon her arrival in England. Just four years later, Francis I would go so far as to describe her as old and deformed, in comparison with Henry's youth and good looks. Worse still, she had sacrificed it in the attempt to provide Henry with a family, but did not even have the string of children to show for it, which would have been worth the pain she had experienced if it secured her position in her husband's affections and earned the respect of the court. She had been young once, and she knew what it was to be loved by a man like Henry. To see his affections transferred elsewhere, even under the guise of honouring her through court entertainments, cannot have been easy. Catherine took refuge in the status of her position. Her marriage and appearance might have changed but she was still Henry's wife and England's queen, and as such she would command the respect and deference that was due to her. She was an integral part of the court, of the country, and as she continued to conceal any pain her life may have caused her, she became even more the embodiment of the role to which she had been born.

Once Catherine's pregnancy was confirmed, Henry may have again sought the attention of other ladies at his court. Jane Popincourt had not yet departed for France and, with possible flirtations with Elizabeth Carew and Bessie Blount established, the king did not have to look far to find attractive young ladies with whom to indulge while he awaited his wife's confinement. He was young, attractive, accomplished and royal; his court was the most splendid in Europe, famed for its chivalry and partying. The royal coffers were still healthy, even after the expenses incurred by Henry's victories in France and in the tilt yard, and the long summer days were filled with pleasure, as the king travelled from one of his beautiful properties to the next, adorned by jewels and cloth of gold. In the eyes of his contemporaries, Henry literally had a touch of divinity about him. He was the embodiment of magnificence. Setting aside the fact that to refuse his advances could have put an end to a promising career and the advancement of a whole family, to be the mistress, or favourite, of such a man would be an honour that few could refuse.

21

Begetting a Boy, 1515–16

Hail, root, bringing forth stems of different colours from your shoot
Along which one stands out, from whose top there gleams a scarlet rose
Where peace and justice stand enclosed and harmonious.[1]

As the autumn of 1515 passed and the New Year arrived, Catherine's fifth pregnancy progressed according to expectation. This was certainly a comfort, although she had experienced few problems before with conception or the development of the child in her womb; time had proven that the critical period for her was the final couple of months. Awaiting her confinement, the devout queen would have prayed regularly and diligently, to God and the saints, in the hope that they would look favourably upon her through the coming ordeal. Catherine would have prayed to St Margaret, the patron saint of childbirth, and perhaps her own name saint, Catherine, but it was the Virgin Mary whose cult dominated pre-Reformation Europe, being the favourite intercessor of women hoping to become mothers, especially those who had experienced loss, as the saint had. No doubt she prayed to be delivered of a healthy child, and that that child was to be a boy.

The determination of foetal gender was thought to depend on theories of the four humours, with warmth creating boys and coldness responsible for girls. By extension, it was believed that impurities cooled the blood, so purging and bleeding could rejuvenate its heat and, as a consequence, became popular treatments for women attempting to produce sons. China root, sassafras and sarsaparilla were also prescribed as blood cleansers. Catherine had proved herself able to conceive male children, although they had not survived, but the credit would have been given to the hot, dry seed of her husband. The right-hand side was also thought to be favourable, with the right testicle and right ovary cleansed by the right kidney before reaching the gonad. Thus, males were believed to be conceived when influenced by this bodily half.

This translated into practical advice that involved keeping the right side warm, having sex lying on the side, or the woman rolling over immediately afterwards. It was also believed that the mixing of sides was undesirable: 'If the semen which comes from the right side of the man falls in the left side of the womb, it produces a boy, but an effeminate one; whereas if the semen from the left side falls in the right, it makes a masculine girl.'[2] It was suggested by one of Henry's later physicians, Andrew Boorde, that the best time to conceive a child was between the first and second sleeps. This involved a common practice of the times, by which people woke during the night as a natural part of their body rhythms, and rolled over before returning to sleep on their other side. This would have involved an early morning visit to his wife's chambers on the part of the king. He would have been accompanied through the dark corridors, past sleeping courtiers, to visit Catherine, before returning to his own bed. Protocol dictated that he awoke in the morning in his own rooms. One folklore suggestion for conception advocated a more direct method of intervention by strapping up the left testicle prior to the act. Catherine would have been no doubt that it was imperative that she bore a son. Perhaps she and Henry attempted to influence their child's gender using one or more of these methods.

Herbals offered a range of advice on the generation of sperm. The ideal aphrodisiac was considered to be any food that was warm, nutritious, moist and created windiness. Pepper, mustard seed, ginger and anise were used, as well as orchids for their supposed phallic resemblance. One broth recommended in a medieval text included nineteen birds' tongues. The genitals of male animals were eaten or dried and used as talismens as they were thought to pass on their qualities of hot, dry masculinity, with the penises of oxen and stags featuring in such recipes.[3] Henry was interested in medicine from an early age and kept a range of doctors, barbers, surgeons and other medical professionals such as astronomers and astrologers at his court. Comments made by his doctors later in his life showed that he was in the habit of confiding intimate details to them, so it would seem likely that he sought advice over conception and perhaps even gender, after so many failures.

Since 1509, Henry had employed Thomas Linacre, an Italian-born doctor who had previously served Prince Arthur and Princess Mary, as his court physician, on a salary of £50 a year. Linacre encouraged Henry to pass the Medical Act of 1512, to help curb the trade in quack medicines, and to establish the Royal College of Surgeons in 1518. At various times he also retained the services of John Chambre, who replaced Linacre on his death in 1524, William Butts, George Owen, Walter Cromar, Augustine de Angustinius, Edward Wootton, Ferdinand de Victoria, Dr Wendy and others. On hand to treat the king whatever his ailment, or just for the general benefit of his health, they prescribed over 230 different remedies for him, including creams, lotions, balms, potions, plasters and enemas, made mostly from herbal sources. It appears that Henry himself contributed his own remedies, as he was a keen amateur apothecary, mixing up roses, pomegranate, bark and nightshade to balance the humours and wine, ginger and violet for a pain-relieving enema.[4] Henry also employed a number of separate surgeons, with John Veyrier being his 'chief surgeon of the body and to the heirs of his body' from 1509 to 1516. Marcellus de la More was his surgeon on the field of battle, accompanying him to campaign in France in 1513 and receiving a lifetime annuity in 1516.[5] His apothecary, whom he kept busy dispensing the necessary medicines between 1509 and 1527, was Richard Brabham.[6]

That summer relations between England and Spain became a little friendlier, with Wolsey negotiating a treaty that would bury previous injuries in 'oblivion' and bind the two countries to defend each other. It was concluded on 19 October, and the following day Henry wrote from Greenwich to thank his father-in-law for the 'splendid presents and jewellery' that Ferdinand had sent to help smooth the deal. According to Catherine, these were a sword, horses in ornate trappings and a jewelled collar. In a very warm response, Henry wrote that 'great as the value of the presents is, he values them principally because they show his [King Ferdinand's] love and benevolence towards him. No one could send such presents who is not animated by the most sincere and tender love towards him.' He saw 'how much [Ferdinand] values and esteems him' and loved him 'as much and as sincerely as he ever did before, and even more'. He had 'forgotten all the disagreeable things which have passed between them' and begged 'to be allowed to regard him as a brother or as a son, often [looking] at the presents, and every time he sees them, his [King Ferdinand's] image is recalled to his mind's eye'.[7] Anti-Spanish feeling had been running high over the previous years, but with their antagonism set aside Catherine could feel more secure in her position and the reputation of her country at her husband's court. Now, as the laces of her dresses were loosened, she could turn her attention to the coming birth.

Henry and Catherine kept Christmas 1515 at Eltham Palace,

watching a performance of *Troilus and Pandarus*, followed by a feast of two hundred dishes, which required the building of temporary kitchens. As a touching gesture of favour, Henry also wore his wife's pomegranate badge while tilting at the ring in the New Year festivities. The queen was aware that her time was approaching; she had planned to lie in at Greenwich and a suite of rooms was prepared for her in her absence that festive season, ready for her formal confinement at the end of January. Around this time Catherine employed a new doctor, Peter Vernando, to whom she awarded an annual salary of £66 13s 4d, before she entered the confinement that would necessitate her leaving the men locked out of the room and relying upon the knowledge and support of her women. Many of them had already been through this process with her several times before.

That January, news arrived at court of the difficult birth experienced by Henry's sister Margaret in Scotland. Having delivered a daughter the previous October, she was still suffering significant sciatic pain in her right leg, with 'no appearance of improvement, in spite of all the doctor can do'. Margaret had two physicians but was anxious for Henry to send her one of his, in the belief that 'if the pain were abated, she would soon be past all danger, and strong enough to stir. There seems to be no danger to life; nevertheless it would be advisable to send a physician immediately.' In the meantime, she was able to eat little more than broth, almond milk, pottage and boiled or roast meat with jelly, but her appetite had been 'destroyed'.[8] This information was probably kept from Catherine so that it did not cause her to worry unduly about her own forthcoming confinement, but there was even more distressing news that was kept from the queen 'on account of the expected delivery'.[9] On 23 January, Ferdinand of Aragon had died in the village of Madrigalejo after falling ill on the way to Andalusia.

Henry was back at Greenwich by the end of the month, which suggests that Catherine was expected to give birth around that time. On 13 February, he was negotiating a treaty of friendship with Ferdinand's heir, Catherine's nephew Charles, who was now King of Castile. The queen went into labour shortly after this, and bore a healthy child on 18 February, at four o'clock in the morning. A reward Henry paid to her Spanish doctor, Dr Victoria, suggests he was present and assisted at the birth. It was unusual for a man to be present, but this breach of protocol may have been due to Catherine's previous experiences of losing children shortly after delivery. It was not the son they had hoped for, but a daughter, whom they named Mary. Henry's hopeful response was that he and Catherine were both young and that 'if it was a daughter this time, by the grace of God, the sons will follow'.[10] A son was to follow, but Catherine would not be his mother.

22

The Quiet Queen, 1516–18

And though a Prince
And a King's son he be
It pleaseth him of his benignity
To suffer gentlemen of low degree
In his presence[1]

Catherine appeared less and less in public. Through his years as Venetian ambassador, between 1515 and 1519, Sebastiano Guistiniani saw her 'but seldom', either in court events or in private. With her daughter's nursery to oversee, her own religious devotion and the loss of her father, Catherine spent more and more time in her private apartments, still with the increasingly slender hope that she would conceive and bear Henry a son. Among those keeping Catherine company while she sat and sewed her husband's shirts was her old friend Margaret Plantagenet, Lady Pole, along with the mothers of two of Henry's future wives, Elizabeth Boleyn and Maud Green, Lady Parr. Among her ladies of the bedchamber, serving her on a more intimate basis, had been one of her original Spanish entourage, Agnes de Venegas, now Lady Mountjoy, but after her death in 1514 Mountjoy had remarried. His new wife was Alice Kebell, who served Catherine along with Anne Bourchier, Lady Dacre; Elizabeth, Lady Scrope; Margaret, Lady Bergavenny; Anne, Lady Percy; Elizabeth, Lady Maltravers; and Lady Ferrers. Of these women whose birth dates are known, with one exception, the majority were in their late thirties and early forties. Perhaps this was a deliberate policy, as their role was more confidential and personal than those chosen to dance in court entertainments. Sometimes the older ladies at court participated in revels, but increasingly these were the preserve of their daughters' generation, with the young Lady Guildford, Elizabeth Carew, Anne Carew, Mary Fiennes Mabel Fitzwilliam, Elizabeth Grey and Elizabeth Dannett taking the key roles.

Catherine's role as Henry's wife was also changing. She had always wanted to be a mother and her devotion to her young daughter and her upbringing gave her a focus outside the marriage. Also, her father's death had ended her position as the intermediary between Henry and Ferdinand. Spain was now being ruled by her nephew Charles, son of Joanna, and although Catherine would always be his advocate, it was no replacement for the position of trust she had occupied as her father's informal ambassador. As Henry's wife, she had also been his counsellor and advisor, discussing events of national and international policy and acting on the king's behalf. Nowhere had this been clearer than during the aftermath of the disastrous 1512 campaign and her role as regent the following year. Now, Cardinal Wolsey's rapid rise and efficient capability meant that Henry increasingly leaned on the older man for advice and that Wolsey took over more of the diplomatic business that the queen had once undertaken. In many ways this allowed her more time to devote to her daughter, but it marked a change in her relationship with Henry and in her role.

The palaces that Catherine most regularly occupied during these years were Greenwich and Eltham, followed by Windsor and Richmond. A fire in the privy chambers at Westminster in 1512 had destroyed the ancient seat of government, which was only slowly rebuilt, and shifted the focus of the court elsewhere. At Eltham, Henry's childhood home, the king undertook significant building work, extending Catherine's suite of rooms in the west range and building a new chapel. In the coming years, her presence chamber, where she sat in state, was enlarged towards the north, along with her private withdrawing room. Greenwich was undoubtedly a favourite retreat, a reminder of the happier days Catherine and Henry had spent after their wedding. One public occasion at which Catherine played a key role was the festivities at Greenwich in May 1516 to honour the visit of Henry's elder sister, Margaret Tudor. Two days of jousts were held 'in the presence of the three queens', Catherine, Margaret and Mary Tudor, after which Catherine hosted a banquet in her chambers. Margaret stayed at the English court through that year and must have been a welcome companion for the queen, being a similar age and having experienced a comparable record of losses in childbirth. She passed Christmas with the royal couple at Greenwich, watching a pageant called Esperance, or Hope, in the great hall, where an artificial garden was filled with roses and pomegranates made of silk and where six knights and ladies danced, followed by a banquet.

It possible that Catherine withdrew more from public life so as not to witness the relationship developing between Henry and Bessie

Blount. In her apartments, she could oversee the conduct of her gentle-women and close the door literally and symbolically on whatever was happening elsewhere in the palace. Sometimes Henry would bring dances and masques into her presence in her honour, and she would venture out with her women to participate in feast days and full-scale court entertainments, but the chronicles show she was not always present, keeping to her rooms. However, this latest amour was more serious. If the king had previously taken lovers for entertainment, or indulged in flirtations with Catherine's women, he now appeared to have fallen in love.

Although it is not clear exactly how long Henry's relationship with Bessie lasted, one later source was of the belief that it had been an affair of significant duration. Lord Herbert of Cherbury wrote of the 'chains of love' that bound Henry to Bessie, 'which damsel in singing, dancing and in all goodly pastimes, exceeded all other, by the which goodly pastimes, she won the king's heart'.[2] He goes on to state that she bore him a son 'at last', which suggests more than a single encounter. Henry's desire to father another child with Catherine would not exclude him from bestowing his affections and attention elsewhere. As one historian has suggested, the birth of Princess Mary was an incentive for Henry to remain faithful to his queen, but faith-fulness was not the guarantee of a successful conception. Rather, to the Tudor mind, the regular engagement in intercourse and the relief of bodily fluids, would be more successful in terms of gynaecological health, especially during periods when Catherine was unavailable. Henry may well have still loved Catherine and been sharing her bed, but it is a misleading modern sentiment that this required him to abstain elsewhere. Especially as the months of 1516 and 1517 passed without Catherine conceiving, Henry himself would have seen no incompatibility between pursuing Bessie and impregnating his queen in order to beget a legitimate heir. The irony of this was that Henry's male child was conceived by his lover, not his wife.

Outside Catherine's household, the world had a turbulent feel. Although Henry had made his peace with Ferdinand before his death, the mood of hostility towards foreigners in London had not diminished but escalated. In late April, a speech at St Paul's Cross called on English men to defend themselves against the wealthy merchants and bankers, mostly Italian, who made their homes in and around Lombard Street. Some disturbances followed, which led to the imposition of a curfew. On May Day 1517, known as 'Evil May Day', gangs of apprentices defied the ruling and ran amok through the streets, causing damage to property and engaging in looting. Henry and Catherine were at

Richmond, removed from the scene, but by quickly dispatching his troops the king regained control of the capital. Most of the hundreds of rioters were released without charge, but a sizeable number were brought before Henry at Westminster Hall, shackled together under the threat of execution. Among them were eleven women. Whether Henry had planned to send them to their deaths, or whether it was a carefully planned scene, it fell to Catherine to plead for their lives, on bended knee before her husband. 'With tears in her eyes', she asked for the people to be pardoned and was described by the papal nuncio who witnessed the scene as 'our most serene and compassionate queen'. The king was magnanimous and Catherine had played a significant conciliatory role in the eyes of her subjects.

Trouble was brewing under the king's nose, too. During 1517–18, Henry's court was becoming increasingly boisterous and causing concern among his advisors. John Skelton's *Magnificence*, a political satire and morality play dealing with the fall of a king from grace into poverty, was probably written during this period in an attempt to counter some of the young man's excesses. Wolsey had become alarmed by the clique of unruly and disrespectful young men or 'minions' who had gathered about Henry, with their scandalous love affairs and boisterous disrespect. Skelton was well placed to comment on it, having been the king's tutor in his youth and the author of at least one previous work aimed at his personal improvement, the now lost *The Mirror for Princes*. Skelton's work depicted the king as the embodiment of magnificence, or generosity combined with grandeur and wisdom. The central eponymous character is tempted by Crafty Conveyance, Courtly Abusion and others, but is brought back to the enlightened path by the figures of Measure and Perseverance.

Magnificence was probably staged in 1519, but it received a new lease of life in 2010 under the direction of Dr Elisabeth Dutton at Hampton Court Palace. It appears that *Magnificence* and other plays and interludes of the time could use the guise of drama to indulge in some poetic satire of the king without fear of reprisals. Also writing at this time were John Rastell, who printed many of these early dramas, and his son-in-law John Heywood, the author of *The Play of the Weather* and *The Play of Love*. Such works and pageants might have provided Henry with a vehicle for flirtation, but he was also not averse to giving his playwrights a similar degree of licence when it came to subtle satire.

If Henry had exploited the element of courtly misrule in order to pursue women, such occasions had also encouraged members of his privy chamber to forget their place. The minions, a sort of private boys' club including William Compton, Edward Neville, Francis

Bryan, Nicholas Carew, Charles Brandon and Henry Courtenay, began causing trouble home and abroad, and some were berated by the conservatives at Henry's court as being 'all French in eating, drinking and apparel, yea, and in French vices and brags'. Their influence over the king was becoming remarked, with Brandon in particular being rumoured to 'rule him in all things'.[3] As personal attendants on the king's body, in terms of dress, sleeping, clothing and bodily functions, they are the most likely to have known about his sexual habits and affairs, to have witnessed his amours and been his confidants. Many of them had known him since his youth, having been the 'henchmen' in his household prior to the death of his father. They had risen with Henry, witnessed him create his own glittering world for the pursuit of pleasure and their arrogance and rakish behaviour was something of an extension of Henry's own unbridled ego. Undoubtedly many of them knew his secrets, just as he knew theirs.

If Henry trusted his minions to collude in his liaisons, creating an intimate core at the heart of his court, he would have further contributed to the manner in which his favourites transgressed the boundaries of acceptable behaviour and blurred the lines of status between themselves and the king: 'certain young gentlemen in his privy chamber, not regarding his estate or degree, were so familiar and homely with him, and played sight touches with him, that they forgot themselves'.[4] If they forgot themselves, it was because Henry failed to maintain the appropriate distance and encouraged their hedonistic antics. Ultimately, though, the influence of these rowdy young men was not as strong as that of Henry's old guard of Wolsey, Thomas Boleyn and the Duke of Norfolk, who moved against them in May 1519, and expelled many from the king's intimate service. It is also significant that many of these young men were executed by Henry in the late 1530s, under the aegis of treason, although in the cases of Neville, Carew and Courtenay it would be little more than suspicion regarding their proximity to him and their reputed designs on his status. By then, Henry was not prepared to tolerate those who encroached upon his royal person.

In the spring of 1518, a whole two years after the birth of Princess Mary, Catherine suspected she was pregnant again. That March she had visited the Priory of St Frideswide at Oxford, whose shrine and relics had particular associations with female health, and probably prayed and left offerings there in the hope of conceiving. Given their history, the royal pair was cautious about making the news public until they knew that Catherine's condition was certain, but as early as April Henry's secretary had informed Wolsey that it was being 'secretly said' that she had conceived again. The king himself confirmed this hope, writing about it 'not as an ensured thing, but as a thing wherein I have great hope and likelihood'.[5] Mindful of Henry's comment following the birth of their daughter, the queen no doubt hoped that Mary's survival was an indication that she would be able to bear a healthy child. She was now thirty-two and considered old for a mother. Hopefully this would be the son the dynasty required.

The royal couple kept well away from London that summer, where an outbreak of the sweat raged through the capital, and travelled leisurely through their countryside properties together and separately. Henry had been staying at Penshurst Place in Kent, the seat of the Duke of Buckingham, before returning to Catherine, who had remained at Woodstock. There, she 'did meet with His Grace at his chamber door, and showed unto him for his welcome home her belly, something great, declaring openly that she was quick with child'.[6] Reports reached them of the extent of the illness in London, which, as chronicler Hall related, 'was so cruell that it killed some within three houres, some within two houres, some merry at dinner and dead at supper'.[7] Henry and Catherine learned that 'many died in the kynges courte, the Lord Clinton, the Lord Grey of Wilton, and many knights and gentlemen and officers'.[8] No doubt this reminded the queen of the terrible outbreak of 1502, which she had survived but Arthur had not. This new outbreak was so virulent that it would last from July to December, before it began to show signs of abating.

In the meantime, Henry was negotiating a marriage for his infant daughter to the dauphin of France, the son of Francis, who bore his name and who had been born that February. Henry risked riding to London to take part in the negotiations and the banquet that followed, hosted by Wolsey at his property of Durham House. Hall's detailed description of the disguisings that followed clearly identifies the key participants. Twelve couples were dressed in fine green satin, covered in cloth of gold, tied on with laces and wore masquing hoods. They danced before pulling off their masks to reveal Henry and his sister Mary, then Brandon and Lady Daubeney, who was possibly Elizabeth Arundell, to whom Henry had given a grant of £100 back in 1510. There was also the Lord Admiral and Lady Guildford, Edward Neville and the Lady St Leger, Henry Guildford and Elizabeth, Lady Walden, and Captain Emery with Lady Anne Carew. Sir Giles Capel partnered Elizabeth Carew, Francis Bryan danced with Bessie Blount, Henry Norris with Margaret Wotton, Francis Poyntz with Mary Fiennes, Arthur Poole with Margaret Bruges. It was clearly an occasion when married couples were encouraged to take other partners, with Brandon, Guildford, Carew and Bryan dancing separately from their wives, and with Norris not paired with Mary Fiennes, whom he would marry the following year.

This was the last court appearance made by Bessie Blount that year. She had fallen pregnant with Henry's child and, with the exact date of her confinement unclear, may or may not have been aware of her condition at this point. The fact that she did not appear in the pageant at Greenwich five days later suggests that her absence was due to the presence of the queen. Either Catherine already knew or, more likely, she stayed away to avoid grieving her mistress in her advanced state of pregnancy. The entertainment followed the preaching of a solemn Mass in favour of matrimony, before the king and queen removed to the great hall to watch a pageant of an artificial mountain topped with five trees. Drawing on the heraldic devices of England, France and Spain, there stood trees bearing olives, pineapples, roses, lilies and pomegranates. Fair ladies and gentlemen in crimson satin were seated around it, some who danced and some who fought. Then a figure named Report, dressed in a gown of crimson embroidered with tongues, entered on a winged horse named Pegasus. A banquet followed, of 160 dishes, followed by 60 plates of spices alone.[9] Henry conceded Tournai to the French and peace was made. It was probably the queen's last public engagement before retiring from the public eye.

It is not clear whether Catherine had formally entered confinement but, in November, according to the Venetian ambassador, she was 'delivered of a daughter, to the vexation of everybody. Never had the kingdom so anxiously desired anything as it did a prince'. The baby girl either died at birth or soon after. It was a terrible blow for Catherine, not only to lose her child but to have felt herself to be the 'vexation of everybody'.[10] She would not conceive again.

23

The Illegitimate Son, 1519

What hope is left for to redress,
By unknown means it liked me
My hidden burthen to express.
Whereby it might appear to thee.[1]

Bessie's pregnancy marked the end of her affair with Henry and of her masked performances at his court. She had been his lover for an unknown period of time, perhaps as long as four years or as briefly as a single night, which would have been around the time of the October celebrations at Durham House. Now, still in her late teens, she had conceived the king's child and disappeared from sight to await the birth. Church records show there was a stigma attached to unmarried mothers, with women who conceived outside wedlock being required to ask for forgiveness in public and sometimes being whipped in the marketplace for fornication. Private letters dating from the period also highlight the cases of pregnant wives whose morality was suspected, when they and their child were repudiated by the husband, although these are rare.

For Bessie, though, the normal rules did not apply. There was no stigma attached to bearing the king's son; in fact, it was a badge of honour. Henry's status gave her protection from the censure of society and the Church; in fact, the Church actively colluded to facilitate her lying-in. She was sent away from court less as an act of disapproval, than as one of discretion. Henry did not want his chivalric reputation to be tarnished by the increasing belly of his mistress nor to incur the wrath of his wife or set the tongues of gossips loose. It was not so much his own prudery as the attention it would have drawn in an arena of foreign ambassadors and politics. In contrast with many of his contemporaries, the king simply did not want his private life to be the subject of gossip.

Thomas Wolsey arranged it all. He was familiar with the need for discretion, as a cardinal and Archbishop of York, who kept his own mistress, or 'non-canonical' wife, contrary to the rule of clerical celibacy, and fathered two children. However, by the time of Bessie's lying-in, Wolsey had decided to distance himself from Joan Larke, arranging a marriage for her to George Legh. Catherine is reputed to have known all about it and deplored the 'voluptuous life' of 'abominable lechery' that he led.[2] Wolsey's relationship was not a very well-kept secret, with John Skelton representing court gossip – 'I tell you what men say' – and making puns on her name in his poem *Colin Clout:*

> And hauke on hobby larkes
> And other wanton warkes
> Whan the nyght darkes[3]

Bessie was taken to Essex, to the Augustinian Priory of St Laurence at Blackmore, near Chelmsford. The prior, Thomas Goodwin, who had held his position since 1513, was someone who Wolsey felt could be trusted to lodge the expectant mother in his own medieval moated house known as Jericho, close to the church. The derivation of the name is unclear, although it has been suggested that the River Wid, running alongside, also bore the name of Jordan, and the existence today of nearby 'Jericho Place', a cul-de-sac lined with modern housing, as well as separate houses called Little Jordan, Little Jericho and Jericho Cottage, indicate a longstanding local connection. Writing in 1768, historian Philip Morant suggested that Jericho House had been Henry VIII's pleasure palace, used by him for secret trysts, as a 'lascivious king ... lost in the embraces of his courtesans'. The priory was dissolved in 1524 but the nave still exists as part of the church, while the house was rebuilt or redeveloped into the private property that stands beside it today.

However, there is a chance that part of Jericho Palace, or at least the ghost of the place, remains. It has been suggested by Pevsner that, while the façade is Georgian, the layout looks more sixteenth century, so the foundations of the original priory may exist under the present house. Standing a little way off from the church, to the east, at the end of Church Lane, the back of the property can be glimpsed from the graveyard. Photographs from the early twentieth century show a redbrick, three-storey property with solid chimney stacks and a series of outbuildings. Part of the tall exterior wall also still stands. In 1766 the village was described as containing around fifty families, so it would have been a quiet, secluded place for Bessie to deliver her baby.

What Catherine was told about her maid's absence is not recorded. That summer, she and Henry stayed in two of their Essex properties that were close to Jericho Priory. Firstly they stayed at Catherine's property of Havering-atte-Bower, where the queen hosted a huge banquet, for which Henry 'thanked her hartely' before he passed the days in shooting and hunting. The house stood less than ten miles to the south-west of Blackmore. In September, they were at the king's new palace of Beaulieu, later called New Hall, for more masked dances and sport. Beaulieu was on the site of an old house that Henry had bought from Sir Thomas Boleyn in 1516 for £1,000; shortly afterwards he began to build a new palace on the site, which was to be known for its beautiful gardens. It was twelve miles east from Jericho, on the other side of Chelmsford. Both these properties were close enough to allow Henry to visit Bessie and his newborn child. Even if he did not go there in person, he could receive news as her labour progressed. A messenger would have been dispatched at once to inform him that Bessie had given birth to a healthy boy. He was named after his father.

The existence of Henry Fitzroy was unlikely to have gone unnoticed in his early years; there may have been some formal celebration to honour the boy which Catherine was forced to attend, and the banquet recorded as taking place at New Hall in August 1519 may have been occasioned by the news of his safe arrival. After his investiture as Duke of Richmond and Somerset in 1525 he frequently came to court, with his household based at his godfather Wolsey's London property of Durham House. In addition, some of the resources employed in Princess Mary's nursery were diverted to that of the new arrival, with the movement of staff from one child to another. The boy's existence was a thorn in Catherine's side, a justification of contemporary belief that her gynaecological failings were her own fault, a reminder of her pain. It also gave Henry confidence in his ability to father future sons, having proven that God would bless him with a male child. Little Fitzroy's arrival raised the question of whether there was something about his marriage that was displeasing.

The evidence suggests that Bessie's relationship with Henry was over by this point, or came to an end soon after. Perhaps it never developed into a relationship at all. It is interesting that he never considered marrying her and legitimising his son, even after Catherine did not conceive another child. Perhaps another woman had already replaced Bessie in the king's bed; an Arabella Parker, wife of a city merchant, has been cited by a late nineteenth-century historian,[4] but there is no evidence to corroborate this. Margery or Margaret Parker was a rocker in Princess Mary's household in 1516 and the Mistress Parker who danced in a court entertainment in 1522 was probably Jane, who went on to marry George Boleyn. It is not impossible that one of these women shared Henry's bed at some point, perhaps on a handful of occasions, which history has not recorded.

Alternatively, Henry might have been devoting his attention more exclusively to Catherine, in a final attempt to father another son now that he had been proved to be capable of it. Bessie would have had little control over the affair; she had yielded to Henry's advances and probably sacrificed her virginity to him, borne his son and served her purpose. It is difficult to know, with the lack of surviving evidence, whether she regretted the loss of the relationship or what, exactly, her expectations had been. Given that Catherine was Henry's established wife, Bessie's role had probably been more opportunist than ambitious, as her family seem to have benefited little from the connection. It is not difficult to read a short-lived love match into their affair, a romantic interlude fuelled by the courtly dance. However, the pain caused to Catherine must have been considerable, even if she did turn a blind eye.

Henry did take care of Bessie's future, though. There was no stigma in marrying the mother of the king's only son and any potential husband she might take would be in a position of strength to influence the boy in whatever direction his life might lead. Therefore, it was important that whoever was to act as his father was chosen, or at least approved, by Henry himself. Additionally, Bessie had proven her ability to bear a healthy male child, which was not an inconsiderable attraction in an era when fertility and childbirth were something of a lottery. Bessie's husband was Gilbert Tailboys, an only son whose father had served Henry in France before being declared insane in 1517. Then aged around twenty, Gilbert had entered Wolsey's household and his marriage was probably arranged by the cardinal too.

However, there is an interesting question of timing regarding the birth of Bessie's second child. The first reference to Bessie as Tailboys' wife comes on 18 June 1522, although their marriage took place before this date, but Bessie's daughter Elizabeth may have been born as early as 1520. If this is the case, and given that Bessie gave birth in the summer, her daughter would have been conceived in the autumn of 1519 or first three months of 1520. If she had married Tailboys that winter, she would have fallen pregnant soon after and the birth simply followed the wedding without any cause for doubt. It is unusual that the Tailboys are not referred to as a married couple until over two years later, though. While it has been suggested that Elizabeth was Henry's daughter, and that their affair continued after the birth of Fitzroy, the king did not acknowledge Elizabeth as his own. The liaison may even have continued after Bessie's wedding, in which case, Henry would not have been certain of his paternity, nor is he likely to have owned the child of a married woman, particularly as it was a daughter. It seems most likely, though, that the amour was over and Bessie was married around 1521, subsequently conceiving and bearing a daughter whose birthdate has been recorded imprecisely.

Two more children were born into the Tailboys' marriage, sons George and Robert, around 1523 and 1528. Bessie's part in the elaborate masked dances of Henry's court was taken by others.

24

The Proud Aunt, 1520

I have been ready at your hand,
To grant whatever you would crave,
I have both wagered life and land,
Your love and good-will for to have.[1]

While her personal life was full of pain, the year 1520 offered
Catherine the opportunity to take her place again in international
politics. Following the death of Emperor Maximilian in 1519, his
grandson Charles, Catherine's nephew, had been elected to the post,
beating his rival Francis I. This established an uneasy new triangle
at the heart of Europe, replacing the old triumvirate of Henry, Louis
and Ferdinand, but it would undergo just as much fluctuation of
fortune in the years ahead. That May, Henry was in the last stages
of planning the most expensive and opulent event of his entire reign,
which would see him cement an alliance with the French king at the
Field of Cloth of Gold. They would meet in temporary palaces where
fountains ran with wine and the walls were adorned with precious
stones, all torn down at the end of the two-week celebrations. Henry's
friendship with Francis was to prove just as temporary; before he
crossed the Channel he had arranged a secret meeting with Charles.

While the Earl of Worcester was writing to Henry from France
regarding the measurements for the camp and tilt yard, the king was
also receiving letters from Margaret of Savoy about her nephew's
delayed arrival in England due to bad weather. As Francis planned
his jousts and suits, his opponent was snatching the opportunity to
consort with his only enemy weeks ahead of their meeting. The queen's
response to the plan was reported by Charles' envoys as ecstatic,
'clasping her hands and raising her eyes unto heaven, gave laud unto
God ... that she might behold her nephew, saying it was her greatest
desire in the world'.[2] On a personal level Catherine would have been
delighted to meet her sister's son, but the move also supported her
ultimate political aim to establish a Spanish future alliance for her
daughter. She had been 'gratified at his success' and was opposed to
forging a closer friendship with France, which went 'against the will
of the queen and all the nobles', being, instead, 'intrinsically in favour
of Spain'.[3] Soon, she hoped, he might become her son-in-law.

On 21 May, Catherine left Greenwich at Henry's side to travel down to Canterbury, where they were to await Charles' arrival. It was still not clear whether the poor weather conditions that had hitherto detained him would disperse, enabling him to make the rendezvous before the English monarchs were obliged to leave for France. Arriving at the Archbishop's Palace four days later, Catherine would have been aware of a city in readiness, with the streets being sanded, the city officials decked out in new gabardines, or cloaks, and the keys to the Westgate being tied with a new ribbon, in advance of being presented to Charles. Preparations were also taking place across the Channel. On 26 May, Francis issued one of many proclamations for the organisation of the Field of Cloth of Gold. Displayed in all thoroughfares and public places, it stated that all vagabonds must clear the appointed place within six hours, or else suffer death by hanging. No one was to be present at the meeting without a ticket signed by their master, and all were to pay homage to the English.[4] On the same day, a ship slipped into harbour at Hythe, battered by storms, carrying the Holy Roman Emperor himself.[5]

Wolsey had been dispatched to the coast to greet Charles as soon as he had been spotted on the horizon. The Imperial fleet had been conducted safely from Hythe to Dover by England's Vice-Admiral, Sir William Fitzwilliam, 'with six of the king's shippes well furnished'.[6] Henry followed swiftly on the heels of his chancellor, meeting the Emperor 'under the cloth of his estate of the black eagle all splayed on rich cloth of gold'[7] at Dover Castle, but Catherine had to wait until the next morning. She remained the guest of William Warham in the Archbishop's Palace, with its fine wooden panelling, marble pillars, gardens and library, of which only an arched doorway remains. On 27 May, Henry and Charles arrived in the city and attended Mass in the cathedral to celebrate the feast of Pentecost before processing along a purple carpet into the palace, where they were greeted by twenty-five of the 'handsomest and best apparelled' court ladies and twenty of Catherine's pages dressed in 'gold brocade and crimson satin in chequers'. It was Charles' intent 'specially to see queen of England his aunt'. Catherine was awaiting them at the top of a flight of fifteen marble steps and wept as she greeted her nephew.[8]

The three attended Mass together, with Catherine having changed into a dress of cloth of gold lined with violet velvet, a headdress of black and gold decorated with jewels, and a string of pearls about her neck, in the centre of which hung a large diamond. Charles also had the opportunity to meet Princess Mary, then the Duchess of Suffolk and the mother of three children, who, but for the quirks of diplomacy six years before, might have been his empress. The Elizabethan chronicler Holinshed adds 'peradventure the sight of the Lady Mary troubled him, whome he had sometime loved, and yet through fortunes evill hap might not have her to wife'. Charles would have been aware that the 'evill hap' was more down to Henry than fortune. The following day, Whit Monday, while the king led the dancing after dinner, Charles looked on, seeming to take little delight 'in pastime and pleasure'. This was followed by a four-hour banquet and entertainments that lasted until daybreak. The festivities continued for four days. Then, on 31 May, Charles bade farewell to his hosts and departed for Sandwich, where he sailed to Flanders. That same day Henry and Catherine set sail from Dover, arriving in Calais at eleven o'clock at night. What followed would be magnificence on an unprecedented scale.

An entry in the State letters and papers for 1520 gives an idea of the nature and opulence of Catherine's wardrobe at this time, in advance of her diplomatic roles. During the months of April and May, a Louis Harpsifield had been paid almost £150 for providing her with two pieces of white satin at over eighty-six yards long, fifty-eight yards of green velvet, seventy-three yards of green Bruges satin, yellow and russet velvet, black velvet, crimson velvet and green cloth of gold. It seemed that Catherine's servants shopped in London's Chepe Street, parallel with the river, its very name deriving from the Old English term for 'market'. Stow's survey of London described it as the centre of the city's wealth, with goldsmiths and merchants occupying houses that could rise to as high as five storeys tall. With their shopfronts filled with luxury goods, these traders attracted custom from the court. In spring 1520, Barker 'of Chepe' supplied the queen with more white satin and his neighbour, Barton 'of Chepe', sold her black sarsenet and green and russet velvet.[9]

Catherine would not have gone to buy these items in person. Overseeing these purchases was an Ellis Hilton, who settled the bills and delegated purchases to other servants and traders. An agent named George Bryggus purchased 14s 4d worth of crimson velvet for her from 'Colier of Chepe', who also received an order for yellow damask from the Lord Chamberlain for the queen's use. Her servants also shopped further afield. A John Norris in Friday Street supplied linen cloth, Master Smith of Watling Street provided red kersey and broad grey cloth was bought from an unspecified vendor at Blackwell Hall. New bedding was also bought for Catherine, perhaps in readiness for her departure to France, as on such occasions it was customary for royalty to dismantle and export their own high-status beds. Over seventy-seven yards of blue sarsenet was purchased to make bed curtains, perhaps in anticipation of being embroidered with gold fleurs-de-lys.[10] On 10 May, the mercer William Lock had supplied the queen with cloth of silver for scutcheons and arms, red stain and yellow damask for lining her chairs, and violet satin for lining a gold valance, all 'paid by me, Elys Hylton'.[11]

Ellis Hilton also made a number of other purchases on behalf of his queen, including green cloth from a Mr Wilkinson in Candlewick Street to make coats for her guard; Catherine did not like them, however, and they were given away.[12] Generally, the queen's retinue were well catered for, with payments made for coats and doublets in the Tudor colours of white and green, and also for an embroiderer named Ebgrave to sew the motif of feathers on to their clothes and for crimson velvet to line their cloaks. Milan bonnets were bought for them from Gerard the capper, at 6s each; the account includes bucklers, swords, shirts and points, as well as orange-coloured boots at 4s 3d a pair, spurs at 6d a pair, coifs of gold for the queen's ladies at 10s each, while eighteen shirts cost 8s each to be made.[13]

Catherine's travel arrangements are also recorded in detail for the month, with a Roger Brown being paid 20s for taking the 'stuff' of the guard from London to Canterbury, and a man named Parker receiving 53s 4d for painting the 'close car'. More 'stuff' for her henchmen travelled by barge to Gravesend at a cost of 5s, then on to Canterbury by road at 2d per mile, for twenty-six miles. Her clothes and linen were likely to have been transported in the five spruce chests with hanging locks which cost 32s 8d and her tailor Thomas Kelevytt made garments for the queen's use at a price of £28 3s 4d. Some of Catherine's items were washed at Dover before she embarked for France, which cost 16d, but the carrying of the same items from the ship to her lodgings in Calais cost 14d.

As befitted her status, Catherine took a large retinue with her to France. It was headed by Thomas Stanley, Earl of Derby, who was Henry's cousin through their mutual descent from the Wydevilles. As his personal allowance, Derby had six gentlemen, three chaplains, twenty-four servants and twenty horses; his wife, Anne, also attended among the queen's party of ladies. Catherine had three bishops accompanying her: John Fisher, Bishop of Rochester; Charles Booth, Bishop of Hereford; and George de Athequa, a Spaniard who had come with her to England in 1510, now Bishop of Llandaff. Each of the three had four chaplains, six gentlemen, thirty-four servants and twenty horses. She had four barons: William Blount, Baron Mountjoy, who had been married to the Spanish Agnes de Venegas, then deceased;

William Willoughby, Baron Willoughby d'Eresby, the husband since 1516 of Catherine's companion Maria da Salinas; Thomas Burgh, Baron Cobham, future father-in-law of Catherine Parr; and Henry Parker, Baron Morley, future father-in-law of George Boleyn. Each had a retinue of their own of chaplains, gentlemen and servants, as did Catherine's thirty-one knights.

The most senior of Catherine's ladies accompanying her to France was the Duchess of Buckingham, Lady Eleanor Percy, followed in precedence by seven countesses – of Stafford, Westmorland, Shrewsbury, Devonshire, Derby and Oxford, as well as the Dowager Countess of Oxford – each of whom had seven servants. Among her sixteen baronesses were Elizabeth, Lady Fitzwalter, whom Henry had sent away from court after her interference in the affairs of her sister Anne, Lady Hastings, who was also present; also, Anne, Lady Grey, and Elizabeth, wife of Sir Arthur Plantagenet, an illegitimate son of Edward IV; Lady Elizabeth Boleyn, Henry's future mother-in-law; and the wives of the barons in her company. Additionally, Catherine was served by eighteen knight's wives, including Lady Compton, Lady Guildford and Lady Parr and twenty-five gentlewomen, among whom were Mistress Carew, Mistress Parker and Mary Boleyn, Mistress Carey. She had three chamberers, who were each entitled to take a servant, fifty Yeomen of the Chamber, with twenty servants between them and sixty people to take care of her horses.

The king's equally extensive retinue included Thomas Wolsey and Thomas Boleyn (who had masterminded the event), the Duke of Buckingham, ten earls, four bishops, twenty-one barons, three knights of the garter, a hundred knights (including his court favourites Sir William Compton, Sir Nicholas Carew, Sir Francis Bryan) along with Sir Thomas More. There were ten chaplains, two secretaries, two clerks of the signet, two clerks of the privy seal, twelve sergeants-at-arms, 200 Yeomen of the Guard, seventy servants of the king's chamber with 150 others at their disposal, 266 members of the king's household, assisted by a further 206, with 205 in the stable and armoury, and an unspecified number of minstrels and trumpeters. These figures give some idea of the vast scale of the operation, as well as the minimum numbers thought necessary to maintain the king's dignity on such an occasion.

Included in this huge retinue, already running into many thousands, were the ambassadors of Emperor Charles, with their twenty servants and twenty-three horses. It was a reminder that Imperial eyes were watching the whole time, and that Charles himself was awaiting Henry and Catherine in Flanders once the French festivities were over.

25

Field of Cloth of Gold, 1520

Fame I am called, marvel you nothing,
Though with tongues am compassed all round,
For in voice of people is my chief living,
O cruel Death, thy power I confound.[1]

On arriving in France, Henry and Catherine had been lodged at the Exchequer in Calais and rested there until 4 June, when they progressed to the field between Guisnes and Ardres that had been designated as the meeting place. The well-known image in the Royal Collection, of Henry arriving at the camp, painted in around 1545, conveys a sense of the transformation that had taken place there in recent weeks and the expense that had gone into creating what was, in effect, a temporary city. The image simultaneously contains the highlights of the visit, with Henry's entry surrounded by his retinue, with Calais, the Channel and a distant England behind; it has a panoply of tents set up in camps, some white, some decorated, some gold. There are fountains flowing with wine, a huge temporary palace and glimpses of Henry and Francis at key moments: wrestling, jousting and feasting. It was the zenith of both their reigns. Although Henry features as the central figure, the picture lacks a clear image of Catherine. She is definitely present to observe the joust, but so small that no detail can be identified, and she may also be the woman dining in one of the small tents, but a clear choice has been made not to place her in the initial procession alongside the king and Thomas Wolsey. It is a stark reminder that, by the time the picture was painted, Catherine had been edited out of Henry's life.

The Field of Cloth of Gold, as it came to be known, must have been dazzling to behold. Its centrepiece was a temporary palace, built by 600 English and Flemish workers, with foundations of stone and a framework of timber imported from the Netherlands. The windows were made of real glass but the walls and roof were of painted canvas. It was described by chronicler Hall as 'the most noble and royal lodging before sene', in the shape of a 'quadrant' 328 feet long. Before the entrance gate, on a green, stood a fountain of gilt and fine gold running with red and white wine, decorated with antique work and topped by a figure of Bacchus. On the other side of the gate stood a pillar wrapped in gold, decorated by the faces of lions and topped with a sculpture of Cupid, with his bow and arrows ready 'to stryke the young people to love'. The arched entrance gate 'of great and mighty masonry' included windows depicting men of war, above statues of Hercules and Alexander richly lined with gold.[2]

The gate led into a courtyard with bay windows on every side. From there, a range of doors marked the extent of the chambers within, which were 'long and large and well proportioned, to receive light and air, with white floors and roofs made of silk. They were decorated with rich cloths of silver, knit and fret with cuts and braids, 'like bullions of fine burned gold' with roses set in lozenge shapes, so that 'no living creature might but joy in the beholding thereof'. Each room was hung with cloth of gold, tissue and rich embroidery, with chairs covered in the same fabrics, decorated with golden pommels and great cushions from Turkey. Inside the palace was a chapel with two closets, or small private chambers, decorated in cloth of gold and tissue with roses, and an altar with gold candlesticks, three rich crosses and all the requirements for Catholic ceremony, in gold and pearls. The first closet was for the use of the king, with a crucifix, an image of the Trinity, an image of the Virgin Mary, two gold candlesticks and twelve other images of gold and precious stones on the altar. The second was for Catherine, with an altar 'so richly apparelled that there lacked neither pearls nor stones of riches', with twelve great images of gold on the altar.[3] These exquisite closets, glittering with gold and gems, serve as a reminder of the intense Catholic faith and ritual of the king and queen and its centrality to pre-Reformation life.

The royal party were lodged in four suites inside the palace, one each for Henry, Catherine, Mary, Duchess of Suffolk, and Thomas Wolsey. There were also a number of administrative offices, for the Lord Chamberlain, the Lord Steward, Lord Treasurer of the Household, the Controller and office of the green cloth, wardrobes, jewel house and the offices of service, including the ewery, confectionery, pantry, cellar, waffry, saucer, buttery, spicery, pitcher house, larder, poultry and all other offices for the craft of 'viands' such as ovens, chimneys and ranges.[4] The Rutland Papers contain more detail of the catering arrangements made for the occasion, with additional housing provided for the scalding house, the laundry by the mill, a hall for the makers of pastilles and subtleties, accommodation for the cooks and a large, circular oven which is shown on the 1545 painting.[5]

Other officers and members of the court were lodged in a sea of tents sprawling out behind the palace. Surviving plans in the British Library depict a variety of complex constructions, echoing the layout of Tudor palaces, with a series of connected galleries leading to a number of private apartments, made up of large and small tents subdivided with curtains. Dressed in red and blue cloth, or green and white, they are fringed with mottoes, sewn and topped with gold, with ridgeboards on the roof bearing golden fleurs-de-lys and Tudor roses. The tent poles are topped with heraldic beasts, holding standards with crowns, royal arms and other heraldic devices.[6] In total, tents outside the palace and small town of Guisnes provided lodgings for 820 people, 'which was a goodly sighte'.[7]

While Henry and Catherine were establishing themselves in their camp outside Guisnes, Francis I and his wife, Queen Claude, were settling into their royal lodgings in nearby Ardres. The suave, sophisticated Francis, with his eye for fashion and the ladies, was twenty-five to Henry's twenty-eight. His wife, counterpart of the thirty-five-year-old Catherine, was Claude, daughter of the old king, Louis XII, once the stepdaughter of Mary Tudor and also Francis' cousin. She was only twenty, very short and suffered from scoliosis, but she had already borne four children, three of whom were still living and two of which were boys. That June, she was heavily pregnant with a fifth, a daughter, who would arrive on 10 August. Among her retinue of ladies was Anne, the younger daughter of Sir Thomas Boleyn, who was a couple of years younger than the queen and may have acted as her translator. Dark-haired, elegant and well educated, Anne had been abroad since 1513, acquiring a European polish at the court of Margaret of Savoy before coming to France for Mary's marriage to Louis, after which she had stayed on to serve Claude. If Catherine had seen the Boleyn's younger daughter as a child, this would have been seven years ago and Anne was now a grown woman. The Field of Cloth of Gold also provided an opportunity for Anne to be reunited with her mother, Elizabeth Boleyn, and sister Mary Carey, who had been married earlier that year to Privy Chamberer William Carey. The queen probably paid little attention to two more of the many attractive young ladies present at the festivities, but the Boleyn girls would prove impossible to avoid in the years to come.

Catherine and Claude were not present at the initial encounters between the two kings, who met and banqueted in a tent between the two camps. Hall gives us a glimpse of Henry as 'the moost goodliest Prince that ever reigned over the Realm of England', dressed in cloth of silver of damask, ribbed with cloth of gold, 'marvellous to behold' and riding a horse likewise trapped in gold. The queens finally met on 11 June,[8] at a field that was decorated with a pageant of two trees. Catherine and Claude saluted each other 'right honourably' and took their places on a stage to watch the men engage in a tournament 'so valiantly that the beholders had great joy'.[9] The women sat in a 'glazed gallery, hung with tapestry and talked about the tourney' and many in their company were obliged to use the services of translators, as they could not understand each other. More days of entertainments followed, interspersed with talks and banquets, with feats of strength and skill including wrestling, fighting with weapons, archery and darts presided over by the queens, with Claude presenting Henry with his prizes and Catherine doing the same for Francis. On 13 June, a treaty was ratified for the marriage of the dauphin to three-year-old Princess Mary, left behind at Richmond under the care of Margaret Pole. This cannot have been Catherine's first choice, as she was still hoping for a Spanish match for her daughter.

On 17 June, Henry dined with Queen Claude in chambers hung with blue velvet and gold, where he met the French ladies, 'the most beautiful that could be', arrayed in cloth of gold, with everything presented 'to ease his delight'.[10] The French queen, dressed in gold, diamonds, pearls and other gems, rose from her chair of state in greeting, at which Henry kissed her on bended knee. Then she led him by the hand to the banquet where they dined on an indescribable number of dishes before retiring to talk in a room hung with gold tapestries and carpeted with crimson velvet.[11] On a second occasion, a week later, Henry visited again for dinner. This time, the ladies 'dressed themselves to daunce' and Henry, apparently just to please them, withdrew and 'secretly' joined the masked company, clad in pale cloth of gold lined with green taffeta, with visors on their faces that sported beards made of gold wire. Along with them, he 'took ladies and danced ... passing the time right honourably'. Then, at Claude's insistence, the revellers removed their masks, revealing their identities. A banquet was served, including spices, fruits and jellies, before the party took their leave. Then, 'in secret places', they put on their masks again 'so that they were unknown and so passed through the French court'.[12] Among those accompanying Henry were the Duke of Buckingham, the Duke of Suffolk, Sir William Compton and Sir Thomas Boleyn. Anne Boleyn would have been present on that occasion too, for translating, feasting and dancing, although she does not appear to have yet captured the king's eye. If Henry had been disposed to flirtation with any of the ladies present, the circumstances of the masque and his departure would certainly have been conducive.

In Henry's absence, Catherine and Mary, Duchess of Suffolk, received Francis in the palace at Ardres 'with all honour that was according'. On display was a 'multitude' of silver and gold plates and vessels, and the finest ingredients had been sourced from local 'forests, parks, field, salt sea, rivers, moats and ponds', men being well rewarded for finding great delicacies.[13] When the plates were cleared away, masked dancers performed and women acted as mummers.[14] A provisional menu survives for the occasion and, although it does not represent the final order of service, it gives a fair idea of the kinds of dishes that were consumed that evening. The first of three courses contained boiled capon, cygnets, carpet of venison, pike, heron and hart, followed by pear pies, custard, cream and fruit. Secondly, kid, capon, sturgeon, peacock, pigeons, quails and baked venison prefaced similar sweet dishes, before a final course introduced storks, pheasants, egrets, chickens, gull, haggis, bream and green apples, followed by oranges, fruit, creamy towers and a cold banquet.[15]

Estimations in advance for consumption by the king and queen in France had allowed for £420 worth of wheat, £770 of wine, £27 of sweet wine, £560 of beer, £24 for hippocras wine, £624 for 340 pieces of beef, £33 for four hogs, £6 for mutton, £200 for veal, £300 for salt and freshwater fish, £440 for spices, £1,300 for all kinds of poultry, £300 for table linen and cloths, £200 for wax, over £26 for white lights, £300 for pewter vessels, £200 for braising pans, turning spits and other essentials plus £40 for rushes. Twenty cooks were to be hired at a fee of 20d a day, twelve pastillers at the same salary, and twelve brewers and twelve bakers at a daily rate of 8d.[16]

In comparison, the expenses paid after the event proved a lot more detailed. Among some of the most evocative entries were 20s 10d paid to Thomas Tayllor for cream for the king's cakes, John Rogers receiving 5s for two hundred pippins (apples), John Busshe being paid 25s for strawberries and junkets and a Mr Dosson receiving 12d for making a lock and key for the spicery door. Antony Carleton carried two loads of the queen's wardrobe from Guisnes to Calais for a fee of 5s 4d, but these were not all of Catherine's clothes, as a Jasper Cope was paid 8s for carrying twice the amount from Guisnes to the camp. A further 2s was paid for a casket for wafers and 12s for two pairs of wafer irons; 9s 1d was paid for fourteen sticks of sugar candy, 6s went to a Margery Bennett for fanning and washing hempseed and 14d to Robert Constantin for supplying line and cord to hang the quails' cages.[17]

On 23 June, a chapel was erected on the field which had witnessed the tournaments, where Wolsey sang High Mass and issued an indulgence, a pardon for any sins, to all present, including both sets of kings and queens. Part way through, a huge artificial dragon appeared in the sky from the direction of Ardres, four fathoms long and full of fire, which scared many of those assembled. It passed over the chapel 'as fast as a footman can go',[18] which might give some clue to the method of its operation. While some thought it a comet or a monster, it was part of the festivities, either as some huge firework or balloon, and was recorded for posterity in the corner of the 1545 painting. Following this, Catherine, Claude and Mary, Duchess of Suffolk, dined together before retiring for the night when guns were fired to mark the vigil of St John the Baptist.[19]

On 24 June, Henry and Francis formally concluded the festivities, with the exchange of gifts: a collar of diamonds for the French king and a bracelet of great price for England. Catherine gave a gift of horses to Claude, who responded with the gift of a cloth of gold litter and mules. It had been a great diplomatic success. As remarked by Martin du Bellai, the spectators believed they had witnessed 'an amity so entire that nothing could ever alter it'.[20] However, they were mistaken. Henry and Catherine were already riding back into the arms of Francis' enemy, the Emperor.

On 10 July, after resting at Calais, Catherine and Henry took a fraction of their entourage to Gravelines, on the French coast, just to the east, over the border into Flanders. There Charles greeted them, with 'such semblant of love',[21] along with his aunt Margaret of Savoy, whom Catherine had not seen since her childhood. Returning with the English king and queen to Calais, Charles and Margaret were lodged at the Hall of the Staple, in anticipation of the completion of an eighty-foot banqueting house built using the masts of ships. Strong winds prevented it from being completed, though, so the banquets and masques were relocated into the Exchequer and the Staple. An agreement was reached that both powers were 'to have the same enemies and the same friends' and neither would enter a treaty without the knowledge and consent of the other.[22] On 14 July, Catherine bade farewell to her family before boarding ship and setting sail again for England. It would be the final golden hurrah of her reign.

26

Mother of the Princess, 1520–22

Adieu my daughter Mary, bright of hue,
God make you virtuous, wise and fortunate.[1]

To Catherine's great delight, Princess Mary was developing into an intelligent and accomplished child. Returning from the Field of Cloth of Gold, she was told by Margaret Pole of the girl's beautiful playing on the virginals to impress a group of French visitors at Richmond Palace. The guests were amply entertained with four gallons of hippocras, wafers and fruit, at a cost of 35s 3d, and departed full of praise for the little princess. The queen was closely involved in her daughter's upbringing, even though she had been given her own household under the careful eye of Catherine's trusted friend. On her return to England she would have examined the accounts for September 1520, where recent payments had been made to individuals for contributing to Mary's larder, for bringing quails and rabbits, chickens and a pig, puddings and bread, strawberries and cherries. It also reveals that Mary's establishment contained six gentlemen and nine valets, six grooms of the chamber and twelve grooms of the household, as well as the ladies charged with her daily care.[2]

At an early stage of the developing alliance with France, a betrothal had been finalised between Princess Mary and the dauphin Francis, third child and eldest son of Francis I. On 5 October 1518, a formal ceremony had taken place in the queen's closet at Greenwich, with the Admiral of France standing in as proxy for the seven-month-old bridegroom. Little Mary had offered to kiss him, mistaking him for her future husband. The Field of Cloth of Gold had had cemented this alliance and established a closer connection between the two mothers. Mindful of the future path laid out for her daughter, Catherine wrote to Queen Claude of France some time in 1521, in response to her 'good and affectionate letters'. She had been 'very greatly consoled' to hear the 'good news, health, estate and prosperity in [which is my] very dear and most beloved good son, and yours, the dauphin'. She expressed the 'good love, friendship and fraternal intelligence and alliance which is now between the two kings our husbands and their kingdoms, which I hold inseparable and pray God that it may continue'.[3]

Catherine had worked diligently to promote the French marriage for Mary when it had suited Henry's international objectives, but privately she had always hoped for an alliance with Spain, or someone connected with her Spanish past who was more sympathetic to the old alliance. She would have been delighted, then, in January 1521, when the match with France was broken in favour of Mary's betrothal to Emperor Charles. As Henry explained to Bishop Cuthbert Tunstall, then on a diplomatic visit to attend the Diet at Worms, 'our daughter will be of age before the French king's, and will be a more advantageous match than the other, by possibility of succession'. In opening Imperial negotiations, Henry was mindful of his daughter's worth: 'It is to be considered that she is now our sole heir, and may succeed to the crown; so that we ought rather to receive from the Emperor as large a sum as we should give with her if she were not our heir.' However, the king was still hopeful that Catherine would conceive again, two years and two months after her last delivery. Henry specified that 'if we have a male heir hereafter', he was willing to give Mary as great a dowry as he had to his sister.[4]

On Valentine's Day 1521, the five-year-old was given a brooch of gold and jewels bearing her fiancé's name, which was noted by the Imperial ambassadors and reported back to Charles, along with Mary's 'beauty and charms'.[5] She also performed a dance, twirling 'so prettily that no woman in the world could do better ... then she played two or three songs on the spinet' with the 'grace and skill ... and self-command' that 'a woman of twenty might wish for'.[6] The considerable age gap of sixteen years meant that they would be unable to wed for at least eight years, so Catherine set out equipping her daughter with the skills she would need for her future life as Holy Roman Empress, ensuring that she learned to dance and sing as well as the more scholarly pursuits she had followed in her own childhood. When Mary was seven, Catherine brought the Spanish Humanist scholar Juan Luis Vives to England, to act as tutor to the princess and commissioned him to write *The Education of a Christian Woman*, a groundbreaking book about female learning. She would also give her approval to his other book, *The Institute of a Christian Marriage*.

In May 1522, Mary had a chance to meet her fiancé. Charles visited England again with a large retinue, on his way to Spain. He arrived at Dover on the afternoon of 27 May and Henry, who had been awaiting him at Canterbury, went to greet him and conduct him to London via Sittingbourne, Rochester and Gravesend. From there, on 2 June, they took a barge to Greenwich, arriving at around 6 p.m.[7] At the entrance to the great hall, Charles was reunited with

Catherine and Princess Mary, expressing 'great joy' to see the pair of them. He was then lodged in Henry's apartments, which were so richly hung that the visitors marvelled at them. Jousting, feasting and masques followed, in which a disguised Henry was among those who 'toke ladies and daunsed'.[8] A letter arriving at court on 5 June from the French ambassador recorded England's deteriorating relationship with France, followed by the declaration that Francis was now Henry's 'mortal enemy'.

On 6 June, the party left Greenwich and headed towards London but, just outside the city, they encountered a rich tent made of cloth of gold, where Sir Thomas More made an 'eloquent oration' on the love between the two princes 'and what a comfort it was to their subjects to see them in such amity'.[9] A series of nine pageants followed, full of historical, mythical and allegorical symbolism for the alliance, before they arrived at Richmond Palace, then on to Wolsey's palace of Hampton Court and then to Windsor, where they passed nine days, between 11 and 20 June. Catherine would have been a participant in the hunting and disguising, even perhaps watching Henry and Charles play tennis, but the council chamber doors were closed upon her while the two men discussed business, which would result in the Treaty of Windsor. However, the queen would have been delighted at its outcome, as it committed Charles to marry Mary within eight years and stipulated that, once she had reached her twelfth birthday, in 1528, the Emperor, who would then be twenty-eight, would send a proxy to London for the first formal wedding ceremony. Wolsey sealed the deal with his authority as a papal legate by adding the condition that if either man broke it, they would automatically be excommunicated.

On 21 June, Charles began his journey to Southampton, via Alresford, Winchester and another of Wolsey's properties, Bishop's Waltham. He had probably already said farewell to Catherine and Mary but Henry had accompanied him to the palace, where they parted on 3 July. Charles sailed from Southampton four days later, having spent six weeks in England. Catherine had now been in England for twenty years, thirteen of which she had spent as Henry's wife, and just before Christmas 1521 she had celebrated her thirty-sixth birthday. Her husband was still sharing her bed, in the hope that she would conceive again but, with each passing month, this appeared less likely. While Catherine could rest assured that all had been done to guarantee her daughter Mary's future marital happiness, her own was now beginning to look less certain.

PART FOUR
Mary Boleyn

27

Kindness, 1520–22

Mankynd is bed schal be undyr the castle
And ther schal the sowle lye under the bed til
He schal ryse and pley.[1]

On the night of 4 March 1522, Wolsey led the Imperial ambassadors into the great hall of York Place, the cardinal's London residence.[2] It was Shrove Tuesday and they had enjoyed several days of jousting and feasting, during which Henry's horse had worn a courser embroidered with the legend 'she hath wounded my heart'. Now, after dinner, a pageant had been prepared for them – an elaborate castle, painted green and decorated with leaves, where banners hung from three towers, decorated with a thinly veiled declaration of love. The first banner bore the image of three hearts torn in half, the second showed a lady's hand gripping a man's heart and the third showed another female hand 'turning' a man's heart. Taking her place to watch the performance begin, what must Catherine have made of these coded messages?

The pageant was entitled the *Chateau Vert*, or, most aptly, *The Assault on the Castle of Virtue*. Eight ladies waited inside the castle, dressed in Milan bonnets and gowns of white satin, each with their role, all abstract virtues, embroidered in gold. The part of Beauty was taken Mary Tudor, Duchess of Suffolk, and Honour was played by Gertrude Blount, the Countess of Devonshire. The daughter of Lord Morley, Jane Parker, was Constance and Mistress Browne, Mistress Dannett and the daughters of Sir Thomas Boleyn also took roles. The elder Boleyn girl, Mary, who had served Mary Tudor in France, either chose or was assigned the part of Kindness, while her sister Anne, recently returned from the court of Queen Claude, played the role of Perseverance.

From under the castle more figures appeared, but these were a grotesque parody of the courtly women trapped within. Played by choristers of the chapel royal and attired 'like to women of Inde', or India, they represented the negative qualities of lovers: Danger, Disdain, Jealousy, Unkindness, Scorn, Strangeness and Malbouche, or bad (harsh) tongue. Then eight lords entered the hall, dressed in blue capes and golden caps, yet not so dazzling as their leader, who took the role of Ardent Desire in a costume of crimson satin adorned with burning flames of gold. For once, Henry was not so unsubtle as to take this role in front of his wife. It was probably played by William Cornish, who was nearing the end of a long career as an actor and musician and Master of the Children of the Chapel Royal. Accompanying him were Love, Nobleness, Youth, Devotion, Loyalty, Pleasure, Gentleness and Liberty. A mock battle followed, an allegory for the overcoming of a lover's scruples, in which the ladies wished to yield to Ardent Desire but were dissuaded by Scorn and Disdain. In their defence, the women threw rosewater and comfits, while the men replied with dates and oranges and the suggestive 'other fruits made for pleasure'.[3] With the women surrendering and being led from the castle by their suitors, Henry was hoping that life would echo art. Indications suggest that it was around this time that his affair with Mary Boleyn began.

Our certainty of this liaison rests on the shoulders of a nineteenth-century historian, John Lingard, as Henry ensured that very little evidence survived to establish the extent of their relationship. Others had refuted the notion before Lingard's 1817 study, which cites Cardinal Pole's letter of 1535 regarding the degree of affinity between Mary and Henry's intended wife, Anne.[4] However, Lingard's evidence was swiftly rejected by his contemporaries. One reviewer of his work suggested the theory was borne out of 'a spirit of determined hostility' towards Anne Boleyn, 'in order to fix a character of greater odium on her marriage with the king'[5] and present his rejection of Catherine of Aragon in a less favourable light. But this was never the historian's intention. In response to this criticism, Lingard defended his position by quoting Pole's words to Henry regarding Anne: 'For who is she? The sister of a woman, who you had long kept as a mistress ... whose sister you have carnally known yourself ... the sister of one who has been your concubine.' As Lingard stated in his defence, Pole's 'language is that of a man who asserts nothing of which he is not assured, and who neither fears nor expects to meet with contradiction'.[6] This leaves little doubt that Mary and Henry were lovers and that their relationship was of some duration.

This nineteenth-century debate serves as an important reminder about attempting to reach a decisive conclusion when it comes to the king's lovers. Trends in historical thinking, and the accidents of survival, illustrate just how far Henry's personal reputation cannot be assumed. Mary Boleyn is now widely accepted as one of the king's known mistresses, but if her relationship was disputed so recently, and is known on such slender evidence, the existence of other possible lovers cannot be ruled out with certainty.

Mary was probably the eldest of the Boleyn children. Sir Thomas, an ambitious and talented man on the rise, had made a politically astute marriage to Elizabeth, daughter of Thomas Howard, 2nd Duke of Norfolk, at a time when the Howard fortunes were experiencing a dip. Having fought against Henry VII at Bosworth, Elizabeth's father had been stripped of his title and lands and committed to the Tower for several years. After a period of being out in the cold, he was permitted to return to court around 1499 and rebuild his career, around which time he agreed to the Boleyn match. The Boleyns had risen through the social ranks two generations back, with Sir Thomas's grandfather, Geoffrey, becoming a successful merchant and Mayor of London, with enough capital to purchase the family seats of Blickling Hall in Norfolk and Hever Castle in Kent.

Situated fifteen miles north of Norwich and just ten miles from the north Norfolk Coast, Blickling Hall was in the possession of Sir John Fastolf in the mid-fifteenth century. It had been built during the reign of Richard II and developed around two courtyards, before the knight sold it to Sir Geoffrey Boleyn in 1452.[7] Some walls of the original medieval manor house still stand but the majority of the house was demolished during the Jacobean period and rebuilt as the Blickling Hall open to visitors today. Ten years later, Sir Geoffrey bought the smaller thirteenth-century property at Hever, conveniently located close to London in the Weald of Kent. His grandson Thomas would extend it considerably as befitted his rank, adding the present entrance hall and later making it a fitting location to entertain a king.

Elizabeth Howard was a talented beauty, if the poet John Skelton is to be trusted. Before her marriage, he included a portrait of her in his poem 'The Garland of Laurel', which sees him walking in a garden led by the allegorical figure of Occupation, who brings him to her mother, the Countess of Surrey. The poem was probably composed when Skelton was a guest at the family property of Sheriff Hutton in the winter of 1494/95. In it, the young Elizabeth Howard is compared to Criseyde for her beauty and Irene for her artistic talents, being 'of womanly features, whose flourishing tender age is lusty to look on, pleasant, demure and sage'. She was married to Sir Thomas Boleyn around 1498/99 and bore him several children, of whom three survived to adulthood. There has been much academic debate about the order of their arrival, but the general consensus is that Mary was the eldest, being born in 1499 or 1500, with Anne following a year later and George in 1503–04. This made Mary around twenty-two at the time she danced the role of Kindness in 1522. It is interesting that Skelton's poem was not published until 3 October 1523, almost thirty years after it was written, which may have been a mark of respect in response to the developing affair between Henry and Mary.

Rumours would later arise that Elizabeth had been the mistress of Henry VIII, either in his youth or as a very young king. She was significantly older than him but, in his early days, Henry does appear to have favoured older, experienced women, so this is not necessarily a barrier to them having had a relationship. However, the same reasons that rule out Elizabeth Denton as the prince's lover also apply to her namesake, with the heir to the throne being carefully guarded and his father's precautions regarding physical health and sex at a young age being observed. The story first arose among the king's enemies in the 1530s, against the replacement of Catherine of Aragon with Anne Boleyn, and must be seen in this context. Princess Mary's confessor, Friar William Peto, made the claim in 1532, followed by a letter by George Throckmorton that describes Henry being accused of meddling 'both with the mother and sister', to which Henry blushingly replied, 'Never with the mother.' It was repeated by Elizabeth Amadas, who implicated a number of men and women of the court as part of her defence against charges of treason and witchcraft fifty years later, and it must be seen in that context.

The most damage to Elizabeth Howard Boleyn's posthumous reputation was done by the hostile Jesuit priest Nicholas Sander, who would go as far as to suggest that Anne Boleyn was the daughter of Henry VIII, the result of an early affair he had with her mother. Writing a biography of Anne during the reign of her daughter, while exiled from England, Sander boldly claimed that 'Anne Boleyn was the daughter of Sir Thomas Boleyn's wife; I say of his wife, because she could not have been the daughter of Sir Thomas, for she was born during his absence of two years in France on the king's affairs'.[8] To blacken Anne's character further, Sander explained that Henry had sent Sir Thomas abroad to 'conceal his own criminal conduct' and followed this with an order to the returning Boleyn, to 'refrain from prosecuting his wife, to forgive her and be reconciled to her'.[9] The problems of this theory are manifold, not least given the purported birth dates of Anne and the fact that Henry felt no need to address this reputed paternity when removing impediments to their match. The absence of Sir Thomas for a duration of two years around the possible time that Anne arrived cannot be established either and the birth of other siblings, who did not survive, might also indicate he was not absent for such a length of time. While the rumours about Elizabeth Boleyn and Henry VIII cannot be completely ruled out, they appear to be little more than part of the later anti-Boleyn smear campaign.

In the early days of Henry's reign, though, the Boleyn family were on the make. Mary's career had seen her travel to France in the train of Mary Tudor in autumn 1514, at around the age of fourteen, remaining there to serve Queen Claude with her sister. It was probably her first official post, beginning with her journey to the court at Greenwich from her childhood home of Hever Castle to witness the proxy marriage in August 1514. It may have been the first time she saw the English king, although the fact that her parents were frequently at court might suggest she had visited before, or previously been presented to Henry if he paid a visit to her parents at Hever. As he was in the habit of staying at the homes of his courtiers while on progress, or while hunting, and given the strategic location of Hever Castle, the young girl may have glimpsed her future lover. The first time they can be put together for certain is at the proxy wedding and the subsequent journey to Dover, although the king's attention was elsewhere at the time. For Mary, these events put her at the heart of court and international politics; she may have been forgiven for thinking the world revolved around the gorgeous, bejewelled figure of the king.

The young Boleyn girl attended the marriage of Mary Tudor to Louis XII at Abbeville Cathedral on 9 October. She was among the retinue of English ladies who were received by Louis' daughter Madame Claude, before she was a queen herself, and conducted to the Palace of the Hotel de Gruthuse, to splendid apartments connected to those of the king via a pleasure garden. She would have attended the ball that was thrown in Mary's honour that evening by the dauphin Francis, 'with dancing and music resounding to the skies', and risen with her the following morning, an hour and a half before daybreak.[10] Mary would have helped the princess dress, in a dress of gold brocade decorated with ermine and diamond clasps, and brushed out her red-gold hair, which was topped with a coronet of gems. Then, the girl formed part of the train that followed her mistress, with each lady in waiting flanked by two gentlemen holding their caps in their hands. The wedding was conducted in a room draped entirely in gold and, after the ceremony, the new French queen and her ladies retired to dine together in her chambers. It was a scene of the most dazzling opulence and ceremony, which cannot but have impressed a young girl new to court life. However, the discrepancy in age between the bride and groom would also have been a stark reminder to Mary Boleyn of the realities of marriage among the nobility.

Mary would also have prepared her mistress for the arrival of King Louis in her bed. With the memories of the proxy match at Greenwich in mind, the beautiful young queen was anticipating quite a different encounter with the ageing French monarch, and as one of her ladies Mary would have gone about the business of making her and the room ready to receive him, before discreetly departing. Here, and later at the court of Catherine of Aragon, she learned the ritual of the bedchamber and perhaps some of the secrets of married life as the ladies whispered among themselves or imparted their accumulated wisdom. If nothing else, she would have witnessed the mixed emotions with which Queen Mary now went to the marital bed.

The literary stereotypes of old men desiring young women are frequent in late medieval poetry, and usually result in the cuckolding or embarrassment of the older lover. Chaucer's Januarie was sixty when he was married to his 'fresh' May:

> And certainly, as sooth as God is Kyng
> To take a wyf it is a glorious thing
> And namely whan a man is oold and hoor;
> Thanne is a wyf the fruyt of his tresor.
> Thanne sholde he take a yong wyf and a feir,
> On which he myghte engendren hym and heir,
> And lede his lyf in joye and in solas.[11]

Louis did lead the rest of his life in joy and solace, but it proved too much for him. After his death, Mary and Anne, who had joined her from the Netherlands, found themselves well placed to witness the end of one French regime and the start of a new one. Another lesson in love followed swiftly on the first. The rapid remarriage of the dowager queen to Charles Brandon showed Mary that women could exercise a degree of control over their lives and marry for love. Matches might be made along dynastic lines, but love would always find a way.

The reputation of the new king preceded him. At the licentious court of Francis I 'both maids and wives do oft-times trip, indeed do so customarily', and he was described in thinly veiled sexual metaphors as 'drinking' from many fountains and 'clothed' in women.[12] Reputed to have created spyholes in his palaces in order to watch women undressing and engaging in intimate acts, Francis would have been very aware of the young women in the entourage of the dowager queen. His extramarital activities and official mistresses were in stark contrast to the modest and pious establishment of the new queen, Claude, in which Mary was now engaged. Handsome and experienced, Francis was then twenty-one and Mary was fifteen, the age at which the king himself had lost his virginity.[13] It is entirely in keeping with what is known about Francis that he may have tried to seduce one of his wife's attractive young maids and succeeded. Later, Francis referred to Mary in the disparaging terms of 'a very great whore and infamous above all'. He also described her as 'more dirty than queenly'.[14]

However, the extent of their relationship is undocumented and recent historians have disputed whether it was of any significant duration or whether it happened at all. Francis' comments derive from 1536, long after Mary had been Henry's mistress, and his possibly unattainable standards for queenly comparison were the regal dignity of Catherine of Aragon and the long-suffering diligence of his own wife Claude. In addition, they formed part of the anti-Boleyn feeling that accompanied Anne's fall and were reported in a letter written by the papal nuncio in Paris. It is not clear whether the author heard these words uttered by Francis in person or whether he was repeating court gossip. The latter seems more likely; although Francis could have a sharp tongue, he also insisted on women being treated with respect and honour. Another reference to the affair comes from a letter penned by the Bishop of Faenza, Rodolfo Pio, who described Mary as Anne's sister 'whom the French king knew here in France', adding that she was 'a great prostitute and infamous above all'. Yet this was written in January 1536 and other statements in the letter are incorrect, such as the assertion of Mary's presence at court when she had in fact been banished to the country. The case for Mary's liaison with the French king suddenly appears to stand on less solid ground.

Perhaps most significantly, Mary did not contract syphilis; Francis was known to have the disease, given all the mercury cures prescribed by his doctors. It is difficult to know exactly when Francis did have the fateful encounter that infected him, but any relationship with Mary would date from the very earliest days of his reign, so the chances are he was still clear of the disease. Based on a single sexual encounter with an infected king, the chances of Mary contracting syphilis herself were between 3 and 10 per cent.[15] She would have displayed symptoms of sores, rashes and swellings that would have been remarked upon at the time. No such reports exist, and there is no evidence that Mary or, by extension her children, were sufferers. It is possible that they had some short-term fling, or even a single encounter, from which Mary emerged physically unscathed, but it is equally likely that these rumours were politically motivated. The surviving evidence is insufficient to allow for a decisive conclusion to be drawn.

Mary remained in the household of Queen Claude for the next five years, with no contemporary comments suggesting any dishonour to her character. It is possible that she was continuing her education at one of the properties of the king, or becoming accustomed to court ritual and life. Of a similar age to Claude, she was likely employed to serve and support her mistress, keeping her company through her continual pregnancies and cheering her spirits as she recovered. Mary reached the age of twenty having eluded more formal documentation, quite late to be married by contemporary standards. Sir Thomas had been negotiating for a suitable husband and she was recalled home in 1519, soon to become the first Boleyn girl to catch the eye of the King of England.

On 4 February 1520, Mary Boleyn married William Carey. Her husband was a gentleman of the Privy Chamber whose maternal family descended from Edward III through the Beaufort line, making him yet another cousin of the king. Henry attended the wedding, making his customary offering of 8s 6d and giving his blessing. Husband and wife had been present at the Field of Cloth of Gold, but it was shortly before the *Chateau Vert* pageant. On 5 February, Carey was appointed keeper of the manor of Beaulieu or New Hall in Essex and bailiff of several nearby manors. As with the sudden sizeable grant made to Elizabeth Blount's father, this might indicate an approximate starting point for Henry's affairs. Even more convincingly, Sir Thomas Boleyn was made treasurer of Henry's household that April. It seems that, by the summer of 1522, Mary Boleyn had found her way into the royal bed.

28

The King's Mistress, 1522–25

Madam, withouten many words
Once I am sure you will or no
And if ye will then leave your bourds
And use your wit and shew it so[1]

The watchwords for Mary's relationship with the king were secrecy and discretion. Yet history has tarnished her with scandal and rumour, insults and aspersions, leaving her with a reputation worthiest of the greatest whore at Henry's court. Just like so many of the facts of Mary's life, her real personality and appearance elude us. Historians and novelists have deduced various things from the known dates of her service in France, particularly her comparative lack of education and the circumstances of her marriage, yet these have often raised more questions than they have answered. Mary is illuminated in history by the light that fell upon her sister and she has suffered from the comparison ever since. Sadly her light will always be dimmer, her biography more nebulous.

Without a surviving authenticated portrait of Mary, it is impossible to draw any satisfactory conclusion about her appearance, beyond the fact that she was sufficiently attractive to engage the attention of the king. She may well have had the same colouring and proportions as her sister, but the two main candidates for her portrait, one by Lucas Horenbout and the other an anonymous image held at Hever Castle, both depict women with rounder, softer faces and perhaps lighter colouring. In fiction and on the screen, Mary has been played as alternately dark and fair, silly and serious, usually as a foil to Anne, but the only contemporary indication of any personal characteristic attributed to her is her role as Kindness, and for all we know that may have been allocated on a chance basis. While the parts of Kindness and Perseverance seem apt to the modern reader, enjoying the dancing of 1522 with a dash of hindsight, we could equally picture Mary and Anne drawing pieces of paper out of a velvet cap and laughing at their unsuitability. Perhaps these roles were even ascribed as a joke, a further disguise, with Mary refusing to be 'kind' to the king and Anne known for her impatience. We will never know.

Taken at face value, the internal evidence of the *Chateau Vert* pageant may suggest Mary's affair with Henry began in the spring of 1522. Again, the exact start, as well as the duration of the liaison, is unknown. It may have been the four years some historians suggest, or it may have been a single night. All we know is that he did sleep with her on at least one occasion, by his own admission. As with his other mistresses, this is the result of Henry's intense desire for privacy. The private and public aspects of his complex role determined the experiences of his mistresses, as well as the degree of ceremony and arrangements by which he shared their beds. For Catherine, as queen, the preliminaries for sex were somewhat formalised due to the dynastic significance of the moment, marked by a degree of ceremony and the involvement of servants. It mattered to the court when Henry slept with Catherine and how often. Once the doors closed, that was another matter. For a mistress like Mary, though, the emphasis was on pleasure. This was not something Henry wanted to be recorded or observed, so a veil of courtly secrecy was woven by the few people in the know.

Apart from the pageant, there is no evidence of Henry's affair with Mary that dates from the early 1520s. No whisper, no rumour, no accusation or gossip survives to shine any light on their connection. It can scarcely be considered the open secret that some historians have suggested, with not a single shred of proof that it was known outside the most intimate court circles. Henry would have put his trust in a few men; as the facts show, his close relative Cardinal Pole was aware of the affair and Wolsey's role in the birth of Henry Fitzroy suggests he would also have been Henry's confidant. An interesting case is that of the Franciscan Friar William Peto, who mentioned Mary when he spoke out against Henry's divorce in 1532. As both Henry and Catherine favoured the Franciscans, frequently using their church at Greenwich, there is a chance that Peto had been trusted as a confidant outside the confessional, or had known someone who was. It is interesting to ponder, though, whether he had learned this information from the king or from Catherine herself. It is not even clear whether Catherine knew that Mary was sharing her husband's favours.

And yet, by Henry's own later admission, Mary was definitely his mistress. How exactly did he achieve this without too much comment? That is the intention that lies at the heart of this book: to challenge the assumption that Henry's extreme desire for privacy and his active love life are incompatible. One method, which he had already established with Bessie Blount, was to remove the focus of his attentions from the gaze of the court. When Henry visited his other properties, outside the main court, physical space dictated that he often took a smaller staff. With William Carey and his wife installed at New Hall in Essex, the king might stay nearby and visit, as he had done in 1519, and entertain Mary in comparative secrecy. The presence of numerous smaller buildings on large royal estates could also provide opportunities for liaisons, as with the Tower in Greenwich Park, a short, safe distance from the main house, or one of Henry's many hunting lodges, where a small and trusted band of companions could conduct a lady under cover of darkness. Chance references in chronicles show just how often Henry managed to escape from the gaze of his court and wife, such as Hall's mention of his visit to Hitchin in Hertfordshire in October 1522, to 'see his hawks fly.'[2] Exactly where Mary and Henry found time to be together is uncertain but, as the case of Bessie proves without shadow of a doubt, if the king wanted to be alone with a woman, he could. And if he wanted it to remain a secret, it would.

Developments in Tudor architecture may also have helped Henry's bid for secrecy. It is likely that Wolsey facilitated Henry and Mary's liaison while the pair was at court. Just as Sir William Compton is suggested to have arranged convenient encounters for the king in Thames Street, the house Wolsey had occupied at Bridewell, behind Fleet Street, from around 1510[3] may have been another location used by Henry. It was here that Wolsey had installed his own long-term mistress and children, setting the tone for illicit encounters that may have encouraged the king's trust. Originally an inn called St Bride's, part of Bridewell Palace had been taken over by Henry in around 1515, when Wolsey moved out to Hampton. From that point, the pair collaborated on a programme of redevelopment worth around £39,000.[4] The cardinal chose Thomas Larke, his close friend and probably a relation of his mistress Joan Larke, to oversee the building works, which comprised two courtyards and a long gallery of two hundred feet, leading down to the Thames.

The king's lodgings were in the south wing of the inner court, most easily accessible from the river, but formally approached by a grand staircase in the outer courtyard. Archaeological evidence shows that Henry's privy chamber sat beside a closet which was attached to his presence chamber. A door from this room led directly down the gallery, past a council chamber and closet, to the watergate.[5] According to Stowe, the palace was further improved specifically to entertain Charles during his visit of 1522, a date which coincides with the start of his affair with Mary. Additionally, the queen's lodgings lay to the north, completely separate from the gallery, privy garden and water access. Although Wolsey was then using the property less, the previous proximity of his household, identifying the building as the repository of secrets and location for sexual discretion, may imply that Henry saw it as a safe house for his extramarital affairs.

There is also the location of Penshurst Place to consider. Lying a little over six miles to the east of Hever Castle and thirty miles south of Greenwich Palace, the fourteenth-century house had been owned by the Duke of Buckingham. Henry's cousin and old friend had entertained him there on many occasions before making reckless comments about his own claim to the throne and asserting that he would physically defend himself against the king should he be arrested. He had been sent to the Tower in 1521, while Henry considered the evidence against him, before being tried before a panel of seventeen of his peers and executed on 17 May. As a result, Penshurst passed to Henry, who used it as a hunting lodge, visiting in the 1520s with Charles Brandon, providing another possible location for him to woo Mary or, at least, close enough for them to coordinate visits to her parental home. Penshurst was a spectacular place to host a court entertainment, with its huge Baron's Hall, sixty feet high, and its quieter withdrawing room; under the pretext of hunting, Henry and a close-knit group of friends could enjoy a degree of privacy there.

Mary Boleyn disappears from the records again after the *Chateau Vert* pageant, perhaps as she left court to take up residence at Newhall or to visit her parents at Hever. This may suggest that her liaison with

Henry was on an intermittent and opportunistic basis, instead of her being a more long-term established mistress. Nor does she appear to have been more than a diversion for the king, who probably took his pleasure with her when circumstances presented an opportunity. She was not established in her own lodgings at court in proximity to the king, as her sister would be, nor was she listed as playing any further role in the court ceremony of these years. As a married woman, she also had the opportunity to entertain the king in her marital home, which raises some interesting questions about the division of her favours between Henry and her husband.

While her affair with the king lasted, Mary would have been sleeping with two men. Perhaps not equally, as Henry would have taken precedence during visits to the Carey home or occasions when they met at court or elsewhere. It is a modern sensibility to question the morality of this; it must be remembered that the Tudors took a far more pragmatic approach to bodily functions, which is how this kind of pleasure-oriented sex was viewed. Dynastic inheritance was important, and this accounts for the double standard that restricted the activities of married women, but the honours that could be accrued by sleeping with the king easily trumped this. William Carey would not have refrained from sleeping with his wife because she was having an affair with Henry. For all the theories of fiction and film, it is not even guaranteed that he knew about it, particularly if it was a single encounter or took place in an opportunistic way in his absence. Equally, he may have seen it as a chance to engage in a little extramarital sex of his own, redressing the balance by sleeping with a mistress of his own, or a woman of the lower classes, who were considered to be more sexually satisfying. Carey would have been Mary's everyday lover, while Henry was her lover for special occasions.

This love triangle, or rather, sex triangle, worked for Henry, Mary and Carey, as far as we know. However, it does complicate matters when it comes to the children Mary bore in the 1520s. Her first was a daughter named Catherine, possibly named out of deference to the queen, whose arrival may have taken place any time between 1522 and 1526, although the preferred date by most historians is 1524. Initially, this would place her conception in 1523 or the spring of 1524, a time which may well have corresponded with her relations with Henry. This does not mean, though, that the king's paternity is guaranteed; in fact, it may imply that Mary herself was not certain about the identity of her child's father, which helps explain the fact that Henry did not acknowledge this daughter as his illegitimate offspring. There are also the possibilities that Henry did know Catherine was his, but did not feel the need to own her, due to her gender, or that he knew for certain that she was not, as the affair had already ended or the dates of their encounters were decisively against it.

Mary's son was born on 4 March 1525, according to the date inscribed on his tomb in Westminster Abbey. This places his conception in late May or early June 1524, requiring his sister's birth date to adjust around it. If Mary had conceived again quickly after delivering Catherine, it would push the girl's conception interval back even earlier into 1523, which creates a timespan of around a year between Henry's veiled declaration at the *Chateau Vert* and the moment of conception, which might indicate the two were not sleeping together with any sort of regularity. According to Hall, Henry was staying at New Hall at the beginning of the year, which was counted as 25 March, and was either still there, or had returned by St George's Day, almost a month later. With the ceremony of the Knight of the Garter traditionally held at Windsor on 23 April, Henry's prolonged stay during this time was an interesting choice. Perhaps his presence there offers a significant piece of evidence that has hitherto been overlooked.

The boy was named Henry, a touching mark of deference that linked him with the king and with Henry Fitzroy, his potential half-brother. Only one contemporary source attributed the child's paternity to the king. The vicar John Hale claimed that Henry Carey had been pointed out to him as the result of the liaison but, unsurprisingly, this dates from 1535, when the author used his best efforts to discredit the king as 'mired in vice' and enjoying 'foul pleasures ... defiling himself in any filthy place ... fully given to his foul pleasure of the flesh and other voluptuousness'.[6] Hale also made the claim that Henry kept his own brothel at Farnham Castle in Surrey, the property of Richard Fox, as Bishop of Winchester, through the 1520s. Situated about thirty miles to the west of Hampton Court, the place passed briefly to Wolsey in 1529, but there had already been some significant alterations made to allow easier access to the castle from the town, with the installation of a flight of steps that was staggered, in easy stages, but this is more likely to have been fashioned to accommodate clergymen's robes than the long skirts of prostitutes.

In every respect, William Carey treated Catherine and Henry as his own children. Their resemblance in portraits to Elizabeth I has been frequently commented on, but this is to be expected as, even if they were not her half-siblings, they were cousins through the Boleyn line. Both made good marriages and established careers at Elizabeth's court, with Catherine serving her cousin as chief lady of the bedchamber and Henry becoming Baron Hunsdon and Knight of the Garter. It is possible that Mary's affair with the king ended when she became pregnant in 1523, in the same circumstances that had signalled the end of his relationship with Bessie Blount, which would have made Catherine his daughter and Henry the son of Carey. The likelihood is that Mary herself was not completely certain. Any challenge Henry might make to the legal presumption of Carey's paternity would have required an Act of Parliament and that was a scandal the king was not prepared to shoulder.

Did Henry love Mary Boleyn? Not in the way he had loved Catherine of Aragon, nor in the way he would love Anne Boleyn. He did not decide to replace his queen with her, with all the consequences that would entail, nor woo her for years without certainty of success or, as far as we know, barrage her with persuasive love letters. He may have loved her for what she represented to him; a pliant, pretty diversion who had provided an easy chase and conquest, in the same way as Bessie Blount. One often remembered fact about Mary is that Henry owned a ship named after her, but he had bought this from her father in 1523, already bearing the name. This might be an indication of his attachment, particularly as he would also later purchase its partner, which was named after Anne.

There is some evidence from the 1530s that he did retain some affection for Mary, writing to intervene when Sir Thomas Boleyn refused to help his daughter in her hour of need, but she was never the king's *grande amour*. However, it is impossible to know how Mary felt about him. As her affair with Henry ran its course, she would have seen his interest in her younger sister deepen into love. Perhaps she welcomed this with relief or perhaps it was difficult for her to see herself replaced. Maybe she advised Anne about how to handle her former lover, or counselled her to be cautious, or avoid his advances if she could: it is impossible now to know.

In around 1524 or 1525, just as Queen Catherine was approaching her fortieth birthday, her ladies-in-waiting would have noticed that her erratic monthly periods had ceased. Six years had passed since she had conceived her last child and the arrival of the menopause was a significant watershed in the life of the queen and the king, signalling that there would be no more children of either gender. It has been suggested that Henry stopped frequenting her bed as a result, but this is not certain, although he may have visited her far less, and with the objective of physical satisfaction alone. Although the poet Lydgate's *Dietary* advised, 'with women agyd, flesschly have not to do',[7] canon law still advised post-menopausal wives to yield up the marital debt, to prevent sin.

The idea of the conjugal debt in canon law related to the husband as well as the wife, but by 1524 Henry wanted to free himself from this obligation. The Apostle Paul stated that 'you must not refuse each other, except perhaps by consent, for a time, that you may give yourself to prayer, and return together again lest Satan tempt you for you lack self-control'.[8] Catherine had taken her marriage vows with sincerity and had endured Henry's humiliating infidelities. Setting aside the question of her queenship, and the rights of her daughter, she was not about to give her consent that Henry might refuse his marital obligations. Sterility or old age were not considered valid impediments to a marriage in medieval law, although the case of a king in need of a male heir was more complicated. It was around this point, as Catherine waited in vain to see if her menstruation would return, that the idea must have been implanted in Henry's mind that he would have to upset the status quo if he were to father a legitimate son. In the meantime, his thoughts turned to his illegitimate one.

On 18 June 1525, Henry Fitzroy was thrust from the privacy of his secluded childhood onto the political stage. He was brought to Bridewell Palace and invested as Duke of Richmond and Somerset in a public ceremony that included many members of the court and clergy. This elevation to peerage had historical significance too, as the title had been devised for Edward, the Black Prince, and had previously been bestowed on John Beaufort, Henry's Lancastrian great-grand-father, who had been born out of wedlock but later legitimised. This was a clear indicator that Henry was considering making the boy his formal heir at some future point. Having narrowly escaped death in a jousting accident in 1524, the king was probably pondering his mortality and the condition of the realm should he die at this point, leaving only his nine-year-old daughter to sit on the throne.

Fitzroy's investiture must have delighted his mother Bessie, whose husband Gilbert Tailboys attended the ceremony, but it also represented a significant blow to Queen Catherine. Fitzroy's quiet childhood may have enabled her to maintain a dignified denial about his existence but this public event, and all that his investiture entailed, made the boy a main figure at court from that point onwards, when he was given his own establishment at Durham House, her former home. A private letter written by Lorenzo Ohio, the Venetian ambassador, described the event and the return of the party to Windsor, wearing gowns lined in lynx fur as it was cold. If Henry had not insisted she attend the ceremony, Catherine may well have waited at the castle, as even Ohio noticed it had been the cause of some tension between them: 'The queen resents the earldom and dukedom conferred on the king's natural son and remains dissatisfied, at the instigation, it is said, of three of her Spanish ladies, her chief counsellors, so the king has dismissed them [from] the court, a strong measure, but the queen was obliged to submit and to have patience.'[9]

Catherine was not just thinking of her own position. The investiture of Henry Fitzroy also posed a potential threat to the succession of her own child, although Mary's status was formally recognised around the same time. Following the custom of male Princes of Wales of the last three generations, the princess was sent to Ludlow Castle, the traditional training place for the heir to the throne. Yet Catherine's memories of her marriage to Arthur and brief life there must have left her in constant fear for her daughter's good health, as well as the considerable pain of separation. Henry's response made it clear that she had no choice but to accept the situation and bite her tongue. For the time being, she complied.

PART FIVE

Anne Boleyn

29

The Other Boleyn Girl, 1513–22

I was quite pleased to see you sing and laugh,
Dance, play, read and write,
Paint and portray, play the monochord,
The strings of which you well make sound.[1]

When Mary Boleyn danced as Kindness in the *Chateau Vert* pageant in March 1522, the part of Perseverance had been taken by her younger sister, Anne. Believed to have been born in around 1501, Anne was probably the middle child of the three surviving Boleyn offspring, although some historians have placed her birth as late as 1507. However, the known events of her early life confirm the likeliness of the earlier date and have been widely accepted by most historians and biographers. Born at Blickling and raised at Hever, Anne was around twelve years old when she was sent to the court of Margaret of Savoy in the Netherlands, arriving in the summer of 1513, shortly before Henry himself, who was on campaign against the French. This was the customary age for sending young members of the nobility into service, or to complete their education, in great households, as is seen by the arrival of maids such as Bessie Blount in Catherine's establishment.

A letter Anne wrote home in 1514 has provided the main piece of evidence for judging her age, although there are numerous difficulties about applying modern standards of spelling and composition to a child's text written over five hundred years ago. In it, Anne apologises for her many mistakes and poor handwriting, explaining that it was the first letter she had written for herself, as her previous efforts had been copied from models supplied for her. However, it must be remembered that Anne was not writing in her native tongue but in French, a language she was still learning, and her age cannot be confidently assessed from the internal evidence of the letter. Even her mentor, Margaret, at the age of thirty-seven was not fluent in Flemish, the language of her city of residence, and had to ask for assistance on occasion.[2] Anne clearly impressed Margaret, though, as she wrote to Sir Thomas that she was 'more beholden to you for sending her to me, than you to me'.[3]

So Anne probably arrived at the court of Margaret of Savoy aged twelve, conveyed there by a Claude Bouton, Captain of the Guard to Prince Charles of Castile, soon to become Emperor. Although Margaret owned considerable properties across the Netherlands, her main residence was in the Hof van Savoye in Malines, a building she was expanding and developing, with its decorative red-and-white brickwork, steep sloping roofs and dormer windows with gable decoration. The impressive new Renaissance palace was a mark of Margaret's taste and her establishment of a centre for leading humanist scholars, artists, musicians and thinkers. In her extensive library was the *Trés Riches Heures de duc de Berry*; her art collection included Van Eyck's Arnofini portrait and she retained Gerard Horenbort as her illuminator and miniaturist. She employed Erasmus, poet Jean Second and physician Cornelius Agrippa among a host of talented men in a range of fields, including Adrian of Utrecht as tutor to Prince Charles. Castiglione referred to her as one of the 'noblest' examples of contemporary womanhood, who governed her state 'with the greatest wisdom and justice'.[4] The extent of Margaret's learning was outlined by her court poet, Jean Lamaire:

Besides feminine work of sewing and embroidery, she is excellently skilled in vocal and instrumental music, in painting and in rhetoric, in the French as well as Spanish language; moreover, she likes erudite, wise men. She supports good minds, experts in many fields of knowledge and frequently she reads noble books...yet not content merely to read, she takes pen in hand and describes eloquently in prose as well as in French verse, her misfortunes and admirable life.[5]

Anne was educated in the nearby Hotel de Bourgoyne on Keyershof,[6] alongside Prince Charles' sisters, the nieces of Queen Catherine. They were Eleanor, who had been born in 1499, Isabel, born 1502, and Mary, born 1505. Antonio Beatis, a papal secretary, visited the city in 1517, only three years after Anne's residence, and thought that it was 'a superb city, very large and well-fortified. Nowhere have we seen streets so spacious and elegant ... a number of canals whose waters follow the movement of the oceans traverse the city.'[7] Beatis described Margaret herself as 'not unpleasant looking and her appearance is truly Imperial and her smile full of charm'.[8] These influences, stemming from a formidable mentor, placed Anne at the heart of the European humanist Renaissance, at a stage of her life when her opinions and tastes were being decisively formed.

Anne's letter of summer 1514 was not composed in Malines,

though. At that point, the court had departed for Veure, a royal palace with 700-acre park and hunting grounds, half a day's ride from Brussels, which was a common Hapsburg family retreat during the warm weather. It had been established in the thirteenth century by Henry I, Duke of Brabant, and developed into a royal palace over the following centuries, before being demolished in 1782. A print surviving from 1726 shows it dominated by a large central building with gabled roof, rising high above the three- or four-storey range with its long windows and turreted towers. A drawbridge gives down onto a small bridge crossing the wide moat, in which an artificial square island is laid out in formal gardens. Margaret is recorded as being in residence there between 1 June and 21 August, at which point Princess Mary's marriage to Louis XII was being planned and Anne was recalled to attend her in France.

Anne would have been reunited with her elder sister in France, although it is not clear whether she arrived in time for the wedding. Following the death of Louis, both girls remained to serve Queen Claude but Anne stayed longer, after Mary had departed for England at the end of 1519. It is likely that, during her time at the French court, Anne encountered another significant humanist scholar, another highly educated and accomplished woman: Marguerite of Navarre, sister to Francis I. Best known today as the author of the collection of short stories called *The Heptameron*, she was described by Erasmus as possessing 'prudence worthy of a philosopher, chastity, moderation, piety, an invincible strength of soul, and a marvellous contempt for all the vanities of this world'. In service to Claude, Anne would have visited the chateau of Blois, which Francis was improving, as well as Fontainebleu and Chambord; she may even have seen Leonardo da Vinci, when he was presented to the court at Amboise in 1516.[9] The queen's court had retreated there after an outbreak of plague. One of Anne's earliest surviving possessions was a Latin book of hours from Bruges, dating from 1450; later she would build a considerable collection of evangelical works in English and French.[10]

In January 1519, Sir Thomas was posted to Paris as ambassador and would have seen both his daughters frequently. That March he stood in for Henry at the christening of Francis and Claude's fourth child and would soon begin work on the arrangements for the Field of Cloth of Gold that would reunite all his family members. By 1521, when relations between England and France had soured, Boleyn left Francis for the court of the Emperor and it seemed expedient to withdraw Anne in the developing political climate. That November he had a suitable marriage for her in mind, writing to Wolsey from Bruges[11] to try to hasten arrangements so that Anne could leave, which she did the following January.

Anne's intended husband was her cousin, James Butler. The family were connected through Anne's paternal great-grandfather, whose co-heiress, Margaret, married into the Boleyn family, bringing with her the Irish title of Earl of Ormond. However, the earldom had been claimed by the Butlers in the absence of a male heir and, by the 1520s, the obvious answer was a marriage between the descendants of each line. The match may have even been suggested by the king himself. Born around 1496, James Butler had been raised in Ireland and arrived at court around 1513. He had fought with Henry in France that year at the age of around seventeen and was seriously wounded in the leg, causing him to limp for the rest of his life.[12] After returning to Ireland for some years, he entered Wolsey's household in around 1520 and would encounter Anne's brother, the young George Boleyn, who would also soon find a position there.[13] It is very unlikely that the pair had met before, given Butler's Irish roots and Anne's foreign education, so, sometime in 1522, they would have been introduced.

Descriptions of Anne vary wildly, with many tainted by later political and religious agendas, or simple hindsight. The portraits of her which survive have some features in common but the lack of surviving images from her lifetime suggest a that process of destruction followed her fall from grace; it is almost inconceivable that, in a court where the master portraitist Hans Holbein was employed, Anne did not sit for him as queen. In fact, the survival of a pen-and-ink sketch identified by Dr John Cheke, who served Anne, which depicts her in a bonnet and state of undress, may well have been in preparation for a larger work. Holbein is known to have designed jewellery for Anne and created sketches for the pageantry accompanying her coronation, so it seems likely that a portrait would have been commissioned from him at some point during Henry's courtship of her or their marriage. A most likely date would be to celebrate the coronation itself. Two other significant portraits, held at Hever Castle and in the National Portrait Gallery, depict a woman with clear facial similarities – a long face, with small and pert mouth, dark eyes and high cheekbones – while the clothing and French gable hood are so close as to suggest one was a copy of another.

It seems to have been the consensus among her contemporaries that Anne was not a conventional beauty, as Catherine had been in her youth. Her best feature, according to the Venetian diplomat Sanuto, was her 'black and beautiful' eyes; apart from these, he described her as having a 'swarthy complexion, long neck, wide mouth, bosom not much raised'. The French diplomat de Carles agreed that her eyes were 'most attractive' and that she knew how to use them to good effect, to send flirtatious messages. The poet Thomas Wyatt referred to Anne in poetry as 'brunet', and the following century his grandson George Wyatt echoed the idea of her dark colouring and added that she had several small moles and the 'little show of a nail' upon one little finger, perpetuating the myth that Anne had six fingers. This, and examples such as Thomas Wolsey's private name for her, 'the night crow', in contrast with the comment from one of his servants that Anne 'stood out for her excellent grace and behaviour', shows how far she was able to divide opinion.

Anne's physical attraction lay in her exotic difference from the English concept of curvaceous, blue-eyed, blonde- or red-haired beauty, but, more than this, she had a European polish and charm, an intelligence, wit and humanist education and an unquantifiable sexual appeal that many would find irresistible. According to French courtier Brantome, she set a new fashion with her European style, devising new clothes that were copied by other ladies at court, but was still 'the fairest and most bewitching of all the lovely dames',[14] perhaps as the prototype of 'Greensleeves' with her long, trailing gowns. George Wyatt elaborates: 'In this noble imp, the graces of nature graced by gracious education ... a beauty not so whitely as clear and fresh above all we may esteem, which appeared much more excellent by her favour passing sweet and cheerful ... her noble presence of shape and fashion representing both mildness and majesty.'[15] However, George Wyatt was born after Anne's death and had never seen Anne in the flesh.

For some reason though, James Butler was able to resist her. The marriage that Thomas Boleyn had planned in order to resolve the Ormond family feud was abandoned at some point in the mid-1520s. This has never satisfactorily been explained, as it provided a convenient resolution and Anne was a good catch, being the daughter of such an important diplomat and courtier on the rise. Perhaps her father realised she had the potential to make a better match, or that her talents would be better served at home. It might be that the young people objected to the union, as they were usually permitted the right of veto in cases of personal dislike, although the 1533 sketch by Holbein the Younger shows a fairly pleasant-looking man. Perhaps there was something in the nickname he attracted of 'the lame', following his injury in 1513, to which the swift-footed dancer in Anne objected. James would go on to marry the heiress Lady Joan

Fitzgerald and father seven sons. Although the marriage between James and Anne was off, the problem of the title remained.

The question of the Ormond/Butler inheritance was settled in February 1527, which was probably after Anne had accepted the king's proposal of marriage. An indenture was made between Henry and the heirs of Sir Thomas Butler, Earl of Ormond, and Sir Thomas Boleyn, Viscount Rochford, for which Wolsey was to act as mediator. From that point forward, the title of Earl of Ormond was to revert to the grant of the king.[16] He would give the title to Anne's father in 1529 and, after the death of Sir Thomas, it passed briefly to Piers Butler and then to his son James and his heirs. Given the dating of this indenture, it might seem that the Boleyn–Butler match was eventually abandoned because of Henry's interest in Anne, although in reality, it had lost its impetus five years before.

Anne was now in her early twenties, an age at which many of her contemporaries were married, her future uncertain. She entered the household of Catherine of Aragon and would have been selected to play a role during the visit of Charles V in the summer of 1522, based on her linguistic abilities and her connection with Margaret of Savoy and the court of Charles's childhood. Anne was also probably present at Eltham, where Henry and Catherine kept Christmas that year, and at Greenwich the following June, where Henry entertained the recently deposed King Christian of Denmark, Norway and Sweden and his queen, Isabella. Anne would have been in attendance while Catherine stood under the cloth of estate in the great hall to receive them before removing to the queen's apartments, where Catherine entertained Isabel, who was her niece, as the daughter of her sister Joanna and Philip the Handsome. With the royal couple came their children, including a two-year-old daughter named Christina, who would feature fifteen years later in Henry's marital plans. After feasting every day at Greenwich 'for a season', the family were lodged in Bath Place in London, before being accompanied to Dover with many gifts from Henry and Catherine.

Henry and Catherine passed the Christmas season of 1523 at Windsor Castle. By this point, with arrangements for the Butler match foundering, Anne had decided to take her future into her own hands.

30

Henry Percy's Fiancée, 1522–23

Lo! what can take hope from that heart
That is assured steadfastly;
Hope therefore ye that live in smart,
Whereby I am the most happy.[1]

In the early 1520s, George Cavendish was one of many young men who entered the service of Thomas Wolsey. He recorded the details of the cardinal's household, which numbered around five hundred people and served as something of a training ground, or finishing school, for young gentlemen wishing to enter the king's service. Included in that number were James Butler, the more experienced Thomas Cromwell, George, only son of Sir Thomas Boleyn, and Sir Henry Percy, son of the 5th Earl of Northumberland and a cousin of William Carey.

Cavendish confirms that Henry used Wolsey's house as a location for his own recreation or pleasure, arriving secretly by river to dance with 'meet', 'apt' or appropriate women, who also served to garnish the place with 'other goodly disports':

And when it pleased the kings majesty for his recreation to repair unto the Cardinal's house (as he did dyvers [many/various] tymes in the yere) at which time there wanted [lacked] no preparations or goodly furniture, with [food] of the finest sort that myght be provided for money or frendshippe. Suche pleasures were than devysed for the kyng's comfort & consolation as myght be invented or by man's wit. The banquets were set forth with Maskes and Mumerreys in so gorgeous a sort and Costly manner that it was an heavyn to behold. There wanted [lacked] no dames or damselles meete or apte to daunce with the maskers or to garnysshe the place for the tyme, with other goodly disportes ... I haue seen the kyng sodenly come in thither in a maske, with a dozen of other maskers all in garmentes like Shepherdes made of fine Clothe of gold and fine Crimson Satin paned and Caps of the same... and other persons attending upon them with visors and clothed all in Satin of the same Colours and at his commyng and byfore he came in to the hall ye shall understand that he came by water to the water gate without any noise where against his coming was laid charged [prepared] many chambers.[2]

Witnessing this atmosphere of courtly dancing, masques and flirtation, the young men of Wolsey's court were conscious of their own marital futures. Cavendish had been married around the time he entered service in 1522, which meant that he was often separated from his wife. Jane Parker, daughter of Lord Morley, who became the wife of George Boleyn in 1525, suffered less from this as she was in the service of the queen. Thomas Cromwell had been wed for around ten years by the mid-1520s, producing three legitimate children and at least one other by his mistress. A suitable wife had been found for Henry Percy when he was fourteen, but his marriage to Mary Talbot, daughter of the Earl of Shrewsbury, had still not taken place by the time he entered Wolsey's household at around the age of twenty. Through 1522, as he attended Henry's court and helped entertain the king at Wolsey's many properties, he fell in love with the beautiful newcomer who had made her debut at the *Chateau Vert*.

Cavendish describes Anne as a maid in Catherine's household, where with 'her excellent behaviour and gesture [she] did excell all other in so much'. While Wolsey attended to court business, Percy 'would then resort for his pastime unto the queen's chamber' and 'fall in dalliance' with her maidens. Quickly he developed a favourite, 'being at the last more conversant with ... Anne Boleyn than with any other'. This preference escalated into more than friendship and 'there grewe such a secret love between them that at lengthe they were ensured together intending to marry'.[3] During the autumn of 1522 or early in 1523, Anne apparently made a promise to Percy to become his wife. Whether this was part of the play of courtly love, or the more formal kind of verbal agreement that was considered legally binding, it made the negotiations for the Butler match more complicated. With Wolsey responsible for the morality of the young men in his house, he could not tolerate the threat of a love match to any established dynastic negotiation for the hands of his charges. The cardinal intervened, calling Percy before him, and berating him in front of the servants of his chamber.

Cavendish takes up the story again:

> I marvel not a little of thy peevish folly that thou wouldst tangle and ensure thye self with a foolish girl yonder in the court. I mean Anne Boleyn. Dost thou not consider the estate that God hathe called thee unto in this world for after the death thy noble father thou art most like to inherit and possess one of the most worthiest Earldoms of this realm and therefore it had been most meet and convenient for thee to have sued for the consent of thy father in that behalf.

Percy had been already matched 'according to your estate and honour, whereby you might have grown so by your wisdom and honourable behaviour in to the king's high estimation that it should have been much to your increase of honour. But now behold what you have done through your wilfulness, you have not only offended your natural father but also your most gracious sovereign.' George Wyatt also confirmed this report during the reign of Elizabeth, but what is interesting about Cavendish's version, is that as early as 1523, he explains that Henry was 'offended' by the engagement 'wherefore he could hide no longer his secret affection but revealed his secret intention unto my Lord Cardinal in that behalf'.[4]

This is often dismissed as incorrect, as Anne Boleyn's relationship with Henry did not begin for at least a couple more years, around 1525 or 1526, but this does not preclude the king's pre-existing admiration. It is quite possible that Henry had noticed Anne already and had hoped to add her to his list of conquests and, without initial success, consoled himself with her sister and perhaps other lovers. This might have been as informal as Anne simply not returning his interest, or using her dark, attractive eyes to show her affections were bestowed elsewhere. After all, Cavendish was present in Wolsey's household at the time, an eyewitness to the development of the king's affairs. He records Anne's history with hindsight, but the notion that Henry had already been drawn to the woman with whom he would soon fall passionately in love is not impossible. If he did intervene in the Percy–Boleyn betrothal, it was probably to restore the Butler match for its political usefulness. In the meantime, though, he was more intent on the pursuit of a more willing lover.

Percy seems to have genuinely desired Anne for his wife, according to Cavendish, as he was prepared to stand up to the cardinal and argue in her favour, even though he was 'weeping', according to the account. Considering himself of good years, Percy 'thought [him]self sufficient to provide me of a convenient wife where as my fancy served me best but that my lord my father would have been right well persuaded and though she be a simple maid and having but a knight to her father, yet she is descended of right noble parentage as by her mother she is nigh of the Norfolk blood and of her father's side lineally descended of the Earl of Ormond'.[5] As Percy explained, the understanding had become common knowledge among the couple's acquaintance, having 'gone so far before so many witnesses that I know not how to avoid myself not to discharge my conscience'.[6] Such a process of formal betrothal was sometimes finalised by the consummation of the match and Percy specifically refers to it, in Cavendish's words, as a 'precontract'. It has been suggested by some writers that Anne and Percy might have slept together, as their vows would have entitled them, but it is unlikely that the king would have continued to pursue Anne for seven chaste years in the knowledge that she had slept with another man.

Wolsey sent for Percy's father, the fifth earl, in order to consult him about ways to avoid 'this ... hasty folly'. He 'made quick speed to court' on hearing of the matter and went at once to the cardinal, meeting him 'in secret communication' in his gallery. The harsh character assassination ascribed to him by Cavendish gives a very one-sided impression of the young man to whom Anne had contracted herself; he 'hast always been a proud, presumptuous, disdainful and a very unthrifty waster ... ' who had now 'misused' himself, with 'no manner of regard to' his father or king by 'ensuring' himself to Anne. Warning his son to 'use thyself more witter hereafter', he assured him that if he did not 'amend his prodigality' he would be the last earl of their house, due to his natural inclination to be a wasteful prodigal. Thankfully, the father had 'more choice of boys' to choose from, whom he trusted to 'prove themselves much better and use them[selves] more like unto nobility'. And with this he obtained Percy's promise that he would be married to the daughter of the Earl of Shrewsbury.[7] Cavendish related that the 'former contract was clearly undone, wherewith Anne Boleyn was greatly offended saying that if it ever lay in her power, she would work the cardinal as much displeasure'. Percy was 'commanded to avoid her company' and Anne was 'commanded to avoid the court and ... sent home again to her father for a season whereat she smoked for all this while she knewe nothing of the king's intended purpose'.

Cavendish's account clearly puts words into the mouths of the key players. It is unlikely, even if he had witnessed these events in person, that he would be able to recall their speech with any degree of precision but, considering his position in Wolsey's household and his later place as one of the few who remained with the cardinal after his disgrace, his version of events contains some approximate truths. The question of hindsight also makes it a difficult source to disentangle, but the basic facts are sound regarding the betrothal. Percy and Anne clearly fell in love at court, as he sought her out in the queen's apartments, perhaps dancing together, playing cards, reading or taking part in court entertainments. Catherine's court in the 1520s has been presented by some historians as being dour and solemn, with women sitting in silence and reading, devoid of lovers, dance and song. This is almost certainly misleading, given the references in *Hall's Chronicle* to Catherine's role in the court entertainments and masques, but while the queen may have withdrawn more from public life, she had not taken up the life of a vowess. Catherine was becoming increasingly religious, and her court may not have been as colourful as it once was, but this image of an overly austere queen belongs more to the coming years; the poetry of Thomas Wyatt attests to the tone of her court at this time, and if her ladies were sewing to excess then they would have been assisting the royal wardrobe by working on the costumes and elaborate disguises that Henry still loved. However, from July 1524, Catherine may have been in mourning following the death of her French counterpart, Claude, at the age of twenty-four and, after 1525, she was feeling the loss of her daughter Mary, who was away at Ludlow. Catherine might set the tone of her household, but Henry set the tone of the court.

There was also a frequent overlap between the households of the king and Wolsey, providing plenty of opportunity for romance, following the lead established by Henry himself. Percy may well have witnessed Anne's performance in the *Chateau Vert*. In fact, it seems very likely that he did, along with a number of other young men, given that it took place at the cardinal's residence of York Place, where his protégées were lodged. The fledgling betrothal was dismissed and Percy's engagement to Mary Talbot was resurrected, with the marriage taking place in 1525 or 1526. Anne disappeared from the records again until 1525, so there seems little reason to doubt Cavendish's explanation that she had been forcibly rusticated to Hever.

If we accept that a betrothal was made and broken, and there seems no reason not to, then the implications for Anne were considerable. In terms of the Boleyn sisters' reputations, it was Anne rather than Mary who returned home disgraced after engaging in illicit emotions. With the Butler and Talbot matches still a possibility, the young couple took quite a daring step in 'ensuring' themselves to each other, to borrow Cavendish's word. Given the way it happened, evolving out his attentions to her at court, and purely of their own choosing, it would seem this is the first occasion when we can genuinely be confident that Anne was in love. Although her feelings on the matter were not recorded, the wrath they incurred and her apparent removal from court might suggest the 'great offense' which Cavendish describes her as having taken. It had been a brutal lesson for her about the boundaries of love at Henry's court and the dangers of letting emotion take precedence over dynastic might.

The question of the pre-contract would raise its head once more. By 1532, when Anne was poised on the verge of becoming queen and Percy's marriage had broken down, his disgruntled wife sought a divorce, citing the previous arrangement with Anne. However, when the allegation was investigated, Percy was questioned about his love affair and the nature of the understanding between them. Under oath, with the potential to derail the king's imminent marriage, he wisely denied that there had been an engagement ten years earlier. Or rather he neatly circumvented it, to the peril of his mortal soul, writing on 28 May that it 'may be to my damnation, if ever there were any contracte or promise of marriage between her and me'.[8]

31

Brunet, 1523–25

What word is that, that changeth not,
Though it be turn'd and made in twain?
It is mine Anna, God it wot,
The only causer of my pain.
Yet is it loved, what will you more?
It is my salve, and eke my sore.[1]

Anne was sent away from court, probably to languish in the Kent countryside, while Henry continued to pursue her sister. Yet Henry Percy was not the only man she had attracted during her brief debut. The reputation of Thomas Wyatt preceded him, both as a poet and as a man. His father, Henry Wyatt, had been a key figure in the life of the king in his youth, becoming a Privy Councillor and Knight of the Garter, and a neighbour of the Boleyns, living at Allingham Castle near Maidstone, about twenty-five miles to the east of Hever. The connection went further, too, as Sir Henry and Sir Thomas had been appointed joint guardians of Norwich Castle in 1511, so it is likely that their children met at some point during the following decade. His eldest son, Thomas, had been born at Allingham in around 1503 and, at the age of eighteen, had married Elizabeth Brooke, a Boleyn cousin, although this match quickly turned sour. By the time Anne arrived at court in 1522, the tall, handsome poet had already been in the king's service for several years. According to the account written by his grandson, George, he was quickly captivated by the new arrival, his old acquaintance, and 'ever more taken with her witty and graceful speech'.[2]

Wyatt's poetry gives an insight into the nature of Henry's court in the early to mid-1520s, shedding light on the nature of courtly love and the flirtations that were conducted in and around the queen's apartments, which were hardly the dour, joyless places they later became. Written to entertain an elite circle, the poems were riddles and games, literary exercises designed to tease and titillate, amuse and suggest, for performance in the chamber, tucked into his lover's pocket or read at a pageant, rather than for publication.[3] He was one of an inner coterie who 'spend their time in vainful vanity, making ballades of fervent amitie'.[4] As such, his poems reflect the intimate courtly culture, the in-jokes of the time and the references to love affairs and affections that would have immediately been understood by those witnessing them unfold.

With some poems referring to one 'Brunet' that 'did set our country in a roar', 'falcon', Anne's badge, and 'Anna', Wyatt paints a world where the need for secrecy in love is essential, particularly when the participants were married, like Henry or Wyatt, or engaged elsewhere, like Anne and Percy.

> Take heed betime lest ye be spied
> Your loving eyes you cannot hide
> At last the truth will sure be tried
> Therefore take heed!
>
> For some there be of crafty kind,
> Though you show no part of your mind,
> Surely their eyes ye cannot blind.
> Therefore take heed.

Percy's courtship of Anne would have been apparent to those observant members of the queen's household as they danced or sang together, or engaged in conversation and whispered secrets. Himself rejected by Anne, Wyatt may have observed her, sitting demurely and sewing, pretending not to notice her lover, or even awaiting his arrival:

> She sat and sewed that hath done me the wrong
> Whereof I [com]plain and have done many a day,
> And while she heard my plaint in piteous song
> Wished my heart the sampler as it lay.
>
> The blind master whom I have served so long
> Grudging to hear that he did hear her say.
> Made her own weapon do her finger bleed
> To feel if pricking were so good indeed.

The evidence of his poems suggests that the married Wyatt's attentions did not find favour with Anne during 1522–23, probably due to her affection for Henry Percy. As a young woman, already in her early twenties, Anne had probably been intent on finding a suitable husband rather than a married lover when Wyatt made his first advances. By the time she returned to court a few years later, however, the situation was different. Percy was either a married man or about to become one, and Wyatt's marital unhappiness was widely known, as he repudiated his wife as an adulteress. It is unclear exactly when Anne did arrive back at Henry's court, but if it had been during the 1524/25 Christmas season then she would have witnessed Wyatt's participation in the pageant of the *Chasteau Blanche*, perhaps even dancing with him or the king on this occasion rife with symbolism.

To honour the ambassadors who had arrived from Scotland, a challenge was delivered to the king in Catherine's great chamber at Greenwich, shortly before Christmas 1524. The participants included William Carey, Thomas Wyatt and his brother-in-law George Cobham, along with other young men of the court who are better known today because of their famous offspring and relations – Leonard and John Grey, Sir John Dudley, Francis Sidney, Edward Seymour and others. A herald delivered their trial on a coat of arms, bearing the device of a castle with four silver turrets, in each of which was a beautiful lady; the captains agreed to 'raise the castle on a mount', in heraldic detail, to form the centrepiece of feats of strength, and it would be known as the *Chasteau Blanche*. It was to have one white shield, and whoever touched it should run six courses at the tilt; the red shield signified involvement in the tourney. Those who touched the yellow shield must answer twelve strokes at the barriers and the blue one represented the assault upon the castle, with a range of weapons. The building work began in the tilt yard.

This pageant was to run for weeks, keeping the court busy, with carpenters sawing, knights rehearsing and ladies sewing; like previous entertainments, it provided a convenient cover for courtship and intrigues to develop under the courtly masque. The castle was an immense twenty feet wide and fifty feet tall, built from timber and fastened with iron. To the north and south were two steep ditches, fifteen foot deep, set with drawbridges and, just like the coded messages about Mary at the *Chateau Vert*, it was said to 'not be wonne by sport, but by ernest',[5] which may have been aimed at a specific lady. This time, though, the metaphor of conquest and surrender, of persistence in the face of great difficulty, was more suited to perseverance than kindness. Henry was 'minded to have it assaulted' and, after St John the Evangelist's Day, 27 December, six men-at-arms and two ladies on palfreys presented Catherine with a note or bill, saying 'that although youth had left them, and age was come, and let them to do feats of arms: yet courage, desire and good will abode with them and bade them to take upon them to break spears, which they would gladly do if it pleased her to give them licence'.[6] Catherine read the letter and consented. Such notes, verses and poems played a prominent role in courtly entertainment, both on a grand scale like this and in the more intimate arenas of courtship.

With the queen's consent, the revellers revealed themselves as Henry and Brandon, followed by Nicholas Carew, Henry Norris, Francis Bryan and others, all dressed in gorgeous costumes. They ran courses and broke spears, before repairing to Catherine's chamber to dine and, after the lords and 'diverse ladies' had danced, the masquers arrived. All sixteen of them were dressed in cloth of gold from head to toe, from their shoes to their caps. Led again by Henry and Brandon, they danced 'a great season' before wine and spices were brought to signal the end of the evening.

It was not until 2 January that an attempt was made on the castle. After Wyatt and his team had taken up their defensive positions inside, the attacking knights attempted to break in, digging their swords into the banks and climbing the walls until they were 'out of brethe', getting up again valiantly until they were overthrown and the attack was abandoned. The castle was attacked again on the following day, with stones being thrown that hurt some bystanders, then again on 5 January, until the king decided to lead the knights in person three days later. Dressed in cloth of silver and black velvet, he proved himself in the tournament, making 'great strokes'.[7] The metaphor of Henry's power over that of his companions is a powerful one here, set against the backdrop of the unassailable castle, yet Hall does not relate whether or not the walls were finally broached. The focus seems to have shifted and the surrender was of far less interest than the chase. Historian David Starkey believes that Anne Boleyn was among the ladies taking part, watching the king perform his feats of skill and strength outside and Thomas Wyatt defending the white castle, with its connotations of purity and innocence. He dates Henry's interest in Anne from this point, which seems entirely logical. Anne, though, was probably unaware at this point that she had made a royal conquest.

Wyatt's grandson, George, would later suggest that a love affair had developed between Anne and Thomas shortly before she attracted Henry's attention, which must imply a date of late 1524 or early

1525, shortly before and during the performance of the *Chasteau Blanche*. Henry's love letters to Anne include the detail that he had been 'struck by the dart of love' for a year, and internal evidence would place composition around 1526, moving his awakening interest in her back to 1525. This would support the notion that she was back at court in time for the Christmas celebrations, perhaps summoned to attend Queen Catherine during the Emperor's visit. It is likely that her friendship with Wyatt was renewed at this point and may have developed into something more. The hostile Jesuit Sanders later went so far as to relate a scandalous account of the poet visiting Anne in her chamber and taking certain physical liberties with her before she fled upstairs at the summons of another lover, but it is so ridiculous as to be easily discounted. A story related by George Wyatt sounds more credible, in which the king recognised a ring or jewel Thomas had taken from Anne during courtship. Recognising the item and its symbolism, Henry declared that he had been deceived, at which point Wyatt realised he must abandon his pursuit, in favour of the king's.

The game of courtly love could be a minefield for young women. Vives outlines some of the difficulties in *The Education of a Christian Woman*, espousing the view of St Jerome that young innocents could fall prey to predatory men and the strong passions their attentions could raise: 'From meetings and conversations with men, love affairs arise. In the midst of pleasures, banquets, dances, laughter and self-indulgences, Venus and her son Cupid reign supreme.'[8] This was more literal than the author might have suspected, with the allegorical figures of love often being portrayed by actors in masks and plays at Henry's court. 'Such things attract and ensnare human minds,' Vives continued,

> but especially those of young women, over which pleasure exercises an uncontrolled tyranny. Poor young girl, if you emerge from these encounters a captive prey! How much better it would have been to remain at home or to have broken the leg of a body rather than of the mind ... although [love] burns with insatiable desire for pleasure, it wastes much time in suspicions, tears and complaints, it makes itself hateful.

Love caused girls to 'hate their parents and relatives because they stand in the way of their' happiness. Citing biblical examples, Vives described how love was responsible for the fall of Troy, how it 'drove mild-mannered David to expose the innocent Uriah to imminent danger so that he could freely possess Bathsheba. It drove Solomon, the wisest of kings, to madness, to the point of idolatry. It weakened Samson, it forced Medea to rend her brother limb from limb and kill her children. It led Catiline to slay his own son so that he could bring Orestilla into an empty house'.[9] Soon the King of England himself might be added to such a list.

Wyatt's awareness of having been supplanted by a superior suitor appears to have inspired his best-known work, a Petrarchan sonnet that exposes the rivalries and darkness beneath the court's glittering exterior. In typical Tudor style, he puns on the notion of his heart and the pursuit of the hart, which he realises has been in vain, and is now only able to follow the crowd of admirers, as she has been won by Caesar, or the king:

> Whoso list to hunt, I know where is an hind,
> But as for me, hélas, I may no more.
> The vain travail hath wearied me so sore,
> I am of them that farthest cometh behind.
> Yet may I by no means my wearied mind
> Draw from the deer, but as she fleeth afore
> Fainting I follow. I leave off therefore,
> Sithens in a net I seek to hold the wind.
> Who list her hunt, I put him out of doubt,
> As well as I may spend his time in vain.
> And graven with diamonds in letters plain
> There is written, her fair neck round about:
> Noli me tangere, for Caesar's I am,
> And wild for to hold, though I seem tame.

In spite of some of Wyatt's more intimate poetry, there is no evidence that he and Anne were ever lovers, or even that she returned his affection before she was thus 'collared' by Henry. Sanders reported that Anne had lived an active sex life before arriving at court, sinning 'first with her father's butler and then with his chaplain', before becoming the 'royal mule' of the King of France, but these slanders are spun out of the Jesuit's desire to blacken the name of a woman who 'embraced the heresy of Luther ... but nevertheless did not cease to hear Mass with the Catholics', which was 'wrung from her by the custom of the king and the necessities of her own ambition'.[10] Sanders also reported a scene where Wyatt confessed his adultery with Anne to Henry in these early days, warning the king away from entering a relationship with such a stained woman, but such a salacious anecdote overlooks the dynamic of the three participants. Writing during the reign of Mary I, Nicholas Harpsfield describes Wyatt dissuading Henry with the line that Anne was 'not meet to be coupled with your grace', which he claims came from a source close to Percy, implying that consummation had taken place with him, or Wyatt, or both, but that Henry did not believe him and dismissed it.

The king would not have made such a wanton woman his second wife, with whom he wished to produce a legitimate heir for the kingdom. There was also Anne's considerable faith to contend with, her awareness of humanist thinking and her understanding of the position of women which she had developed under the influence of Margaret of Savoy and Marguerite of Navarre; experiences that her sister had not absorbed. It was Anne's faith, coupled with her future role, that lay behind these colourful stories; her stigmatisation as sexually voracious and deceptive fit the later Catholic dialogue about her position as a catalyst for the Reformation and the driving force behind Henry's cruelty to his elder daughter. No genuine evidence for any scandalous behaviour or sexual activity survives for Anne's early life, and had she indulged in any affairs similar to those of her sister it would have provided rich meat for her later detractors.

The evidence in Wyatt's poems suggests that his desire for Anne went unrequited, although this may not have prevented him from imagining it. Separating from his wife by the mid-1520s, citing her adultery and lies, he was to take mistresses of his own from among the court circuit and fathered at least one illegitimate child. One of his most famous poems gives a glimpse of the kind of transition from courtly entertainment to sex that signalled the shifting boundaries of intimate relations between ladies-in-waiting and their lovers:

> Thanked be fortune it hath been otherwise
> Twenty times better, but once in special
> In thin array after a pleasant guise,
> When her loose gown from her shoulders did fall
> And she me caught in her arms long and small,
> Therewithal sweetly did me kiss,
> And softly said, 'Dear heart, how like you this?

But while the poem suggests a tone of easy licentiousness at court, Anne's recent experiences, her awareness of her sister's relationship with Henry and her own unmarried status caused her to tread a far more cautious path. Through the second half of 1524 and into the following spring Mary was pregnant and unavailable, then lying in for the customary month and recovering. At some point in 1525 Anne became aware that Henry was interested in her, initially as another mistress to share his bed, perhaps to bear him another bastard before being replaced by a younger, prettier face. She chose to resist.

32

A Vanishing World, 1525–26

Why come ye not to court?
To which court?
To the king's court
Or Hampton Court?[1]

By 1525, Henry's coffers were feeling the strain of sixteen long years of partying. To save unnecessary expenses, Thomas Wolsey undertook a series of reforms of the royal household, which were published as the Eltham Ordinances in January 1526, after the palace where the idea was conceived. Although they were ultimately unsuccessful in reducing spending, the surviving document is invaluable in providing a record of Henry and Catherine's household at the moment just before it began to disintegrate.

Catherine's world was about to crumble under her feet. For twenty-six years she had lived as a queen, with all the advantage and adulation of her court and country, dressed in luxurious cloths of gold and draped in jewels, living in the finest fairy-tale palaces, dining on the best the country had to offer, waited on hand and foot, at night and day, heading diplomatic missions abroad and being the envied wife of the dazzling, accomplished king. Yet there was another side to her life. Over the years, her personal relationship with Henry had grown increasingly stale as she turned a blind eye to his infidelities, even when they had been paraded in public under her nose. As two monarchs on the international stage, she and Henry had been a match of equals, able to discuss law, religion, poetry, history and politics, and Catherine's regal dignity had reinforced her position at her husband's side. Her only area of failing had been her inability to provide the country with the surviving male heir that Henry craved. Even as 1526 arrived, with the king freshly infatuated with a new love, the daughter of Ferdinand and Isabella could have been forgiven for thinking that her long years of service made her situation inviolable.

The previous autumn, Catherine had opened up her establishment to the scrupulous eyes of her husband's chief minister. Ever conscious of status, exactly what she thought of being scrutinised by a man of humble origins is unclear but, as ever, she complied with Henry's wishes and laid the mechanics of her household bare for his pen to scratch out in ink. In minute detail, the ordinances list exactly who was fed what and when, how much money was allocated to each of the various household offices, where the supplies came from and at what cost. Not a single herring or a half-burned candle went unaccounted for.

Wolsey's observations mark the increasing privacy which Henry was creating for himself by developing a more exclusive set of inner rooms. Here, he and Catherine could retreat from the world, with protocol and a series of doors dictating who was allowed access to his person and when. The ordinances outline the timings for the king's and queen's 'outward' chambers, with the pages rising at seven, making up the fire and preparing the room. The esquires for the body were called for at eight, who then had to tidy away the nightclothes and wait outside the door to be summoned into the inner chambers, with the clothes the king was to wear. At the same time, a yeoman was to be present at the door, to admit only lords, knights, gentlemen, household officers and those of an honest disposition, reporting all doubtful cases to the Lord Chamberlain. If they were to perceive anyone unsavoury present in the king's chamber, any 'mean' persons, they were to act to 'expel and avoid them from the same'. If the king or queen chose to dine or sup outside the hall, then they would be fully attended by a specified number of servants and no others should be 'suffered to tarry' nearby. All servants, rascals, boys and other foes would be expelled from the place outside the doors and the area was to be kept clean, with no 'ale, water, broken meat or other thing conveyed out of the king's chamber be cast or remain there to the filthiness and annoyance' of Henry, so that a 'large passage to the queen's chamber' was created.[2]

The final point about passage to the queen's chamber is an interesting one. Following on from comments about cleaning up after meals, the implication is that Henry may wish to visit Catherine in the hours of the evening or night. Undoubtedly, the king was entitled to attend the queen for discussion and company, but there may have been a suggestion that Henry was still sharing Catherine's bed at the time the ordinances were drafted, or else that he did not wish to contradict the belief that he was. Given the routine that accompanied his nocturnal visits, though, with the elaborate disrobing and preparations for the night, it was a process that would have involved a significant number of staff, both in the king's and queen's households, and those responsible for clearing and guarding the route along the way. The rituals for making the king's bed also involved the constant fear of assassination, so, even at these most intimate moments, Henry would have been led to his wife's chamber, while her maids quickly scurried away. The Eltham Ordinances capture their relationship in a moment of flux. With the queen's women aware of the moment that she had ceased her menstruation, and Wolsey's instructions regarding the passage to the queen's chamber, it remains unclear exactly when Henry ceased visiting his wife's bed. Most likely he visited less and less, as his attention drifted elsewhere and her erratic periods gradually slowed to a halt.

Henry's own privy chambers operated along lines designed to preserve his own secrecy. For the 'quiet, rest, comfort and preservation of [his] health', it was judged 'convenient that the king's highness have his privy chamber and inward lodgings reserved secret, at the pleasure of his grace, without the repair of any great multitude thereunto'. No one was to be admitted except those 'his grace shall from time to time call for or command'.[3] Apart from servants in their specific capacities as ushers or grooms, the exclusive guest list included the Marquess of Exeter, Henry Courtenay, a grandson of Edward IV and Henry's cousin, who 'hath been brought up as a child with his grace in his chamber'; then Sir William Tiler, Sir Thomas Cheyney, Sir Anthony Browne, Sir John Ruffell, Henry Norris and William Carey. Carey's position as a gentleman waiter would have facilitated any arrangements for his wife, Mary, to meet with the king in secret while her husband obligingly turned a blind eye. Six grooms were named, including Sir William Brereton, along with the king's barber, Pennye, and his page 'young Weston', Sir Francis Weston, then aged about fifteen.

The days of the minions' old intimacy and presumptuous behaviour towards the king were long gone. These men were charged to do Henry 'humble, reverent, secret and lowly service about all such things as his pleasure shall be to depute and put them to do'. The grooms were not to be lodged in the king's chamber, but were to be provided with their own accommodation and none was to 'presume to enter, or be suffered to enter into his said privy chamber ... under paine of incurring the king's displeasure and looseing of their service'.[4] The Eltham Ordinances made it possible for Henry to get up to whatever he wanted in his bedroom, with whomever he wanted, taking only a small and reliable handful of people into his trust. Bearing in mind the letter from Etiennette de Baume in 1514, describing how Henry referred to her as his page, it would have been possible for the king's intimate servants to smuggle a disguised lover into his bedroom at the king's request. The two grooms charged to sleep on pallet beds in his chamber could easily retire to the next room, as Catherine's women did when Henry paid her a visit. Sir Henry Norris was given the ultimate control of the king's privacy, charged to prevent all the other named gentlemen from 'presum[ing) to enter or follow his grace into the said bed chamber, or any other secret place, unless he shall be called ... by his grace'.[5] The old argument that if it was happening at court then people must have known about it is cast into a different light by these pieces of evidence.

As Groom of the Stool, the privacy of Henry Norris' position is obvious; he would literally stand guard while the king was on the toilet, yet by the extension of the concept of 'privy' and 'privacy' he was also well placed to facilitate the king on other intimate occasions. The 'other secret places' referred to in the Eltham Ordinances can cover the padded close stools for Henry's use, his bedroom and other closets. A 'closet' was literally a room that could be closed, and was not necessarily of a specific size or function. In the early 1540s, the behaviour of Catherine Howard would prove that closets also could provide a location for an illicit romantic encounter. With Sir Henry Norris guarding the door, Henry's privacy was guaranteed whatever he chose to do behind closed doors.

Norris had been present at Henry's court for at least a decade before the ordinances described him taking this important role. Possibly a relative of Richard III's close friend and chamberlain Francis Lovell, his grandfather had fought at the Battle of Stoke Field and Norris himself was about a decade older than the king, having been born around 1482. He had been one of the original minions of 1517 but survived the cull and attended Henry at the Field of Cloth of Gold. At the time of the publication of the Eltham Ordinances he replaced Sir William Compton as the Groom of the Stool, a move which indicates his closeness to Henry. For at least ten years, Norris would be the king's closest personal friend, the man in whom Henry could confide, who would have known his most intimate secrets.

As well as the king's increasing desire for privacy, the Eltham Ordinances shed light on the nature and composition of Catherine's household at the point before her power and position began to be eroded. Wolsey provides a list of those 'ordinary' members of the queen's establishment who were entitled to eat in her chamber. Her carver was Henry Semer, probably Henry Seymour, one of the less well-known brothers of the king's third wife, then in his early twenties and, as yet, unmarried. Catherine's sewers were Robert Warner and Nicholas Frogmorton, whose brother was her cup-bearer, Clement Frogmorton. These were probably from the Throckmorton family, the young sons of Sir George, who had served with Henry in France in 1513 and had been present at the Field of Cloth of Gold. Henry Webb was the gentleman usher of Catherine's privy chamber. In addition, she had four gentlemen ushers and three gentlemen waiters. All of these men were entitled to draw a salary of £11 8s 1d and to have bouche of court. Catherine's household contained an additional three servers of the chamber, who received a wage but no entitlement to be fed at her expense.[6]

Also well rewarded were those of the queen's personal waged servants who received bouche of court and an allowance of meat. They included William Herper or Harper, her clerk of the court on £6 15s 3d, and her groom porter, William Uxenbridge, who drew eleven shillings. She had three men overseeing her robes, the yeoman Ralph Worsley on £4 11s 3d, the groom Thomas Firten on 11s and the page Arthur Belfield on 26s 8d. A similar triumvirate governed her beds. Yeoman of her beds was Edward Floyd on £4 16s 3d, his groom Thomas Neverell, or Neville, received 11s and the page Thomas Harrison got 26s 8d. Bouche of court was also granted to the queen's laundress, for wood and lights.[7] In addition, Catherine had twenty-two Yeomen of the Chamber, drawing a salary of £15 4s 2d, five grooms of the chamber who received £2 but no food and four pages who only got £1 6s 8d. A higher value was placed on her messenger, John Grove, whose reward was £4 2s 3d. Eight others were listed as having no manner of allowance within the queen's household: her surveyor, auditor, attorney, solicitor, clerk of the council, clerk of the wardrobe, clerk of the closet and sergeant-at-arms.[8]

Arrangements were made for the provision of food, the 'bouche of court', for those entitled to eat in the queen's chamber. Catherine herself made do with only one serving at breakfast, with two to be shared between her attendant ladies; this still came in at an annual cost of £70. Sitting in her chamber while she ate, her Lord Chamberlain, her vice-chamberlain and 'other' of her council shared one 'mess' or course. A further three messes were to be divided between her four chaplains, her ushers, waiter, sewers and a handful of other officials. Her ladies were granted seven messes to share and her maidservants only three.[9] Described like this, the allowance of messes sounds a little meagre, but this is misleading as the ordinances also describe what constitutes a 'mess', giving a sense of the diet that Catherine and Henry were enjoying in 1525–26.

Above: 1. Lady Chapel, Westminster.
Catherine's mother-in-law, Elizabeth of
York, died shortly after giving birth in
February 1503, meaning that the young
Spanish princess lost an important ally.
She was buried in the chapel built for her
by her husband, Henry VII, who now lies
entombed beside her.

Right: 2. Map of Westminster. Westminster
Palace was the seat of the court and of
government, situated to the west of the
City of London. Catherine would have
known it well, visiting many times until a
great fire destroyed much of the complex
in 1513. The present buildings date from
the nineteenth century.

Scotland Yard

Great Hall, by Wolsey, 1528

Tennis court

Preaching place

'Holbein' gate

King St Gate

Westminster Hall (the seat of the law courts)

Abby

State Chamber

House of Commons
(formerly chapel of St Stephen's)
from 1547 until the fire of 1834

House of Lords

Court of Requests

The Queens bridge

Henry VII's chapel

Above: 3. Letter from Catherine of Aragon to the king's almoner (Thomas Wolsey), 2 September 1513. Dated at Richmond and signed 'Katherine the Qwene' the letter recommends that Louis d'Orleans, Duke of Longueville, who had been taken prisoner at the Battle of the Spurs fought on the 17 August, be conveyed to the Tower 'as sone as he commethe' for 'it shuld be a grete combraunce to me to have this prisoner here.' At this time Henry VIII was in France and Catherine of Aragon was ruling England as regent in his absence. The Battle of Flodden was not fought until a week later.

Opposite: 4. Catherine of Aragon. In her youth, Catherine was considered a great beauty, with her curvaceous figure, fair skin, pretty features and long, red-gold hair. The early years of her marriage appear to have been happy.

KATHERINA VXOR HENRICI . VIII.

Opposite: 5. The famous Hans Holbein cartoon of Henry VIII as he has been remembered ever since. Drawn in black ink on paper as a preliminary study for the mural painting in Whitehall Palace that was destroyed by fire at the end of the seventeenth century.

Above: 6. Henry Fitzroy. Later dating evidence suggests that Bessie Blount's son was born in June 1519. He lived a quiet childhood until the age of six, when he was invested as Duke of Somerset and Richmond, after which he played an increasingly prominent role at court, with Henry considering making him his heir. His tomb is at St Michael's church, Framlingham, Suffolk.

Above right: 7. Funeral effigy of Bessie Blount.

Below: 8. Hever Castle. Sir Thomas Boleyn inherited Hever Castle in 1505, after the death of his father, Sir William, Lord Mayor of London. Anne spent much of her childhood there until 1513, when she was sent abroad. It was at Hever, set amid the Kentish countryside, that Anne retreated during Henry's courtship of her, and where he is reputed to have wooed her. The property was later granted to Anne of Cleves.

Above left: 9. Anne Boleyn. This sketch by Hans Holbein the Younger is reputed to be of Anne, although its inscription was added in the seventeenth century. An etching of Anne by Wenceslaus Hollar appears to have been made as a copy of this image.

Above right: 10. Mary Boleyn, the woman who supplanted Bessie as the king's mistress.

Below: 11. Grave of Catherine of Aragon. Catherine died on 7 January 1536 at Kimbolton House and was buried in Peterborough Cathedral on 29 January. Even at the last she was not afforded the ceremonial due to a queen; she was laid to rest as the widowed Princess of Wales.

ANNA BOLLINA · · · VXOR HEN VII

12. Anne Boleyn as queen. The only contemporary image thought to represent Anne is on a medal struck to commemorate her coronation in 1533. This portrait, which hangs in Ripon Cathedral, is thought to date from the late Elizabethan period and may be a copy of a lost original. Henry probably ordered the destruction of Anne's image, as it seems unlikely that she would not have sat for Holbein during the 1530s.

Above: 13. Great Hall, Hampton Court. An artist's impression of the Great Hall, the very centre of Hampton Court, during Henry's lifetime, with hammer-beam ceiling, tapestries and flags.

Below left: 14. Hampton Court. The palace's site was acquired in 1514 by Thomas Wolsey and rebuilt in the renaissance style, to make a residence that rivalled the king's own. Court poet John Skelton reflected this in his verse 'why come ye not to court, to the king's court, or Hampton Court?' Wolsey handed the property over to Henry in 1528, in an attempt to save his skin.

Below right: 15. Anne Boleyn's gateway, Hampton Court. Henry expanded the palace considerably in the early 1530s, building larger kitchens, great hall and tennis courts, although work on Anne's lodgings, over this gateway, was still incomplete at the time of her execution.

MARIA : REGINA

16. Princess Mary. Separated from her mother since 1531, Princess Mary was almost twenty when Catherine of Aragon died. Having initially refused to accept her illegitimacy, she spent several difficult years estranged from her father and suffering from ill health, before the pair were reconciled and she was a more frequent visitor at court in the late 1530s.

17. Tower of London. Traditionally the Tower was the location from where coronation processions began. Anne Boleyn had stayed here in May 1533 and, on her arrest in 1536, was shocked to be conducted back to the same rooms, weeping and saying they were 'too good for her'.

Above: 18. Site of execution, Tower of London. On 17 May, George Boleyn and four others were beheaded on Tower Green, followed by Anne two days later. Their cousin Catherine Howard would also lose her head on the same spot, on 13 February 1542, shortly followed by George's widow, Jane Rochford.

Opposite: 19. Jane Seymour. Jane Seymour was a lady-in-waiting to Anne Boleyn when she attracted Henry's attention. While Anne languished in the Tower, Jane stayed at Beddington Manor, then at Chelsea, becoming betrothed to Henry the morning after her predecessor's execution. She married Henry at York Place ten days later.

Left: 20. Edward VI by Hans Holbein. Edward was born on 12 October 1537, and this drawing was made some time before Holbein's death in 1543.

Below left: 21. Anne Shelton. Sir Thomas Boleyn's sister Anne married Sir John Shelton and bore him six children. In 1533 she and her sister Alice were put in charge of Princess Mary, while her daughters Margaret (Madge) and Mary became ladies-in-waiting to their cousin Anne Boleyn.

Below right: 22. Mary Shelton. Labelled as Lady Henegham, or Heveningham, this sketch by Holbein is thought to depict Mary Shelton, poetess and possible amour of Henry in the late 1530s.

Above: 23. Richmond Palace. Built by Henry VII, Richmond was frequently used during his reign and Catherine of Aragon stayed there often, especially in late 1501, during the celebrations of her marriage to Arthur. It was Anne of Cleves' principal residence, where she was informed of the annulment of her marriage, and was granted to her as part of her settlement.

Right: 24. Anne of Cleves. Raised in a Lutheran household in Germany, Anne was considerably different from Henry's previous wives and he pursued the match to create an alliance against France and the Empire. This portrait, painted by Hans Holbein the Younger in 1539, portrays her in the heavy clothes that Henry found so unattractive, although it does not convey exactly what he objected to on a personal level.

Left: 25. Catherine Howard. Like her cousin Anne Boleyn, Catherine Howard came to court to serve a queen. Raised in the household of her step-grandmother, she had already had been promised to her lover, Francis Dereham, by the time Henry made her his wife. She was married to the king at Oatlands Palace, soon after his union with Anne of Cleves was declared invalid.

Below: 26. The Bishop's Palace, Lincoln. During the summer progress of 1541 Henry and Catherine Howard stayed in the Bishop's Palace from 9 August, where Jane Rochford helped arrange the queen's tryst with Thomas Culpeper.

Above: 27. Rochford Hall, east façade. Sir Thomas Boleyn inherited Rochford Hall, Essex, from his mother Margaret Butler and was elevated to Viscount Rochford in 1525. In 1534, following Mary Boleyn's marriage to William Stafford, the couple were granted Rochford Hall as their principal residence.

Below: 28. Rochford Hall church. Just a stone's throw from Rochford Hall, most of St Andrew's church dates from the fifteenth century, although an earlier church stood on the site. It is likely that Mary Boleyn was buried here, having died in the hall in 1543, but no evidence remains of her final resting place.

Above left: 29. Catherine Parr. Having already been twice widowed, Catherine Parr returned to court in the spring of 1543, in the hopes of being married to Sir Thomas Seymour. She soon attracted a more prestigious suitor though and, after Seymour was sent abroad, became Henry's queen that July.

Above right: 30. Catherine Willoughby, Duchess of Suffolk, widow of Charles Brandon. Henry may have considered making her his seventh wife in 1546.

Left: 31. Princess Elizabeth. A portrait of the princess at the age of thirteen, painted shortly before the death of her father. Catherine Parr brought Henry's three legitimate children together and helped repair their difficult relationships with the king and each other.

On a flesh day, the days in the religious calendar that did not observe a restricted diet, king and queen were amply served in the great hall with a two meals a day: dinner, which was at ten in the morning, and supper, at four. When they were not dining in the hall but in other places in the palace, the two daily meals were served at eleven and six.[10] On the dinner menu were £16 worth of the finest white 'cheat and manchett' bread, pottage, beef, venison, mutton, young veal, swan, goose, capon, rabbits, carp, custard and fritters washed down with beer, ale and wine.[11]

Supper saw the arrival of more of the first-course staples: bread, beef, capon and rabbit; chicken, larks, sparrows or stewed lamb with mutton chunks; mutton or venison topped with cloves; pheasants, plover, cockerels or gulls, followed by oranges, quince and pippins, with the usual beer, ale and wine. The second course comprised kid, lamb or pigeon, partridge or quail, teal or pullets, rabbit or lark, venison and baked meats, butter and eggs, blancmange and fruits.[12] On holy days, the main dishes were replaced by salmon, herring, crab, porpoise, pike, whiting, trout, eels, lobsters and, surprisingly, seals, which were deemed to be of the sea and therefore fish.[13] The total cost of providing the two daily meals, with two courses, for the king and queen was calculated at £4 3s 4d a day, or £29 3s 4d a week, or £1,520 13s 4d annually.[14] Whatever was left over was to be gathered by the almoner and distributed to the poor at the outer court gate.[15]

Separate diets or messes were drawn up for the Masters of the royal household, for the gentlemen of the Privy Chamber, clerks of the green cloth, the cofferer, the controller, the clerk of the kitchen and others, while the royal physicians and surgeons had a separate bill of fare. Those entitled to the queen's board were fed an average dinner of bread and pottage, three different types of meat, green goose and capon, fritters and custard, followed by a similar second course, at a daily cost of 19s, with a two-course supper priced at 14s. The queen's Lord Chamberlain and her gentlewomen were served with a daily diet worth 7s 4d, featuring fewer dishes and no sweets. The maids, servants and children ate only bread, ale, beef and veal on flesh days, with ling and other sea fish substituted on Friday and Saturday.[16]

In addition to meeting these demands, Wolsey estimated a further £113 6s 8d annually for the expenses incurred by grinding wheat and baking bread, £227 for the cellarage costs of storing and serving beer and wine, £713 6s 8d for spices and candles, £103 6s 8d for preparations, repair and maintenance in the kitchen, £163 6s 8d for salting, curing and storing food in the Accatry, £150 to transport and house poultry, £506 14s 3d for the scullery, £54 for making sauces, £516

3s 4d for contributions made by the woodyard, including rushes, plus alms, offerings and fees, making a total of £4,445 2s 6d.[17] And this was only one additional department.

Yet while Wolsey was busy trimming down the king's household in such exacting detail, his own wealth was expanding exponentially. Having carved himself a meteoric path to success by virtue of his own ability and desire to serve, the cardinal had accumulated properties and wealth that rivalled the king's own. The most famous of these was the palace he built at Hampton, on the Thames, to the south-west of London, a site which he acquired from a religious foundation in 1514. Investing a huge sum of money, he had built up a Renaissance palace by around 1521, where he entertained the king on such a lavish scale that it gave rise to satire. John Skelton's poem of 1523 depicts Wolsey presiding over the offices of the Chancery, Chequer and Star Chamber, dismissing dukes, earls, barons and lords and almost outshining Henry in his magnificence:

> Why come ye not to court?
> To which court?
> To the king's court,
> Or to Hampton Court?
> Nay, to the king's court!
> The King's court
> Should have excellence
> But Hampton Court
> Hath the pre-eminence,
> And York's Place,
> With my Lord's Grace!
> To whose magnificence
> Is all the confluence,
> Suits and supplications,
> Embassades of all nations.[18]

When the cardinal's devoted servant and confidant George Cavendish wrote his detailed biography of his old master in the 1550s, he described the role the astute courtier took at Henry's court:

> The kyng was yong and lusty, disposed all to myrthe & pleasure and to followe his desire and appetyte no thyng myndyng to travell in the busy affayers of this Realme the whiche the Almosyner perseyved very well, toke vppon hyme therfore to disborden the kyng of so waytie a charge and troblesome busynes puttyng the

kyng in Comfort that he shall not nede to spare any tyme of his pleasure for any busyness.

This was such a successful policy that Wolsey's household swelled to require a staff of hundreds, including a Mr Cooke in his privy kitchen 'that went daily in damask, satin or velvet, with a chain of gold about his neck', footmen apparelled in 'rich running coats' and a keeper of his tents.[19]

Yet Wolsey's popularity was beginning to turn. He had often incited criticism and dislike because of his background, but in 1525 his new moneymaking scheme alienated the nobility further. When news arrived at court of the capture of Francis I at the Battle of Pavia, Henry saw an opportunity to seize the French throne. To raise the necessary funds, Wolsey devised the Amicable Grant, a 'benevolence' or 'gift' from the clergy and nobility to the king of between a sixth and tenth of their revenue. In the end, hostility to this plan ensured its failure, and Wolsey negotiated a peace treaty with Francis' mother, Louise of Savoy, but he had made some powerful enemies along the way. Soon Wolsey and Catherine would both find themselves eclipsed by a more formidable enemy. The king was in love again.

33

Love Letters, 1526–27

Nothynge yerthly to me more desyrous
Than to beholde youre bewteouse countenaunce:
But, hatefull absens, to me so enuyous,
Though thou withdraw me from her by long dystaunce.[1]

Anne Boleyn's royal suitor was undergoing a period of transition. The years 1524–26 had been a time of intense personal challenge for the king and queen, bringing them to the recognition that their relationship had permanently changed. Their hopes of another child had been dashed and the future path of the Tudor dynasty was uncertain. Henry was no longer the 'green' young man who had wooed women entirely for pleasure, as sexual adventures and playthings, as parallels for the hart he hunted in the forest, and outlets for his physical needs. After each previous romance he had returned to Catherine as his wife and equal, whose breeding and position meant that none of his paramours could really offer any competition. By 1526, those days were gone. Henry was thirty-five and his wife was forty. In these years, the king was facing some difficult decisions about his future.

Henry appears to have fallen in love with Anne by early February 1526. At the Greenwich Shrovetide jousts, he dressed in embroidered gold and silver bearing the device of a 'mannes harte in a presse, with flames about it', and the motto 'declare, I dare not'. His opponents, headed by the king's cousin Henry Courtenay, Marquis of Exeter, were dressed in green-and-red velvet decorated with burning hearts. Over this image was that of a woman's hand 'commyng out of a cloud, holdyng a garden water pot, which dropped silver drops on the harte', giving relief. This symbolism revealed a new object of affection, the pair of concealed love and the remedy, which was within the reach of the right woman.

During the celebrations, Henry 'did service' to the queen and her ladies. This would have included Anne, to whom his cryptic message was directed. It is likely that, by this time, she was aware of his meaning. Equally Catherine may have seen the signs but not known the identity of her rival; it is impossible to know just how aware she was of the flirtations taking place in her household. However, the joust then took a violent and shocking turn. In an accident reminiscent of that Henry himself had endured in 1524, when a lance splintered against his helmet, Sir Francis Bryan was injured by the 'chance shivering of the spere'.[2] He lost an eye and would always wear a patch as a consequence. Such an accident would kill the French king Henri II in 1559. It was another reminder of the fragility of life and that death could strike at any time, even in the royal circle. If the king was to meet an untimely end, the realm would be left in the hands of a ten-year-old girl.

Henry's embroidered motto may have stated that he dared not declare his love, but this was only in a public arena. He knew the queen was watching. In private, though, he did not hesitate to make his feelings plain. At some point early in 1526, he found an opportunity to speak to Anne alone, perhaps as she sewed costumes of silver and gold or sat reading in a garden or alcove; the scene has been imagined many times by historical novelists. He also ordered his goldsmiths to make four gold brooches that continued the motifs of desire and hope, using the visual symbols of hearts and hands, tongues and eyes, which poets like Wyatt deployed in verse. It was part of the playful romantic games of the age to send symbolic messages in gifts that represented some virtue or desire to be decoded by the recipient. Another method was to use the language of flowers, selecting particular blooms for a nosegays or bouquet. As Shakespeare reminds us in *Hamlet*, there was rosemary for remembrance, pansies for thoughts, daisies for unhappy love, violets for faithlessness. The royal wardrobe in 1532 included a range of such symbols once created as messages before having lost their context: eight separate legs made of silver, a silver hand, a tooth of silver and two silver breasts. Perhaps at some point they had been lovers' tokens.

Placed in order, the four brooches Henry commissioned relate a narrative that makes a promise to Anne. There was a brooch of Venus and Cupid, another of a lady holding a heart in her hand, a third portraying a man lying in a lady's lap and a fourth, which foreshadowed her future, of a lady holding a crown. Was Henry considering making Anne his wife as early as spring 1526? It is more likely at this stage that the crown was symbolic of Anne's rule over Henry as a lover rather than making any specific promise, although that was only a year away.

The song 'Greensleeves', traditionally thought to have been written about Anne, includes lists of more of the type of gifts that the king may have sent to his lover in an attempt to persuade her to yield to him:

> I bought thee kerchiefs for thy head,
> That were wrought fine and gallantly;
> I kept thee at both board and bed,
> Which cost my purse well-favoredly.
>
> I bought thee petticoats of the best,
> The cloth so fine as it might be;
> I gave thee jewels for thy chest,
> And all this cost I spent on thee.
>
> Thy smock of silk, both fair and white,
> With gold embroidered gorgeously;
> Thy petticoat of sendal right,
> And these I bought thee gladly.

In the meantime, Henry continued to try and talk Anne into his bed. Vives describes the ways in which experienced men might woo and seduce innocent virgins:

He approaches smoothly and persuasively; first he praises the girl, says that he has been captured by her beauty, and last of all he says that he is perishing of his uncontrollable love. He is well aware of the vain minds of many women, who take singular pleasure in being praised. In this way the fowler deceives the bird with birdlime and the decoy's cry. He calls you beautiful, charming, clever, eloquent, noble, and perhaps you are none of these things, but you like to hear those lies ... He swears that he will die and even ... that he is dying.[3]

Vives then cites the case of a 'certain French girl [in] the retinue of those who accompanied Marguerite of Navarre' who was tired of hearing men saying they were dying for love and replied to one, 'Well, die and be done with it so that I can see some lover die of all those who say that they are going to die.'[4] By 1524, Vives' work was complete, dedicated to Catherine of Aragon and available in her household, so it is not impossible – in fact, it is more than likely – that it was read among her ladies. With Anne's wit and experience of the courts of Europe, though, she is likely to have been more like the example of the French girl, far more sophisticated than the audience Vives addresses. Anne would have been aware of the warning that 'your lover will deceive, either because he is used to deceiving or because this is the reward for an illicit love or because satiety of pleasure will persuade him to do so'. But Anne was no fool; she knew that accepting the advances of a married lover necessitated deception. She may not have been naïve, but she was human.

Exactly how welcome were Henry's attentions, though? Assuming the birth date of 1501 is correct, Anne was approaching her mid-twenties; she had already seen two potential husbands disappear, and had been wooed by a married man who could not offer her a respectable future. In 1525–26, Anne was in no position to anticipate that Henry could offer her the ultimate prize of becoming his wife and it had probably not yet occurred to the king himself that this was a viable route. While his attentions were flattering, he was ultimately attempting to talk her into his bed, to yield up the virginity that she probably still retained. Henry was no longer the young romantic figure who had attracted such admiration and universal praise in his youth, yet nor had he become the obese invalid of his later years. He was older and wiser than he had been; an experienced lover who still retained much of his good looks, although they were tempered by maturity.

Seventeen love letters survive from Henry VIII to Anne Boleyn. Lodged in the Vatican archives, they were penned by a self-confessed reluctant writer at various points when they were apart between autumn 1526 and 1528. No replies from Anne survive. It is only possible to estimate her feelings by using the limited evidence of Henry's responses. Equally, the nature and frequency of her replies is unknown, punctuated by the couple meeting in person at intervals. Between some of the letters, Henry and Anne had conversations and amorous encounters in palace gardens and secret corners of the court. We cannot know what passed between them then, although the letters leave some clues.

There are also problems of scholarship with the letters. The authenticity of some is still under dispute and some were written in French. Additionally, their uncertain dating has resulted in various acts of editorial resequencing. Even under such circumstances, though, these letters provide a valuable snapshot of the techniques Henry used to woo women; we can hear the voice of the king as lover, whispering his secret desires to Anne Boleyn, through a language of rhetorical devices, conventions and promises.

Much of Henry's prose is romantic and tender, decorated by his drawings of hearts and coded initials, but it belies the true dynamic of their relationship. Professing himself her 'loyal servant and friend', the bombardment of Anne by passionate letters actually tells a more sinister story. Ultimately, did she really have a choice in the matter? By the letters' internal evidence, she resisted him for over a year, frequently absenting herself from court and his presence. Henry's presentation of the trope of courtly love, of the pursuit of the unattainable woman, is belied by his desire to make her his. At some point in 1527, the pretence of role play was dropped and he offered her the unprecedented position of his official mistress. She declined. Are these the records of a developing love affair, or the gradual wearing down of a woman's resistance, who had no option but to submit to the demands of her king? Was Anne bullied into becoming Henry's lover?

The first letter is conventional enough, drawing on the usual motif of the pining lover, parted from the object of his desires and asking to be remembered by her. He hopes that absence will not lessen 'her affection', which would increase his pain, 'of which absence produces enough'. Henry uses the imagery of astronomy, an accessible metaphor for courtly poetry, to remind Anne that although the sun might be distant, it is hotter; 'so it is with our love, for by absence we are kept a distance from one another, and yet it retains its fervour'. But he is unsure of her feelings, adding 'at least on my side, I hope the like on yours'. As he could not be with her, he sent a gift of his 'picture set in bracelets ... wishing myself in their place, if it should please you'.[5]

Anne does not appear to have replied to Henry in full, or to have seen him in person, before the composition of the second letter. In the event that she received a gift of jewellery from the king, protocol dictated that she would have sent some grateful reply, possibly along formal lines. She probably composed a reply, which is now lost, which failed to satisfy him. 'Since my parting from you,' Henry wrote, 'I have been told that the opinion in which I left you is totally changed.' He had been informed that she would not come to court, with her mother 'or in any other manner', to which report 'I cannot sufficiently marvel at'. Here, the voice of the king overrules that of the man. Even though Henry plays the lover, the tone of his 'marvel' subtly stresses her obligation and his failure to recall what he may have done to 'offend' her implies that he has, in fact, done no such thing. He believes he had done all he could to be of service and to please. It is not permissible for his declarations of love to have caused offence. Henry's letters show him to be a master of the literary technique of litotes, the employment of negatives and the irony of understatement, to highlight the tension between what he might ask of Anne and what he might command. He continues by saying that her aloofness 'seems a very poor return for the great love which I bear you' and that he hoped she loved him 'with as much affection as I hope you do ... though this does not belong so much to the mistress as to the servant.'

What this second letter makes clear, is that Anne needed to negotiate a fine line to walk with Henry. His use of phrases suggestive of the love that she should bear him juxtapose the context of sovereign and subject uncomfortably with that of man and woman. Had she received such a missive from Percy or Wyatt, Anne's responses would have been more her own; from the king, they raised the question of just how much autonomy she really had in the relationship. With Henry switching between roles, as man and king, she had to work out just how much licence he was prepared to give her to rule him and where she needed to step back and submit to his authority, in the interests of herself and her family. Her lack of response and the coolness Henry complains of may well have been less the hard-headed manipulator that Sanders suggests, playing the long game to hook the king, than a confused young woman unsure how she should respond, or how she wanted to. Perhaps Anne stayed away from court and from Henry because this was too dangerous a game, one she initially did not want to play. Her king, though, was not going to allow her that choice.

Henry wrote again, about the 'uneasiness my doubts about your health gave' him. The sweating sickness that terrified him had broken out afresh and a number of the royal servants had fallen sick, including George Boleyn. It appears that Anne was at court in Surrey, which might be a reference to Hampton Court, which Wolsey would formally make over to Henry in 1528 although it was frequently used as a venue by the king before then. By the time of writing, word had reached Henry that Anne had 'as yet felt nothing' in the way of illness and he reassured her that 'few or no women have been taken ill', so she should not be frightened 'nor be too uneasy in our absence'. He advised her to 'avoid the pestilence as much as you can', but also that 'we must sometimes submit to our misfortunes, for whoever will struggle against fate is generally but so much the farther from gaining his end'.[6] For the time being, though, Anne continued to struggle against the fate that Henry was urging her towards.

It is clear from Henry's fourth letter than Anne had now sent him at least two replies. However, these had not put his mind at rest. Rather, he had been 'turning [them] over in my mind' in 'great agony', not knowing how to 'interpret them'. Anne's message must have been ambiguous; perhaps it was still clouded by doubt as she remained uncertain about how best to receive the king's advances, 'whether to my disadvantage, as you show in some places, or to my advantage, as I understand in some others'. He beseeched her 'earnestly to let me know expressly your whole mind as to the love between us'. Henry's demand could hardly be ignored, as 'it is absolutely necessary for [him] to obtain this answer, having been for the whole year stricken by the dart of love'. This lengthy pursuit can hardly have been typical of the king's conquests and his request, with its use of the term 'necessary', attempted to bring the waiting to a close. Then, however, he appeared to soften and give Anne a way out. He asked her to declare whether she only loved him with 'an ordinary love' or if she could 'give up yourself body and heart to me' and thus be worthy of the title of mistress. Henry's promise that he would take Anne 'for my only mistress, casting off all others besides you out of my thoughts and affections, and serve you only'[7] echoed the marriage vow, and must have reminded Anne that she was dealing with a married man. Equally, Henry's words are the most powerful evidence so far that he had, up to that point, had a number of mistresses. Perhaps they suggest that, until recently, he had been enjoying the attentions of more than one woman, all of whom he was now willing to cast off in Anne's favour. At this point, something between them changed.

Following the use of imagery, symbolism and metaphor in courtly play, Anne sent the king a gift with a coded message. The details of it only survive in Henry's next letter, along with his 'cordial' thanks for 'a present so beautiful nothing could be more so'. First, Anne sent a the conventional gift of a fine diamond. With it, though, was a statue made of silver, depicting a solitary damsel tossed inside a ship set on stormy seas; a metaphor for her internal struggles. She sent it with a letter, including 'demonstrations of your affection' and 'beautiful mottoes ... so cordially expressed' that they obliged Henry 'for ever to honour, love and serve you sincerely'. Anne had clearly given the reassurance the king had been seeking, but without the evidence of her letters it is impossible to know whether she did so willingly, or out of a sense of obligation after his relentless pressure. She was being asked to distinguish between her feelings for him as her monarch and as a man, weighed against whether or not she wanted to enter into a relationship with him. This might have been a straightforward question for Anne, or it may have been difficult. The length of his courtship before her capitulation suggests the latter.

In response to her gift, Henry promised that 'henceforward my heart shall be dedicated to you alone. I wish my person was too.' It would appear that some kind of understanding had been reached, tantalisingly in private, or in a letter that does not survive, as the king then raised the first possibility of Anne becoming his wife. He hoped to be hers in person, assuring her that 'God can do it, if He pleases, to whom I pray every day for that end'. This may date letter five in the sequence to the early months of 1527, when Henry first began to make legal enquiries about the validity of his marriage, or the end of 1526, when the idea may have germinated. For Anne, this was a glimpse of a dazzling future, the first exciting moment when it began to sink in that one day she really might become Queen of England.

34

Anticipation, 1527

My trust alway in him did lie
That knoweth what my thought intends
Whereby I live the most happy.[1]

Christmas 1526 was a colourful affair, with entertainments held at Greenwich and York Place. A 'great plentie of victuals' was served between the revels, masques and banquets, spiced wine was drunk, sweetmeats were consumed and the lamps blazed late into the night. The jousting began on 30 December, with the usual combatants dressed in their finery of velvet, tissue and cloth of gold, and no doubt Anne was watching Henry compete again on 3 January, when three hundred spears were broken during the course of the day. Yet there was something different about the festivities that year. Henry was good at concealing his feelings but as he danced, rode and feasted, those who were closest to him, including his gentlemen of the Privy Chamber, his grooms and close companions, may have noticed a change in his mood. The king had a secret.

The night after the jousts ended, Henry took a small band of young gentlemen to Bridewell Palace where they donned masks before climbing into a barge on the river. Under cover of darkness, it took them to Wolsey's residence of York Place, where the king dined with a 'great compaignie of lords and ladies'. After the meal, much 'good pastime' was made, before the disguises were removed and the identities of the players revealed.[2] Surely, with Wolsey's connivance, Anne was among them, taking the opportunity to be with Henry away from the eyes of the main court. This may have been the point at which the king managed to overcome her reluctance to his suit and convince her that his intentions were serious. Equally, it might have been at the Shrovetide jousts that year, or the banquet in the queen's chambers that followed. Either way, Henry had decided that his marriage was over. With the help of the Pope, Anne would become his new wife – but he was not yet ready to pull off the mask of his private life and reveal his true intentions to the world.

On 17 May, Wolsey convened a secret ecclesiastical trial at York Place to investigate the validity of the royal match. The building was transformed from a place where masked dancers feasted and flirted to the legal arena in which Queen Catherine's marriage would be examined and judged. It should have been a fairly simple, quick matter. There was the precedent of Louis XII's first marriage, which had been annulled to allow him to make a better dynastic match. Only that March, the Pope had done the same for Henry's own sister Margaret, who was released from her marriage to the Earl of Angus on the grounds of his earlier pre-contract with Lady Janet Douglas. The king had every reason to believe that Pope Clement would readily do in May what he had in March. The trial should really just be a formality.

With Henry seated beside him, Wolsey began by raising Catherine's first marriage to Arthur. If that union had been consummated after all, then the failure of the queen to bear healthy sons was explicable according to certain Biblical verses. His main justification was a passage from Leviticus (20:21) that condemns marriage to a brother's wife as unclean and destined to remain barren: 'If a man shall take his brother's wife, it is an unclean thing: he has uncovered his brother's nakedness. They shall be childless.' Yet the Bible contradicts itself. A verse in Deuteronomy states that 'the wife of the deceased shall not marry to another, but his brother shall take her and raise up seed for his brother' (20:6), but Henry's council advised him that Leviticus took precedence over Deuteronomy in canon law. Henry and Catherine were not exactly childless either, with the existence of Princess Mary, but this was conveniently circumvented by manipulation of the text, where 'childless' was substituted for lacking a male heir. As related by Hall, the issue was formally first 'raised', probably at Wolsey's instigation, by the president of Paris during the negotiations for a match between Francis and Princess Mary. Concerned about her legitimacy, he 'doubted whether the marriage between the king and [Mary's] mother, being his brother's wife, were good or no'.[3] Thus, the future of Catherine's daughter was being used as a pretext to undermine her past. Catherine must have been furious when she heard. The assembled clergy and lords met at York Place on two further occasions to debate the validity of Catherine's marriage, before admitting on 31 May that they were unqualified to reach a decision. The next day, some devastating news arrived in England.

The Pope would not be annulling any marriages in the near future. Hundreds of miles away, over thirty thousand mutinous Imperial soldiers had been left unpaid and unfed for weeks, during the war Charles had been waging against Francis. Partly inspired by their condition, and partly by a swell of anti-Catholic feeling, they attacked the walls of Rome and burst into the city on 6 May, embarking on a campaign of destruction, murder and pillage that would last for days. Symbolically, they ransacked the tomb of Julius II, the very pope who had issued the dispensation for Henry and Catherine back in 1503. By the time Henry's secret court met, Pope Clement, on whom he was pinning his hopes, had been driven to flee to safety in the Castel Santangelo. Effectively, the Pope was now Charles' prisoner. This made the Emperor the most powerful man in Europe. He was also a devoted nephew. Under different circumstances, Henry's first marriage might have been quickly swept away, but the conjunction of these events on the European stage tied such a Gordian knot of diplomacy and legal wrangling that it would take years to unravel.

At this stage, Wolsey was unaware of the new object of the king's affections. Henry allowed his servant to believe that he was pursuing an annulment because of his religious doubts and that, at this stage, any remarriage was only theoretical. Soon after the trial, Wolsey departed for France. His joint missions were to work towards a European peace and negotiate a match with Princess Renee of France, daughter of Louis XII. The latter was a deliberate wild goose chase. When Henry applied to the Pope for a dispensation to remarry that August, Anne was not named, although the conditions did cover a woman related to him in the 'first degree of affinity ... from ... forbidden wedlock'. This clause allowed him to wed a woman whose sister he had already 'bedded' and must have been phrased with Anne in mind. It is also a critical surviving source of our evidence for the king's relationship with Mary Boleyn. The following month, Henry wrote to Wolsey, who was still in France, thanking him for his good service 'which ... cannot be by a kind master forgotten, of which fault I trust I shall never be accused, especially to you ward, which so laboriously do serve me'. He added that they had 'never sent to the Pope since his captivity, and have no one resident there, lest the queen should anticipate us in our great matter'.[4] Henry was trying to keep secrets from everyone: he may have succeeded in keeping Anne's name out of things but his wife had too many loyal servants at court for his plans to remain hidden for long.

Henry may have hoped that Catherine's current preoccupation with her daughter's future would blind her to his activities. Mary's betrothal to Charles V had been abandoned with the breakdown in Anglo-Imperial relations in 1525 and the Emperor had gone on to marry his cousin Isabella of Portugal, who bore his first son, Phillip, a year later. It was a great disappointment for Catherine, who could not have predicted that the infant Philip would one day go on to marry her daughter. The broken alliance proved to be a significant turning point. It pushed Henry into the arms of the French, with the suggestion that Mary could become the second wife of Francis I. Catherine was aware of Francis' reputation as a lover and, by this time, his syphilitic state may have been suspected among the European courts. Memories of Queen Claude, with her repeated pregnancies and early death, added to the concerned mother's determination to resist the proposed match. By March 1527, matters had progressed as far as discussions about the dowry, whether the ceremony was to be held at Calais and the desirable age of the princess at the time, which was judged to be fourteen. As Mary had just passed her eleventh birthday, it meant that the wedding could go ahead in just three years.[5]

Catherine was also aware that the marriage would sideline Mary in terms of the English succession. She probably suspected that it was with this in mind that the king was considering making Henry Fitzroy heir to the throne. Imperial ambassador Mendoza wrote to Charles on 18 March that 'the King of England has here a natural son, whom he much wishes to make King of Ireland, bestowing upon him other large estates besides; that the king holds this son in such affection that he would show the same honour and regard to anyone entering into an alliance with him as with the princess, his daughter'.[6] With Henry now secretly resolved to make Anne his wife, the plans he was proposing for Princess Mary and Henry Fitzroy make dynastic sense. Mary would make a suitable royal marriage outside the realm and, considering what had happened to Prince Arthur, Fitzroy would be Henry's reserve heir until such time as Anne provided him with a new legitimate son. To secure the boy further in the world of international politics, a wife was currently being sought for him within the Danish royal family. Later the same month, Wolsey had approached Mendoza as Henry's advocate regarding his son's future, which was met with contempt by the ambassador: 'The cardinal's overtures to [Mendoza] respecting the king's illegitimate son and the intention of conferring upon him the title of king, together with the proposal for his marriage, might be considered in the light of a joke, were it not that the cardinal's presumption and folly are well known. Such proposals would be unworthy of an answer.'[7] Listening to the various rumours leaking out of York Place, Catherine may have begun to consider Wolsey with similar contempt.

That May, Henry was anticipating a quick conclusion to his first marriage when he hosted a huge joust and banquet to be held for the French ambassadors at Greenwich. Nicholas Carew, Robert Jerningham, Anthony Browne and Robert Harries acted as challengers, wearing costumes embroidered with the word 'loyaltie' and the motto that 'by pen, pain nor treasure, truth shall not be violated'. Henry Courtenay and his men responded to their challenge, dressed in gold and silver set with images of mountains and olive branches, and the two sides ran 'fair courses' for two and a half hours in spite of the rain. A special banqueting house was built to Henry's specifications on one side of the tilt yard. It was an impressive hundred feet long and thirty wide, but it seems ironic that Henry had proposed to Anne and been accepted while the dynastic symbols of the rose and pomegranate were still combined in its purple cloth roof. And it was Catherine, still keeping her mouth shut, who sat beside Henry under the 'goodly' cloth of estate, hung with the royal motto *'dieu et mon droit'*.

Visiting Venetian Gasparo Spinelli described the queen's ladies, 'whose various styles of beauty and apparel, enhanced by the brilliancy of the lights, caused me to think I was contemplating the choirs of angels'. Inside the pageant, the women were more beautiful still, 'as to be supposed goddesses rather than human beings. They were arrayed in cloth of gold, their hair gathered into a net, with a very richly jewelled garland, surmounted by a velvet cap, the hanging sleeves of their surcoats being so long that they well nigh touched the ground, and so well and richly wrought as to be no slight ornament to their beauty.' This might seem to echo the old legend that Anne instigated the fashion at court for long, trailing sleeves, perhaps even 'greensleeves', either as a French fashion or to cover the little extra nail that reputedly grew on one of her fingers.[8] Anne could well have been among these women who danced around the bejewelled mountain, or perhaps was claimed by the king when he suddenly disappeared and returned in gold Venetian masks.[9] Predictably, the end of the evening saw all the masks removed, but greater secrets would soon be made public.

35

The King's Darling, 1527–28

He is so blindly in love with that lady that he cannot see his way clearly.[1]

Henry had seriously underestimated his wife. Catherine was popular, 'much beloved in this kingdom',[2] with her own network of loyal servants. When it came to such a critical issue as the validity of her own marriage, she soon found out what he was planning. In fact, she had been informed by a 'reliable authority'[3] of the secret meeting at York Place barely hours after it had first met and passed that information on to Mendoza, who wrote it down in a letter to Charles. Soon, the whole of Europe was aware of the King of England's delicate moral conscience, while Henry himself believed that his secret was only known to a select few. Yet it appears that his motives were unknown at this stage. Catherine still believed her husband's doubts were political rather than personal, and she therefore retained hope.

In a private letter to Charles, though, it was clear that Catherine was placing her hopes on her nephew. Ambassador Mendoza's account of events at the English court primarily attacks Wolsey for 'scheming to bring about the queen's divorce' rather than recognising Henry's personal desire or the level to which he was driving the issue. He described to Charles how the queen was 'so full of apprehension on this account' after hearing 'that the king is so bent on this divorce that he has secretly assembled certain bishops and lawyers that they may sign a declaration to the effect that his marriage with the queen is null and void on account of her having been his brother's wife'. Mendoza was fearful that the captive Pope Clement might be influenced or tricked by 'some false statement to side against the queen, or that the cardinal, in virtue of his legatine powers, may take some step fatal to the said marriage'.[4] He was right to suspect that the Pope could do little independently of the Emperor and to fear that, as his prisoner, Clement could possibly be led to act against Henry's wishes.

Catherine believed 'that the principal cause of all that she is made to suffer is that she identifies herself entirely with the Emperor's interests', having taken Charles's side when Henry wished to ally with France. Her mistake suited Henry. Writing to the Emperor, Mendoza asked for the Pope to be 'put on his guard in case any application should be made to Rome against this marriage; also that His Holiness should tie the legate's hands, and by having the cause referred entirely to himself, should prevent him from taking part in it, or appointing judges in this kingdom'. This is exactly what Charles would do, forbidding Clement from making any ruling and attempting to delay Henry's investigation into the marriage in any way that he could. After discussion with the queen, the ambassador believed that if Henry met with any success he would soon make the affair public, 'but should the king see that he cannot succeed, he will not run the risk of any of the preliminary steps being known'. Until then, 'the queen desires perfect secrecy to be kept in this matter, at least for the present'.[5] It worked to Catherine's advantage for Henry to believe her in ignorance of her plans, buying her some much-needed time. With all these secrets seething beneath the surface at court, a dramatic confrontation was brewing.

When Catherine was officially informed of Henry's doubts concerning their marriage, on 22 June, it came as no surprise. Through the intervening weeks, she had been planning and preparing her response and defence, hoping that the matter would be dropped, dreading the moment when her husband might broach the topic. Official records show that Henry was at Windsor on that day, so it seems likely that he broke the news to Catherine there. He knew his wife to be proud, intelligent, devout, determined and loyal; at one time, these had been traits he had admired in her, traits that became a queen well. However, it must have also made him uneasy about exactly what her response would be.

Outlining the questions of conscience that had been troubling him, Henry informed his wife that they had been living in mortal sin since 1509 and that she must retire into a convent. Although Catherine had been aware of his 'great matter' for over a month, she had believed it would be put aside when Henry's attempts to annul the marriage failed. This interview convinced her that he was serious. This question was not going away. To be confronted with Henry's desire to part in this way, for it to have finally become an acknowledged reality, must have been devastating for Catherine. Yet she was accustomed to tragedy; for decades it had been strengthening her will.

The *Spanish Chronicle* includes an account of events composed by an author who was possibly an eyewitness at court during the 1520s and 1530s, or who had access to someone who had been. Into the mouth of the 'sainted Queen Catherine' on 22 June it puts this reasoned speech:

> My good Henry, I well know whence all this comes, and you know that the king, Don Ferdinand, when he gave me in marriage with the Prince of Wales, was still young, and I came to this country a very young girl, and the good Prince only lived half a year after my coining. My father, the king Don Ferdinand, sent at once for me, but King Henry Vii. wrote and asked my father that I might marry you. You know how we were both agreed, and how my father sent to Rome for the dispensation, which the Pope gave, and which my father left well guarded in Spain.[6]

Other sources claim that Catherine burst into tears. It must have been an emotional encounter. Henry then asked her to keep the matter a secret, little knowing that it was already the worst-kept secret in Europe.

It must have been around this point that Catherine became aware that Henry was intending to replace her with Anne Boleyn. After eighteen years of marriage, she was adept at reading her husband's moods and observing his affairs running their course. This was a new challenge. With the recent elevation of Henry Fitzroy she had been reminded that Henry would not tolerate her commenting upon certain aspects of his personal life, but she now knew she was fighting for her future. If Cavendish is to be believed, she had learned to keep her enemies close, almost to appreciate them, holding Anne in 'great estimation' and accepting 'all things in good part and with wisdom and great patience'. She had weathered the storm thus far and would refute these allegations with obstinate certainty. As an anointed queen, stepping aside to enter a convent was insult enough; leaving the throne empty for her lady-in-waiting was unthinkable. Catherine was the daughter of two monarchs, with Plantagenet blood in her veins and connections to the great ruling houses of Europe; Anne was the descendant of a merchant. There was also the question of religion and the supremacy of the Church. Catherine represented the old faith, with its Catholic ritual and the guidance of papal authority; Anne's background was reformist, 'more Lutheran than Luther himself'. She leaned towards France rather than Spain and the Holy Roman Empire. Thus, she represented a threat to the entire world that had produced and nurtured Catherine, which she had proudly represented for decades. Anne must not replace Catherine. Such a move would redefine England.

Yet that was indeed the direction in which Henry and Anne were moving, with his letters becoming more passionate and committed to their future together. He impatiently anticipated the time he and Anne would be together as husband and wife, 'the approach of the time for which I have so long waited rejoices me so much, that it seems to almost have come already'. It was also clear at this point the relationship had taken on a more physical dimension, as Henry wished Anne 'were in mine arms, or I in yours, for I think it long since I kissed you'.[7] Later, he wished himself 'privately' with her and that he might spend an evening 'in my sweetheart's arms', whose pretty 'dukkys' (breasts) he longed to kiss. To facilitate this closeness, he arranged lodgings for Anne at Greenwich which were close to his own. Ironically, it was Wolsey, now appraised of the situation, who helped find a suitable place 'which could otherwise not have been hired'. This was a role the cardinal had certainly played before, on at least one occasion, to help the king's love life run smoothly. Yet Catherine was still in residence at Greenwich in the queen's apartments and Anne's presence must have created an uneasy atmosphere. As Du Bellay reported, 'Open house is kept by both the king and queen, as it used to be in former years. Mademoiselle de Boulan is also there, having her establishment apart, as I imagine, she does not like to meet with the queen.'[8]

As a lover, Henry was affectionate and full of small attentions. His letters allow us to glimpse the kind of language and flattery, the promises and presents he used in wooing a woman – we hear his technique as a lover. He sent Anne a buck which he had killed himself, hoping it would make her think of him; he longed for her rather than her brother, who was the bearer of the note, and begged her to ask her father to bring her back to court sooner than planned. Henry showered her with gifts, of material, jewels and other items that may have taken her fancy, but reassured her that she was a greater comfort to him than 'all the precious jewels in the world'. However, as an experienced man in his thirties, Henry would have been hoping for comfort of a different sort.

Having managed to reach an agreement with Henry about the future of their relationship, Anne was now faced with the challenge of setting boundaries regarding their physical closeness. From the letters it is clear that she had allowed him to kiss and caress her, but there must have been a point at which she refused him. The tradition of Anne holding Henry at bay and inflaming his desire is a well-established one and rings true for this phase of their connection. After all, they expected their marriage to be imminent, so they could control themselves for a few months. But the boundaries Anne imposed – assuming they came from her and not Henry – also raise the question of her motives and governing emotions.

Did Anne resist falling in love with Henry, either for personal reasons or an awareness of the wider implications of her actions? Vives' advice to young women was to tread cautiously, as 'it is in your power to let love in, but once you have let it in, you no longer belong to yourself, but to it. You cannot drive it out at your pleasure, but it will be able and will take pleasure in ousting you from your own house ... while this passion violently sweeps away all human hearts, it does so all the more with women's feelings, which are more tender than men's.'[9] Vives clearly paints women as the victims in love, but this raises the questions of just who was steering Anne and Henry's relationship and the extent to which Anne's decisions were reactionary or whether she took the initiative. With Henry's letters making his desires clear, was Anne intimidated by his courtship and status into complicity? Could any female subject really give Henry a decisive refusal? Did she see an opportunity and take it? Or had she, by the end of 1526, fallen in love with the king, or with the idea of becoming queen?

A number of possible interpretations for her actions could make sense, depending upon different readings of the tone of the king's letters. If Anne was not in love with Henry, she may have agreed to marry him as the ultimate prize in the marital stakes. This would not have been a cynical move; it would be entirely consistent with the arranged matches that families made to advance their fortunes and establish strong dynastic connections. Everyone was looking to 'marry up', and Anne was no exception. Perhaps she was exhilarated by the rewards Henry could offer and decided to play the game. She may also, along the way, have developed feelings for him. She may have not. This would make her an absolutely typical woman of her times and no different from Henry's other wives. However, the romantic possibility remains that she fell in love with him; either at the start while resisting his advances out of loyalty or belief that they would not lead to marriage, or as their relationship developed. We will probably never know.

Just how far did Henry and Anne go during their early courtship? Henry wrote of the pleasure of having her in his arms, or being in hers; he also longed to kiss her pretty breasts, although this may well refer to the portion of chest above the bodice, or even just be a fantasy he was anticipating making into fact. When Anne moved into rooms at Greenwich, in close proximity to Henry, this would have allowed them greater privacy and may well have marked a great stage of intimacy. Furthermore, Anne was not occupying them as the king's mistress, but as his intended wife, his fiancée, even if their intention to marry was still secret. In this respect, she had the same legal status as she had after having given promises to Henry Percy, an act that was often considered binding by the Church and considered sufficient licence to allow the couple to indulge in various acts of foreplay, or 'bundling'. It is very unlikely that Henry and Anne slept together this early, as they would have wanted to be certain of the legitimacy of any child she may conceive. Rudimentary forms of contraception did exist, and perhaps Anne may have taken the risk and yielded once, in order to make their betrothal legally binding and secure her position. However, it seems more likely that they indulged in some intimate acts that allowed Henry to glimpse their future sex life without them fully becoming lovers.

By the summer of 1527, when Henry broke with Catherine, he had apparently not slept with her since her menopause, in 1524. Although it is difficult to ascertain exactly what happened once their bedroom door was closed, a number of historians repeat the assertion that he still 'shared her bed' for the sake of appearances. Does this mean that he was still having sex with his wife, or visiting her room, or literally sleeping beside her, to prevent court gossip? In 1527, Wolsey wrote to his representative in Rome, Gregorio Casale, that sexual relations were now impossible between Henry and Catherine, as 'certain diseases in the queen defy all remedy, for which, as well as for other causes, the king will never again live with her as a wife'. Some intimate illness, Wolsey suggested, meant that Henry was 'utterly resolved and determined never to use' her again and that 'danger ... may ensue to the king's person by continuing in the queen's chamber'.[10] This was quite a dramatic claim. It implied that Catherine had some infection, illness or condition that affected her sexual organs and that this might be transmitted to her husband, or that the queen was capable of doing violence to Henry. Was this really true, or were Henry and Wolsey prepared to use whatever weapon they thought might prove successful in severing the king from his wife? Considering that Wolsey also lied to the Pope that the bloodstained sheets from her 1501 wedding night had been sent to Spain and defamed Catherine as frenzied with desire for sex, his argument about her disease appears in a less credible light. There is no other surviving source for the queen's 'illness'.

That autumn, Anne, who was noted for her fluency in both French language and French graces, would have been indispensable at the reception of the Lord Montmorency at Greenwich. The Grand Master of France had been at Francis' court since 1515 so it is likely that Anne already knew him and would have been selected from among Catherine's attendants to form part of the official welcoming party. This took place at Greenwich, being followed by jousts and a feast in another new banqueting hall of gold and satin silver, where ninety dishes were served before a pageant of a white marble fountain flanked by hawthorn and mulberry trees, set with gold gargoyles and winged serpents. If Anne's powers of translation had served their purpose, she may have been one of the eight 'fair ladies in straunge attire' with whom the king and his companions danced 'very lustily'. No doubt she and Henry enjoyed watching the tragedy performed in Latin by the Children of the Chapel Royal, depicting the imprisoned Pope being rescued by a cardinal, who appealed to the king of England for assistance. The subsequent entertainment of dancing, masquing and banqueting followed predictable lines, but the surviving expense account gives a delightful insight into the world of courtly pageantry, into the wheels that turned behind the scenes, the labour required to create the illusion of magic.

The provisions for the palace of pleasure had been made by a Richard Gibson. In the second week of November, he submitted the list of costs incurred, including the wages and payments to men 'working day and night', as well as such fascinating details as sixty-six pounds of old lead for leaves, pomegranates, fleurs-de-lys and 1,700 'little long leaves cast in lead'; four dozen measures of rushes for 'raising of the dust' in the banquet chamber, half a pint of aqua vitae, 14*d* for a piece of cord to draw the curtains and 8*d* for eight long canes to put out the lights. It also mattered that the event smelled nice, with 6s 8d spent on half a pound of sweet powders put among the king's napery (table linen) and 6s 8d for perfumes put under the pageant, and forty-two gallons of sweet water were purchased at 5s per gallon to run in the ornamental conduit.[11]

The verses needed to be written on clean paper too, with quires of paper royal costing 4d per quire, while the works were recorded on seven reams of inferior brown, at 12d per ream. It must have been a colourful affair. To mix their tints, the painters required ninety-eight pounds of verdigris green, 12d of white lead, 12d of red lead, 12d of Spanish white, 12d of ground black, over two gallons of pink, half an ounce of saffron, one pound of vermilion, 6s 8d of sap green, one pound of yellow ochre, bound by 22d worth of hens' eggs, mixed in four dozen earthenware dishes. They used thirty-six pairs of scissors and four pairs of great shears, four pounds of bristles, 130 pounds of glue, eight pounds of gum Arabic, three gallons of vinegar for tempering green paint, a bottle of what flour for paste, eleven yards of satin, two ounces of red ribbon, twelve leaves of gold paper and six dozen of silver paper, all to make trees, bushes, branches, roses, rosemary, hawthorn, mulberries, panes of gold and stars. The work was begun on Friday 11 October and completed a month later, on 10 November.[12]

Details of the ladies' clothing for the occasion survives too, from the twenty-one ounces of flat gold of damask used by the tailor's wife in Bowe Lane and her maidens, for piping eight cauls for the princess and the ladies, to the eight great cauls of Venice gold, bought from Elizabeth Phelype for the princess and the ladies; 14s was paid for the gold damask for piping the ladies' cauls and 12d for six hair-wigs. A John Skut was rewarded 20s for making alterations to the women's clothing. Other clothing expenses survive from the play. Almost thirty-seven yards of white sarsenet were made into a 'train mantle' for the actor or actress playing Lady Peace and wide Spanish sleeves for Quietness and Tranquility. Five crimson gowns with wide sleeves were made for the ladies and seven pieces of black buckram provided twelve mantles and eight more gowns. Some 3s 8d purchased red-and-white kersey hose (tights) lined with yellow and 8d bought sufficient narrow ribbon to make hair laces.[13]

From this surviving account, it is clear just how much work went in behind the scenes to create the glittering façade of a single entertainment. It can provide a parallel with the main court, shining a light on a microcosm of the huge machinery of daily life in the royal palaces. With thousands of servants working behind the scenes in so many departments, Henry was at the apex of a vast and complex establishment; the corresponding cogs of his kitchen, or his privy chamber, were used to serving his daily needs from the moment he woke to the time he fell asleep at night and securing his safety and comfort all through the hours of darkness. It must have bred a sense of divine entitlement and privilege that led the king to confidently expect that all his wishes would as easily be met. However, he was soon to discover that, outside his kingdom, those who opposed his will were not prepared to be so accommodating.

36

Ménage à Trois, 1527–28

*It did not seem to me to be a time to guard myself
against Love's blows: so I went on
confident, unsuspecting; from that, my troubles
started, among the public sorrows.*[1]

In October 1527, Emperor Charles declared that he would support his aunt in her refusal to acquiesce to Henry's request and demanded that Pope Clement took no further steps towards granting an annulment. Effectively, Charles had his uncle in checkmate. Wolsey had returned to England in September to find that another ambassador had been dispatched to Rome, and there was no sign of the warm welcoming committee he had expected. Worse still, when he met with Henry at Richmond to discuss his mission with the king in private, Anne Boleyn was the one to summon Wolsey to Henry's presence and accompanied them into the closet for the duration of the interview. It was a sign to the cardinal that his influence over the king was slipping. Perhaps he recalled the occasion when he had forbidden Henry Percy to honour his betrothal to Anne and regretted that she was not now Countess of Northumberland. There was a powerful new player at court and Wolsey recognised that she was able to give Henry much that his old friend could not.

The issue rumbled on into the New Year, with an uneasy triangle of Henry, Anne and Catherine under the same roof in their separate establishments at court yet meeting frequently in the public arena. Often the three dined together in the same hall. According to Cavendish, Catherine employed various methods to keep the lovers apart, 'the oftener had her at cards with her, the rather that the king might have the less her company', on which occasion Catherine reputedly uttered the ironic line that Anne had 'good hap to stop at a king, but you are not like others, you will have all or none'.[2] Again, time played to the queen's advantage, allowing her to take advice, communicate further with Charles and prepare her case.

Early in the New Year, though, news arrived in London that Clement had escaped from captivity, allowing him to act independently of the Emperor. Perhaps this, or Catherine's stubbornness, acted as a catalyst. In February 1528, Wolsey applied for a commission to allow proceedings to go ahead for the trial in London, in order to appease Henry's 'troubled conscience'. In response, Catherine sought the advice of William Warham, Archbishop of Canterbury, John Fisher, Bishop of Rochester, Dr Henry Standish, Bishop of St Asaph's, Cuthbert Tunstall, Bishop of London and John Clerk, Bishop of Bath and Wells, ultimately, to defend her against the papal legate Henry had requested to hear his case.

Catherine watched Anne closely. She had seen other rivals come and go before; younger, more beautiful women whose fertility was untested, who could dance all night with the king and compose poems and music. She knew that some of them had shared his bed but, by maintaining her position and devoting herself to God, she had preserved her dignity. That June, though, an enemy of a different kind made an appearance, which might have seemed like the answer to her prayers. The dreaded sweating sickness broke out again in London, and, while Henry and his wife left for the country, Anne sought the shelter of Hever. The disease was notorious for the swiftness by which it claimed its victims and the terrible nature of their suffering, which Catherine had experienced herself as a young woman at Ludlow. Slipping back into the old daily routine, with Catherine sewing Henry's shirts and the two attending Mass and confession together, it may have seemed to the queen that the mistress was out of sight and out of mind. The public façade continued. Yet, as Henry's letters indicate, he was still in regular contact with Anne, and was soon writing out of concern for her health, having heard 'the most afflicting news' and saying he would 'gladly bear half your illness to make you well'. He sent her one of his own physicians and beseeched her to 'be guided by his advice.'[3]

When Anne fell ill with the sweat, it may have seemed to Catherine that divine judgement had been enacted upon her ex-servant for immorality. Such terrible epidemics, often claiming hundreds of lives apparently at random, could only be explained in the sixteenth-century mind as an act of God, as a reaction to sin. The queen would not have needed to look far to identify what that sin might be. Catherine must almost have held her breath in anticipation of the news. With her rival neatly removed, her marriage might even have a chance of recovery and the passage of a few years might even lessen the pain and erase the memory. But Anne did not die. God chose to answer the king's prayers instead of the queen's. By the end of the summer Anne had begun to recover, and, although he wanted to see her, Henry wrote that she knew 'best what air doth best with you' and that she should 'do therein as best you like'.[4] For the time being Anne stayed on at Hever, surrounded by its rolling Kent countryside, away from the pressure and judgement of the court.

Anne survived the illness but her brother-in-law William Carey succumbed, dying on 22 June at his house of Plashey in Essex. Anne was granted the 'custody of the lands of William Carye, deceased, during the minority of Henry Carye, his son and heir, with the wardship and marriage of the said heir',[5] but not of his sister Catherine, then aged fourteen. Carey's death left Mary in considerable debt and Henry's old fondness for her prompted him to write to Anne, asking their father to help as 'it cannot stand with his honour, but that he must needs take her his natural daughter now in her extreme necessity'.[6] Meanwhile, the news was looking better for Anne on another front: the Pope had agreed that Wolsey might hear the case of Henry's marriage in London, along with a second papal legate, to ensure fairness and accountability. The trial was on.

The second cardinal was appointed that June. Henry wrote to inform Anne that Lorenzo Campeggio, 'whom we most desire', had recently arrived in Paris and was, therefore, expected to soon reach Calais, and then he would 'enjoy that which I have so long longed for, to God's pleasure and both our comforts'.[7] The aged Campeggio, travelling slowly and suffering from terrible pain as the result of his gout, had reached Paris in mid-September, but had to be carried to Calais on a litter; he did not arrive in London until 8 October 1528, with the express purpose of finding a solution that would suit all parties and to delay proceedings as long as possible. At once, he took to his bed. In a subsequent letter to Anne, Henry was frustrated by the 'unfeigned sickness of this well-willing legate', which did 'retard this access to your person', but trusted that God would restore him to health and that Cardinal Campeggio could with 'diligence recompense his demur'.[8]

In the meantime, Henry arranged for them to meet midway between Hever and London at Beddington Place, the 'fair house' or 'paradise of pleasure'[9] of her cousin and Henry's obliging courtier and friend Sir Nicholas Carew. Then it would have been surrounded by countryside but today only the great hall remains, sitting in the London borough of Sutton, as part of Carew Manor School. Between 10 and 14 November 1528, Henry and Anne were guests of Nicholas and Elizabeth, enjoying some rare privacy in the gardens, deer park and comfortable rooms before Henry returned to London and they were parted again. It had been a chance to reaffirm their mutual desire but there was still a long way to go before the king could call Anne his own. If Henry thought his wife would quietly accept his wishes and step aside, he had seriously underestimated her.

On 24 October, Catherine and Campeggio finally met. Hoping to find an ally, the meeting would have been a disappointment for her once she realised the approach the cardinal was going to take. She resisted his attempts to persuade her to enter a convent, saying that she 'intended to live and die in the state of matrimony, to which God had called her, that she would always remain of that opinion and that she would never change it'. Two days later she visited the cardinal at his lodgings at Bath Place, where he was again incapacitated. Henry had agreed to the pretext she offered of making a confession to Campeggio, but her words can hardly have been those he had hoped she would utter. Catherine 'affirmed on her conscience that from her marriage with Prince Arthur ... she had not slept in the same bed with him more than seven nights and that she remained as intact and uncorrupted as the day she left her mother's womb'. As in the years of her widowhood, duress pushed Catherine to dramatic extremes, embracing the notion of martyrdom, claiming that 'although she might be torn limb from limb, should compel her to alter this opinion; and that if after death she should return to life, rather than change it, she would prefer to die over again'.[10] She was aware that she was not just fighting for herself, but for the future of her daughter too. Campeggio believed her.[11]

Then, Catherine produced her trump card. The sons of a long-dead Spanish ambassador from her youth, Rodrigo Gonzalez de Puebla, had uncovered a crucial piece of evidence among his papers. It was a papal brief, a copy of the original dispensation that had been issued allowing Henry and Catherine to marry, which she now presented as irrefutable evidence that the marriage had been legitimate, as this paperwork even covered the eventuality that consummation had taken place. Thus, Henry's scruples should be eradicated regarding the legality of the match, which Catherine maintained was unnecessary anyway, as no prohibitive affinity had been established between her and Arthur. On 7 November, the queen made a declaration in the presence of Warham, the Archbishop of Canterbury who had married her to Henry, and John

Fisher, Bishop of Rochester, to the effect that she had been a virgin on her marriage to Henry, rejecting the words that had been inserted in the brief to allow for the consummation of her first marriage. It was a formidable setback for Henry and Anne's cause. The king's response, the following month, was to follow through with a threat he had made earlier in the year and separate Catherine from her daughter.

37

The Blackfriars Trial, 1529

O wavering and new fangled multitude! Is it not a wonder to consider the inconstant mutability of this uncertain world.[1]

On 22 June 1529, Catherine of Aragon prepared to give the performance of her life. The setting was the Dominican monastery of Blackfriars, a complex of cloisters and religious buildings connected to the palace of Bridewell by a long gallery of over seventy metres. Summoned to appear before Wolsey and Campeggio, three weeks after the legantine court had been convened, she instructed her ladies to dress her with care and walked with dignity along the passage from the inner court into the packed hall. Having previously lodged a complaint to Rome about the legitimacy of the court, Catherine sat down before the audience to listen to the 'scruples' Henry claimed to have felt 'from the beginning' but had not raised for the 'great love he had and has, for her'. Henry claimed to desire 'more than anything else that their marriage should be declared valid', and argued that the 'queen's request for the removal of the cause to Rome was unreasonable, considering the Emperor's power there; whereas this country is perfectly secure for her, and she has had the choice of prelates and lawyers'.

Catherine knew what she had to do. Rising from her seat, she knelt before Henry, addressing him only, appealing to him as her husband and as the only other person in the court of equal rank.

'Sir,' she began,

I beseech you for all the love that hath been between us, and for the love of God, let me have justice. Take of me some pity and compassion, for I am a poor woman, and a stranger born out of your dominion. I have here no assured friends, and much less impartial counsel. Alas! Sir, wherein have I offended you, or what occasion of displeasure have I deserved? I have been to you a true, humble and obedient wife, ever comfortable to your will and pleasure, that never said or did any thing to the contrary thereof, being always well pleased and contented with all things wherein you had any delight or dalliance, whether it were in little or much. I never grudged in word or countenance, or showed a visage or spark of discontent. I loved all those whom ye loved, only for your sake, whether I had cause or no, and whether they were my friends or enemies. This twenty years or more I have been your true wife and by me ye have had divers children, although it hath pleased God to call them out of this world, which hath been no default in me. And when ye had me at first, I take God to my judge, I was a true maid, without touch of man, and whether it be true or no, I put it to your conscience. If there be any just cause by the law that ye can allege against me either of dishonesty or any other impediment to banish and put me from you, I am well content to depart to my great shame and dishonour and if there be none, then here, I most lowly beseech you, let me remain in my former estate and receive justice at your hands. The King your father ... and my father, Ferdinand, King of Spain ... thought then the marriage between you and me good and lawful. Therefore, it is a wonder to hear what new inventions are now invented against me, that never intended by honesty ... I most humbly require you, in the way of charity and for the love of God, who is the just judge, to spare me the extremity of this new court, until I may be advised what way and order my friends in Spain will advise me to take. And if ye will not extend to me so much impartial favour, your pleasure then be fulfilled, and to God I commit my cause![2]

Henry attempted to raise Catherine from her knees twice but she would not move. Finally, she rose, curtseyed, and turned to walk straight out of the courtroom. An official called to her to return, but she responded that 'it makes no matter, for it is no impartial court for me, therefore I will not tarry. Go on!' With her head held high, she never returned to the courtroom. Henry, moved, echoed that she had indeed 'been to me as true, as obedient, and as conformable a wife as I could in my fantasy wish or desire. She hath all the virtuous qualities that ought to be in a woman of her dignity ... she is also a noble woman born.'[3] But he went on to outline his suspicions, after 'all such male issue as I have received of the queen died incontinent after they were born, so that I doubt the punishment of God in that behalf'. He explained that he wished to 'take another wife in case that my first copulation with this gentlewoman were not lawful, which I intend not for any carnal concupiscence, nor for any displeasure or mislike of the queen's person or age, with whom I could be as well content to continue during my life, if our marriage may stand with God's laws, as with any woman alive'.[4]

The issue continued to be debated without resolution. In mid-July, Campeggio and Wolsey visited Catherine again to make one last attempt to convince her that she must retire from life and enter the convent of her choice, but they found her adamant. Receiving them in her rooms at Bridewell, the queen appeared with a skein of white thread about her neck, as she had been interrupted sewing with her ladies, 'thinking full little of any such matter' as the steps they urged her to take. She appealed to their better natures, claiming 'I am a poor woman lacking both wit and understanding sufficiently to answer such approved wise men as ye be both, in so weighty a matter ... I am a simple woman, destitute and barren of friendship and counsel here in a foreign region'.[5] Yet Catherine was anything but a simple woman.

Amid the heartbreak and uncertainty she was feeling, she threw herself into maintaining the legitimacy of her marriage and the justification of her position as Henry's wife, Mary's mother and her country's representative of the Church of Rome. She would not deviate from this position for the rest of her life.

In Catherine's absence, the investigation continued for a further two months. Henry attempted to prove that Catherine and Arthur's marriage had been consummated, but Bishop Fisher proved a formidable opponent, countering the king's arguments with the queen's sworn statements of virginity and corresponding passages from the Bible. As he had done by inventing the disease Catherine was reputed to be suffering from, Wolsey decided to fight with whatever weapons he could. He now drew on a number of statements he had gathered from those who had been witness to the 1501 marriage, as servants, pages and companions – those placed to repeat the worst kind of gossip that can arise out of the bawdy jokes and tone of the moment. The chief witness was Charles Brandon, who spoke of Arthur's boast the following morning at being tired after spending the night 'in the midst of Spain'. Wolsey also found William Thomas, who had helped Arthur to undress and accompanied him to Catherine's chamber, although this could only prove that he passed the night there, not that the pair had actually had sex. Eventually, it was concluded that what had transpired between Catherine and Arthur could not be proven either way, especially in the light of the queen's sworn statements. On 1 September, to Henry's great frustration, Campeggio referred the question back to Rome.

Henry had not stayed at Blackfriars to hear the full proceedings of the court. Through the summer months, he had seized the opportunity to be with Anne on royal progress, taking her with him in the place of Catherine. This must have provided her with some reassurance, as the clergymen and witnesses tied themselves in increasing knots about the legal rights of the case. They did not travel far, though, allowing Henry to receive news from court, spending August at Waltham, Barnet, Tittinghanger, Windsor, Reading and Woodstock and licking their wounds that September slightly further afield at King's Langley, Grafton, Notley, Bisham Abbey and Buckingham, where they stayed with the recently widowed Mary Carey. It allowed the king a chance to see his potential illegitimate children by his former lover: Henry, who was three, and Catherine, who was aged between four and six, Anne's niece and nephew. This itinerary also gave them some privacy in which to plan their next move. They had stayed at Waltham Abbey for nine nights from 2 August and returned from 11 to 20 September, probably to the adjoining house called Romeland, where Henry discussed the matter with the triumvirate of Cambridge clerics Thomas Cranmer, Edward Foxe and Stephen Gardiner, who suggested that he appeal to the universities of Europe about the finer points of canon law. It was a good idea that allowed Henry and Anne some hope for the future. However, they were also looking for someone to blame for the failure of the Blackfriars court and their gazes rested on Thomas Wolsey.

Cavendish described what he 'heard reported by them that waited upon the king at dinner', with Anne outlining 'what debt and danger the cardinal hath brought you in with all your subjects' and the 'things [he] hath wrought within this realm to your great slander and dishonour'.[6] It must be remembered that his account was written as a vindication of Wolsey, but it would seem from Anne's letters of 1529 that her relationship with the cardinal had reached an impasse after an initial period of friendship. Acknowledging that Wolsey had 'quarrelled with the queen to favour me at the time when I was less advanced in the king's good graces', she proceeded to tell him he 'cannot avoid being censured by everybody for having drawn on yourself the hatred of a king who had raised you to the degree'. Neither she nor Henry could 'comprehend ... how your reverent lordship, after having allured us by so many fine promises about divorce, can have repented of your purpose ... to hinder the consummation of it'. He had 'broken and spoiled' their plans and betrayed Anne by pretending 'to enter into my interests only to discover the secrets of my heart' and only the fact that she had believed him sincere restrained her 'in avenging myself'.

That autumn, Wolsey was stripped of his titles, offices and properties, including Hampton Court, although he was permitted to remain Archbishop of York. The great seal was taken from him by the dukes of Norfolk and Suffolk at 6 p.m. on 17 October in the gallery of his house at Westminster, and an inventory was made of his goods.[7] According the the report of the newly arrived Imperial ambassador, Eustace Chapuys, Henry 'returned to Greenwich by water secretly, in order to see them, and found them much greater than he expected'. With him to look over Wolsey's confiscated wealth were '"*sa mye*" [his darling, Anne Boleyn], her mother, and a gentleman of his chamber' who might have been Sir Henry Norris.[8] Henry also summoned the first sitting of what would become his Reformation parliament, which would debate his great matter and his relationship with Rome for the next six years.

A week later, in the privy chamber and Greenwich, the king formally handed the great seal to Thomas More, 'a good servant of the queen', who assumed the job of Lord Chancellor. Writing pitifully to Henry, Wolsey cried 'daily to you for mercy', and beseeched the king 'that you will not think it proceeds from any mistrust I have in your goodness, nor that I would molest you by my importunate suit. The same comes of my ardent desire, that, next unto God, I covet nothing so much in this world as your favour and forgiveness. The remembrance of my folly, with the sharp sword of your displeasure, have so penetrated my heart.' Cardinal Jean du Bellay visited Wolsey 'in his troubles' and judged him to be 'the greatest example of fortune that one could see'. He wept and prayed, with his countenance having 'lost half its animation' so that even his enemies 'could not help pitying him, yet they do not desist from persecuting him to the last'. He was prepared to 'give up everything, to his shirt, and to go and live in a hermitage, if this king will not keep him in disfavour'.[9] But it was the king's rising favourite whom Wolsey had most offended., as he acknowledged, writing that 'none dares speak to the king on his part for fear of Madame Anne's displeasure'.[10] Finally, on 27 October, Wolsey was 'definitively condemned by the council, declared a rebel, and guilty of high treason for having obtained a legatine bull, whereby he had conferred many benefices in the king's patronage. He has been deprived of his dignities, his goods confiscated, and himself sentenced to prison until the king shall decide.'[11] He would die on his way to his trial the following year.

Through the final months of 1529, the king showered his lover with gifts, making Anne increasingly look like a queen. As the first of his publicly acknowledged mistresses, she must look the part now that the eyes of the court, the country and, indeed, Europe were watching them. The Privy Purse expenses for November and December 1529 show that 12s 8d was paid to Cecil for a yard and a quarter of purple velvet for Mistress Anne, followed by Henry paying £217 9s 8d to Walter Walshe for 'certain stuff by him prepared' for Anne and settling the bills of his jewellers, with over £24 going to John Crepye and a similar sum to William Hoyson.[12] On 29 November, a third jeweller named Morgan Fenwolf received £26 16s 3d for nine-and-three-quarter ounces of Paris work. December saw a further jeweller's payment of £10 for a ruby and an emerald and £100 went to Cornelius Hayes, Henry's goldsmith.[13] A more substantial reward was soon to follow, though, as on 9 December Anne's father was elevated to the status of Viscount Rochford, Earl of Wiltshire.

In spite of this, the pretence of harmony was being maintained at court. For Catherine, at least, it was proving an impossibly difficult arrangement and, when Henry dined with her on St Andrew's Day, 30 November, her composure snapped. Reported by Chapuys to Charles, the queen 'said to him that she had long been suffering the pains of Purgatory on earth, and that she was very badly treated by his refusing to dine with and visit her in her apartments'. Henry replied that she had no cause to complain, as she was 'mistress of her household' and could 'do as she pleased'; furthermore, that he had been busy recently cleaning up the mess that Wolsey had left. He added that 'as to his visiting her in her apartments and partaking of her bed, she ought to know that he was not her legitimate husband, as innumerable doctors and canonists, all men of honour and probity, and even his own almoner, Doctor Lee, who had once known her in Spain, were ready to maintain'. Catherine replied that Henry knew full well 'that the principal cause alleged for the divorce did not really exist, as he himself had owned upon more than one occasion'.[14] She went on to challenge him that 'for each doctor or lawyer who might decide in your favour and against me, I shall find 1,000 to declare that the marriage is good and indissoluble'.[15]

After a 'good deal of talking and disputing', Henry abruptly left Catherine at the table and headed off to sup with Anne, 'very disconcerted and downcast'. According to Chapuys, Anne reproached him with the words,

Did I not tell you that whenever you disputed with the queen she was sure to have the upper hand? I see that some fine morning you will succumb to her reasoning, and that you will cast me off. I have been waiting long, and might in the meanwhile have contracted some advantageous marriage, out of which I might have had issue, which is the greatest consolation in this world; but alas! farewell to my time and youth spent to no purpose at all.

It is difficult to know how accurate these recorded speeches are, passed on second or third hand and composed for an audience hostile to Anne, but there may be something in the sentiment expressed about her age and the passage of time. At well past the age that many women were already mothers, to their 'greatest consolation', and with two broken engagements behind her, Anne must have been conscious that her 'time and youth' were passing while the great matter was being debated. By her age, Catherine had already had five pregnancies. There may well have been times when, in spite of Henry's attentions and her position at his side, she experienced doubts about her future.

This may have been the occasion that prompted Henry to send Catherine away from court. The queen was obliged to leave Greenwich and go to Richmond, although she was permitted to return for the Christmas season. Presiding over the usual festivities, Henry showed Catherine 'more consideration than was his wont', with Anne not making an appearance, although the queen had, by this time, 'lost all hope of bringing him to a sense of right and duty'.[16] 'She never could think that her affairs would fall so low as they are at present. She always fancied that the king, after pursuing his course for some time, would turn away, and yielding to his conscience, would change his purpose as he had done at other times, and return to reason.'[17] Sadly, from this point, Catherine had to face the unpalatable truth that Henry considered their marriage to be over. Through her remaining six years, life would only become more and more unhappy.

38

The Other Women, 1525–32

> *My lyf not chast, my lyvyng bestyall*
> *I forced wydowes, maydens I did deflower*
> *All was oon to me, I spared non at all*
> *My appetite was all women to devoure*
> *My study was bothe day and hower*
> *My unlawful lechery, howe I might it fulfil*
> *Sparyng no woman to have on her my wyll*[1]

After the failure of the Blackfriars court, Henry and Anne would have to wait three more years before becoming man and wife. Assuming that their daughter Elizabeth arrived after a full-term pregnancy of around nine months, her conception can be dated to December 1532, pinpointing the latest moment in time when Anne could have yielded up her virginity. This would assume that she conceived straight away, as Catherine had done in 1509, but Anne was in her early thirties at this point, so may have been sharing Henry's bed for longer before she conceived. Anne's virginity also had a political dimension – as the future mother of an heir to the throne, she must be seen to be chaste and able to swear the effect of her own purity.

This still leaves a stretch of seven years, from 1525 until the autumn of 1532, when a number of questions need to be asked about Henry's sexuality. If we accept that he was not sleeping with Anne, does it then follow that he was chaste, that he abstained from intercourse completely, for the entirety of that time? Did King Henry VIII not have sex at all between the ages of thirty-four and forty-one? If we reject this as unlikely, even ludicrous, considering the medical and cultural mores of his day, then just whom was the king sleeping with?

These are the years from which the most rumours of royal bastards seem to stem. All are worthy of investigation, even though some sound more plausible than others, but regardless of the individual details of each case it remains that not a single one of these children were publicly acknowledged by Henry. This could be taken as an indication that he was unsure of their paternity, or that they were born to lower-class women and therefore would not be a desirable liaison to admit to, or of sufficient status to provide him with an alternative heir. Equally, Henry already had a perfectly good illegitimate male heir in Henry Fitzroy, whom he anticipated making his sole inheritor in the event of Princess Mary being married abroad. The boy's premature death in 1536 left Henry without a son for fifteen months before the birth of Prince Edward. It is possible that some of these claims to royal blood date from this period of uncertainty, when existing or imaginary bastards sought to exploit the vacancy beside the throne.

The first of three possible offspring of Henry's casual encounters was born in around 1530. The birthdate of Thomas Stukley is usually calculated backwards from his employment as a standard bearer in 1547, a job that was typically given to a boy in his mid- to late teens, although earlier dates have also been suggested. This timeframe would date his conception to the period of Henry's official abstinence between Catherine and Anne, while the earliest theoretical date suggested, 1520, would place his conception between Henry's affairs with Bessie Blount and Mary Boleyn. Officially, he was the son of Sir Hugh Stukley, a knight of the royal body of Affeton Castle in Devon, and Jane, daughter of Sir Lewis Pollard, who owned a number of local properties including the Manor of Oakford, thirteen miles away. Jane and Sir Hugh were married around 1520 and had a large family; quite how rumours of royal paternity were particularly attached to one of these children in preference to any of the others is not clear, although Thomas' colourful past is likely to have been an influential factor. Henry is reputed to have stayed at Affeton Castle, and presumably it would be during one of these encounters that Thomas would have been conceived. The possibility of Henry receiving hospitality from Sir Hugh and then quietly bedding his wife certainly follows the interpretation of the king as an irrepressible, irresistible force. It seems unlikely that Sir Hugh did not know what was going on under his roof, or that he found out soon afterwards, if this encounter did in fact take place. Might he have been complicit in the encounter, or unable to refuse even if he opposed it? It is just as impossible to imagine what negotiations were made between host, wife and king as it is to prove the authenticity of the story.

Rumours of his royal paternity made an appearance during Thomas Stukley's lifetime, recorded by a James Fitzgerald who, after making his acquaintance in Rome, recorded that he was 'said by some to be an illegitimate son of Henry VIII, King of England', although he also recorded at least two other stories about his parentage. A 'Sir Thomas Stucley' is mentioned along with Lewis Pollard in the 1524 collections of the Subsidy Tax for 1524, and again his servant was rewarded 2s for the gift of a buck, but this would be far too early given his potential birthdates.[2] However, the grant of livery of lands in Thorne, Devon, to 'Thomas Stucley' in June 1526 are more likely to relate to him. Possibly placed in the household of Sir Charles Brandon at a young age, Stukley's subsequent life was a controversial mix of mercenary warfare, imprisonment, debt, piracy and scandal. He is reputed to have referred to Elizabeth I as his sister. Such figures attract rumour, even consciously court and create it. It is rather a chicken-and-egg scenario to question whether his life evolved as it did because of his rumoured paternity or whether his actions led to certain speculations. His claim appears to have rested on his physical likeness to the king and the poems and plays written about him after his death at the Battle of Alcazar. Setting Thomas aside, little more is known about Jane Pollard, the woman who may have been the king's lover.

Slightly more is known about Mary Berkeley, the mother of John Perrot, who was reputed to have been another of Henry's illegitimate offspring. Having been born around 1511 to James Berkeley and Susan, *née* Fitzalan, Mary had been orphaned by the age of ten and went to live with her uncle at Berkeley Castle in Gloucestershire. She was married to his ward Thomas Perrot in around 1526, when she was about fifteen, and bore him three children, including a son, John, in November 1528. This would place the boy's conception in early February of the same year, after Henry had been committed to Anne for over a year. This is not a point against the possibility of the king's paternity; rather it would fit the scenario of a temporary liaison after Anne had been keeping a frustrated Henry at bay.

Although there have been claims that Mary was a member of Catherine of Aragon's household, no evidence survives to support this claim and she appears to have been mostly at the family seat in Pembrokeshire, Wales, rather than at court. On 13 February 1528 Henry was at Greenwich, from where he wrote to James V of Scotland and the Earl of Angus, but there is always the possibility that Mary travelled to court or that she and the king happened to meet at some other place, by accident or design. Sir Thomas Perrot was reputedly a great hunter and had been knighted by him in 1526, so it is possible that Henry encountered him and his wife again through their mutual passion. Mary remarried when her son was around five and her new husband bought the boy's wardship. Again, Thomas' secret identity turned around his resemblance to Henry and the colourful story that the king intervened to prevent him being punished for brawling within one of the royal palaces.[3] John went on to have a similar series of brushes with piracy, debt, deception and scandal to that of Thomas Stukley. In later life he may have invented, embellished or resurrected the story of his birth in an attempt to prevent his execution for high treason.

A third illegitimate child reputed to the king, Ethelreda, Esther or Audrey Malte, has the most unusual story. Her mother was a Joanna or Joan Dingley, possibly a royal laundress, on whom Henry fathered a child in the late 1520s or early 1530s before asking one of the cutters in his great wardrobe, John Malte, to claim her paternity as his own. Plenty of evidence exists for the career of Malte through the previous decade and for the life of Ethelreda, who went on to marry in 1547, when she was probably in her late teens or around the age of twenty. The case for her paternity rests on a royal grant she received on 17 January that year, just eleven days before Henry's death, by which 'John Malte, tailor, and Awdrye his base daughter' received a large £1,312.[4] It may be that Henry made deathbed provision for his illegitimate child, or that he was rewarding a loyal servant.

Joanna Dingley is more difficult to trace. If she was working as a laundress to Henry VIII she would have been the only woman within his exclusively male household, but she certainly was not the chief napery laundress mentioned in the 1526 Eltham Ordinances, who was responsible for washing the king's table linen. Detailed provision was made then for an Anne Harris, who was to deliver daily seven long and seven short breakfast cloths, eight towels and three dozen napkins, and to remove that which had been soiled the previous day. She was to 'discretely' peruse and view 'the stuff how it hath been used and ordered and return any substandard pieces to the offices of the counting house'. She was given two standard chests, one for clean and one for dirty linen, and given allowances of wood and soap.[5] No mention is made in the ordinances of any assistants of Anne's, although these may have operated behind the scenes. It is also possible that Joanna served the queen, as Catherine's laundress for 1526 was listed as receiving 2*d* a day and bouche of court. However, it is far more likely that any laundress the king would attempt to seduce would be the one washing his shirts and underclothing, who therefore had access to his privy chambers and knew the intimate secrets of his body. No record of Joanna exists in that department either.

If we reject the premise that Henry was chaste for seven years, then he had to be sleeping with someone. Given his romantic devotion to Anne and his intention to make her his wife, it is likely that he did exactly what many noblemen of his day did and sought physical relationships on a one-off basis with women of the lower classes. It is likely that he would not have wanted Anne to be aware of this, so such encounters would have taken place either while they were apart, on occasions when she was at Hever, or when he was a guest in the houses of courtiers or friends. Once she had moved into apartments close to his the opportunities would have been less, so the king may have sought out women with whom he had a reason to be in intimate contact, such as a laundress. Elements of plausibility in all these stories mean there is a fair chance that they represent the types of encounters Henry had in 1525–32, but the lack of definite evidence prevents them from being asserted as fact.

There is also the possibility that Anne and Henry deceived the world when it came to their intimate relationship, and continue to do so. After all, no one knows for certain what happened between them when the bedroom door closed. In 1528 she had her own suites at Greenwich and in London, and the following year she was granted rooms in Hampton Court, despite the fact that it was 1531 when Anne moved into lodgings adjoining the king's, allowing a degree of access that was usually reserved for spouses. In this scenario they could either have used contraception until such a point that they felt secure in their imminent marriage or, more credibly, Anne simply may not have fallen pregnant until winter 1532, whereupon Henry married her. Given the ardour of his letters in 1526–27 and the years they lived with adjoining rooms, coupled with Anne's premarital pregnancy, the evidence actually points towards the fact that they were lovers, whether consistently or infrequently. The early nineteenth-century historian Lingard certainly believed that they were, citing their physical proximity and living arrangements as an indicator that they were living as man and wife:

> We find the king attempting to seduce a young and beautiful female. To overcome her objections, he promises her marriage, as soon as he can obtain a divorce from his wife. The cause is brought into court: but the delay of the judges irritates his impatience. He expels his wife, he sends for the object of his affections from the house of her father, he allots her apartments contiguous to his own, he orders his courtiers to pay to her all the respect due to the queen, he suffers her to interfere in matters of state and to claim a share in the distribution of favours. Thus they live for three years under the same roof. We find them taking their meals together. If the king rides out, we are sure to discover her by his side, if he changes his residence, she accompanies him and when he crosses the sea, he cannot leave her behind him. Let the reader couple all this with the amorous temperament of Henry, with his impetuous disposition, with his indelicate allusions in his correspondence with her and he will not want evidence to teach him in what relation they lived.[6]

The true nature of Anne's premarital relationship with Henry cannot be established, but through 1531 the Privy Purse accounts give a glimpse of their life together. The year started for her at Greenwich, with games and pleasures: over £200 was spent by Henry on gambling at dice or cards, in addition to the £450 he lost at dominos; £80 11s was paid to the milliner Christopher for 134 pearls and an emerald; 10s went to the gardener from Richmond for bringing sweet water and fruit, 50s to Charles Brandon's minstrels; and £4 15s for hay and oats to feed the deer in the park. On 21 January, they removed to Wolsey's old palace of York Place. There, 30s was spread among four poor people 'whom the king healed of their diseases'; the royal horses were also healed, at a cost of £8 15s, and Henry lost over £4 at bowls. The following month, Henry incurred expenses in being rowed back and forth between Hampton Court, Greenwich, Battersea and York Place; he paid £16 4s for three tons of white wine and over £3 for six Mass books and velvet to cover them. In March, servants received small rewards for bringing him gifts of baked lampreys, fresh salmon and orange pies. Those bringing him letters were given 7s or 10s, labourers who cleaned the alleys in the park at Windsor got 10s 8d, while Hugh Latimer, soon to be Bishop of Worcester, was paid £5 for preaching 'before the king on the second Sunday of Lent'.[7]

That April, the court removed to the Manor of the More in Hertfordshire, another property that had passed from Wolsey's possession into the hands of the Crown. There George Boleyn and Francis Weston played four games of tennis, at each of which George won £4 from the king, and a servant of Anne's was paid 3s 4d for catching a hare. Three pairs of virginals were brought to the More for £3 20s and Thom, the jester, was given £25 for his livery. In May, Catherine was feeling more confident, encouraged by support from Charles and reports that Anne was unpopular among the common people and much of the court. She may have influenced Henry's spending that month, with 10s going to one of her servants for bringing Henry his spaniel, Cut, and 4s 8d to a servant of her gentle-woman Maud, Lady Parr, who brought the king a coat. Another dog, named Ball, got lost in Waltham Forest and was brought back, earning the man 5s. A servant of Lord Berkeley brought fresh sturgeon to York Place for 40s, establishing a further link with the family of Mary, mother of John Perrot. Jasper, the gardener of Beaulieu, once the residence of Mary and William Carey, received 6s 8d for bringing the king strawberries. Anne was not forgotten, as the bills of her tailor and skinner were paid and 23s 4d was given to a man named Scawesby for her to have bows, arrows, shafts, broadheads, bracer and a shooting glove.[8] In June, she also received cherries from a servant of the Mayor of London, four bows for 13s 4d and one of her servants was given money to pass on to another at Penshurst Place.

Summer was a season of abundance and more gifts arrived for the king wherever he happened to be: cherries, lettuces, cheeses, cakes, capons, bucks, herbs, artichokes, cucumbers, carp, partridges, pears, puddings and a glass of rosewater, brought from Guildford to Windsor, for which the bearer was rewarded with 5s. Henry was at

Hampton Court on 14 August to receive philberts and damsons from the gardeners of Richmond and at Easthampstead hunting lodge in Berkshire three days later, where he received fruit from York Place. A day later he had moved on to Ashridge Priory, where a servant was rewarded 7s 6d for bringing a buck and another got 8s 4d for making dogs draw water from a well. At Ampthill in Buckinghamshire at the end of the month, the king recompensed the keeper and his wife 10s for fishing and oranges and lemons reached him at Hertford on 6 September. Anne received linen cloth costing £10 but had to pay out 10s for a cow killed by greyhounds she owned.

In November 1530, Catherine fell ill at Richmond and remained behind there when Henry and Anne went to York Place and then on to Hampton Court. The news also reached London of the death of Cardinal Wolsey, who had passed away at Leicester, following his arrest. It meant there would be no trial. The mingling of his loyalties and transitions of his career are glimpsed in an inventory of the goods at Cardinal College, Oxford, which included a lockable jewel in the shape of a blue heart, bearing the letters H and K in white, with two hands holding a heart and a hanging pearl, which had been given to him by the queen; garters decorated with gold castles, roses and pomegranates; a white falcon on a mount, with a crown and ruby about its neck, which was Anne's symbol; a pomander decorated with 'H and K', a crimson satin bag embroidered with the same initials and one of black velvet, sewn with a pomegranate.[9]

That same month, Anne was given £20 to redeem a 'jewel which my Lady Mary Rochford [Carey] had' and almost twenty yards of crimson satin were purchased for her at 16s the yard. Anne and Henry may well have been discussing the finer points of canon law, as three separate individuals were rewarded for bringing the king's books from York Place to Hampton and another was paid 5s for making an inventory of the titles. By this point, they had already received the learned opinions of the Universities of Orleans, Paris, Angers, Padua, Bourges, Bologna and Toulouse and Henry had commissioned treaties and studies.

In December, Anne received a payment of 20s in silver, £5 for 'playing money' and £13 for linen cloth, for 'shirts and other necessaries', while £80 went to the skinner Adyngton for the furring of her gowns. The Privy Purse records further expenses that might have contributed towards Anne's gifts that season, with Italian jeweller John Baptist receiving an initial 1,225 crowns, followed by 1,601 for pearls and an Alart Plymmer being paid a huge 7,437 crowns for various jewels. Anne received £100 to contribute towards the purchase of gifts she would distribute at New Year.

Catherine had recovered and arrived at Greenwich in time for the Christmas celebrations and those at Twelfth Night, dining with Henry and sitting beside him in estate in the great hall, 'where as were divers interludes, rich masks and disportes, and after that a great banquet'. Briefly, the appearance of royal harmony was resumed. However, Anne was not going to accept defeat, as Chapuys explained to Charles on 1 January 1531:

I have just heard from a well-informed man that this marriage will undoubtedly be accomplished in this Parliament, and that they expect easily to pacify your Majesty. I cannot tell upon what they rest this expectation, as I have always told them distinctly the opposite, and shall do still before the game is concluded.

The lady [Anne Boleyn] feels assured of it. She is braver than a lion. She said to one of the queen's ladies that she wished all the Spaniards in the world were in the sea; and on the other replying, that, for the honour of the Queen, she should not say so, she said that she did not care anything for the Queen, and would rather see her hanged than acknowledge her as her mistress.[10]

39

Rejected Queen, 1531–32

In days of old here Ampthill's towers were seen
The mournful refuge of an injured Queen;
Here flowed her pure but unavailing tears,
Here blinded zeal sustain'd her sinking years,
Yet Freedom hence her radiant banner wav'd
And Love aveng'd a realm by priests enslaved
From Catherine's wrongs a nation's bliss was spread
And Luther's light from Henry's lawless bed.[1]

By the summer of 1531, the painful triangle of Catherine, Henry and Anne had reached an impasse. Something had to give and, inevitably, it was the queen. Recently her situation had appeared to improve, with Henry dining with her more frequently and visiting her chamber, in order to give the appearance that he was not separating from her through choice. Chapuys was able to report on 14 May that 'there was nothing but courtesy and kindness on the part of the king, although the following day he refused to consent to Catherine's request that Princess Mary visit her mother at Greenwich, saying that the pair might meet elsewhere.[2] Then, late on a June evening, she had been interrupted in her chambers shortly before bedtime by a delegation of thirty noblemen, who made a final attempt to persuade her to submit to her husband's demands. Catherine replied that she would 'never consent to it as long as she lived' and would continue to obey her ultimate sovereign, the Pope. By the middle of July, the court was at Windsor. Henry and Anne rose early one morning and rode away to Woodstock, ostensibly on a hunting trip. Catherine was left behind, without having had a chance to say goodbye. She would never see her husband again.

Woodstock was one of the six largest royal properties at the time and could easily have accommodated the queen and her household in a way that the smaller houses could not. There were two courtyards, the great outer one measuring 3,339 metres squared,[3] around a fountain of heraldic beasts. The inner courtyard was still very large, if a bit smaller than its partner, measuring 2,023 feet squared and overlooking the tennis courts and privy garden. A late sixteenth-century survey counted ninety rooms.[4] It was therefore a conscious choice to leave Catherine behind, whether or not Henry had intended it to be final. The summer days passed with Anne and Henry engaged in hunting and hawking, always side by side, as Chapuys reported.

From this point onwards, Catherine was shunted along a string of increasingly smaller and more uncomfortable properties, with her household gradually scaled down. When Henry wanted to return to Windsor for hunting that October, she was asked to leave and occupy the More, in Hertfordshire, while Mary, who had been staying with her, was sent away to Richmond. A possession of the Abbot of St Albans, the More was a sizeable property, built around two court-yards, considered by the French ambassador Jean de Bellay in 1527 to be more impressive than Hampton Court. Catherine's new home had been considerably expanded by Wolsey during his ownership, with formal gardens and new wings being added to enclose the existing inner court. The queen's watching chamber overlooked the moat and privy gardens, with the long gallery that led down to the entrance gate.[5] According to the visiting Venetian Mario Savorgnano, it was large enough for her to retain a court of around two hundred people, although she confided in Chapuys that she would rather have been locked in the Tower, as then at least everyone would have been aware of her misfortune. She wrote to Charles that her 'tribulations are so great, my life so disturbed by the plans daily invented to further the king's wicked intention' and although she had offended neither 'God nor the king' they continued to treat her in a way that 'is enough to shorten ten lives'.[6]

That month Henry's councillors visited her again to persuade her on bended knee to resolve the matter amicably. Again, Catherine was adamant, answering with 'sweetness and frankness'[7] but repeating her previous arguments in favour of the validity of her marriage and queenship. Almost all her attendants were present and she spoke up, in order for them to hear, leaving scarcely a dry eye in the room.[8] As Chapuys related, 'on retiring they told her that the king would give her a choice either of staying where she was, or retiring to a small house of his, or to an abbey. The queen replied, it was not for her to choose, and that wherever the king commanded her, were it even to the fire, she would go.' Catherine's willingness to embrace martyrdom demonstrates her complete belief in her cause and her absolute refusal to relinquish her anointed position. She was obeying a higher authority than her husband. However, his wishes still counted for something, as on 13 November an awkward situation arose when both Henry and Catherine attended a feast for the sergeants-at-arms at Ely House. The king managed to avoid his queen by insisting they dine in separate rooms and Catherine went away again without having seen him.[9]

Catherine was still at the More by the time Christmas arrived in 1531. Henry observed the season with Anne at Greenwich 'but all men said there was no mirth ... because the queen and the ladies were absent'.[10] In the list of New Year's gifts for 1532, Sir Thomas Boleyn and George, Lord Rochford, received gilt bowls, goblets and cups, and Bessie, Lady Tailboys, Mary Rochford and Anne's mother were given gifts from a range that included gilt cruets, bottles, cups, salts and goblets. In return, Anne's parents gave their future son-in-law a box of black velvet with a steel glass set in gold and a coffer of needlework containing three silver collars and three gold, while the widowed Mary Boleyn gave Henry a shirt with a black collar. In the records, a space was left by the queen's name. For the first time this year, Henry gave Catherine no gift and had forbidden her to send him anything for Christmas. However, he had not mentioned anything about New Year, so Catherine sent him a gold cup. It was intercepted before the official presentation and therefore went unrecorded in the privy accounts. Henry returned it to her with the message that, because they were no longer married, it was not an appropriate gift for her to have sent.[11] Anne gave Henry a set of rich and exotic boar spears or darts from the Pyrenees and 'in return, he gave her a room hung with cloth of gold and silver, and crimson satin with rich embroideries. She is lodged where the queen used to be, and is accompanied by almost as many ladies as if she were queen.'[12]

In May 1532, Henry ordered Catherine to leave the Manor of the More and move to Hatfield, in Hertfordshire, 'a house much farther off than where she now is, and with bad accommodation. The queen is vexed, because the house belongs to the Bishop of Lincoln, who has been the principal promoter of these practices' but, as Montfalconet pointed out to Charles, she was retaining her dignity: 'The queen, although surrounded by vile persons devoted to the king, has never in any way given any occasion for slander, and even those who endeavour to damage her in the estimation of the king are struck with admiration for her virtue.'[13] Hatfield had been built around a central courtyard in 1497 by John Morton, Bishop of Ely, with its impressive decorative red brickwork and banqueting hall, and would later be used as a home for Princess Mary and the rest of Henry's children. In 1532, though, it represented the increasing isolation of a queen who was considered an inconvenience.

That month, support for Catherine grew. It was said that 'all love the queen' and her supportive clergymen, including John Fisher, Bishop of Rochester, 'preached daily in her favour', even though some ran the risk of arrest, with her chaplain Thomas Abel publishing a book, *Invicta Veritas*, in her favour, and Chancellor Thomas More resigning his position over Henry's proposed supremacy over the Pope. Even Charles Brandon, the king's closest companion and brother-in-law, whose wife's dislike of Anne Boleyn was an open secret, declared that it was time for Henry to be talked out of his folly. The turning tide must have been uncomfortable for Anne. In July, she and Henry headed north on an extended hunting trip that included a five-day stay at Waltham, where the French ambassador accompanied Anne hunting and watching the deer run. Henry was concerned for their privacy, as later Privy Purse payments show 40s being paid 'to the smith, for bolts and rings to the king's chamber door all the time of the progress'.[14] Was this more to repel potential intruders, or to keep the secret of what was going on within? Although 'great preparations' had been made, the trip was cut short and they returned to London. According to Chapuys, 'some say the cause is that, in two or three places that he passed through, the people urged him to take back the queen, and the women insulted the Lady [Anne]'.[15] Yet Henry and Anne were planning a far more significant conquest, in the form of Francis I.

40

Calais, 1532

To bed them were they brought
That night on his lady mild
As God would, he gat a child
But they of it wist nought.[1]

On Sunday 1 September at Windsor, Anne Boleyn was created Marchioness of Pembroke. She was conveyed by a party of noblemen and the castle's officers-at-arms into the king's presence for the honour designed to prepare her for the trip to France. The whole process mirrored the rituals of the coronation. Anne's cousin, Mary Howard, daughter of the Duke of Norfolk and soon to become the wife of young Henry Fitzroy, carried the coronet and a crimson mantle lined with ermine. Anne wore a corresponding crimson surcoat with straight sleeves, also with ermine, and with her hair traditionally loose. She knelt before Henry to receive the patent of her creation and another of £1,000 a year. Then, no doubt exhilarated by the significance of her new status, she bade the king a dignified thanks and 'returned to her chamber'.[2]

It was important for Anne to look the part in France, to be accepted as Henry's consort and, to this effect, new clothes and jewels were ordered for her wardrobe. Back in June, £4 had been paid for thirteen yards of black satin to make a cloak for Anne, with black velvet for edging and lining. A further thirteen yards of black satin went to make her a nightgown, at 8s a yard, with taffeta, buckram and velvet for its lining,[3] and over sixteen yards of green damask were acquired for John Skut for her use, at the same price. Perhaps they planned their trip enjoying the suckets and marmalade brought to the king by a servant of Cromwell's, or listening to the singing of the nightingales that had been given to them by George Boleyn.[4] However, there were also a number of old jewels that Henry and Anne had in their sights.

In late September, Catherine received a message from the Duke of Norfolk stating that Henry wished her to return her jewels, which were needed to adorn Anne for the coming visit. Her collection of gems included some state pieces, gifts from her husband and inheritances from other family members, but also some that she had brought with her from Spain. They were far more than just wealth; their possession was a critical indicator of status and a connection to her past, both as queen and the legacy of her parents; they were also heirlooms for her daughter. Catherine responded with righteous passion, refusing to 'give up my jewels for such a wicked purpose as that of ornamenting a person who is the scandal of Christendom'. She would only relinquish them if Henry issued a direct order, so Henry did. A record dated 24 September shows a further removal of jewels from storage at Greenwich to the king at Hampton Court, including a gold chain, Spanish fashion, enamelled red, white and black; an excess of diamonds, rubies, emeralds, pearls, sapphires and garnets were received by Cromwell a week later.[5] It was another humiliation for Catherine in a long line of humiliations; she was permitted to keep a small gold cross that reputedly contained a shard of wood from the real cross, but the knowledge that her jewels had gone to her rival, who was about to be feasted and treated as a queen in France, must have made a bitter day indeed for her.

Henry and Anne were excited about their forthcoming trip, which represented a significant recognition of Anne's status in the eyes of Europe. Her acceptance by Francis as Henry's consort, as Catherine's replacement, would be a final step towards making her Queen of England, with a political and diplomatic role. If not exactly an old friend, Francis was well known to them both and his own understanding of the complexity of marital relations would ease Anne's foreign debut. As Chapuys wrote, 'the king seems never to have desired anything so much as this journey, for he does not care to talk of anything else. No one else wishes it except the lady, and the people talk of it in a strange fashion.' It is understandable that the trip set tongues wagging, only twelve years after Henry had departed in pomp with Catherine by his side, yet the king's excitement suggests that they may have intended this to be an important private step as well as a public one. If they had not already slept together by this point, this might have been the moment he, or they both, selected in advance of their trip; perhaps they went as far as to plan their wedding. Catherine believed they would take the opportunity to marry, although Chapuys thought it unlikely, as Anne would want it to be done by the book: 'The queen was very much afraid that the king would marry the Lady at this meeting; but the Lady has assured some person in whom she trusts, that, even if the king wished, she would not consent, for she wishes it to be done here in the place where queens are wont to be married and crowned.'[6]

One occurrence in the late summer might have removed the final barrier to their restraint. In August, Catherine's staunch supporter Archbishop William Warham had died, leaving the See of Canterbury vacant. Henry's choice for the job was the pro-Boleyn Reformist Thomas Cranmer. He was travelling through Italy as ambassador to Charles' court when he received a letter on 1 October 1532, informing him that he had been appointed. He would have known what Henry's expectations of him were. If the Pope would not give Henry the divorce wanted, he was resolved to break with Rome and head his own Church of England, where all such matters would be referred to his sympathetic appointees.

While one barrier was removed, another potential problem arose. This was the moment that Mary Talbot, now Countess of Northumberland, chose to seek an end to her unhappy marriage to Henry Percy. Relations between the couple had broken down in the late 1520s, with both making allegations against the other ranging from unkindness and deception to the claims made by Mary's father than Percy might attempt to poison his wife. The countess's pretext for divorce was her husband's pre-contract with Anne Boleyn, and, regardless of whether this was entirely privately motivated or was employed by the Aragon faction to prevent Henry from marrying Anne, it might undermine any union he had with Anne in the same way that his grandfather Edward IV's marriage had been. Henry could take no chances and summoned Percy to his presence to undergo a rigorous questioning, which the king himself led. The countess's request was denied on the basis that there had been no pre-contract, to which Percy swore an oath, undermining his own chance of gaining freedom from a woman he had reluctantly wed. The couple lived apart after this, until Percy's death finally freed Mary, who lived until 1572.

On 10 October, Henry and Anne arrived at Dover and stayed overnight in the castle. Early the next morning they set sail in a ship named *Swallow*, arriving in Calais for an 'honourable reception'. They were lodged at the Exchequer, where Henry and Catherine had stayed in 1520, and awaited the arrival of Francis. Dressed in a coat of riches, 'in braids of gold laid loose on russet velvet and set with trefoils full of pearls and stones', Henry met the equally gorgeous

Francis, who had chosen a coat of crimson velvet with the gold lining pulled through the slashes. Anne remained behind in Calais, awaiting their return, with her thirty of her ladies, including her sister-in-law, Jane Boleyn, for company. In a twist of fate, Anne's former admirer Thomas Wyatt was also present – perhaps somewhat reluctantly if his poem on the occasion is to be trusted – but he would have accompanied Henry rather than remained behind with Anne. Two weeks passed before the kings rode triumphantly back and Francis was lodged in the Inn of the Staple, in rooms hung with tissue and velvet, embroidered with flowers, where he dined on 'all manner of flesh, fowl, spice, venison, both of fallow deer and red deer, and as for wine, they lacked none'.[7] Francis sent Anne a diamond as a gift of friendship and welcome but his wife was less warm. The widowed French king had been married to Eleanor of Austria on 4 July 1530, a daughter of Philip the Handsome and Joanna and a niece of Catherine of Aragon. Although she had shared a schoolroom with Anne Boleyn in the household of Margaret of Savoy, Eleanor could not now accept her as her aunt's replacement and declined to meet Anne at all during the visit. Another version of her absence has Henry refusing to meet her because of her background and his dislike of Spanish dress, but this would have been a considerable insult to a queen in her regnal country and it is unlikely that the rejection was on the English side, given Henry's keenness to receive the blessing of Francis. Anne suggested that Francis' sister, Marguerite of Angouleme, who she 'ever hath entirely loved', might attend in Eleanor's place, but the new Queen of Navarre was ill and unable to travel.

On Sunday 27 October, when the kings' business was concluded, Anne finally made her international debut as Henry's partner. That night, Francis came to dine with Henry in a chamber hung alternately with panels of silver and gold tissue, with seams covered with embroidered gold, full of pearls and gems. A cupboard with seven shelves displayed plate of gold and gilt, while white silver branches bore chains from which were hung wax lights. Three courses were served, totalling 150 dishes of 'costly and pleasant' food, with the meat dressed in the French style for Francis and in the English styles for Henry. Then, Anne entered the chamber with seven ladies, all masked, wearing crimson tinsel satin with cloth of silver 'lying lose' and caught up in gold laces. Every lady 'took a lord', with Anne partnering Francis, before her identity was revealed.[8] After she removed her mask, the pair talked 'for a space' before the French king retired for the night.

On 29 October, they bid farewell to Francis and prepared to leave Calais. The weather, though, was terrible, with storms making it dangerous to cross the channel and 'such a winde, tempest and thunder that no man could conveniently stir in the streets of Calais'.[9] Waiting for two weeks at the Exchequer in their fine rooms, linked by a connecting door, this may well have been the moment that Henry and Anne consummated their love. If they had not slept together before, this event had been eagerly anticipated for seven years and a lot was riding on it. If Anne had successfully held Henry at bay all that time, protecting the virginity she now yielded to her experienced lover, it must have signified that she felt certain of their future. They finally left Calais at midnight on 12 November and, after a terrible crossing, sailed into Dover early in the morning of 14 November, St Erkenwald's Day. According to Hall and Sanders, they got married the same day, probably in the chapel or their apartments at Dover Castle.

Two months later, when they suspected Anne was pregnant, another ceremony took place on 25 January 1533. This lessens the likelihood of the November wedding, which may have been suggested in order to provide retrospective evidence that their daughter had been conceived within wedlock rather than before it. The January ceremony was a private affair. Cranmer was unaware it had happened until two weeks later, so it was probably Rowland Lee who presided over it at York Place; he was promoted to Bishop of Coventry the following year. It was witnessed by Anne's gentlewoman Anne Savage and Henry's close companions Henry Norris and Thomas Heneage. This momentous step remained a secret from the nation for the time being, but the arrival of the child Anne conceived in late November or early December, would necessitate their love being displayed in the most public of forums.

41

Rise of the Falcon, 1533

Behold and see the Falcon White
How she beginneth her wings to spread
And for our comfort to take her flight
But where will she cease, as you do read?[1]

On Thursday 29 May 1533, a flotilla of boats took to the Thames. The first bore the model of a huge dragon 'continually moving and casting wild fire' across the waves 'and round it, terrible monsters and wild men casting fire, and making hideous noises'.[2] The barge of the mayor followed it, at the head of a fleet of fifty others, hung with banners and gold and silk cloth, bearing dignitaries dressed in the scarlet and crimson robes of office. The sound of hundreds of tiny tinkling bells and the playing of musicians on each barge reached observers on the shore. On the left-hand side of the mayor stood a statue of Anne's emblem of the white falcon, standing high on a mount, dressed in a gold crown and surrounded by red and white roses. In a long procession, they headed downriver towards Greenwich where they moored, played music and waited.

At three o'clock, Anne appeared from the palace dressed in rich cloth of gold and accompanied by her retinue. She entered her barge and the noblemen accompanying her joined the procession in boats of their own to accompany her back along the Thames to the Tower, where they were met by a salute of guns. Henry was awaiting her at the waterside gate and greeted her with a 'loving countenance',[3] before she turned and thanked the mayor and disappeared into the Tower. The following day, Friday, Henry created eighteen new Knights of the Bath, including Francis Weston and Henry Parker, brother of Jane, Anne's sister-in-law. Anne had a day of rest before the ceremonies that would place her at centre of national focus, as Henry's wife and the country's new queen, began again. As she waited in the Tower, watching the hours pass, did she reflect upon the journey that had taken her to this point, from the moment she first attracted the king's attention seven years before? Now she was six months pregnant with the heir he had longed for, a child she hoped would be the future King of England.

On Saturday, Anne left the Tower to process through the streets of London to Westminster. Dressed in his crimson robes and the golden chains of his office, the mayor, Stephen Peacock, rode to greet her, with two footmen clad in red and white damask. The sheriffs rode ahead, along streets that would have been swept, cleaned and sanded, with the pressing crowds railed back on both sides. Next came a company of twelve Frenchmen dressed in blue and yellow velvet, in the employ of the ambassador, Jean de Dinteville, who was immortalised in Holbein's famous memento mori picture that year. Two by two after them came gentlemen and knights, followed by Judges and Knights of the Bath in violet gowns and miniver-lined hoods, before the abbots, bishops, barons, earls, marquises, then Sir Thomas Audley as Lord Chancellor, Thomas Cranmer as Archbishop of Canterbury, Lord William Howard as deputy marshal during his brother's absence in France and Charles Brandon, Duke of Suffolk, as high constable.

Anne followed, in a vision of white. She sat in a litter of white cloth, pulled by two palfreys covered from head to toe in white damask, and wore a surcoat of white cloth of tissue, an ermine mantle and on her loose hair, a coif with a circlet of rich stones. Sixteen knights carried a canopy of gold cloth and bells above her head. Her ladies wore crimson velvet adorned with gold and tissue, their horses draped in gold. Four chariots followed, of red cloth of gold and white, carrying her female relations and more of her ladies. Thirty more gentlewomen followed and the procession was brought to a close by the guards at the rear.

The first pageant awaited them at Fenchurch, where children dressed as merchants sang verses of welcome in English and French. At Gracechurch Corner, a mountain of white marble flowed with four streams running with Rhenish wine and Apollo and Calliope sat with four muses, playing music and praising Anne in epigrams. At Leadenhall, another mountain under a gold canopy was set with red and white roses, with a crowned falcon, and St Anne 'made a goodly oration to the queen about the fruitfulness of St Anne ... trusting that like fruit should come of her'.[4] The three graces met them by the Conduit of Cornhill and the Cheap was hung with banners of arms and painted images of kings and queens were displayed. At the Cross, Anne was presented with a purse of gold containing a thousand marks, 'which she thankfully accepted with many goodly words'.[5] She received a golden ball from the figure of Mercury at the Little Conduit and wafers inscribed with welcome messages were showered down from St Paul's Gate. Two hundred children recited verses, a male choir sung new ballads and melodious chimes sounded before they reached the final pageant of a tower with four turrets. Anne then retired to Westminster, where the hall was hung with arras and the windows freshly glazed. There, she was served with spices and subtleties, hippocras and wine, before retiring with her ladies to private rooms in Whitehall, where she was dressed, before heading back to spend the night with Henry.

Verses for the occasion were composed by John Leland and Nicholas Udall, who produced the definitive poem celebrating Anne through the use of her falcon device:

This White Falcon,   No bird compare
Rare and geason,   May with this Falcon White.
This bird shineth so bright;   The virtues all,
Of all that are,   No man mortal,

Of this bird can write.
No man earthly
Enough truly
Can praise this Falcon White.
Who will express
Great gentleness
To be in any wight [man];
He will not miss,
But call him this
The gentle Falcon White.
This gentle bird
As white as curd
Shineth both day and night;
Nor far nor near
Is any peer
Unto this Falcon White,
Of body small.
Of power regal,
She is, and sharp of sight;
Of courage hault
No manner fault
Is in this Falcon White,
In chastity,

Excelleth she,
Most like a virgin bright:
And worthy is
To live in bliss
Always this Falcon White.
But now to take
And use her make
Is time, as troth is plight;
That she may bring
Fruit according
For such a Falcon White.
And where by wrong,
She hath fleen long,
Uncertain where to light;
Herself repose
Upon the Rose,
Now may this Falcon White.
Whereon to rest,
And build her nest;
GOD grant her, most of might!
That England may
Rejoice always
In this same Falcon White

The verse is conventional and formulaic, as would be expected, but its imagery highlights the qualities that Henry was most keen to see associated with his new queen in the popular imagination. By stressing the falcon's, and by extension Anne's, incomparability with any other mortal, the poem comments on her worthiness to rule beside Catherine, while the bird's immortal virtue is a reminder that the Church had ruled in favour of her marriage, thus Anne was approved by God. The simile that she was white as curd, and therefore pure, and shone at day and night, suggests an attempt to present Anne's chastity during her daily life and in Henry's bed, 'more like a virgin bright' an irony that cannot have been lost on the crowd as the pregnant queen passed by. Anne had been 'wronged so long' regarding the king's marriage to Catherine that she would now 'herself repose upon the rose', indicating the nature of relief, ease and intimacy in her relationship with Henry, and build a nest there for her fruit.

Early the following morning, between eight and nine, Anne processed from Westminster Hall to the abbey on the traditional ray cloth, surrounded by the nobility and clergymen of England. She wore a surcoat and robe of purple velvet, with the jewelled circlet on her loose hair again and her long train carried by the Duchess of Norfolk. The ladies and gentlemen following were all clad in scarlet, powdered according to their degrees. Anne prostrated herself at the high altar before the waiting Cranmer, then being anointed on the head and breast and having the crown of St Edward briefly placed upon her head before it was substituted for a lighter one of her own. After hearing Mass, she made an offering at the shrine of Edward the Confessor before placing her right hand in that of her father and being led out to the sound of trumpets. The king himself watched the proceedings from a little closet, accessed by the cloisters.⁶ In a break with the usual tradition, the banquet that followed was held at the newly refurbished Whitehall, reputedly Anne's favourite house, as it did not contain lodgings for Catherine.⁷ The new queen was served three courses, each of thirty dishes or over, served by the nobility of Henry's court, including Sir Thomas Wyatt, who took the role of chief ewerer. Anne finally withdrew at six in the evening and the couple were reunited, to share their excitement and joy about the day's proceedings and the forthcoming birth of their child.

It must have been a dark day for Catherine. That March she had been moved to Ampthill in Bedfordshire, forty miles from London, to be out of sight, although not out of mind. Weeks before Anne's coronation, she had been summoned by Thomas Cranmer to attend a court at Dunstable Priory, to be examined regarding her marriages to Arthur and Henry. Catherine had refused to attend. In her absence, the momentous step was taken that Henry, Anne and Catherine had been preoccupied with for so long: as head of the new Church of England, Cranmer fulfilled his king's expectations and pronounced that Henry's first marriage was null and void, making Anne his first legitimate wife. Contrary to the descriptions of popular history, Henry's separation from Catherine was never a divorce; the marriage was annulled on the grounds that it was invalid from the start.

Lord Mountjoy, Catherine's chamberlain since 1512, was charged with the task of delivering the bad news to her. She was no longer to be referred to as queen, but must revert to the title of princess dowager, her status on the death of Arthur. Mountjoy was instructed to inform her that

the king, finding his conscience violated, grudged, and grieved by that unlawful matrimony contracted between him and the Dowager, which was defined and determined by a great number of the most famous universities and clerks of Christendom 'to be detestable, abominable, execrable, and directly against the laws of God and nature,' was therefore lawfully divorced, and by advice of all his nobles, spiritual and temporal, and all the commons of his realm, was married to the lady Anne, who has been crowned Queen.

As the king cannot have two wives he cannot permit the Dowager to persist in calling herself by the name of Queen, especially considering how benignantly and honourably she has been treated in the realm. She is to satisfy herself with the name of Dowager, as prescribed by the Act of Parliament, and must beware of the danger if she attempt to contravene it, which will only irritate the feelings of the people against her. If she be not persuaded by these arguments to avoid the king's indignation, and relent from her vehement arrogancy, the king will be compelled to punish her servants, and withdraw her affection from his daughter. Finally, that as the marriage is irrevocable, and has passed the consent of Parliament, nothing that she can do will annul it, and she will only incur the displeasure of Almighty God and of the king.

Catherine refused to comply. She insisted on still being referred to as queen and scribbled out any written references to her as dowager princess. A number of her staff supported her loyally, stating they had taken an oath to serve her as 'queen' and would be committing perjury if they now referred to her by another title.[8] At the end of July, she was moved on again, from Ampthill to Buckden House in Cambridgeshire, but the local people gathered outside the house as she left, to cheer and encourage her. The loyal Chapuys painted rather a dramatic picture of the occasion – 'they begged her with hot tears to set them to work and employ them in her service, as they were ready to die for the love of her' – but there were other examples of support being publicly demonstrated for Catherine that summer. Across Henry's palaces, the initials H and K were being rapidly cut away and replaced with the onomatopoeic H and A that Anne's enemies found so risible. Buckden Towers was almost thirty miles north-east from Ampthill, representing a step further away from London, from the court and Princess Mary, who had been suffering from ill health for much of that year. While Catherine was separated from her own child, Anne was preparing to welcome hers. If she could bear a boy, the line of Tudor succession would be unquestionably settled and the Boleyns' power inviolable. Writing to celebrate the coronation, John Leland requested that 'heaven bless these nuptials and make her a fruitful mother of men-children. Fruitful Saint Anne bore three men, the offspring of her body ... by her example, may you give us a race to maintain the Faith and the Throne.'⁹ As summer progressed, Anne waited for her son to arrive. Her coronation medal had carried the legend 'the most happy'. And she probably was.

A suite of rooms were prepared for Anne at Greenwich, hung with tapestries depicting the life of St Ursula, and the magnificent bed given in ransom for the Duc d'Alencon in 1515 was moved out of the royal treasury. With Charles' council discussing intervention by force and Pope Clement threatening to excommunicate Henry if he did not leave Anne and return to Catherine, Henry faced a potential international crisis. However, this was kept secret so that it 'may not injure the Lady and endanger a miscarriage'. This also makes it seem unlikely that Henry and Anne quarrelled in the way that the hostile Chapuys reported, presenting the marriage on the verge of collapse after Anne discovered that Henry had been unfaithful. The king's sharp response that she needed to keep her mouth shut, as her betters had done, may be an exaggeration but Henry's infidelity is not completely impossible. If Anne had been a virgin until late autumn 1532, she must have conceived almost at once. Having anticipated their full sexual relationship for seven years, they quickly found themselves in the position of not being able to enjoy this for very long, as Anne's pregnancy advanced. The unborn child, no matter how desired, put an end to their honeymoon period before it had run its course. On 26 August, Anne retired to her rooms and went into labour about ten days later. Chapuys wrote that 'the king, believing in the report of his physicians and astrologers, that his Lady will certainly give him a male heir, has made up his mind to solemnize the event with a pageant and tournament', and horses had been ordered from Flanders.¹⁰ Between three and four o'clock on the afternoon of Thursday 7 September, she was delivered of a healthy child. It was a girl.

42

A Familiar Story, 1533–34

I saw a wound at first susceptible of cure
*But neglected, suffered the bane of long delay*¹

The arrival of a daughter was a setback for Anne, but at least she had survived the process and proven to Henry that she was capable of bearing a healthy heir; all she had to do next was to provide Princess Elizabeth with a brother. Still, the mood of disappointment lingered at court. The celebratory jousts were cancelled and the paperwork announcing the birth was altered to reflect the child's gender.

Elizabeth's christening was held at the Grey Friars' church at Greenwich on 10 September, just three days after her birth. Anne did not attend, as she was still in confinement, recovering from the ordeal, so the arrangements were handed over to the princess's godparents, Archbishop Cranmer and the Marquess of Exeter, the dowager Duchess of Norfolk and the dowager Marchioness of Dorset. Catherine had refused to give permission for the use of a piece of 'rich and gorgeous' ceremonial cloth that had been used at the christening of Princess Mary in 1516, on the grounds that it was her personal possession from Spain. This did little to prevent the pomp of the occasion, though, for which new cloths were ordered along with the silver font from Canterbury, hangings of arras and the formal procession of mayor, aldermen and nobility that accompanied Elizabeth as she was anointed with holy water and prayers said for her future. Then she was returned to her mother, who received her 'joyfully', 'lying on her great French bed with the king at her side'.

It was a less than happy time for Henry's former wife. That December, in an attempt to break her will, Catherine was threatened with another move, this time from Buckden to Somersham Palace in Cambridgeshire. It was a place surrounded by fens and marshes, thought to be very unhealthy, which fed Catherine's fears that her very life was in danger. Indeed, the records of disputes between the bishops of Ely and abbots of Ramsay regarding the site do describe the nearby Crowlodemoor and Hollode as 'marshes',[2] which might explain the place's rapid recent decline. The Tudor palace had been constructed on the site of an earlier manor with extensive gardens by James Stanley, Bishop of Ely, whose 1515 tomb records that 'he builded Sommersome the byshoppe's chief manor'. It quickly fell into disrepair after his death, though, and by 1520 the palace was in a state of disrepair bordering on the dangerous. The next incumbent, Bishop Nicholas West, described it as his 'poor house at Somersham' and in a letter to Wolsey said that he was so surrounded with water that he could not leave and no one could go to him without great danger except by boat. The banks were in 'great danger of collapsing and five hundred men were working on them to prevent the low country there from being drowned, while a further hundred watched at night, in case the water should break through'.[3] In 1533, an accumulation of building material at the property indicates that preparations were being made to patch over the problems in readiness for the royal arrival, but Catherine had other ideas.

When Henry's officials arrived to load her baggage and evict her, the ex-queen locked herself in her room and challenged them to break the door down and carry her away. This was a serious test of her strength and status – there was no guarantee that Henry's servants would not carry out such an act of violence. Yet Catherine's birth, her years as their queen and their respect for her prevailed. Waiting behind her locked door, she heard them ride away. It was a small victory, and rather a pyrrhic one; Catherine would never live at Somersham, but Henry was intent on breaking her by moving her to another, less convenient place. He soon settled on a new location, and this time his former wife was given no choice but to comply.

In May 1534, Catherine was relocated from Buckden House to Kimbolton Castle in Cambridgeshire. This was a far less hazardous residence, even if it was not suitable for a woman of her status. Work in the 1480s had improved the original twelfth-century castle and in 1521 it was described as 'a right goodly lodging contained in little room, within a moat well and compendiously trussed together in due and convenient proportion, one thing with another, with an inner court ... lodgings and offices for keeping a duke's house in stately manner'. However, like Somersham, the place desperately needed some essential repairs 'by occasion of the old wall, the hall there well builded is likely to perish; and through the said castle is and will be great decay, by occasion there is no reparations done.' Sir Richard Wingfield was granted the castle by Henry in 1522 and rebuilt the affected areas as well as adding to the building, allowing Leland to report that 'the Castelle is double dyked and the building of it is ... strong ... [with] new fair lodgings and galleries upon the olde foundations of the Castelle'. Later inventories list a 'great hall with screens, a long gallery, a chapel, dining room, drawing room, upper round chamber, lower round chamber, queen's chamber, and many other rooms, a gatehouse, stables, the Castle Court, Dial Court, the Great Garden, and the Little fountain Garden'. The bedchamber and closet allocated to Catherine are reputed to have survived the castle's later modernisation. With the former queen out of sight, Henry could anticipate the arrival of his next child by Anne. Aware of the impending arrival, it must have been a low point for Catherine, still separated from her daughter, the court and the majority of her servants and friends. As she had before, she found solace in her faith, clinging more closely to the very rituals of Catholicism that the failure of her marriage would undermine.

Far away from Catherine's seclusion, Anne was keen to see her daughter's position secured and her longstanding connections with France led her to seek a match for Elizabeth with one of Francis I's sons. The one-time suggestion of a French match for Princess Mary was long forgotten and the new royal baby was displayed in all her naked glory to the visiting ambassadors at Greenwich. Anne and Henry suggested Prince Charles, Duke d'Anglouleme, as a potential bridegroom, who was then aged twelve and reputed to be handsome, although smallpox had left him blind in one eye. Francis, however, seemed reluctant, beginning to veer away from the English alliance towards a union with the Emperor. This possibility was finally abandoned in 1535, and Anne interpreted it as the vote of no confidence in her queenship which it was probably intended to be. However, Francis had clearly learned something from Henry's great matter, as when his second son, the fourteen-year-old Henry, had been married to Catherine de Medici in October 1533, Francis remained in their wedding chamber to ensure that the match was consummated. He is supposed to have commented, in a crude metaphor, that each had 'shown valour in the joust'. Henry was offended by Francis' increasing coolness but there were plenty of other potential husbands out there for Elizabeth, particularly once she was the sister of the future King of England.

Anne's second pregnancy is something of a mystery. At New Year 1534, her gift to Henry had been a 'goodly gilt basin' containing a fountain set with three naked women amid pearls, diamonds and rubies, with water flowing from their breasts. This overt symbol of fertility, a reminder of the main reason for their marriage, may have been coupled with the news that she had conceived, as rumours followed to this effect through the month of January. By early March the pregnancy was common knowledge, with preparations being made for a nursery at Eltham 'against the coming of the prince'. This would suggest that the child had quickened by this point, to allow for Anne's condition to be diagnosed with certainty, and pushes the moment of conception back into the previous November. With Anne's churching taking place in early October, her menstrual cycle must have quickly returned as she conceived again within weeks.

This rapid timescale is consistent with Catherine's early conceptions and the protocol that prevented Anne from breastfeeding, with its contraceptive benefits. Through April to June she was reported as having a 'goodly belly', and by the summer Henry had declined the opportunity to visit France in anticipation of the child's arrival. Yet no child came. There are no records of Anne entering confinement or the usual preparation of a suite at rooms, which would have been expected to take place at Greenwich. Nor are there any surviving reports of a miscarriage or stillbirth, although this is the most likely explanation of what happened.

It remains uncertain just how far this second pregnancy progressed, although a November conception and August delivery would seem to fit the known evidence. With the final observation of Anne's growing belly dating to June, though, it is surprising that preparations do not appear to have been made for her lying-in. Building work was taking place in the queen's apartments at Hampton Court, but this appears to have been part of a scheme planned in 1533, to abandon the existing lodgings in favour of new ones on the same floor level. It would appear that Anne lost the child before the usual preparations began, which would usually be initiated around the seventh month. This would place her loss in late June or early in July. To Henry, this must have seemed worryingly close to the experiences of Catherine, who had lost children in the final trimester. Did he start to wonder whether God was as displeased with his second marriage as he had been with the king's first? That summer the marriage was around eighteen months old, and even though Henry was turning forty-three and Anne was now in her early thirties there was still every chance of them having more children. Anne, though, must have been keen to fall pregnant for a third time. It must have seemed to her that, after all those years of waiting at Henry's side, her tenure on the throne was being shaped, perhaps spoiled, by a desperate race to produce a son.

What is most surprising is that none of Anne's enemies, so far as we know, capitalised on this latest loss in order to claim that the marriage was invalid. It is not impossible that courtiers hostile to the Boleyns exploited the situation by forwarding other candidates for the king's affections; Catherine still had a number of loyal vocal supporters in high places and had been a popular queen, and she was also seen as the figurehead for Orthodox Catholicism, the old alliance with Spain and the Emperor, as well as an advocate for centuries of English submission to the Pope. It was to be expected that there would be rumours of discontent against Anne, but they tended to voice the usual criticisms of the new queen on a moral and dynastic level; her miscarriage of summer 1534 is not mentioned. Perhaps this means it was not common knowledge. One of her most vocal opponents that year was another woman.

In January 1534, an Act of Parliament had made it treason to 'impugn' the marriage of the king and queen, specifically to deal with Elizabeth Barton, the Holy Maid of Kent, who had previously been welcome at Henry's court on account of her prophetic abilities. Her harmless predictions had been amusing enough, and fitted a wider context of consulting astrologers, astronomers and mystics when it came to anticipating events such as the genders of royal children. In around 1532, though, Barton had taken to criticising the king's great matter, predicting his imminent death and having visions of the place reserved for him in hell. Among other claims, she said she had been present, in spirit, in Calais to witness an angel refusing to administer the sacraments to Henry, as a clear sign of divine displeasure. She had crossed the line and her public profile was sufficiently high that it was necessary for harsh measures to be taken. The usual accusations of sexual immorality and mental instability were levelled against her, just as they had been with women of previous centuries whose unruly speech had threatened the legal or temporal order. Now, Barton would suffer the ultimate penalty for 'impugning' the marriage, by a law brought into place after her words were spoken.

Barton had been arrested in the autumn of 1533 and, upon examination, a number of others were revealed as ready to preach her 'revelations' as soon as she received 'notice from God that it was time'. The Act of Attainder was passed in January, enabling her to be condemned without trial and, automatically guilty, she was hanged at Tyburn on 20 April 1534. However, Henry soon had bigger fishes to fry. The Act of Attainder describing Barton's treason had also named a number of her associates, including John Fisher and Thomas More, who Henry had never forgiven for their support of Catherine and the old faith. Fisher had been imprisoned at the time of Anne's coronation but More had refused to attend and now produced evidence to show that he had advised Barton to stop meddling in state affairs. It was too little, too late; Henry had devised a new net in which to catch them. A week before Barton's death, both men were asked to attend to sign the First Act of Succession, and later the Act of Supremacy. They refused and were sent to the Tower. Remaining steadfast in their beliefs, More and Fisher would lose their heads in June and July 1535 respectively.

Although comments about the miscarriage of 1534 may not have survived, it is likely that any coolness between the king and queen was manipulated by hostile forces at court. With Anne hoping for a new pregnancy in the autumn of 1534, a rumour surfaced about Henry's infidelity with a woman referred to as the Imperial Lady. Chapuys wrote that the king had 'renewed and increased the love which he formerly bore to another very handsome young lady of his court', at which Anne had reputedly 'attempted to dismiss the damsel from her service'. Apparently, this had occasioned harsh words from the king about the queen's position, with Henry cautioning her that 'she ought to be satisfied with what he has done for her, for, were he to commence again, he would certainly not do as much; she ought to consider where she came from'. These words cannot be verified but, if true, they represent an ominous harshness in the relationship, quite a contrast to what Henry was offering in his letters to Anne of 1526–27, where he offered to put aside all others for her. Those letters represented an attempt to convince Anne that they would enjoy an exclusive and honest relationship, more like a modern companionate marriage based in romantic love. If Anne's eyes had not been opened by then, they were in autumn 1534. Henry had not scrupled to be unfaithful to Catherine, even during her childbearing years, despite maintaining the fact that he was in love with her; Anne came to the bitter realisation that her marriage would be no different.

43

The Shelton Sisters, 1535

Queen Anne, behold your servants, the Three Graces
Giving unto your Grace faithful assistance
With their most goodly amiable faces.[1]

If Anne had attempted to dismiss the 'Imperial Lady' in the autumn of 1534, this woman must have been one of the ladies in her household. Chapuys' account also includes the details that it was someone with whom Henry had a history, as he refers to the king increasing the love he had formerly borne, and adds that the lady's sympathies leaned towards Rome and the cause of Princess Mary. Who exactly could this paramour have been? An examination of the women in Anne's household dating from January 1534 allows the search to be narrowed down somewhat.

Firstly, the lady in question would not have been Mary Boleyn, as this would certainly have been commented on at the time and Anne's reaction would have been more specifically aimed. Henry's affections for Mary appear to have already run their course, and he would not have been so foolish to resurrect the relationship that had necessitated a dispensation for his second marriage. In addition, Mary also made her own marriage for love in 1534, becoming the wife of William Stafford in a secret ceremony. The young Mary Howard, Henry's daughter-in-law since her marriage to Henry Fitzroy, can also be ruled out, as can the child Mary Norris, son of Henry. Another of Anne's ladies, Elizabeth Holland, was the mistress of Lord Howard for twenty years, commencing around this time, so she was also probably not the Imperial woman of 1534. Another woman who had been in Anne's household since 1533 was Frances de Vere. Her pretty features were sketched by Holbein, but given that Anne helped arrange the girl's marriage by overruling her parents' wishes, it seems unlikely that Frances was the lady who incurred the queen's wrath the year before. Likewise, Anne Savage had witnessed Henry and Anne's marriage in 1533, and was heavily pregnant throughout the autumn of 1534, giving birth late that November, so she was not Henry's amour. Jane Parker is an interesting case, as there had previously been a rumour of a Mistress Parker receiving the king's attention, but Anne appears to have been close to her sister-in-law, displaying trust in her and asking for her assistance to remove the Imperial Lady from court.

A number of Anne's waiting women have the potential to have been the mystery woman of 1534, although there is nothing to link them directly to the king. Grace Newport had been married at the age of eight to Henry Parker, son of Lord Morley, and bore him a child in 1533. The Holbein picture usually identified as her leaves little doubt as to her personal charms. Anne Bray, Lady Cobham, would have been in her early thirties at this point and was frequently pregnant at this time, possibly delivering at least one child in 1533 and another in 1535, which would rule her out. She may also have been the Nan Cobham who later testified against Queen Anne and, if so, a quashed flirtation with Henry in 1534, between her pregnancies, might have provided a motive if motivation were required. Another woman of a similar age to the queen was Elizabeth Browne, Countess Worcester, whose debt of £100 to the queen was outstanding in 1536. She would also later testify against Anne, making more direct accusations about her infidelity, in attempt to divert attention away from her own illegitimate pregnancy. It is stretching supposition too far to speculate whether the child Elizabeth was carrying in 1536, at the time of Anne's fall, was fathered by the king.

Another possible candidate was Anne's waiting woman Margaret Gamage. She was approaching twenty in 1534 and had been married for a year to William Howard. The ceremony had taken place at Whitehall, for which Henry mounted a mock sea battle on the Thames, although the festivities were tainted by tragedy when several were injured and at least one man drowned. Margaret is reputed to have supported Princess Mary and according to Eric Ives was sent to the Tower for it briefly in 1535, but there is nothing to link her to the king in a romantic sense, either during the Imperial Lady incident of 1534 or before. Then there is Mary Zouche, another sitter for Holbein, who is believed to have entered royal service in her late teens to escape the cruelty of her stepmother. Aged around twenty in 1535, she was favoured by Jane Seymour but her future, including her possible marital status, is uncertain. There is nothing either to link the king with Eleanor Paston, Countess of Rutland, already the mother of six children and approaching forty by 1534, or Margaret Stanley, who bore two children between her marriage in 1532 and her husband's remarriage in 1537 after her death.

Also in Anne's household were two women who did become the object of the king's affection: Margaret or Madge Shelton and Jane Seymour. But their day had not yet come. Jane certainly was sympathetic to Princess Mary, but the suggestion that Henry had previously shown interest in this mystery woman rules them out. That leaves one woman out of the queen's retinue who appears to be the most likely candidate.

Jane or Joan Ashley was born around 1517 and definitely served as a maid of honour to Anne and then to Jane Seymour, before marrying Peter Mewtas in 1537, when she was aged around twenty. A surviving Holbein chalk sketch of her depicts a typical courtly lady of the time, with open face, large eyes and narrow mouth. It also contains a separate sketch of her hands, placed to the right of her head, where a heart-shaped leaf is featured on one of her fingers, a device that also appears in her oval pendant. Frequently used at the time as a symbol to depict the colour green among German portraitists, and perhaps representing an emerald ring, could this image be a clue to her identity as the king's secret lover in 1534? The ring, in the Tudor colour of green, may have been a gift to the seventeen-year-old unmarried Jane, whose favours Henry may have been seeking before her marriage. She bore her husband at least four children and outlived the king by a couple of years. No direct evidence survives that she was Henry's lover, but her age and profile, plus the detail of the heart leaf, might fit the unknown lady of 1534. It is the sort of coded message that portraitists and poets employed to hint at their secret affections. Whether Jane had caught the eye of the king before 1534 is not known, unless she was the same woman referred to in Chapuys' report of the previous autumn, whom Henry had pursued during Anne's pregnancy.

There is always the possibility that both of these reports were fabricated by the ambassador, whose intention was to present the Emperor with the news he wished to hear about Henry's 'concubine'. Having initially raised the matter in September, Chapuys repeated the story in December, although stating that the 'king's passion for the young lady' was not a threat to Anne's marriage, unless it was to increase. He reported that he had been told by a Squire of the Body that Anne had 'addressed certain remonstrances' to Henry, complaining that 'the young lady in question did not treat her with due respect in words or deeds'.[2] This may have arisen because of the Imperial Lady's support for Princess Mary. Apparently she sent a message to the princess, stating herself to be a 'true friend and devoted servant' and telling her to 'take good heart', because 'her tribulations will come to an end much sooner than she expected'.[3] This sounds very much like a concerted effort to challenge Anne's hold over Henry, with the ultimate aim of replacing her on the throne or ousting her, rather than an idle flirtation on the part of this unknown love. It suggests that her affair with Henry was politically motivated, perhaps encouraged by other orthodox Catholics, as a conscious plot against Anne.

In the same month, Chapuys reported an occasion, passed on to him by Nicholas Carew, when Anne laughed at a banquet in front of French Admiral de Brion. When challenged, she admitted that her outburst was caused by Henry meeting with a lady and forgetting the time.[4] This was surely less a laugh of amusement than of irony and despair. The Bishop of Tarbres, visiting England that October, formed an impression that Henry's affairs were undermining his marriage, writing to Francis I that the king's love for Anne was 'less than it had been, and diminishes day by day, because he has new amours'.[5] However, John Husee's letter to Lord Lisle presents a different picture of Anne and Henry that Christmas, keeping 'a great house' and appointing a Lord of Misrule to oversee the festivities.[6] Chapuys thought that Anne had enlisted the help of her sister-in-law, Jane Parker, to annoy Henry by quarrelling with the Imperial Lady, in the hopes that she would be sent away from court for the sake of a quiet life. The plan backfired, though, and it was Jane who was dismissed for a while. In the end, Anne had to be patient as the king's affection for the mysterious woman soon ran its course. By the end of February the following year, the romance of the Imperial Lady was over. Henry had found himself a new love.

On 25 February 1535, Chapuys recorded that 'the young lady who was lately in the king's favour is so no longer. There has succeeded to her place a cousin of the concubine, daughter of the present governess of the princess.' At that point, Mary's household at Hatfield was being run by Anne Shelton, *née* Boleyn, the sister of Sir Thomas Boleyn. Her two elder daughters, Margaret or Madge, and Mary, were among the gentlewomen of their cousin Anne's household. Although only an image of Mary remains, sketched in three-quarters profile by Holbein, her elder sister Margaret was also reputedly a beauty. This reputation is often based in her likeness to Christina of Milan, whom Henry was desirous of marrying, but actually it is not clear which 'Mistress Shelton' was meant. It may well have been Mary. In fact, in December 1537, John Hutton wrote to Cromwell that Christina 'resembleth much one Mistress Shelton, that sometime waited in the court of Queen Anne' and a month later John Husee specifically named Mary as a candidate for Henry's next wife. Margaret was sufficiently good looking to catch the eye of Sir Francis Weston and Sir Henry Norris, but it may have been her accomplished sister who attracted a more royal suitor.

Margaret was reputedly the elder of Sir John and Anne Shelton's children, born in 1510, with Mary arriving around five years later. However, the similarities between their names and the possible confusion over the abbreviation 'Marg', which could easily be read as Mary, has led historians to wonder which sister was the recipient of Henry's advances, and whether he may have had affairs with both of them, or even if they were, in fact, the same person. It has been suggested also that Anne asked one of her cousins to divert Henry's attention from the Imperial Lady, or from Jane Seymour, who was noticed by the king in 1535, but there is no evidence to support this theory, nor that Anne was particularly close to either Margaret or Mary. This idea is included as a note in a Shelton family history book dating from a later period. Both ladies, assuming there were two of them, were younger than Anne and unmarried when they joined her household. They appear to have been part of the circle of poets and courtiers engaged in writing the kind of symbolic love poetry that Thomas Wyatt composed about Anne. Anecdotes exist about the queen chiding a Mistress Shelton for doodling in a religious text, and that one or both of them contributed to an anthology of poetry known as the *Devonshire Manuscript*. This work, compiled by numerous authors over a period of several years, contains poems by leading courtiers such as Wyatt and Lord Howard, but around eighty items remain anonymous, or identified by initials alone, as well as copies of works of earlier medieval poets. It has been suggested that the collection was compiled primarily by women: Henry's daughter-in-law Mary Howard, his niece Margaret Douglas and either Mary or Margaret Shelton. It also contains poems written in beautiful handwriting by the son of Margaret Douglas, the future husband of Mary, Queen of Scots, Henry, Lord Darnley.

Mary Shelton is identified by most scholars as being the owner of the handwriting of six poems in the *Devonshire Manuscript*. They follow the conventional themes of love, loss and the need to conceal the poet's true feelings. One is a transcription of a poem by Edmund Knyvett, who had married Anne Shelton, sister of Mary and Margaret, in 1527. Another is a copy of an earlier poem, leaving four that are potentially Mary's own compositions. One of these is a short lyric signed with Mary's name and describes a lost love, which she yearns for and will rejoice when she has regained:

> A wel I hawe at other lost
> not as my nowen I do protest
> bot wan I hawe got that I hawe mest
> I shal regoys among the rest[7]

One of the anonymous poems in her hand describes the need to conceal her feelings, 'to counterfit a merry mood', using the metaphor of wearing a cloak in rain, although this proves ultimately ineffective for the narrator. The same image appears in another of her works, where it is used 'to cloke my greffe wer yt doth grow' when her one-time friend has become her foe.[8] Whether or not they relate to an affair Mary may have had with the king, or to the love affair she had with Thomas Clere, they illustrate the atmosphere of the inner circle of Anne's court, of love games, poetry, innuendo and concealed affections, as well as the tension between public and private that would lead directly to the events that brought Anne's reputation into question.

In 1535, one of the king's former mistresses created a new scandal. Back at court in the household of her sister, Mary Boleyn's secret marriage to William Stafford could no longer be concealed as her pregnancy began to show. As the queen's sister, her marriage to a man of lower status was an unforgivable move, casting shame on the king and eliminating Mary as a valuable marital commodity. Mary was cut off from her furious family and forced to leave, a 'poor banished creature' who approached Cromwell for assistance. 'Love overcame reason,' she wrote, regarding her marriage to Stafford. 'For my part I saw so much honesty in him, that I loved him as well as he did me ... [I] could never have had one that should have loved [me better] though I might have had a greater man of birth and a higher.' She would rather 'beg my bread with him than be the greatest queen in Christendom'. Her family were 'so cruel against us', and she felt she was 'never like to recover her grace's favour', that she threw herself on Cromwell's mercy. The king had little patience with his former lover's disgrace and Anne would run out of time before she could be reconciled with her sister. Ironically, in a sense, it would be Mary who ended up as 'the most happy' of all her immediate Boleyn family, escaping the brutal downfall of her siblings, married to a man she loved, who loved her in return, and living out her final years at Rochford Hall, in Essex, before her death in 1543.

Back at court, the king's attention was drawn by his mistresses of the present rather than the past. Any relationship Mary or Margaret Shelton had with Henry was brief. They were a pleasant diversion of six months' duration at the most, by which point his interest in Jane Seymour had begun to develop. Anne's own relationship had established a precedent, whereby an attractive and unmarried woman in the queen's employ might win the hand of the king and the nation's crown. Such a thing had been unthinkable within living memory before her rise, but Anne's meteoric success opened the door for her ladies to do the same; now the Margaret or Mary Sheltons and the Jane Seymours could aspire to much more than Mary Boleyn or Bessie Blount had. Anne was fully aware of this. Just as she had carved out her own career, the new queen was, to an extent, the author of her own demise. It was her playful courtliness and magnetic sexuality that had attracted Henry, which also gave him ammunition to rid himself of her once he had determined to marry again. When, in April 1536, Anne joked with Sir Henry Norris that the marriage he hoped to enter with Margaret was being delayed because he preferred Anne and 'looked for dead men's shoes', courtly flirtation crossed the line into treasonous talk and precipitated her own fall.

PART SIX
Jane Seymour

44

Death of a Queen, January 1536

Thou couldst desire no earthly thing,
But still thou hadst it readily.
Thy music still to play and sing;
And yet thou wouldst not love me.[1]

During the summer of 1535, Henry and Anne went on annual progress out of the claustrophobic court during the warmest summer months, which were also the most dangerous for the spread of illness and disease. Leaving Windsor early in July, they passed through Berkshire, Oxfordshire and Gloucestershire, staying at the houses of courtiers and leading noble families of the day before arriving on 3 September at Wulf Hall in Wiltshire. There, they were received by Sir John Seymour, a Knight of the Body and Groom of the Bedchamber, and his wife Margery Wentworth, who had borne him six surviving children, who entertained the royal party for around a week. This destination may have been chosen by Henry for more than its size and convenience, its large courtyard, chapel, long gallery and picturesque gardens; he may have visited in order to see the home of the woman with whom he was falling in love.

Jane Seymour had been born at Wulf Hall in 1507 or 1508 and raised as a Catholic noblewoman, with the emphasis of her upbringing placed more on practical accomplishments than the European reformers' texts and disputes that had formed Anne's education. This was not her only difference to the queen. Pale where Anne was dark, quiet where she was outspoken, modest where she was ambitious and demure where she was flirtatious, Jane's appeal lay precisely in the very fact that she was opposite of Henry's second wife. She may have come to court to serve Catherine as early as 1526 and therefore witnessed the breakdown of the royal marriage and Anne's ascendancy at first hand, from the start. However, the exact date of her arrival is unknown. For a number of years, Jane had escaped the king's attention and his growing interest coincided with an unfolding sequence of events that had already placed the royal marriage under pressure. What made her more successful than the Imperial Lady or the Shelton sisters was that she was in the right place at the right time. As Henry would come to see over the next nine months, she offered a complete contrast to the woman with whom he was becoming rapidly disillusioned. Jane might have been Anne's opposite but, by refusing to become his mistress and returning his gift of a purse of coins, she showed that she could also master Anne's methods. When the court returned to London in October, it seems that Henry was not considering Jane as more than a fling, or flirtation, hardly a wife or new queen. He already had one of those and she was expecting his child. In the autumn and winter of 1535, Anne's throne was still secure.

Different writers provide widely varying pictures of Anne's household while she was queen. The hostile account by the orthodox Jane Dormer, Duchess of Feria, presents her at the head of a court steeped in frivolity, in 'masques, dancing, plays and such corporeal delights, in which she had a special grace, temptations to carnal pleasures and inventions to disgrace such and ruin them who were renowned for virtue'. No doubt there was a continuation of those festivities to which the court had been accustomed since Henry's succession in 1509, but Anne was hardly the corrupting moral force Dormer portrays. Those of her letters that survive from her period of queenship relate mostly to the reformed faith, as she attempted to advance those sympathetic to the new thinking. Writing to the magistrates of Bristol in 1535, she recommended her candidate for his 'right good learning ... virtue and good demeanor', writing that his 'good life and spiritual conversation' would promote charitable order, concord and unity for the benefit of the city.[2] The same year she wrote from King's Langley to Cromwell, asking for his assistance in promoting Robert Power to the position of abbot at Wallryale, and also writing to the Abbot of St Mary's, York, in favour of John Eldmer, bachelor of divinity, 'of good learning, sad demeanor and virtuous governance'.[3]

Anne's ladies may have been dancing but she also required them to hear divine service daily and is reputed to have presented them all with devotional books of prayer and psalms.[4] For her own use, Anne owned a copy of Tyndale's translation of the scriptures, inscribed with '*Anna Regina Angliae*', and Miles Coverdale's 1535 translated English Bible, which had been dedicated to 'the most victorious Prynce and our most gracious sovereign Lorde, Kynge Henry the eight [and] your dearest just wife and most virtuous Pryncesse, Quene Anne'. She also appointed her household chaplains from among those who favoured studying the Bible in English, including William Betts and Matthew Parker. According to Hugh Latimer, she visited nuns at Syon Abbey and questioned their use of the Bible in Latin. Although the country had not strictly divided into the dichotomic

'Catholic' and 'Protestant', still being very much differing branches of the same faith, Anne's inclinations and patronage make her position as a reformer, a member of the 'new faith', very clear. Thus, she represented a very different force, religiously and culturally, to her predecessor and this is one of the reasons why she polarised opinion among her contemporaries.

At Kimbolton Castle, Catherine's health was rapidly deteriorating. She had been ill in the early part of 1535, begging Chapuys to intervene with Henry to permit Mary to visit her, whom she had not seen in a long time. Henry refused the request but did allow their daughter to move closer, to Hundson, which was thirty miles from Catherine and conveniently further away from the court. Henry was hoping they would be out of sight and out of mind. Early in 1536, Catherine rallied a little, allowing Chapuys to believe that she would recover, before rapidly declining after 2 January. Yet she had already written out a list of her final wishes, about her burial and provision for her servants, which she handed to the ambassador before he left. Her last letter to Henry, dictated on the morning of 7 January, was dignified and restrained, but remained steadfast to the belief that she was his lawful wife and that he had committed sin in the eyes of God:

> My most dear lord, king and husband,
>   The hour of my death now drawing on, the tender love I owe you forceth me, my case being such, to commend myself to you, and to put you in remembrance with a few words of the health and safeguard of your soul which you ought to prefer before all worldly matters, and before the care and pampering of your body, for the which you have cast me into many miseries and yourself into many troubles.
>   For my part, I pardon you everything, and I wish to devoutly pray God that He will pardon you also. For the rest, I commend unto you our daughter Mary, beseeching you to be a good father unto her, as I have heretofore desired. I entreat you also, on behalf of my maids, to give them marriage portions, which is not much, they being but three. For all my other servants I solicit the wages due them, and a year more, lest they be unprovided for.
>   Lastly, I make this vow, that mine eyes desire you above all things.

Catherine's final wish of seeing Henry again came too late, even if he had been minded to set out at once for Kimbolton. Four and a half years since their last meeting, Catherine can hardly have expected a deathbed reconciliation, although the years she had spent at his side as his queen and love may have led her to hope. It was a desperately sad ending for Catherine, for all she had been and what she had represented. After receiving the last rites, she died at two in the afternoon of the same day, at the age of fifty. A post-mortem examination carried out that evening revealed the most likely cause of her death: her heart was covered over by a black growth. This gave rise to the rumour of poisoning but today is understood to be a symptom of cancer.

The news reached London the following day. It would have come as a relief to Anne, although the significance of Catherine's death went far beyond what she may have anticipated. Finally free of her longstanding rival, she was now the only Queen of England, lifting the threat of Imperial invasion and the Pope's insistence that Henry's first marriage was valid. However, while Catherine had been alive, she had provided an essential safeguard to Anne's position, as any desire Henry may have entertained to divorce her would have necessitated his return to his first wife. Henry's feelings over Catherine's death were more complex than is indicated by the anecdote of him dressing from head to toe in yellow and dancing. Yellow was the colour of mourning for the royal family of Spain and Henry's mind was certainly on mourning rituals. Within days he had appointed the principal mourners for her funeral, issuing them with instructions, yards of black cloth and linen for their heads and faces,[5] although he insisted that a hearse was not suitable, as Catherine was the 'princess dowager', not a queen.[6] Even Chapuys admitted the change in his mood from dancing with 'great demonstrations of joy' to a quieter subsidence, which sent him out into the tilt yard. A pregnant Anne may be forgiven for having thought that her most formidable opponent was now out of the way, as she could not have foreseen that Catherine's downfall would pave the way for hers. Within months, Henry had already lined up his next queen.

Yet Anne may have grieved for the loss of her former mistress, or realised what her death represented. One source informed Chapuys that Catherine's death had indeed plunged Anne into uncertainty, for although she had shown joy on hearing the news and gave a 'handsome present to the messenger', since then she 'frequently wept, fearing that they might do with her as with the good queen'. He had also heard that Henry 'had said to someone in great confidence, and as it were in confession, that he had made this marriage while seduced by witchcraft, and for this reason he considered it null'.[7] Henry appears to have been reflecting on his experiences with Catherine and come to the conclusion 'that this was evident because God did not permit them to have any male issue, and that he believed that he might take another wife, which he gave to understand that he had some wish to do'.[8] Although the ambassador's reports are coloured by his desire to please Charles, this revelation foreshadows the allegations that would be levelled at Anne in May and could explain Anne's distress at Henry's developing relationship with Jane Seymour. It was always a volatile relationship and it is impossible to know just how secure Anne felt at her husband's side.

Her position appeared less certain following an accident that January. Henry was taking part in a joust at Greenwich when he lost his seating, slipped from the saddle and the horse fell on top of him. He was lucky not to have been killed but the blow left him unconscious for two hours. During that time, while the court waited to hear his fate, rumours must have been flying about the succession. Everyone from the Privy Council down would have to choose whether they were going to back the eighteen-year-old Princess Mary or the infant Elizabeth. It was a scenario that might descend into civil war, or at least the factional infighting that could oust the Boleyns and their supporters. Henry's doctors watched over him. The shock of the news, insensitively delivered by Norfolk, may have had caused Anne to miscarry. This would be her explanation of what happened five days later. An alternative theory is that she interrupted Henry with Jane Seymour sitting on his knee and became hysterical despite his advice to 'peace be sweetheart and all will be well'. But all was not well.

Catherine's funeral took place on 29 January at Peterborough Cathedral. Her coffin was brought into the mourning chapel, which was hung with eighteen banners to illustrate her many connections with the ruling houses of Europe. The chief mourner was Eleanor Brandon, Henry's niece, and the king himself was represented by Sir William Paulet. On the same day, Anne suffered a miscarriage. The child had the appearance of being a male, of about three and a half months' development. Later Catholic writers would claim the foetus showed signs of deformity, which was seen at the time as the result of sexual immorality, but there is no contemporary evidence for this. As Chapuys wrote, she had 'miscarried of her saviour'.

But just how far did Anne's miscarriage of 1536 really seal her fate? Historians have interpreted the months of February to April in very different ways and, as Anne herself said that year, 'if any person will meddle with my cause, I require them to judge the best'. However, seeking the truth almost five hundred years later, amid the extremes of rumour and slander, is a difficult task. Many questions remain unanswered, as well as the sequence of events that determined Henry's thinking. Although the events are inextricably linked, it is unclear which came first out of his desire to rid himself of Anne and his perception of Jane as a potential new queen. On one hand, the pattern of the queen's childbearing was starting to look uncomfortably familiar and the king is alleged to have stated that God would give him no more children by her in the aftermath of her loss. At a secret meeting with Cromwell that spring, Chapuys raised the question of another marriage, as Henry had 'hitherto been disappointed of male issue and ... knows quite well that this marriage will never be held as lawful'. Cromwell admitted that Henry was 'still inclined to pay attention to the ladies' but hoped that he would 'henceforth live honourably and chastely, continuing in his present marriage'. At this point, Cromwell concealed a smile behind his hand. This may have been conscious irony, as he was aware of cracks in the marriage, or a comment on the likelihood of Henry living chaste; equally he may have taken pleasure in feeding Chapuys the opposite information to that which he clearly wanted to hear. For the time being, the king's intentions towards Anne and Jane remained secret.

A turning point appears to have been reached in the third week of April. Henry had granted Sir Thomas Boleyn rights to the town of King's Lynn and its lands as recently as 14 April, so it was unusual that, on 23 April, George Boleyn was passed over in the ceremony of Knights of the Garter. Ominously, his role was given to Nicholas Carew, of the Catholic Aragon faction. The following day, Henry signed a commission presented by Cromwell to investigate 'unknown treasonable conspiracies' although, according to hostile witness Geoffrey Pole, he had already sought advice from Bishop Stokesley regarding a divorce from Anne. Apparently the answer given was that adultery was the easiest method.[9] By this point, Edward Seymour was appointed a gentleman of the Privy Chamber and he and Jane were lodged in Cromwell's old rooms at Greenwich, which connected with Henry's by a secret corridor.[10] On the other hand, arrangements went ahead for Henry and Anne to visit France in early summer, creating the outward appearance that the marriage was not in trouble. Also, on 25 April, the king informed his ambassador in Rome that he was opposing Charles' latest demands, due to the 'likelihood and appearance that God will send us heirs male ... through our most dear and entirely beloved wife, the queen'.[11] The sands may have shifted, but, as late as the last week in April, Henry's mind was still not made up.

Until it was, the blonde, demure Jane played queen-in-waiting. She would not have long to wait. Jane's rise was due to Henry's fondness for her, although, as some have suggested, she may have been tutored or schooled in behaviour that would attract and retain his interest. The Seymours were clearly on the rise, with Jane's brother Edward appointed to the Privy Chamber on 3 March, and by April it appeared that cordial relations between Anne and Cromwell had broken down forever when he allied himself with the Seymours, recognising that either he or Anne would fall. Combining forces with Nicholas Carew, who knew Henry's private passions of old, they may have selected Jane with the specific purpose of replacing Anne. Chapuys clearly thought so. However, as a virtuous Christian woman in the Vives model, Jane would have understood exactly what was required to maintain her virtue, even if this did serve to inflame the desire of her royal suitor. Whether she passively received Henry's wooing or was groomed for the job of the next queen, she achieved it because it was what Henry wanted; no servant, courtier or mistress could have brought about such a coup against his will.

On 30 April, the strain on Henry and Anne's marriage erupted, with Scottish visitor Alexander Alesius witnessing the couple arguing through a window, when Anne, holding Elizabeth in her arms, appeared to be entreating Henry: 'The faces and gestures of the speakers plainly showed that the king was angry, although he could conceal his anger wonderfully well ... it was most obvious to everyone that some deep and difficult question was being discussed.' The impending visit to France was also cancelled on this day. Anne did not know it, but the first of a series of arrests had already taken place. A young and handsome musician from her household, Mark Smeaton, whose melancholy she had remarked upon just a few days before, had been removed to Cromwell's house at Stepney and questioned. He may also have been tortured, as the *Spanish Chronicle* relates, as he admitted to the charge of committing adultery with the queen. This played directly into the notion of Anne as an upstart, of deviant sexuality, who sought corrupt pleasures with a man far beneath her station. The argument that Alesius witnessed can only be guessed at but the timing suggests that, in Henry's mind, the seeds of her adultery, or the weakness of Cromwell's scapegoat, had already been sown. After this, the end came very quickly.

The independence and wit that had initially attracted Henry to Anne later began to irritate him. It had been charming in a mistress, but he wanted obedience and tradition in a wife. The sacrifices he had made for her weighed heavily upon him and he was aware of the extent of Anne's lack of popularity, which continued to manifest in cases of treason and libel among the common people. Anne's rise to fame had been unprecedented, even meteoric; she was an over-reacher in the classic sense, rising through the social ranks to an unanticipated position as queen. There is no denying Anne's aristocratic, privileged background, but a significant distance still separated those in her social position from royalty, or aspiring to enter the royal family, as is shown by Henry's furious response to his sister Mary's marriage to Charles Brandon. The king had forgiven his best friend and, after all, that match was presented to him as a *fait accompli*, but Anne's rise was further complicated by her gender. As Henry's own grandfather Edward IV discovered, for a king to wed a commoner exposed a woman to all the latent misogyny of the era and would forever colour interpretations of her character. By becoming queen, Anne was breaking a complex set of social codes.

At the time, 'upstarts' who achieved a similar career arc, like Wolsey and Cromwell, were treated with derision and suspicion. Like them, Anne was able to soar while she had the king's backing; with Henry's blessing, there was little that anyone could do to challenge her position, nor the titles, properties, wealth and influence she accrued. Just like the king's other two chief servants, though, once Henry withdrew his support, the end was swift and dramatic. The king's backing was their life force but it was freely given, underpinning every part of his favourites' success. Its sudden withdrawal whipped away the scaffolding under these careers, as Henry abandoned them to the hostile forces he had previously kept at bay. Anne's dazzling rise to the top was less forgivable than that of Wolsey and Cromwell; her power and influence were more offensive to her contemporaries, because she had transgressed the boundaries of gender roles. She was an intelligent, educated and brilliant woman whose abilities far outstripped those of many of the men at court, and her fall unleashed the misogyny of her enemies. The labels of whore, adulteress, witch and incest were weapons aimed specifically at Anne as a woman who had dared to aim for the throne.

The following day, Henry and Anne took their places on the royal stand to watch the jousts at Greenwich. Among the participants on that hot day were Henry Norris and George Boleyn. Halfway through the tournament, a message was brought to Henry, perhaps with the news of Smeaton's confession and the list of names of others he had incriminated. The king rose and rode away without explanation. Anne would never see him again.

45

A Little Neck, May 1536

And thus farewell each one in hearty wise!
The axe is home, your heads be in the street;
The trickling tears doth fall so from my eyes
I scarce may write, my paper is so wet.[1]

Waiting overnight at Greenwich, Anne must have wondered what had happened and where her husband was. She was still queen and was treated as such as she dined, said her prayers and prepared for the night. In her decorated apartments, surrounded by her waiting women, did she lie awake as the hours passed, uneasy about her fate? The following day, 2 May, she was summoned to appear before the council, and was taken by barge to face Henry's commissioners, headed by her uncle, the Duke of Norfolk.

Norfolk informed Anne that she stood accused of adultery and incest, and that the investigation into her conduct had already begun, with the finger of suspicion pointing at Smeaton and Norris. Perhaps Anne recalled the recent conversations she had had with both men and offered her explanation or protested her innocence and loyalty, but Norfolk would not listen. The whole occasion must have had a nightmarish unreality about it; surely, Anne must have hoped, if she could speak with her husband, or explain herself, all would be resolved? The misunderstanding would be cleared up. That morning she had woken in her royal bed and been waited upon as a queen, the queen Henry had begged her to become for years. Now she was a prisoner at his command.

A barge was waiting. Anne was conveyed down river to the Tower and, on seeing the solid walls appear, she broke down and became hysterical. By a cruel irony, which was perhaps deliberate, she was lodged in the same rooms that she had occupied for her coronation just under three years before. In 1533 she had emerged as queen, still carrying the unborn child she had predicted to be a boy, in anticipation of a glittering future. How had the wheel of fortune cast her down so low in such a short space of time? Anne is alleged to have noticed the contrast, saying that she was 'received with greater ceremony last time [she] was there'. It was already decided that she would not be leaving alive. The swordsman from France who would take her life may have been summoned as early as a week later, given that he had to cross the Channel, making it clear that her death was a foregone conclusion.

Over the next few days, six other arrests were made. Her co-accused were her own brother George, Henry Norris, Francis Weston, William Brereton and Richard Page, who were all members of Henry's intimate household, along with Thomas Wyatt and Mark Smeaton. On 12 May, Norris, Weston, Brereton and Smeaton were put on trial for high treason at Westminster Hall. The jury members included Sir Thomas Boleyn, obliged to attend despite his personal involvement in the case, but the remainder were largely hostile to the defendants and the Boleyn cause, with affiliations to the Seymours, Cromwell, Princess Mary and the old faith. While the queen's arrest may have been shocking to the court, it elicited little sympathy. Records of the trial's proceedings have not survived but the four men had little chance to defend themselves, with the emphasis on them to prove their innocence without access to the range of evidence stacked against them. Norris, Weston and Brereton pleaded not guilty while Mark Smeaton pleaded guilty to 'violation and carnal knowledge of the queen', or, as Chapuys put it, that 'he had been three times with the said *putain* and concubine'.[2]

Mark Smeaton was an unusual choice of defendant, given that he was outside the inner circle of the Privy Chamber and of a different class to the other men. He was probably unfortunate in having a recent conversation with Anne overheard and being observed flaunting possessions that were above his station. Perhaps his good looks and musical talent, or a streak of arrogance in his character, had alienated someone. According to the *Spanish Chronicle*, Smeaton accepted Anne's offers of love so readily because he was a 'base fellow' and 'waited in her sweetmeat cupboard until she summoned him after dark by the coded message to bring her some marmalade'.[3] Alone with him, she 'grasped the youth's arm, who was all trembling, and made him get into bed. He soon lost his bashfulness and remained that night and many others', with Anne going on to shower him with expensive gifts. A far tamer version of their relationship was reported to Cromwell, after being overheard that April in her chambers. Anne reputedly chided Smeaton with the words, 'You may not look to have me speak to you as I should do to a nobleman, because you are an inferior person', to which he replied miserably, 'No, no, Madam. A look sufficeth, thus fare you well.' At least one of the dates on which Smeaton confessed he had slept with Anne at Greenwich was impossible, as she was at Richmond; likewise, Alison

Weir has conclusively proven that the majority of the dates on which all the men stood accused can be ruled out in a similar way.[4] It did not make any difference. Scapegoats were needed. If Anne was to be accused of adultery, she needed to have accomplices. All four men were condemned to death.

On 14 May, Anne's marriage was declared null and void, meaning that technically she could not have been committing adultery. This did not prevent her trial and that of George from going ahead the following day. Her brother defied the charges and daringly read out the note he had been requested to keep secret, that Anne and Jane Parker had allegedly discussed the king's inability in the bedroom, claiming he lacked 'vertu' and 'puissance', or ability and power. Although he did not confirm the account, it was an act of rebellion that counted against him, as did the report that he had spread rumours that Princess Elizabeth had been fathered by Henry Norris. Witness Lancelot de Carles wrote that 'one never saw a man respond better' and that he was eloquent and knowledgeable. Despite onlookers betting ten to one that George would be acquitted, given the lack of evidence, he was sentenced along with the rest.

Anne's turn followed. The trial took place in the King's Hall at the Tower and was presided over by her uncle, the Duke of Norfolk. Also on the panel of jurymen along with her father was Sir Henry Percy, the lover she had not seen for years, after their secret engagement had been ended by Wolsey. She was charged with twenty acts of adultery, three of which were also incest, with her brother George, in November and December 1535. When the inevitable guilty verdict was read out in court, Percy collapsed and had to be helped from the room. In a twist of cruel irony, Anne was condemned under the same statue of 1534 that had been created to protect her and her daughter. Tudor law had decided that she was the 'onchaste wife, the spotted queen, causer of all [Henry's] strife', as she was described in a poem by George Cavendish.[5]

Anne returned to the Tower to await her death. Her state of mind can scarcely be imagined, having gone from queen to traitor in two traumatic weeks, reputedly passing through different stages of shock and hysteria, alternatively laughing and weeping, and reliving past conversations in an attempt to discover where and how she had offended. A letter reputedly written by Anne, although not in her handwriting, was found among Cromwell's effects in 1540 and seventeenth-century historian mentions a second letter, in which Anne states that she could not confess to that which she had not done. While the authenticity of these are seriously in doubt, the sentiment of the first contains some emotional truth, that Henry had 'chosen [her] from a low estate to be your queen and companion, far beyond my desert or desire' and if he had then found her worthy, he should not 'let any light fancy or bad counsel or [her] enemies withdraw [his] princely favour'. The letter also refers to Henry's affection for Jane ('your affection already settled on that party') and suggests that it had been a cause of grievance between them ('your grace not being ignorant of my suspicion therein').[6] Anne was attended by women appointed to observe her behaviour and report her speech, and although her aunts Lady Shelton and Elizabeth Boleyn were present they were charged to act as her gaoler and spies. Through the first week of May, Anne offered to enter a nunnery and remained, reported her gaoler, Sir William Kingston, 'in hope of life'. As the days passed, she realised it was a vain hope.

On 17 May, George Boleyn, Norris, Brereton, Weston were executed. Anne was then informed that she was to die the following day, with her sentence commuted to death by the sword. After having spent the night in prayer and preparation, her end was delayed for a further twenty-four hours and further night stretched ahead of her. By the following dawn, she had celebrated Mass and dressed herself in a French gable hood and a gown of black or dark-grey damask trimmed with ermine over a red kirtle. The Constable of the Tower led her on the short walk to the scaffold on Tower Green, where she mounted the steps and looked down at the crowd. A document in the Vienna archive records that she 'looked very frequently behind her', perhaps in anticipation of a reprieve, and was 'much exhausted and amazed'.[7] Her final speech was traditional but dignified:

Good Christian people, I have not come here to preach a sermon; I have come here to die. For according to the law and by the law I am judged to die, and therefore I will speak nothing against it. I am come hither to accuse no man, nor to speak of that whereof I am accused and condemned to die, but I pray God save the king and send him long to reign over you, for a gentler nor a more merciful prince was there never, and to me he was ever a good, a gentle, and sovereign lord. And if any person will meddle of my cause, I require them to judge the best. And thus I take my leave of the world and of you all, and I heartily desire you all to pray for me.

Before an audience that included Cromwell, Brandon and Henry Fitzroy, the Queen of England removed her hood and tucked her hair under a cap. Then she knelt in the straw and the executioner removed her head with one stroke of the sword. It was an unprecedented moment in national history; never before had a queen been treated in this way.

Present at the Tower throughout this time, Sir Thomas Wyatt and Richard Page were never called to trial and managed to escape death. It seems strangely fitting that, having written about court life in his poetry since Anne's arrival, through to his affection for her and her developing relationship with the king, Wyatt was now present to record her final days. Perhaps his most simple and evocative response lies in the following verse:

> These bloody days have broken my heart.
> My lust, my youth did them depart,
> And blind desire of estate.
> Who hastes to climb seeks to revert.
> Of truth, *circa Regna tonat* (it thunders round the realm).

Wyatt and Richard Page were released that June, after the death of Anne, but the experience broke the poet. In a few brutal and bloody weeks, the inner core of Henry's court, with its glittering young people fond of dancing, flirting and poetry, donning masks to dance into the small hours while dressed in cloth of gold, had all been swept away. Wyatt had witnessed the bloodshed of his close friends and the woman he had loved, scarcely able to believe the charges laid against them or the manner of their deaths. Escaping to his family home at Allington, he composed a moving longer poem as he struggled to accept their fates:

> In Mourning wise since daily I increase,
> Thus should I cloak the cause of all my grief;
> So pensive mind with tongue to hold his peace'
> My reason sayeth there can be no relief:
> Wherefore give ear, I humbly you require,
> The affect to know that thus doth make me moan.
> The cause is great of all my doleful cheer
> For those that were, and now be dead and gone.
> What thought to death desert be now their call.
> As by their faults it doth appear right plain?
> Of force I must lament that such a fall should light on those so
>   wealthily did reign,
> Though some perchance will say, of cruel heart,
> A traitor's death why should we thus bemoan?

But I alas, set this offence apart,
Must needs bewail the death of some be gone.
As for them all I do not thus lament,
But as of right my reason doth me bind;
But as the most doth all their deaths repent,
Even so do I by force of mourning mind.
Some say, 'Rochford, haddest thou been not so proud,
For thy great wit each man would thee bemoan,
Since as it is so, many cry aloud
It is great loss that thou art dead and gone.'
Ah! Norris, Norris, my tears begin to run
To think what hap did thee so lead or guide
Whereby thou hast both thee and thine undone
That is bewailed in court of every side;
In place also where thou hast never been
Both man and child doth piteously thee moan.
They say, 'Alas, thou art far overseen
By thine offences to be thus deat and gone.'
Ah! Weston, Weston, that pleasant was and young,
In active things who might with thee compare?
All words accept that thou diddest speak with tongue,
So well esteemed with each where thou diddest fare.
And we that now in court doth lead our life
Most part in mind doth thee lament and moan;
But that thy faults we daily hear so rife,
All we should weep that thou are dead and gone.
Brereton farewell, as one that least I knew.
Great was thy love with divers as I hear,
But common voice doth not so sore thee rue
As other twain that doth before appear;
But yet no doubt but they friends thee lament
And other hear their piteous cry and moan.
So doth eah heart for thee likewise relent
That thou givest cause thus to be dead and gone.
Ah! Mark, what moan should I for thee make more,
Since that thy death thou hast deserved best,
Save only that mine eye is forced sore
With piteous plaint to moan thee with the rest?
A time thou haddest above thy poor degree,
The fall whereof thy friends may well bemoan:
A rotten twig upon so high a tree
Hath slipped thy hold, and thou art dead and gone.

And thus farewell each one in hearty wise!
The axe is home, your heads be in the street;
The trickling tears doth fall so from my eyes
I scarce may write, my paper is so wet.
But what can hope when death hath played his part,
Though nature's course will thus lament and moan?
Leave sobs therefore, and every Christian heart
Pray for the souls of those be dead and gone.

Despite the best efforts of historian G. W. Bernard[8] to suggest Anne probably committed adultery, most modern historians are of the belief that she was guilty of little more than indiscretion. She exploited the flirtatious traditions of courtly love to make suggestive remarks to at least one male companion, Sir Henry Norris, insinuating that he was in love with her and hoped to marry her if she was widowed. Imagining, or 'encompassing' the king's death was, in fact, treasonous at the time. It was poorly judged but if Anne had retained Henry's support then it would probably never have come to light, or she could have explained it away as a misguided convention. Most damning in terms of the adultery charge were the comments made by her lady-in-waiting Lady Worcester, who cast aspersions on the queen when her own immorality was exposed. Technically, a queen's adultery was also considered treason, as it threatened the line of succession. However, various slanders had been levelled against Anne before but with Henry's support she could ride them out. Henry either knew these allegations were not true but saw them as a means to an end or chose to believe them because they suited his purpose.

Various explanations have been put forward for Henry's brutality, but what lay at the heart of this was his sense of autocracy. Anne Boleyn had been his project, from the moment he had spotted her at court and desired her to his heaping titles and gifts upon her, from the rules and hearts he had broken to her magnificent coronation. She may have exploited his desire for her, but ultimately any power she held over him had been by his permission. It had been an elaborate game of love played according to courtly conventions, and when Anne failed to produce a male heir Henry had tired of it. The notion that Anne wielded any sort of real control in the relationship was an illusion that he had granted her out of genuine affection. At court he had been her defender, her loyal knight and protector. His repudiation of her in 1536 was based in his belief of her ingratitude, her gynaecological failing and a personal desire for revenge.

Henry was ruthless in his personal relationships. His treatment of

Catherine, Wolsey, More and Cromwell, show a similar behavioural pattern. Once-beloved favourites were rejected suddenly, almost overnight, being sent away from court with little warning, never to be seen again. Once he had made up his mind, he never went back. He could no longer tolerate their existence and had a need to close a door upon them. As a king, he could close the ultimate door without any judicial reprisals. The greater the love he had felt for them, the greater the suffering he needed to inflict upon them. Without resorting to modern psychology to diagnose a sixteenth-century king, it appears that Henry had a need to punish Anne, to exact a complete revenge on her that owed less to her reputed crimes than to his own monocracy. Thus, as he had dictated the path of her rise, he had to end it decisively. He had controlled and shaped her as a mistress and queen; she was his subject, his plaything, and he could not resist imposing the ultimate authority when he had tired of the game.

46

Queen Jane, 1536–37

Here take thy queene, our King Harry
And love her as thy life
For never had a king in Cfhristentyne
A truer and fairer wife.[1]

Anne's replacement, Jane Seymour, had led a sheltered life in the Wiltshire countryside. Her mother, Margery Wentworth, was a descendant of Edward III but she had married into a family of the minor gentry, with her husband Sir John holding various minor positions at court. Jane was her mother's seventh child and her eldest daughter, with three surviving brothers arriving before her and two sisters to follow. Her upbringing typified a traditional pre-Reformation girlhood, shying away from the sort of intellectual pursuits and European sophistication that had transformed Anne from a docile, demure country girl into a figure who could hold her own on the international stage. There is no evidence to support the claim made by the full-length portrait of Jane on display at Versailles that she was a maid of honour in the French court of Mary Tudor, as she would have been far too young; nor can it be inferred that she finished her education under Queen Claude, along with Anne and Mary

Boleyn. In contrast, Jane stayed at home. Steeped in Catholicism, schooled by her mother on the virtues of wifely skills and talents, Jane was prepared to become the wife of a Knight Banneret, or similar position, just like her sister Elizabeth, who had married Sir Anthony Ughtred before 1531. Chapuys described Jane as not having a 'great wit, but she may have good understanding'. While Anne had broken the mould when it came to the accomplishments of her gender, Jane conformed to it perfectly.

It may have been the marriage of her younger sister in the late 1520s that had prompted Jane or her parents to send her to court, perhaps in search of a husband of her own.[2] It has been suggested that Jane had already been through a broken betrothal by the time she came to court, but in this eventuality Henry would surely have sought legal confirmation that she was now free to marry. She was following a family precedent by travelling to London as Margery had served Catherine of Aragon in the early days of her marriage, and this connection, as well as her father's position as Knight of the Body, helped place her daughter in the queen's household. When that establishment began to fracture, dividing loyalties between those who supported Catherine and those who supported Anne, Jane would have remained firmly in the former camp, with her orthodox faith, her family connection to Catherine and the years she had seen Princess Mary growing up at court. Watching the process by which Anne became queen, Jane witnessed an unfolding drama on which it would have been impossible for her not to have held an opinion. In 1535, when she transferred to Anne's household, according to Jane Dormer, she had observed exactly how a mistress could make the transition to the throne and, although she shared a great-grandmother with Anne, Jane probably had little love for the reformist and ambitious Boleyns. A conversation reported by Chapuys indicates the sort of approach favoured towards Henry and his daughter, by the woman the ambassador came to call the 'pacifier' or peacemaker:

I hear that, even before the arrest of the Concubine, the king, speaking with Mistress Jane Semel [*sic*] of their future marriage, the latter suggested that the Princess should be replaced in her former position; and the king told her she was a fool, and ought to solicit the advancement of the children they would have between them, and not any others. She replied that in asking for the restoration of the Princess she conceived she was seeking the rest and tranquillity of the king, herself, her future children, and the whole realm; for, without that, neither your Majesty nor this people would ever be content.

When Henry fell in love with Jane she was in her late twenties, 'of middle stature and no great beauty, so fair that one would call her rather pale than otherwise'.[3] Chapuys wondered how Jane had managed to keep her virginity intact amid the reputedly licentious court, but there is no gossip to connect her with any other man and there may be some truth in the ambassador's cynical comment that 'he may make a condition in the marriage that she be a virgin, and when he has a mind to divorce her he will find enough of witnesses'. Chapuys also crudely punned on the possibility of her possessing a grand 'enigmé', usually meaning a secret or riddle but also contemporary slang for the female genitals.[4] Yet there is no doubt that Jane's purity and untarnished record counted in her favour. It was to preserve her from scandal that might have arisen at the time of Anne's fall, and to 'cover his affection' for her, that Henry moved Jane out of the court to Carew Manor in Beddington Park, Croydon, the family seat of Nicholas Carew. With the matter privately decided between them, Henry's public actions were quite different, however.

Stating in public that he had 'no desire in the world to get married again unless he is constrained by his subjects to do so', Henry was enjoying a brief moment of freedom. Chapuys reported how he was 'banqueting with ladies, sometimes remaining after midnight, and returning by the river' and had lately dined with 'several ladies in the house of the Bishop of Carlisle', where he had shown an 'extravagant joy' and claimed to have written a tragedy about himself and Anne.[5] The day after Anne's execution, the French ambassador offered him the hand of the Princess Madeleine, the young and beautiful sixteen-year-old daughter of Francis I, but Henry replied that she was too young for him and 'he had had too much experience of French bringing up and manners'.[6] Yet, despite his protestations, he had become engaged on the very same day.

Jane had been brought from Beddington to More's old house at Chelsea on 14 May and 'splendidly served by the king's cook and other officers' as well as being 'splendidly dressed'.[7] Five days later, on Anne's death, a dispensation had been issued by Thomas Cranmer to allow Henry and Jane to marry without the need to publish their banns, despite being related in the third degree of affinity. The betrothal took place on 20 May and the wedding was solemnised in the queen's closet at York Place. Hearing of the match, Princess Mary, who had resisted Anne's few attempts at reconciliation, wrote from Hundson to her father, congratulating him on his new marriage, at which she 'rejoiced', and asked to be allowed to come to court to serve Jane, as well as praying to 'God to send you a prince'.[8] No doubt Henry was praying for the same but, eleven days after Anne's death, was he possibly regretting the speed at which he had replaced one woman with another? That summer, while placing his hand on Jane's belly and saying, 'Edward, Edward', although she was not yet pregnant, Henry confided to Chapuys that he was not certain that the queen would provide him with children, adding that he had recently seen two beautiful new women arrive at court and wished he had waited a little before remarrying.

Might these two women have come from Jane's own household? There had been some continuity from Anne's court, with several ladies transferring their allegiance from one queen to another, including Mary Zouche, Eleanor Paston, Mary Brandon, Mary Norris, Margery Horsman, Jane Ashley and even George Boleyn's widow, Jane Parker, but the comment suggests they were newcomers whose arrival was timed with the establishment of the new queen's household. The two beauties are unlikely to have been the Bassett sisters, Anne and Catherine, the stepdaughters of his uncle Arthur Plantagenet, Lord Lisle. Still in their teens, the pair had applied to become part of Jane's household, only to be told they were too young: Anne was given a place in 1537 but Catherine was at a slightly further remove from the queen when she joined the retinue of Eleanor Paston, Countess of Rutland. One of the two would become Henry's mistress later but they had not yet left Calais for England, firmly ruling them out at this stage.

However, a letter written by John Husee to their mother, Lady Lisle, on 25 May 1536 suggests a Bassett family connection for the two mysterious beauties, who may have been their cousins: 'Your ladyship hath two nieces with the queen, which are daughters unto Mr Arundell.'[9] Lady Lisle's sister Jane did indeed marry a Sir John Arundel of Trerice and bore him a daughter, Mary, who may be referred to here; he also had two daughters, Elizabeth and Jane, from his first marriage, but she had died by this point, as her widowed husband Sir Richard Edgecombe took a second wife in 1535. Born in or before 1507, Jane would have been at least thirty when she took up at place in the new queen's household. However, Lady Lisle's other sister, Philippa, took Sir John's brother as her second husband, marrying Humphrey Arundel sometime after 1509, allowing plenty of time for her to produce two daughters of suitable age before she died in 1524. Of all the possible Arundel nieces of Lady Lisle, it seems most likely that the half-sisters Jane and Mary are being referred to by Husee and, given the timing, providing strong possible identities for the women who drew the king's admiration. For the moment, though, Henry had a new wife to whom he must attend.

There seems to be no reason to doubt that Jane was a virgin on her wedding night. Awaiting the arrival of her new husband at York Place, on the night of 30 May, she was not old enough to have seen the youthful bridegroom of 1509 who sped to Catherine of Aragon's chamber, fleet of foot and with a beauty that was celebrated across Europe. With Jane stripped down to her nightgown, pale and untouched, her ladies melted away as Henry approached. He was hardly love's young dream, with his expanding girth and ulcerated leg, but he was the king, and that counted for a lot. As Thomas More once wrote, 'The king has a special way of making every man feel that he is enjoying his special favour ... just as the London wives pray before the image of Our Lady ... till each of them believes it is smiling upon her.' No doubt it was true for women too. Asserting that he was a 'man like any other', in spite of his age and the lack of ability that Anne had hinted at, Henry was an experienced lover. Now he consummated his marriage to Jane in the hope that, like his previous wives, she would quickly fall pregnant.

Assuming that Henry had not resolved to marry Jane until spring 1536, although he may have been involved with her since the previous year, it had been a very swift journey from maid of honour to queen. As Philip Melanchthon wrote, 'What a great change has suddenly been made.'[10] Jane must have felt it too. Only eleven days had elapsed between Anne's death and Henry sharing the bed of his new wife. Now she was quickly established in her new role, expected to pick up where Anne had left off, almost to fill her shoes, although in a very different style. On 3 June, Sir John Russell wrote from to Lord Lisle that Jane's servants had been sworn in on the day that the king and queen returned to Greenwich, with Jane and her ladies in 'the great barge'. He clearly approved of Henry's choice, assuring Lisle that 'she is as gentle a lady as ever I knew, and as fair a queen as any in Christendom. The king hath come out of hell into heaven for the gentleness in this and the cursedness and the unhappiness in the other. You would do well to write to the king again that you rejoice he is so well matched with so gracious a woman as is reported.'[11]

Jane made her public debut at Henry's side at Whitsun, 4 June, when her brother Edward was elevated to Viscount Beauchamp. According to Thomas Wriothesley, she was proclaimed queen with a great train of ladies after her, attended Mass and dined in her presence chamber under the cloth of estate. Chapuys, though, stated that she was quickly overwhelmed and needed to be 'rescued'. After he had addressed Jane, Henry, 'who in the meantime had been talking with the ladies of the court, approached us, and began making excuses for the queen, saying that I was the first ambassador to whom she had spoken; she was not used to that sort of reception'.[12] Jane was certainly not bred for the limelight as Catherine had been, or as experienced and poised as Anne; she had no parallel experience to the years Catherine had spent as Arthur's widow, observing the mechanisms of the court from within, or the long years of courtship by which Anne had grown accustomed to Henry as a man and lover. The new queen was rushed into position in a matter of weeks. On 7 June she attended a water pageant held in her honour on the Thames outside York Place, sharing Henry's barge as part of a great procession saluted by guns. As they sailed past the Tower, streamers and banners were hung from the walls and more musicians saluted them as they passed under London Bridge. The following day, Cranmer, still reeling in shock over Anne's demise according to his letter to Henry,[13] declared that the king's previous two marriages had been unlawful. She had then been married to Henry for a week.

Another reason for Henry's marriage to Jane has been suggested by some historical writers, one which raises a mind-blowing possibility. At least one novelist has suggested that Jane was pregnant at the time of her marriage, having conceived as a result of an affair with the king in spring 1536. This may have occurred in February, after his disappointment arising from Anne's miscarriage and during a possible period of estrangement that had arisen between the king and queen. Jane would have suspected her condition by March or early April, which would explain Henry's sudden need to remove Anne and place Jane on the throne in order to legitimise her child. He had married Anne when she was pregnant, an event which had proved the catalyst for his wedding of January 1533, and the removal of Jane from court during the process may have been to conceal her symptoms. Suddenly, the timescale of events in 1536 appear in a very different light.

This theory would mean that Jane would be expecting to deliver her child in mid-autumn. She would have been three or four months pregnant at the time of her marriage and still perhaps able to conceal this fact under her clothes. The lack of other evidence is not necessarily conclusive, as the precedent of Bessie Blount's pregnancy and delivery establishes the degree to which such an event might be covered up. It may also offer a different explanation as to why Jane appeared nervous before Chapuys in early June 1536 and needed to be rescued, in case her condition might be determined by hostile witnesses. Obviously, if Henry had impregnated Jane during his marriage to Anne, and ordered the removal and death of his queen in order for the unborn child to be legitimate, the damage to his reputation would have been serious. It seems that any pregnancy was kept secret until such a time that it could no longer be concealed, at which point the drastic steps of May 1536 could no longer be reversed. But then, there was nothing. Just like Anne's miscarriage or stillbirth in the summer of 1534, a veil of silence descends.

If she was pregnant, Jane would have lost this child in June or July 1536. It must have happened in private, in her privy chambers and probably at night, when there were fewer witnesses. Miscarriages in the early months were not always recorded and may have been known to only a small circle of the queen's ladies, such as when Catherine had lost a daughter at seven months in January 1510. The court had known nothing about the event then, so it could easily have known nothing of Jane's in 1536, nor that there had even been a pregnancy to lose. It may have been the prompt for the king and queen to head off on progress through Kent, as a change of scene for Jane, although there is the chance that she miscarried while they were away. This shocking theory would rewrite Henry's reputation for adultery, his marriage to Anne, Anne's fall, Jane's reputation and their marriage. It is difficult to know just how news of such a scandalous pregnancy would have been received at the English court or in the country in general, and further afield on the international stage. Henry had barely managed to stave off an Imperial invasion when he repudiated Catherine but Anne Boleyn had no such powerful relatives to avenge her fall. If a pregnancy had been announced in June 1536, it is hard to imagine just who would have been in a position to object or create a scene worse than that which had already been enacted between Henry, the Emperor and Rome.

A miscarriage at this early stage would have been a dreadful blow to Henry after he had placed so much upon the survival of this child, as with Elizabeth in 1533. Worse still, it would have put Jane under intense pressure, perhaps also in a state of fear that she might prove as disposable as her predecessor if another courtly beauty was to catch her husband's eye. There are no signs in the behaviour of either king or queen that support this outcome. Evidence does exist against the theory, though. Given the doubts of a number of onlookers that Jane would conceive and bear a child, coupled with what is known about her character, it seems far-fetched in the extreme. The truth of this theory will probably never be known, unless fresh evidence comes to light after almost five centuries; in the meantime, the story derives from historical fiction and is better left there in the absence of solid proof.

However, Henry was to suffer a real loss that summer, the facts of which are documented and indisputable. That July, the king and queen were staying at Dover Castle when they received the terrible news of Henry Fitzroy's death at the age of seventeen. In recent months, Henry Fitzroy had taken a more public role at court and on state occasions, even attending Anne's execution. The king was proud of his son, now on the verge of adulthood and married, and his most likely successor in the event that no other male heir was conceived. As recently as early June the likelihood of him succeeding Henry was raised, in the light of Princess Elizabeth now being considered a bastard: 'The Earl of Sussex in the Privy Council proposed to the king that as the princess was a bastard, as well as the Duke of Richmond, it would be right to prefer the male to the female; and as this opinion was not opposed by the king, it may be that some will hereafter favour it.'[14] The young man was accustomed to staying at court and bidding his father goodnight as, during Anne's imprisonment, this was the occasion when Henry gave his son his blessing and wept, saying that he and Princess Mary had escaped her attempts to poison them. Cruelly, though, the young man did fall ill within weeks of this conversation, reported as being ill that July. On the 23rd of the month, he died at St James' Palace, possibly of tuberculosis. Henry was distraught. Having placed his hopes on the boy in spite of his illegitimacy, he was now without a son at all. Sharing his bed, Jane was aware of his expectations of her.

A magnificent coronation ceremony was planned for Jane that October, to outstrip those of Henry's previous wives, with Jane travelling from Greenwich to the Tower in a huge ship made in imitation of the Venetian *Bucentaur*, the state galley of the doge. Its latest incarnation, created in 1526, had two decks and forty-two oars, and bore a sculpture of Justice on the prow, sculptures of lions and a canopy of red and blue with gold stars. Although it never took place, a pageant planned in 1536 featured Jane's badge garnished with her motto, 'Bound to serve and obey', along with a true love knot and a figure representing the Holy City being shown to St John, the stories of Adam and Eve, Martha and Mary Magdalene, as well as 'cages with quick birds to be set in a meadow'.[15] According to Thomas Wriothesley, the date was fixed for the Sunday before All Hallow's Eve, so Sunday 29 October 1536. However, the events of that summer and autumn put the coronation on hold, as Henry's religious reforms brought about the most significant threat to his rule yet: a full-scale rebellion in the north that would come to be known as the Pilgrimage of Grace.

With the king occupied by the demands of the rebels and the

uprisings that spread into the following year, all thought of Jane's coronation was put to one side. However, she would never get to ride down the Thames in all the pomp that had been envisioned. By the time the rebel leaders had been brutally quashed, the queen had fallen pregnant.

47

A Prince at Last, 1537

God save King Henry with all his power,
And Prynce Edward, that goodly flowre
With all his lordes of great honoure,
Synge trolle on away, synge trolle on away.
Heve and how, rombelowe, trolle on away.[1]

Jane must have been very relieved to find that she was with child. The lives of her predecessors had been defined by their gynaecological histories, and as the months had passed without her conceiving, the court began to ask questions. Given Henry's age, size and ulcerous leg, this was no real surprise; perhaps there was some truth in the claim raised at Anne's trial that she had cast doubt on his ability to perform and the king's own defiant response that he was 'a man like any other'. This concern was echoed by Dr Ortiz, in a letter to the Empress in September 1536 when he wrote that no children were expected 'on account of the complexion and disposition of the king',[2] and also by Chapuys, who wrote in October regarding Jane's 'coronation, which was to have taken place at the end of this month, is put off till next summer, and some doubt it will not take place at all'. This was immediately followed by the comment that 'there is no appearance that she will have children',[3] suggesting a connection between the two statements. Although the Pilgrimage of Grace in the north had provided a valid enough reason for delay, it is not impossible that Jane's coronation, the celebration of her as queen, was being put off until she had proved herself fertile.

Jane had conceived early in January 1537, so she probably became aware of her condition within weeks, with her certainty growing through the month of February. Having watched two wives go through this process, Henry probably recognised the symptoms and called in the royal physicians to give their opinion. Many of her ladies were also mothers themselves and had seen Anne through her pregnancies. The queen's condition was made public that April, being referred to in Parliamentary proceedings on the third of the month, when provision was being made for Mary and Elizabeth. Three days later, Sir William Eure wrote to Cromwell that the rumours of the pregnancy 'gave the greatest possible satisfaction', with all men 'rejoicing', and at the end of the month John Husee wrote, 'Jesu send her a prince!'[4] In May, Jane wore an open-laced gown to announce the child's quickening at Hampton Court and special Masses were said in St Paul's Cathedral for her good health and that of the child; the records make clear that she had inherited Anne's dressmaker, John Scut, who would have known how to accommodate her growing belly in suitably regal style. Husee related in May that she would be 'open laced with stomacher by Corpus Christi Day [10 June in 1537] at the farthest'.[5] In the early stages of the pregnancy she developed a passion for quails, which were then out of season. Henry wrote to Lord Lisle in Calais in search of a supply, ordering the net to widen to Flanders if insufficient amounts could be found.

The provision of quails for the pregnant queen was taken by the Lisle family as an important part of the negotiations to smooth the way of Anne Bassett into her household. Husee wrote to Lady Lisle in May that Queen Jane was 'content to take her at the later end of the progress when all heats and dangers of sickness be past'.[6] A week later, Sir John Russell wrote to Anne's father asking for some 'fat quails' 'for the queen is very desirous to eat some but here be none to be gotten ... I pray you in anywise that ye will send some with as much speed as may be possibly [sic] but they must be very fat.'[7] Husee followed this with a letter to Lord Lisle, adding that 'her Grace loveth [quails] very well, and longeth not a little for them' and that Husee 'looked hourly' for Lisle's answer regarding the order of two or three dozen birds that should be killed at Dover and 'speedily conveyed' to Hampton Court.[8] When the first of a large consignment arrived at court that May, a dozen were roasted for the royal dinner and a further dozen for supper. The efforts of the Lisles to satisfy the queen's pregnancy cravings did not go unnoticed, with the queen commenting in July, while eating the quails, that Lady Lisle should send Anne and her sister Catherine over from Calais, 'for her Grace will first see them and know their manners, fashions and conditions, and take which of them shall like her Grace best'.[9] Anne clearly impressed the queen more, as she was sworn in as Jane's maid in mid-September.

It was around this time that Hans Holbein completed a mural at Whitehall Palace that contained the portraits of Henry, Jane and

Henry's parents, Henry VII and Elizabeth of York. Designed to demonstrate the dynasty's lineage, the confidence of Henry's pose suggests his anticipation of the birth of a son, as his astrologers predicted. It is likely that Jane's pregnancy was, in fact, the reason for the work being commissioned. There is no direct reference to her condition in the picture, although this may well have been considered injudicious considering she was in the early stages and there was no guarantee she would carry the child to term. However, the pregnancy did proceed according to plan and the tradition of Henry's wives lying in at Greenwich was broken when a suite of rooms was prepared for Jane at Hampton Court. Plans for a royal progress that summer were abandoned and Jane remained in the palace instead, to avoid an outbreak of the plague in London. It was still raging early in October when the Duke of Norfolk wrote to Thomas Cromwell that 'the death' was still 'extremely sore' in the capital and the 'young folks', traditionally the worst afflicted, were kept away from the palace gates. Jane had already entered her confinement by then, to await the onset of her labour.

It was during these final weeks of Jane's confinement that an interesting case arises in the State letters and papers for 28 September 1537 that may shed some further light on the question of Henry's methods as a lover. In line with the common practice of highborn men taking lower-class mistresses, especially while their wives were sexually unavailable, one of the king's amours was brought to the attention of the council when some gossip was reported within the sanctuary of Westminster. According to a Morris Bull, Henry had taken a passing fancy to a 'wench' of loose morals and claimed her for his own, in what appears to have become a longstanding arrangement, setting her up in some household or secret establishment. Bull explained that 'there was one rode upon a fair gelding and a pretty wench behind him, and a king met them and plucked down her muffler and kissed her, and liked her so well that he took her from him ... and so lived and kept her still in advowtry [adultery]'.[10]

Upon questioning by the king's councillors, the gossip divulged that the man upon the gelding was a William Webbe, who had lived with the 'wench' for two years and now cried vengeance upon the king. The incident had taken place near Eltham, and was witnessed by Kendal, a servant of the king, and the wife of one Robert Sharp of Westminster.[11] The identity of the woman remains unknown, as does her future as Henry's lover. If true, this incident, which only became known through the spread of a string of mutating rumours from one man to the next, exposes something of Henry's methods and sense of entitlement. When it came to women he wanted, particularly lower-class women, he simply took what he wanted.

On the morning of 12 October, Jane was finally delivered of a healthy son. It was the eve of St Edward's Day, although the couple had already chosen this name in advance. Henry was not alone in his delight; celebrations were held all over the country and contemporary letter writers spoke of the 'exceeding goodness' and 'strength of gladness' they felt at the prince's arrival. Hugh Latimer wrote that there was no less rejoicing than if John the Baptist had arrived![12] Initially, Jane appeared to be well. It was a personal triumph for her, having provided Henry with the son he had desired since he came to the throne twenty-eight years before. The birth had been arduous, lasting two days and three nights, but later reports that she had undergone a caesarean or that her limbs had been broken to allow for delivery were wildly exaggerated. She was in recovery when Edward was christened, three days later, in the chapel at Hampton Court, where she sat, wrapped in velvet and furs, to receive visitors in the waiting chamber. The baby's sisters, Mary and the four-year-old Elizabeth, displaced by his arrival, played ceremonial roles as their brother was blessed and anointed.

Jane would also have been pleased to hear, on 18 October, that Henry had elevated her brother Edward to the title of Earl of Hertford, while her younger brother Thomas was knighted.[13] Plans were already being made for the queen's churching when she fell ill a few days later, with one doctor reporting that 'all this nyght she hath bene very syck'.[14] Prayers were said for her at St Paul's but, after briefly rallying, her condition rapidly deteriorated. Her end was different from Anne's in every conceivable way: Sir Thomas Palmer wrote to Lord Lisle that 'if good prayers can save her, she is not like to die, for never lady was so much plained with every man, rich and poor'.[15] However, no amount of prayers could save the queen now.

Six doctors were called in. Among them were William Butts, Henry's chief 'doctor of physic' and one of the founders of his 1518 Royal College of Physicians, and George Owen, who would become chief physician to the newborn child. They witnessed the queen suffer a 'natural laxe', a heavy bleed, on the night of 23/24 October. Postpartum haemorrhaging could be caused by internal injury, perinatal tears or the retention of part of the placenta following delivery. The signs were so disturbing that her confessor had been called by eight that morning and, as anticipated, Jane died that day, at around midday. Writing to Cromwell, Norfolk urged him to keep a watchful eye on the king: 'My good lord, I pray you to be here tomorrow early to comfort our good master, for as for our mistress there is no likelihood of her life, the more pity, and I fear she shall not be on lyve at the time ye shall read this. At viij at night, with the hand of[your] sorrowful friend, T. Norffolk.'[16] But the king's servant did more than comfort his master. Investigating her final days, Cromwell criticised the decision of those attending her 'who suffered her to … eat such things as her fantasy in sickness called for',[17] although, by that point, her diet would have had little effect. Meanwhile, Henry wrote to Francis I, who had long promised to be godfather to any Prince of Wales, expressing his joy at the boy's birth and the 'bitterness of the death of her who has brought me this happiness'.[18]

Jane's case is an unusual one. Midwifery was usually left to women during this period but her status may have made her an exception. While medical manuals were written by men, for men, they dealt with an abstract, academic knowledge about the anatomical process. This was no substitute for the literally hands-on approach of women who had attended births for decades and accumulated practical knowledge from the previous generations of mothers, grandmothers and other relations from whom they learned their skill. Theirs was essentially an oral tradition, which remained behind closed doors. Perhaps it was Henry's caution over the arrival of this child that led the usual gender relations in the birth room to be subverted. It is clear that Jane was attended by male doctors, whom protocol may have prevented from handling her body too roughly or intimately. An examination of the records that survive of her symptoms suggest that a fundamental error was made as a result of this lack of practical experience. A midwife would have known the importance of ensuring that the placenta was removed whole, as even tiny pieces left in the womb could trigger fatal infections. Experienced female attendants would have employed a number of techniques to ensure it was expelled, from herbal drinks, massage and tourniquets to physical examinations. The timescale and nature of Jane's decline strongly suggest that this did not happen.

Detailed evidence survives in the State letters and papers about what happened to Jane's body after her death. Henry put Norfolk and Sir William Paulet in charge of the funeral arrangements and 'retired to a solitary place to pass his sorrows', while he studied the arrangements made for the burial in 1503 of Elizabeth of York, the last queen consort to have died in office.[19] Jane was first given to the wax chandler, who removed her entrails 'with searing, balming, spicing, and trammeling in cloth', before the plumber (literally a worker in lead) 'leaded, soldered, and chested' her and her entrails were honourably interred in St George's Chapel, where the rest of her body would join them two weeks later.[20] From Friday 26 October she lay in a hearse in the presence chamber at Hampton Court, surrounded by twenty-one tapers and her ladies, who had 'put off their rich apparel' and knelt during Mass in the morning and afternoon. A nightly watch was then kept over her body until the end of the month. On 1 November, the route to the chapel was hung in black cloth and Jane's hearse was conveyed there, garnished with eight banner rolls. A train of mourners heard Mass again, saw the area censed and then departed to the queen's chamber. The Masses, offerings and prayers continued for eleven days.[21]

Henry's third queen left Hampton Court for the chapel at Windsor on 11 November 1537. Her mortal remains lay in a casket but, according to custom, a wax effigy of a crowned Jane lay on top, resting on a golden pillow and dressed in robes of state, with embroidered stockings and gold shoes, a sceptre in the right hand and fingers adorned with rings. All along the road to Eton, Jane's passing was marked by lighted torches carried by two hundred poor men, banners and almoners distributing alms. From there they passed over the bridge, where the mayor and brethren were waiting, and climbed the hill up to the castle, where the coffin was lifted from the hearse and taken into the chapel. Jane's stepdaughter Mary took the role of chief mourner, with her train carried by Jane Boleyn, while twenty-nine others, representing Jane's twenty-nine years, made up the procession in five chariots, among them Henry's nieces Margaret Douglas and Frances Brandon, Lady Morley, Jane Ashley, Mary Norris, Anne Bassett, Mary Zouche, Elizabeth Carew and Jane's own sister Elizabeth, now married to the son of Thomas Cromwell. Her other ladies had gone on ahead to Windsor. That night her body was watched over while her mourners stayed in the castle. The service of interment was carried out the next day, followed by the offering of the palls, when her ladies lay expensive cloths over her coffin. Most gave two or three, but Frances Brandon gave four and Princess Mary gave seven. Jane was then laid to rest and the mourners were 'sumptuously provided for' in the castle.[22] She was the only one of Henry's wives to be buried with the ritual of a queen.

The cataloguing of Jane's effects upon her death helps shed a little light on her otherwise shadowy stint at queenship. Many of the items had been given or lent to her ladies, including strings of beads, jewels, pomanders and tablets, girdles and borders enamelled with various colours, bracelets, gold buttons, chains and gold brooches which had been bestowed on her brother Thomas, the king's apothecary Cutberd and Lady Shelton. She also had in her possession a glass with the images of Henry VII and others.[23] A list of her lands and debtors showed that she owned the prestigious and ancient royal properties at King's Langley and Berkhamsted, as well as at Whaddon (which was run by her brother Henry), Bodiam, Cookham, Bray, Hampstead, Walton, Stamford and the forests of Exmoor, Rache and Mendip, as well as Catherine's favourite Essex home of Havering-atte-Bower and a number of properties in Kent. Jane was also receiving rent from the king's palace at Southwark, with a 'barysgardeyn', perhaps a bears' garden, one of the bear-baiting gardens located on the south bank. The value of these was estimated at £938 6s 8d.[24]

Jane's son, Edward, remained in the royal nursery at Greenwich before being set up in his own establishment in the north range at Hampton Court, at a cost of £6,500. Having lost so many children, Henry was leaving nothing to chance with this new son. Under the care of Mistress Margaret, Lady Bryan, recently in charge of his sister Elizabeth's household, Edward's world was run under strict guidelines to prevent infection and injury; serving boys and dogs were forbidden as the most clumsy of creatures and a daily programme of washing was followed, with walls, floors and ceilings scrubbed down. No food or dirty utensils were to be left lying around and anyone falling ill was to immediately leave the palace. Visitors needed the king's written permission to approach the cradle and none were allowed to travel to London in summer, in case they acted as carriers of some terrible infection. The prince's clothes were washed, brushed, tested, perfumed and dried before the fire to kill any lurking pestilences. A new kitchen and wash house were constructed especially to serve Edward's establishment and prevent cross-contamination from the rest of the court. His cradle of estate lay in the presence chamber, where he was displayed to visitors who had been allowed access through the heavily guarded watching chamber. He actually slept in the rocking chamber, where a canopy hung over his cradle to protect him from the sun.

Prince Edward's arrival marks the end of a phase in Henry's life in which his increasing need for a son underpinned many of his actions. It had seen him take drastic action to rid himself of two wives, doubt his own standing in the eyes of God and break with Rome in an unprecedented way. Yet his son's arrival had cost him his queen. Remaining in mourning until the following February, it was the first time the king had not been in a hurry to take a wife.

PART SEVEN
Anne of Cleves

48

Vacancy in the Bed, 1537–39

Thy niece, thy cousin, thy sister or thy daughter
If she be fair, if handsome be her middle
If thy better hath her love besought her
Advance his cause and he shall help thy need[1]

Henry may not have been rushing to the altar, but his minsters were keen to see him married for a fourth time. Jane was scarcely cold when Cromwell proposed a new wife for the king. On 31 October, he had written to Howard and Bishop Gardiner that Henry was 'little disposed to marry again', but 'some of his council have thought it meet for us to urge him to it for the sake of his realm'. Apparently Henry had 'framed his mind, both to be indifferent to the thing and to the election of any person from any part that with deliberation shall be thought meet'. In the light of the king's ambivalence, Cromwell had already come up with two candidates to share the royal bed, 'the French king's daughter [said to be not the meetest] and Madame de Longueville, of whose qualities you are to inquire, and also on what terms the King of Scots stands with either of them'.[2] Now he just had to get Henry interested.

The first candidate Cromwell suggested was Margaret, seventh child of Francis I and Queen Claude, who was then fourteen years old to Henry's forty-six. Raised by Marguerite of Navarre, who had been greatly admired by Anne Boleyn, Margaret's age and French background probably counted against her in Henry's eyes. He had dismissed a potential French bride in 1536 based on a newfound dislike of her nationality and manners. Madame de Longueville, though, was a far more likely candidate. Born Mary of Guise in 1515, she had been widowed at the age of twenty-one, with two sons, one of whom arrived after the death of his father. Her ability to bear healthy male children was an advantage to the King of England, as was her physique, as Henry stated that he was 'a large man who had need of a large wife'. Mary, though, seemed less keen, reputedly referencing Anne Boleyn's comment before execution by saying she may 'be a big woman but she had a very little neck'.[3] In any case, the likelihood of Mary accepting Henry was slight, as she was already committed to a match with a handsome young man half his age.

In the autumn of 1537, negotiations were well underway for Mary to marry the recently widowed James V of Scotland, and while Henry may have wished to steal this eligible bride from under the nose of his young nephew, he was competing against an existing bond of affection between a couple in their twenties. Keen as he was for an English match, Francis I made it clear that Mary of Guise was off-limits, writing to his ambassador Castillon that December. It was 'a great honour if the king take a wife in his realm, and there is no lady who is not at his commandment except Madame de Longueville, whose marriage with the king of Scots has been arranged.'[4] A proxy marriage took place between Mary and James in June 1538, putting an end to any final hopes Henry still entertained. He would have to look elsewhere for a new wife.

Francis then proposed two of Mary's younger sisters, either of whom might make a suitable match for the King of England. Louise and Renee of Guise were then aged seventeen and fifteen respectively and both were considered beautiful. Renee, the youngest, was destined for the Church, but Louise was described by a visiting Scotsman as 'the most beautiful creature that he ever saw'. Castillon crudely urged Henry to 'take her ... she is still a maid, with her you will be able to shape the passage to your measure'.[5] Francis also dangled the carrot of a second marriage, between his youngest son Charles and Princess Mary, in spite of her illegitimate status. Yet neither Guise lady was considered a serious candidate by Henry, nor did he want Francis' cousins Anne of Lorraine and Mary of Bourbon, who were also proposed. The likelihood of him making a French match had seemed doomed once he crassly asked the French ambassador, Castillon, if a number of beautiful women could be assembled for his perusal at Calais, 'especially of the houses of Lorraine or Vendome or Nevers'. Francis was outraged, saying it was not their custom to display women of such noble rank 'as if they were hackneys for sale' and that if Henry was interested in a particular lady he could 'send his envoys to report on her manner and appearance in the traditional way'. The ambassador then wryly suggested that the king might like to 'mount them one after another, and keep the one you find to be the best broken in. Is that the way the Knights of the Round Table treated women in your country in times past?' The dig at Henry's past chivalric ideals was well chosen. Castillon reported that the king blushed, laughed and changed the subject.

Cromwell was already hard at work as international matchmaker. On 30 November 1537, he had written to Thomas Wyatt, mentioning another possible bride, this time drawn from the same pool as Catherine of Aragon. Clearly he considered that sufficient time had passed since Henry's repudiation of his first wife for a mutually beneficial union with the Empire to be possible. Personal memories could be set aside for the good of diplomatic relations. Upon Jane's death, the Imperial ambassadors 'made an overture for the daughter of Portugal', but it seemed they acted without consulting Charles, as Cromwell added 'it was thankfully taken, but would have been more so had it come anew from the Emperor, but it appears they did it upon an old commission'.[6] The family tree of the ruling House of Aziz under John III displays a mysterious lack of suitable Portuguese princesses at the time, with Maria, the eldest granddaughter of Catherine of Aragon's sister Maria and her husband Manuel I, being only ten. However, Manuel's daughter by his third wife was unmarried at the age of sixteen and proves a far more likely prospect. Born in Lisbon in 1521, Mary of Portugal was five years younger than her English namesake and potential stepdaughter, Princess Mary. Her mother, Eleanor, was the sister of Charles V, who had been suggested as a bride for Henry when they were children, back in 1498. She was also, therefore, Catherine of Aragon's niece and, by her mother's second marriage, stepdaughter of Francis I. The match would neatly tie together Henry's interests in France, Spain and the Empire. No doubt this was Mary's attraction. However, it came to nothing. Perhaps Charles was reluctant to commit another female relative to the English king, or perhaps Eleanor, who had previously avoided Anne Boleyn, rejected the idea. Mary never married and no more information appears to exist regarding a potential match between her and Henry.

On 4 December 1537, Ambassador John Hutton was in Brussels and, although admitting his lack of experience when it came to women, summed up the available candidates on offer:

> There is in the Court, waiting upon the Queen, the daughter of the lord of Breidrood, 14 years old and of goodly stature, virtuous, sad, and womanly. Her mother, who is dead, was daughter to the cardinal of Luike's sister; and the Cardinal would give her a good 'dote.' There is the widow of the late earl of Egmond, who repairs often to Court. She is over 40, but does not look it. There is the duchess of Milan who is reported a goodly personage and of excellent beauty. The duke of Cleves has a daughter, but there is no great praise either of her personage or her beauty.[7]

The 'daughter of Lord Briedrood' Hutton refers to was the fourteen-year-old Margaretha, whose father, Lord Reinoud III van Brederode, was captain-general in the Emperor's army, as well as his Privy

Councillor and chamberlain. His daughter was an attendant of Mary, Regent of the Netherlands, and was described by Hutton as 'of a goodly stature ... virtuous, sad and ... womanly', but her beauty was only 'competent'.[8] Coupled with her age, this made her a less likely candidate for Henry's hand. Age also ruled out Frances van Luxembourg, widow of Jan von Egmond, although she was a 'goodly personage'[9] who did not look her forty years. She had already borne a daughter and two sons but was considered too old to provide Henry with the string of heirs he desired.

Hutton's letter contains references to the two women on whom Henry would choose to focus in the coming months: the beautiful Duchess of Milan, whom he wanted to make his wife; and the woman he would later marry, Anne of Cleves. For the time being, though, Henry was enjoying the bachelor life, in the company of different women, while potential wives were discussed. And there were a good number of them. For the first time since 1509 he was an eligible bachelor, although his marital history and his increasing girth – from a thirty-two inch waist in his youth to the fifty-two inches of his later years – made him perhaps slightly less eligible than he had been in his youth. Refusing to take a wife without having some idea of her appearance, Henry dispatched his court painter Hans Holbein on a whirlwind tour of the courts of Europe to paint the pictures of likely beauties. Unexpectedly, one of them would capture the king's heart.

On 10 March, Hans Holbein and diplomat Philip Hoby arrived in Brussels. There, after much bargaining, they were allowed a three-hour sitting with the Duchess Christina. She was the daughter of the exiled Christian II of Denmark and his wife Isabella of Austria, Catherine of Aragon's niece. Having been widowed at the age of thirteen, she was living in the household of her aunt, Mary of Hungary, dressed in deepest mourning and her rooms hung in black. Reports of Christina's charms had already arrived in England, with the young widow described as tall, 'gentle of countenance' and 'soft of speech', with something of a lisp, although this 'did nothing misbecome her'. Also, she had dimples that appeared when she smiled; 'two charming pits in her cheeks and one in her chin, the which becometh her right exceedingly well'.[10] Hutton reported that 'there is none in these parts for beauty of person and birth to be compared with the duchess. She is not so pure white as the late queen ... but she hath a singular good countenance.'[11] Wriothesley added that she 'was a goodly personage of stature higher than either of us and competently fair but very well favoured, a very good woman's face, a little brown'.[12] Beside this, she had a reputation for being 'the wisest of the wise' and spoke French,

Italian and German. Henry was confident in his belief that marriage to him would be an elevation she deserved. Writing to Wyatt that January, he stated he might 'honour [her] by marriage, her virtues, qualities and behaviour being reported to be such as it worthy to be much advanced'.[13] However, the king's reputation had preceded him and the duchess was less convinced.

Christina was interviewed by Thomas Wriothesley, whose overenthusiastic praise of Henry's temper – that the king was 'the most gentle gentleman that liveth', with such a benign and pleasant nature 'that I think to this day no man hath heard many angry words pass his mouth' – was received by an incredulous duchess. Anyone who had witnessed Henry's recent rages (or his physical attacks upon Cromwell, whose ears he regularly boxed), let alone the cold treatment meted out to his first two queens and daughters, knew that this was nonsense. Wriothesley reported that Christina found it difficult to keep a straight face, as she appeared 'like one that was tickled'.[14] Holbein's full-length portrait depicted a young, pale woman in mourning, with a gentle, intelligent and attractive face; Henry found her captivating and urged his ambassadors to bring the negotiations to a conclusion. With the backing of Mary of Hungary, Christina declined his offer. She is reputed to have said that if she had two heads, she would happily put one of them at Henry's disposal. There was a further, convenient, impediment for the duchess. She was, as she stated, at the disposal of the Emperor. And, as Christina was the great-niece of Catherine of Aragon, Henry would require a papal dispensation to marry her, which would be difficult given that he was excommunicated in 1538.

Smarting from Christina's rejection, Henry consoled himself with the ladies who had belonged to Queen Jane's court. Having been sworn in only weeks before her mistress's death, Anne Bassett was now seventeen and references in the Lisle letters make clear that she had a family reputation for beauty. Anne had been born in 1521 in Cornwall but raised in Calais after her mother remarried to Henry's uncle, Arthur Plantagenet, Lord Lisle. She had been educated in the French manner, following the example of the Boleyn daughters, being placed in the household of Thybalt de Rouaud, or Riou, and his wife Jeanne, near Abbeville. There she learned French, and a wealth of letters testify to the clothes and jewels provided for Anne and her sisters in order for them to look the part. She had returned to Calais in September 1536, at the age of fifteen, with a yearly allowance of £6 13s 4d and a marriage portion of over £66.[15] It is clear that her good looks had impressed the king soon after her arrival.

On 9 October, as Jane went into labour, Peter Mewtas wrote to Lord Lisle that Henry had spoken of nothing but him and his daughters for the past two days, stating that he thought 'mistress Anne to be the fairest'.[16] It should have been the start of an illustrious career, during which she could attract a suitable husband, but the queen's death just five weeks later meant that her household was dissolved. Anne and her newly arrived sister Catherine were forced to rely on the hospitality of other previous ladies-in-waiting to the queen. Her mother, Honor, Lady Lisle, wrote from Calais on 14 November to their cousin Mary Arundel, who had become Countess of Sussex in January that year and was expecting her first child:

Commendations to my lord and you. I have received your letter and perceive your sorrow for the death of the Queen, yet her Grace was fortunate to live the day to bring forth such a prince. I perceive my lord and you have taken my daughter Anne until, by your good suit, she may obtain place again. If she cannot I will send for her and recompense your charges. I did not send them to put you or any of my kin to charge, but to have them with the Queen. Where you write that but for your great charge of kin and other gentlewomen you would have taken Kateryn too; it was never my mind to put you to any charge, yet if I were in England and you sent me even three or four I would accept them. I pray you prefer Anne because she was sworn to the late Queen. Where it has pleased my lord of Rutland and my lady at your suit to take Kateryn for the time, I trust they shall be no losers. 'Very glad to hear of your great belly, beseeching God to make you a joyous mother.'[17]

Anne would also live in the households of Jane Ashley, who was then married to Peter Mewtas, and Joan Champernowne, the wife of Anne's distant cousin Anthony Denny. However, as John Husee wrote in December 1537, Henry was fond of Anne and promised her a position in the household of any future wife he might take: 'The king is good lord to Mrs Anne, and has promised she shall have her place whenever the time comes ... It is yet unknown what his Grace intendeth, but it is judged she shall come out of France.'[18] He also sent her the gift of a horse and saddle, perhaps to facilitate them meeting as if by chance while out riding. By June 1539, Anne may have entered the household of Princess Mary as, according to John Husee, who enquired of Peter Mewtas, she had her 'board and charges' taken care of, as 'she was there at the king's setting ... I think they look for some pleasure. As the king set her there, I know the charge will be requited, yet some remembrance may not be forgotten.'[19] Anne would continue to be high in the royal favour and resurfaced again as another candidate for queenship later in Henry's reign. In October 1539, Henry took an interest in Anne's health as 'it was the king's grace's pleasure' that she visit her cousin Jane Denny, who had 'fair walks and a good open air' and 'the physician doth say that there is nothing better for my disease than walking'.[20] By this time, Anne did not consider herself to be in line for the position of Henry's wife, if she had at all, writing to her mother that 'I trust in God that we shall have a mistress shortly ... which I hope to God will not be long.'[21]

On 3 January 1538, John Husee mentioned yet another lady of the court on whom Henry's gaze had alighted. 'The election lieth betwixt Mrs Mary Shelton and Mrs Mary Skipwith. I pray Jesu send such one as may be for his Highness' comfort and the wealth of the realm.'[21] Mary Skipwith was, in fact, Margaret Skipwith, the daughter of Sir William Skipwith of Ormsby, Lancashire. During 1538, when she was around eighteen, she was rumoured to have been a mistress of Henry. Perhaps he helped arrange her marriage to George, the eldest son of Bessie Blount and Gilbert Tailboys, which was being planned in April 1539, but, as John Husee wrote to Lord Lisle, 'please your Lordship to keep secret until you hear more'.[22] Was this secrecy essential because of Margaret's connection with the king? It would be entirely possible that Henry was marrying off his paramour to a pliable, complicit young man. After all, this would only be repeating the pattern established by George's father, Gilbert, and his wife Bessie Blount.

The Tailboys marriage only lasted a few months, though, with George dying on 6 September. By that point, arrangements for Henry's fourth match were well underway and Margaret had missed any chance she may have had of becoming queen. She remained at court for the next couple of years and Henry's interest in her is demonstrated again with his intercession of 1546 to persuade her to marry Sir Peter Carew. With Henry aware of his worth on the international marriage market and keen to secure a diplomatic alliance against the new peace between Charles and Francis, it is probable that he considered a brief liaison with ladies of the court to be a diversion before a foreign bride was secured. Like the others, Margaret would have been pleased to be singled out by the king, as it meant she would receive significant material advantages, in the shape of gifts, accommodation and expenses, but whether or not she was a willing participant in the game of love is another matter entirely. Perhaps Mary, Margaret and their fellow ladies were doing their duty and enjoying the perks of the job; perhaps they were actually enthusiastic players, jostling for the position of Henry's next wife.

The year 1538 marked the height of Henry's bachelor years. He was out of mourning and not yet committed to an alliance; he could simply enjoy himself with whichever women happened to take his fancy. That April, he began work on a new pleasure palace in Surrey. The fairy-tale palace of Nonsuch would become Henry's greatest building project, intended as a hunting lodge, but which grew on an epic scale until it was large enough 'to receive the nobility of the king and horsemen in great numbers'.[23] Designed to rival the most magnificent castles of Francis I, Nonsuch was surrounded by a huge park, although it was the details of its garden that made it an ideal place for the king to woo women. Around the banqueting house, where the king could feast and party late into the night, were dells and hidden paths, concealed jets of water to surprise guests and a grove of Diana, where a statue of the huntress could be glimpsed in her bath. Henry also established similar pleasure gardens at most of his palaces, with tennis courts, heraldic beasts, bowling greens and archery butts overlooked by fruit trees, fringed arbours and hedged walks.

A poem written by Henry Howard, Earl of Surrey, gives a description of the pleasures of one such spot at Windsor:

> When Windsor walls sustain'd my wearied arm;
> My hand my chin, to ease my restless head;
> The pleasant plot revested green with warm;
> The blossom'd boughs, with lusty very [spring]-spread;
> The flower'd meads, the wedded birds so late
> Mine eyes discover.[24]

These outdoor rooms, rather like the early Italian Renaissance gardens in their playfulness, facilitated an intimacy and sense of high-spirited games among Henry and his courtiers. It was a 'privy palace', built for Henry's personal entertainment, lavishly decorated, for an elite group of his most intimate friends.

Now in his late forties, Henry had always been strong and robust, taking a keen interest in his health and medicinal cures. In his youth he had survived smallpox and malaria, as well as injuries sustained in jousting, riding, vaulting and playing tennis, after which he was forced to wear a black slipper to lessen the pain of a wrenched tendon in his ankle. He also endured sore and painful legs, which had become ulcerated by 1538, possibly as the result of one of his accidents or the tight garters he wore. In May that year, they were to give him a powerful reminder of his mortality. The fistulas in his legs were usually kept open to allow the noxious matter to be drained, but on this occasion one closed over, sending it into his bloodstream, which either triggered or contributed to a potential blood clot. After writhing in agony for ten days, black in the face, he recovered quickly and proved just as determined to throw himself into a hedonistic pursuit of pleasure. Those who had proclaimed his death across the country were publicly whipped for spreading false, treasonous reports. He would fall ill again the following Easter, attending church on his knees as the pain in his legs was so great. Yet, each time he recovered. There was life in the king yet; life enough for three more wives.

Henry passed the Christmas of 1538 and New Year at Greenwich, with his Privy Purse expenses recording that he made an offering of 33s 4d on 6 January and a further 100s to the heralds-at-arms. The wages paid to members of the king's court showed that his focus was still on pleasure and entertainment. Trumpeters might receive either 12s or 8s daily, lute players Philip and Peter Welder were paid 66s and 31s respectively, players of the rebeck might get 40s or 20s, a harper was worth 31s, a minstrel 20s 8d,the small drum and viol 33s, minstrels and players of sackbuts between 20s and 55s. A writer with the French-sounding name Maurice Dufresne was paid 33s 4d, probably for interludes or plays composed for the festive season. Paul Freeland, a feather maker, received 22s 2d, probably for the 'new feathering of liverey sheafe arrows in the castle of Windsor and for making of new bowstrings, and for drawing, heading, and burning of spears called demi launces', and the artist Lucas Horenbout was paid 55s 6d. A number of payments were also made to falconers, keepers and grooms of the crossbow, and 20s went to a priest named Sir John Wolfe for devising the arbours. It would appear that the seasonal festivities had been no less splendid for the absence of a queen.[25]

In the summer of 1539, Henry organised a trip for some of the ladies of his court to see his fleet at Portsmouth as part of his royal progress. On 1 July, he and his retinue left London for Beddington, once the home of Nicholas Carew, then on to Hampton Court until 8 July, from where he travelled south, arriving at the coast on the following day, where he signed various papers.[26] Among the women who accompanied him were Jane Ashley, now Mrs Mewtas, Margaret Skipworth and Anne Bassett. On 12 July, Richard Graynfeld reported to Lord Lisle that Henry had gone hunting and that Graynfeld's 'cousin Anne [Bassett] is merry and I was so bold as to bring her to my wife, whose bedfellow she was four or five nights when I was in court. I visited her in her lodging, with Mrs. Metas [*sic*] who was very kind to her.'[27] On 4 August, ten ladies of the court, including Jane, Margaret and Anne, wrote to Henry thanking him for arranging the trip, as the ships were 'so goodly to behold that in our lives we have not seen (excepting your royal person and my lord the Prince your son) a more pleasant sight'.[28] Also present on the *Harry Grace à Dieu* that day were Mabel Southampton, Margaret Howard, Alice Brown, Margaret Tailboys, Jane Meows, Elizabeth Tyrwhitt, Anne Knyvett, Jane Denny and Elizabeth Harvey. The trip may have had another purpose, though, as, while the women danced and feasted, Henry was examining the ninety warships that he had assembled in the case of a French invasion. With diplomatic relations across the channel turning sour, he sought a new bride from northern Europe instead.

In June 1539, instructions were given to Henry's ambassadors for their visit to Duren, in northern Germany, midway between Aachen and Cologne. Their task was to seek an audience with the Duke and Duchess of Cleves, with the aim of securing a marriage alliance between Henry and their daughter Anne. Interestingly, Henry told them to approach her mother first and use 'all their wisdom and dexterity to kindle them to the desire of this matter' and bring about a 'speedy conclusion'.[29] The ambassadors were to examine the appearance of both daughters of Cleves; Anne and her younger sister Amalia, and assess their personal charms. However, they were to be disappointed, as the customs of Cleves only permitted the ladies to appear heavily veiled. Still, it was reputed that Anne's beauty eclipsed that of Christina of Milan 'as the golden sun did the silver moon' and that everyone at court 'praised her beauty'.[30] Holbein was dispatched again to capture another likeness but this controversial painting was to spark a process that incurred the king's wrath and brought about the downfall of his chief minister. The portrait arrived back in England that August for the king's inspection. He liked what he saw. The ambassadors from Cleves arrived in London on 16 September, and by early October the marriage contract had been drawn up. Anne of Cleves had beaten off all the competition to become Henry's fourth wife.

49

I Like Her Not, 1539–40

I am a woman right fair, as ye see,
In no creature more beauty then in me is,
And, since I am fair, fair would I keep me.[1]

Anne had been born in 1515, the second of the three daughters of John III and Maria, Duchess of Julich-Berg, and raised at the Schloss Berg, near Solingen. At the age of eleven she was betrothed to Francis, son of the Duke of Lorraine, which lasted almost ten years until it was broken off in 1535. It had, however, been commensurate with most of her education. Destined to become a duchess, it is not surprising that the instruction Anne received from her mother failed to prepare her to be Queen of England. She only spoke German and could not sing, dance or play an instrument; her knowledge of games and sport was very limited. The court of Cleves, with its heavily moral tone and Catholicism tempered by Erasmian theories, did not encourage the sort of merrymaking, masques and lavish celebrations which had set the tone of Henry's court since his succession. More unforgivably, no one had instructed her about the marital duties of a wife and she arrived in England quite ignorant about sex, to the extent that she was not just virginal and inexperienced, but may have been unaware of the act itself.

A marriage to the king of England was a considerable victory for a daughter of Cleves. Anne set off overland to travel to Calais, so that a long sea voyage would not harm her complexion. Henry had planned to send his fleet to the Cleves-run port of Harderwijk, on the Zuiderzee, in order to avoid the necessity of asking Charles' permission for her to travel through his territories. Cleves favoured the overland route, though; Anne had already survived smallpox but her mother was unwilling for her to risk a journey that not only threatened her life on the dangerous midwinter seas, but also might damage her complexion prior to her arrival in England. Anne's servants, ranging from her ladies and translators to her horsemen and wardrobe, began to pack and prepare themselves for a journey of over 275 miles that would take them through the autumn into the winter.

Permission was granted from the Emperor and Anne set out with a retinue of 263 people but, as she did so, Charles and Francis met at

Loches and rode together to the Louvre Palace, where they consolidated their new alliance with pledges of loyalty, feasts and talks. Thomas Wyatt was the king's eyes and ears on this occasion, although he was made less than welcome, 'in evil-favoured lodging and worse bedding',[2] sending a clear message that the English were not welcome. The new Hapsburg–Valois friendship was a blow to Henry, making the Cleves match all more important, as relations between the Emperor and Anne's brother William, the new Duke of Cleves, were at an all-time low. Fearful of a French invasion, Henry needed a new European force at his side. It was a happy bonus that it also brought him an attractive young bride. He awaited her impatiently at Greenwich, pondering the Holbein miniature with its hooded eyes and serene expression, imagining the moment of their meeting.

Anne would also have wondered about her betrothed. She must have heard some reports of his appearance, character and marital history, but these are likely to have been as flattering as those told to Christina of Milan by Wriothesley the previous year. She was twenty-four, ignorant of the ways of the world, heading to an unknown country to become the fourth wife of a man twice her age. There was plenty of time on the journey for her to contemplate her future, but at every stage she had a taste of what her life would be like as Queen of England. The first leg of the journey took her from Dusseldorf to Antwerp, where English merchants in velvet coats and gold chains conducted her to her English lodgings in the city. From there she travelled to Gravelines, where the town captain rode out to meet her amid a volley of gunshot. Local man Antonine Brussett wrote to Lord Lisle that he had 'got her the best lodging I could in the town' and requested the 100 quarters of malt he had been promised for such a service.[3]

Finally, on 11 December, Anne's party rode into Calais but terrible weather prevented any plans for her to cross the Channel. She was lodged in the Exchequer, the residence used by Henry on previous occasions, and was the third of Henry's Queens to have stayed there. Wriothesley was able to show her the ship prepared for her departure 'trimmed with streamers, banners and flags, and men on the tops, shrouds and yard arms',[4] but two more weeks would pass before the storms subsided enough to make it safe to embark. While there, the Duke of Cleves sent presents to Wriothesley, asking him 'to advise my lady as to her behaviour, to which he replied by expressing his satisfaction at the marriage and his intention to promote love and affection between the parties'.[5] Also, Cromwell asked him 'to cheer my lady and her train so that they may think the time short.'[6] It was something of a delicate commission; Wriothesley responded by trying to teach Anne to play Henry's favourite card game, 'cent'. He related that she 'played as pleasantly, and with as good a grace and countenance as ever in my life I saw noblewoman'.[7] Wriothesley also had a quiet word with Anne's steward Hoghesten and envoy Olisleger, to explain that it was Henry's 'most godly desire and affection to have more children' in case 'God fails us in my Lord Prince'.[8]

Anne was clearly conscious of a difference between the culture of Cleves and that of her adopted country. She requested that Wriothesley come to supper and 'bring some noble folks to sit with her after the manner of her country',[9] wishing to observe 'the manner and fashion of Englishmen sitting at meat.'[10] Telling her it 'was not the usage of our country to do so', the earl complied nevertheless, taking George Tailboys, Francis Bryan, Henry Knyvett, Edward Seymour, Gregory Cromwell and others with him. Anne's manner, he reported, 'was like a princess'. Gregory wrote to his father a week later, informing him that 'my lady Anne, my lord Admiral, and the rest are in good health', but the weather continued to be 'too bad to cross'.[11] The admiral reported to be 'in good health' was George Carew, a relation of the Nicholas Carew to whom Henry had once been close. However, Cromwell also reported from Calais the same day that Carew's wife, Thomasine Pollard, sister of Jane Stukley, had died in the night and was about to be buried in the town.[12]

At Calais, Anne was welcomed and entertained by Lord Lisle and his wife Honor. Lady Lisle wrote her impressions of the Princess of Cleves to her daughter, Anne Bassett, who was then at York Place awaiting the arrival of the new queen. Anne replied on 22 December, reassured about the character of her new mistress and her own 'continuance in the king's favour':

> I humbly thank your ladyship of the news you write me, of her Grace that she is so good and gentle to serve and please. It shall be no little rejoicement to us, her Grace's servants here, that shall attend daily upon her, and most comfort to the king's majesty, whose highness is not a little desirous to have her Grace here ... He [Henry] likes so much the conserves you sent him that he commands me to write to you for more of the codynack of the clearest making, and of the damsons. York Place, Monday before Christmas day.[13]

Early in the morning on 27 December, Anne's fleet set sail from Calais, arriving in Deal, just down the coast from Dover, at around five in the evening. According to Suffolk, who was awaiting her, 'the day was foule and wynde with muche hayle ... contynuelly in her face', but Anne was 'desirous to make haste' to her husband. She was met at by a party of ladies including Catherine Willoughby, Duchess of Suffolk, Lady Hart, Lady Cobham, Lady Haulte, Lady Finche and Lady Hales, whose residence in nearby Canterbury made her a convenient choice. In fact, most were local, as chronicler Hall relates that she was met by 'a great number of Knights and Esquire and Ladies of Kent'.[14] A banquet was held in her honour at Deal Castle, where she also had the chance to change her clothes after her long journey. Her first glimpse of an English castle was the squat, defensive grey-stone bastion facing the stony beach at Deal, built in the shape of a flower with six circular petals. Her next stop gave her a far more imposing example. Suffolk and his wife rode with Anne to Dover Castle, which would have been far more on the scale of the European castles she was used to. After resting at Dover, Anne's retinue headed north-west over the seventeen miles to Canterbury. There she was met under torchlight by the mayor and conveyed to St Augustine's Abbey, which, after Dissolution, had been rapidly converted into the king's palace. Forty or fifty 'gentlewomen of the town' awaited her in her chamber, dressed in velvet bonnets. Anne took this 'very joyously, and was so glad to see the king's subjects resorting so lovingly to her that she forgot all the foul weather and was very merry at supper'.[15]

The meeting between Henry and Anne had been planned for 3 January but, knowing that his bride had arrived in the country, the king could not contain himself and set off from Greenwich to greet her ahead of schedule. His love of games, masques, plays and disguises was well known to his courtiers; it had been the staple of court entertainment for decades, allowing for chivalric role play and flirtation, often in the guise of an allegorical figure, a stranger, foreigner or folkloric hero. And it always worked beautifully, with the entire room complicit in the 'secret,' feigning surprise when the king finally removed his mask. Now Henry saw the opportunity to enact such a game for real. Anticipating a romantic readiness in his spouse, he hoped to catch her unawares, with his identity concealed. True to the plot of a French romance, she would be overwhelmed by the impressive stranger and fall in love at first sight. Anne, of course, knew nothing of this. It was a completely different custom to that she was used to in Cleves, and although she would not have anticipated it there were plenty of precedents for such meetings. Perhaps someone close to Henry should have warned her.

On New Year's Eve, Anne had passed through Sittingbourne and reached Rochester, where she stayed at the Bishop's Palace. The following day, she was relaxing by watching a bull-baiting through her window when a party of nine disguised men entered the room. They all wore hooded cloaks and the effect must have been quite sinister in comparison with the other welcomes she had received. Completely reliant upon her translators and still uncertain of courtly protocol, let alone Henry's penchant for disguise, she was taken by surprise when one of the men approached her, took her in his arms and attempted to kiss her. In fact, considering the close closeting of her childhood, and the strict way in which she had been covered up for the viewing of the ambassadors, this behaviour was probably scandalous to her. On her way to be married to the king, she had been as good as assaulted by a stranger, whose familiarity showed disrespect to her rank and threatened her reputation. No wonder she did not respond and turned away coldly. In Henry's insensitivity and conviction of his own personal charm, he had overlooked Anne's possible feelings. If she really had swooned in the arms of a romantic stranger, without knowing it was her intended, surely it would not have been a good sign regarding her future fidelity?

Henry's attempt to 'nourish love' had failed. Abashed at the failure of his romantic gesture, he retired and changed into regal purple, before returning and declaring his true identity. Recognising her mistake, Anne bowed low and, according to Wriothesley, the pair 'talked lovingly together', although Lord Russell reported that he 'never saw His Highness so marvellously astonished ... as on that occasion'. Hall related how 'she with most gracious and loving countenance and behaviour, him received and welcomed on her knees, whom he gently took up and kissed', after which, they dined together.[16] Anne's reaction had disappointed the king, but her appearance had been even greater a surprise. In his opinion she was not as attractive or as young looking as he had been led to believe, and although he afforded her the respect her position demanded, his growing anger seethed behind his diplomatic mask. The disguise he had adopted in the hopes of sparking romance necessitated him retreating behind another to conceal his dislike. Riding back to Greenwich, he informed Cromwell in no uncertain terms that he did not like Anne. They were ominous words indeed to the man who had invested so much in arranging the marriage.

50

The Unwanted Bride, 1540

Noon other life is worth a bene
For wedlock is so easy and so clene
That in this world it is Paradys[1]

On Saturday 3 January, Anne travelled from Blackheath to Shooter's Hill. One of the highest points in London, named after the medieval archery practice that used to take place there, it was just two miles from Greenwich Palace, where Henry was already pressing Cromwell to find a loophole to allow him to avoid honouring the marriage. Yet the massive wheels of hospitality had been set in motion. The bushes and firs in the park had been cut down to allow for the huge retinue which greeted her, of knights, city dignitaries and gentlemen pensioners. There were also serving men, 'in good order, well horsed and apparelled, that whosoever had well viewed them might say that they, for tall and comely personages and clene of limb and body, were able to give the greatest Prince in Christendom a mortal breakfast'.[2] Dignitaries, clergymen and servants lined the lane in their ranks, from the park gates to the cross of Blackheath, to welcome Anne. Henry's retinue alone numbered between 5,000 and 6,000.[3] As news arrived at the palace that the new queen-to-be had been sighted, the king climbed reluctantly into the saddle, conscious of the contrast with his eager dash out to Rochester only forty-eight hours before.

Anne arrived at about midday, drawn in a chariot, flanked by a hundred horsemen. Dr Day, who had been appointed as her almoner, made a welcome oration in Latin, to which her brother's secretary made a suitable response. Then, Lady Margaret Douglas, Lady Frances Brandon, Lady Mary Howard, Duchess of Richmond, and other 'ladies and gentlewomen to the number of' sixty-five, welcomed her and led her into a gorgeous tent or pavilion of rich cloth of gold that had been set up for at the foot of the hill, in which fires burned and perfumes scented the air. They helped her dress in a rich gown of raised cloth of gold, with a round skirt and no train, in the Dutch fashion. On her head she wore a round bonnet or cap, set with orient pearls 'of a very proper fashion',[4] a black velvet cornet and about her neck, a partelet, set full of rich glistening stones. She was then helped onto a 'faire horse, richly trapped', while her footmen wore 'goldsmith's work embroidered with the black lion' and a gold carbuncle on the shoulder.[5] This time she had been informed of Henry's approach.

Much had been written about the king's response to Anne of Cleves, but there is rarely any significant thought given to what her feelings were towards her new husband. This is mostly because Henry was so vocal in his dislike, which developed into such a significant matter that summer that it required investigation and recording. Neither Anne nor her ladies wrote down their responses to the unscheduled meeting in Rochester, or the appearance of the king, so it has generally been assumed that she raised no objection. Such objections probably never even occurred to her. To reject Henry, Anne would have caused a diplomatic scandal as well as incurring the wrath of her brother, not to mention the terrible insult she would be giving to her host. In all likelihood, Anne accepted Henry warts and all, willingly, even happily. He was a majestic figure and she was about to become Queen of England. He was king; that was sufficient. She knew it was not a love match and had not anticipated any romance, hoping instead for dignity and respect, perhaps with affection developing over time. Such was the way with most arranged marriages, as she had witnessed between her own parents. Anne's opinion of Henry is probably a misleading and anachronistic question to raise.

However, as she awaited him on 3 January, their meeting at Rochester was fresh in her mind. She may not have been able to speak English, and was not skilled or experienced with men or in the arts of flirtation and love, but that does not mean she was insensitive. Did she sense that he was disappointed? If she was able to detect any coolness or distance in his second welcome, she did not know enough about the man to be able to interpret it. Given his concerns over the Franco-Imperial alliance, Henry was not about to risk alienating the Duke of Cleves. It seems most likely that she rode forth across Shooter's Hill in eager anticipation to embrace her future as the Queen of England, with an optimism that marital cordiality could develop over time. Anne was there to fulfil her duty; it is probably rather misleading to consider whether Henry's looks and her personal preferences tallied. She had no way of knowing that her hopes were to be as disappointed as his had been.

Shimmering with jewels and studded with pearls, Anne was in a better position to impress than she had been at Rochester. However, just as Catherine of Aragon's Spanish clothes had caused a stir in 1501, Anne's Germanic costume failed to overturn national tastes for native and French fashions. Marillac commented that Anne 'was clothed in the fashion of the country from which she came' as were her ladies of honour, 'a thing which looks strange to many'. To his (French) eyes, these women were 'inferior in beauty even to their mistress and dressed so heavily and unbecomingly that they would almost be thought ugly even if they were beautiful'. Anne's looks did not meet with his approval either: 'She looks about thirty years of age, tall and thin, of medium beauty, and of very assured and resolute countenance ... according to some who saw her close, [she] is not so young as was expected, nor so beautiful as everyone affirmed. She is tall and very assured in carriage and countenance, showing that in her the turn and vivacity of wit supplies the place of beauty.'[6] Henry's performance was convincing, coming forward to meet her 'with most lovely countenance and princely behaviour'. He 'saluted, welcomed and embraced her, to the great rejoicing of the beholders'.[7] She, in turn, received him with 'most amiable aspect and womanly behaviour', with 'many sweet words and great thanks and praisings given to him'.[8] Placing her on his right, he accompanied her to Greenwich Palace. In the outer court, he embraced and kissed her again, bidding her 'welcome to her own'.[9] With Anne settled in her privy chamber with her ladies, Henry then hurried back to Cromwell, to seek a path by which he could avoid having to make her his wife. There was one glimmer of hope: Anne's pre-contract with Francis of Lorraine.

Despite Cromwell's best efforts to dissuade Henry from repudiating Anne, claiming he 'thought she had a queenly manner',[10] the king directed the council to examine her previous contract. This had already been investigated the previous autumn by the English ambassadors at Cleves, who had then been entirely satisfied with the explanation that the engagement had been entered into when the parties were both below the age of consent and that Anne was now free to marry where she wished. Now, her secretary could only repeat this information, promising to summon the relevant legal paperwork from Cleves at once. Anne must have been surprised that such a question had raised its head again at this stage in the proceedings. She willingly swore an oath to the effect that she was not obligated to Lorraine, and there was nothing Henry could do unless he wanted to send Duke William of Cleves into the arms of the Emperor. While Anne eagerly anticipated her wedding day, her bridegroom felt the net close in around him, knowing he must put his head 'into this yoke'. Seething with rage, backed into a corner, he decided that he was 'not well handled'.

The wedding took place on 6 January, in the queen's closet at

Greenwich. Anne was dressed in the round-skirted Dutch fashion again, this time in a gown of rich cloth of gold, ornamented with large flowers and pearls and her fair, long, yellow hair hanging loose. On her head she wore a coronet of gold set with jewels and decorated with sprigs of rosemary, a common medieval wedding custom that signified love and loyalty. With the most 'demure countenance' she passed through the king's chamber into the gallery, and closet, where she greeted her future spouse with three curtseys. His heart might not have been in it, but Henry had at least dressed the part. His gown of cloth of gold, with raised silver flowers and black fur, a coat of crimson satin tied with diamonds and rich collar, were part of the mask of royalty that he hid behind on that day. Cranmer officiated and the Earl of Overstein gave Anne away. Henry placed a ring on her finger that bore the legend, 'God send me well to keep.' From there, they walked hand in hand back into Henry's chamber to hear Mass and take wine and spices.[11]

Soon after, at nine in the morning, Henry changed into a gown of tissue lined with red velvet, and collected Anne from her chamber where she had been waiting, and they dined together. Then it was the queen's turn to change again, with her choices yet again prompting criticism; this time, it was 'a gowne like a man's gown', and a cap she had previously worn at Blackheath, although chronicler Hall conceded that her apparel was 'rich and very costly'.[12] The hours between then and supper, probably served mid-afternoon in winter, are unaccounted for, but Anne and Henry emerge at that point to attend Evensong, eat together again and enjoy the banquets, masques and 'diverse disports' until 'the time came that it pleased the king and her to take their rest'.[13] It probably pleased Anne considerably more than it pleased Henry, but, if he was displeased with his bride, things were about to get much worse. They retired to their chambers and were ceremonially undressed for the wedding night. It would prove a disaster.

PART EIGHT
Catherine Howard

51

The King's Infatuation, 1540

Give place, ye lovers, here before
That spent your boasts and brags in vain;
My Lady's beauty passeth more
The best of yours, I dare well sayen,
Than doth the sun the candle light,
Or brightest day the darkest night.[1]

The royal wedding night may have been a disaster, but Anne was still Henry's wife. As such, her household was now appointed to anticipate and supply her needs. The Earl of Rutland was her chamberlain, Sir Thomas Dennis her chancellor, Sir John Dudley became her master of horse, with others appointed as secretaries, surveyors, auditors, solicitors and attorneys, as well as the more prosaic roles of cup-bearer, sewer, usher, clerk and sergeant. She was allowed to retain one of her Flemish doctors, Dr Cornelian, given the need for her to communicate over delicate matters in her native tongue, as well as a cook and footman from home. Her wardrobe was placed under the care of Henry Cryche and Dr Malett and Dr Oglethorpe became her chaplains. Perhaps someone dropped a hint to Henry Cryche about Anne's clothing. On 11 January, she appeared to watch the day's jousting dressed in the English fashion, with a French hood, 'which so set forth her beauty and good visage that every creature rejoiced to behold her'.[2]

The list of Anne's female attendants included many of those who had served Jane Seymour and had been biding their time since, until the arrival of a new queen would again give them a formal role at the heart of the court. There were Henry's nieces Frances Brandon and Margaret Douglas, as well as Mary Arundel, Countess of Sussex; Eleanor Paston, Countess of Rutland; Elizabeth Howard, Duchess of Richmond; and Elizabeth Grey, Lady Audley. The new queen's privy chambers required a more intimate set of waiting women, who were the ones to change her clothes, assist with bodily functions and supervise her bedtime. The jobs went to Jane Parker, Lady Rochford; Jane Guildford, Lady Dudley; Catherine St John, Lady Edgecumbe; Isabel, Lady Baynton; and Susanna Horenbout, the sister of Flemish miniaturist Lucas Horenbout, who often depicted Henry VIII. Little did they realise just how important their proximity to Anne would become in the months ahead. Her gentlewomen included Jane Ashley, Lady Mewtas; Jane Cheney, Lady Wriothesley; Jane Seymour's sister Elizabeth, Lady Cromwell; and Margaret Skipwith's sister Catherine, Lady Heneage. Anne Bassett, Mary Norris, Ursula Stourton and Dorothy Bray found positions as Anne's maids of honour, as did Catherine Carey (possibly Henry's daughter by Mary Boleyn) and a plump, pretty young granddaughter of the Duke of Norfolk named Catherine Howard.

The pretence of marital harmony was still being maintained. Queen Anne was happy among her new ladies at Greenwich, according to John Norris, writing to Lady Lisle to report that her daughter Anne Bassett was 'merry' along with them.[3] On 18 January Henry wrote to Anne's brother, William of Cleves, to the effect that he had 'spoken to his ambassadors about his negotiations with the Emperor and concealed nothing' and would 'act sincerely in matters concerning their friendship and the marriage'.[4] Yet, behind this diplomatic façade, the king was still hoping that the Lorraine pre-contract would allow the marriage to be declared invalid. Three days later, Anne's vice-chancellor, Henry Olisleger, wrote to Cromwell in a mixture of Italian and French to establish that he was working to produce the paperwork: 'We have received the letters to the dukes of Saxony and Cleves, but the copy of the letters patent of the dower of our mistress [Anne of Cleves] is left behind. Please send it to-night to Gravesend or to-morrow night to Dover that we may take it with us, and we will advance the business of our mistress as rapidly as possible.'[5] It could not be rapid enough for Henry.

Shortly afterwards, the majority of the Flanders retinue departed, having been feasted well and received their share of a huge £1,405 16s 15d that had been set aside for parting gifts. Four or five gilt cups were given, but the majority were given purses of coins; £102 to the Earl of Overstein, £100 to Grand Master Hoghensten, £99 to Vice-Chancellor Olisleger and various other amounts to her ladies and gentlemen, with £19 to her surgeon and £9 to her messenger.[6] On 4 February, Henry and Anne departed Greenwich and travelled by barge to Westminster. They were welcomed by a flotilla of merchants on barges, with flags and pennants flying, guns shot at the Tower and the mayor and aldermen dressed in their robes of office and gold chains. According to Marillac, it was 'more honourable than any magnificence made at the coming of the said lady'.[7]

On 9 February, Sir Nicholas Wooton arrived back at Schloss Berg, at the court of William, Duke of Cleves. A letter he sent back to

Cromwell at the end of the month sheds the first light on Anne's view of the marriage. On telling 'Ghogreve how well the king liked the queen's Grace, he rejoiced greatly that the affection was mutual, for lady Keteler had written that, on leaving the Queen, she was desired to report to the Duchess, her mother, and the Duke, her brother, that she thanked them most heartily for having preferred her to such a marriage that she could wish no better'.[8] At Easter, the ladies and gentlewomen waiting upon the queen were paid wages totalling over £194, while the royal goldsmith Cornelius Hayes received twice this, claiming an impressive £403 6s 8d for spangles made to decorate costumes and clothes. Two silkwomen, Cope's wife and Lettice Woursop, were paid £80 and £177 respectively for adorning the king's and queen's bodies.[9] That April, a Bill confirming Queen Anne's dower was passed through Parliament and, in spite of his failure to rid his master of his unwanted wife, Cromwell was elevated to the Earldom of Essex. It was the calm before the storm, though. With the queen's household full of attractive young ladies, it was only a matter of time before history began to repeat itself.

Back in the autumn of 1539, as the Cleves negotiations were reaching their conclusion, Cranmer, in his capacity as Henry's personal chaplain, suggested to Cromwell that the king should 'marry where that he had his fantasy and love, for that would be most comfort for his Grace'.[10] He obviously knew his master well but the archbishop's was the lone voice of reason. Having masterminded the alliance, Cromwell dismissed him angrily, saying that 'there was none meet for him within this realm'. Within weeks, though, Henry was to do exactly as his chaplain had suggested. It would cost Cromwell his head.

The date and location of Catherine Howard's birth went unrecorded. Like Anne Boleyn and Jane Seymour, no one could have anticipated that she would ever become queen. She was one of at least six children born to Edmund Howard and Joyce Culpepper, although her mother already had five others from a previous marriage. Estimates for Catherine's birth usually err on the side of caution, placing her arrival in the early to mid-1520s, usually around 1522/23. She was definitely born before 1527, when she was mentioned in the will of her grandmother Isabel Legh, but she did not appear in that of her grandfather John in 1524. However, this does not mean Catherine had not been born by that point; it may have been down to caution, which advised against recognising infants, particularly girls, in family wills.[11] Her father was the brother of Elizabeth Howard, mother of Anne and Mary Boleyn, making her their first cousin; Edmund's own cousin Margery was the mother of Jane Seymour. Catherine was still young when her mother died in 1531 and her father was appointed to the position of Comptroller of Calais.

Catherine's first years were spent at Norfolk House in Lambeth, the London home of the Howard clan. Early in the reign of Elizabeth, it was described as having been two inns, 'formerly called the George (west) and the Bell (east)', which had been annexed to a medieval mansion house, which came with about forty acres of land, meadow and a marsh, called 'the hopes'.[12] In 1531, she was moved into the household of her step-grandmother, Agnes Tilney, the dowager Duchess of Norfolk, at Chesworth House, Horsham, in Sussex. The large property provided shelter for a number of young people from less wealthy backgrounds, who were supposed to learn and make themselves useful until such time as they could find their way in the world of their own accord. For Catherine, it proved to be a period of sexual awakening; her years at Chesworth would come back to haunt her and be the cause of her downfall as queen.

Still standing today, Chesworth House is located half a mile south of Horsham, in the middle of twenty-three acres and preserves much of its original Tudor character. In 1549, it was described as comprising a hall, great chamber, dining chamber, chapel and at least twenty other rooms and service quarters, incorporating the present day north and south wings. Here, the young Catherine Howard was lodged in one of the attic dormitories known as the maiden's chamber with the other young women, while the men had separate sleeping quarters. There were also visiting servants and staff who came to the house on a regular basis during Catherine's youth. One of them was the music teacher Henry Manox, who had been employed by the duchess to teach the girl to play the virginals in 1536. Manox later admitted he 'fell in love' with Catherine, who was then in her early teens, and that the pair exchanged kisses and caresses. He would claim he had touched her intimately, 'feel the secret parts of her body' and would know her by a 'secret mark' on her body. Conscious of her status, though, she refused to allow him to consummate the match, allowing him instead to enjoy certain favours. When the duchess discovered them alone in a chamber, she gave her charge 'two or three blows' and forbade the pair to be alone together again.

Manox was soon replaced in Catherine's affections by a far more ardent suitor, a Howard cousin named Francis Dereham, who arrived at Horsham from Norfolk. If Catherine had wisely held Manox off because of the discrepancy between their social positions, she now had no reason to deny the advances of the dashing Dereham, who wooed her by bringing gifts and making sweet talk. The door to the maiden's chamber was locked every night by the duchess, who took the key away with her until the morning, but one of her waiting women, Mary Lascelles, managed to steal the key and allow a group of gentlemen to enter. Bringing 'wine, strawberries, apples and other things to make good cheer', Dereham quickly progressed to Catherine's bed. The girls slept two to a bed, as was common at the time, so with Catherine's usual bedfellow evicted, the development of the relationship was witnessed by those who shared the chamber.

This arrangement was to prove Catherine's downfall in years to come, when the eyes and ears of her past resurfaced. Privacy was a luxury reserved for the rich. Public sex and courtship must have been common in large establishments after hours, when temporary beds appeared and the majority of young people slept communally. Court records dating from this time are full of examples of servants having sex in dormitories or the various rooms of their masters' house, which usually come to light when a pregnancy resulted. Witnesses would later cite how Catherine and Dereham would 'hang together' by the belly 'like sparrows', leaving little doubt of what was occurring. One, Alice Restwold, who was herself married, knew 'what belonged to that puffing and blowing' that took place under cover of night. Catherine later admitted that Dereham 'lay with [her] naked and used me in such sort as a man doth his wife, many and sundry times'.[13] As the relationship progressed the pair entered an informal betrothal, a promise to become man and wife in the future, referring to each other in those terms. Gifts were exchanged, Dereham giving Catherine fine materials to make dresses from and Catherine sending him a band to wear upon his sleeve, perhaps as a remembrance of her.

Jealous of his rival, Manox informed the duchess by leaving an anonymous letter in her pew at chapel:

Your Grace,
    It shall be meet you take good heed to your gentlewomen, for if it shall like you half an hour after you shall be a-bed to rise suddenly and visit their chamber you shall see that which shall displease you. But if you make anybody of counsel you shall be deceived. Make then fewer your secretary.[14]

The duchess upbraided her charges over their 'misrule', which might 'hurt [Catherine's beauty]'[15] but this served to unite her and Dereham against a common enemy, seeking out the letter from its hiding place in a gilt coffer and making a secret copy. Dereham confronted

Manox, calling him a knave whom neither he nor Catherine loved, but a greater threat was soon to arise. Late in 1539, Catherine was granted a position at court, to be in attendance upon Anne of Cleves. Dereham knew that this would signal the end of their relationship but Catherine was happy to move on to bigger and better things, later saying, 'All that knew me, and kept my company, know how glad and desirous I was to come to court.'[16]

Of two surviving portraits claimed to depict Catherine, one is far more likely to show the new queen's maid of honour. Recently, David Starkey has identified a Holbein miniature of an unknown woman as Catherine, by matching the jewels she is wearing to records of those in her possession. The sitter wears gold and brown against a blue background, her auburn hair pulled back under a gold French hood lined with pearls. More pearls and golden embroidery line her bodice and a further string and pendant sit around her neck. The sitter's face is pale and serene, with heavy-lidded eyes, delicate lips and rounded chin. She wears a gold wedding ring, indicating that the portrait was probably painted between mid-1540 and late 1541. It is less certain that the full-length Holbein *Portrait of a Lady in a Black Dress* depicts Catherine as, although the features are similar, the sitter appears to be older than Catherine is thought to be.

At some point early in 1540, Henry's and Catherine's paths crossed. She may have been coached by her Howard relatives, her grandfather the Duke of Norfolk and her step-grandmother Agnes Tilney, to attract the attention of the dissatisfied king. As longstanding enemies of Cromwell, recognising that the royal marriage was unlikely to last, they might have encouraged Catherine once it was clear that Henry was interested. The duchess believed that it happened almost as soon as she arrived at court, perhaps even as late as autumn 1539, saying that 'the king's highness did cast a fantasy to Catherine Howard the first time that ever his Grace saw her'.[17] The relationship may have developed at one of the midnight banquets held by Bishop Gardiner at Winchester Palace in Southwark which, reputedly, 'far outdid the impromptu entertainments in the maiden's chamber at Horsham or Lambeth'.[18]

By late April the king was smitten, making the first grant of land to his new mistress, indicating a possible time when the affair was consummated. From that point, the possibility of Catherine becoming pregnant meant that Anne's days were numbered. When she took her seat to watch the May Day jousts at Westminster, followed by a week of tournaments and feasting at Durham House, Anne could not have anticipated it would be her last public engagement as queen. On 9 May, Henry summoned Cromwell to Westminster, 'desiring his presence immediately on weighty business concerning the honour and surety of the king's person and the tranquillity of his subjects'. The king's servant can have been in little doubt about what this 'weighty business' was. His efforts appear to have not been enough for Henry, who ordered his arrest for treason on 8 June. Heading to a Westminster council meeting, Cromwell was – literally – stripped of his chain of office by Howard and Wriothesley, and carried away to the Tower. Henry would keep him alive long enough for him to push through the necessary paperwork for his divorce, before he signed the earl's death warrant.

On 24 June, 'the kyng caused the queen to Richmond', purportedly for 'her health, open air and pleasure' and to escape the illnesses that often broke out at court during the summer months. It was a beautiful palace and Henry promised that he would be joining Anne there shortly. The days passed and she waited patiently. Instead, though, her husband established a commission to investigate the legality of his marriage, with the aim of securing a divorce and easing the path of Catherine Howard into his bed. The resulting investigation allows us an insight into the intimate nature of the marriage, a glimpse through the keyhole of the bedroom door, as Henry had reluctantly climbed into bed with Anne of Cleves.

52

The King's Sister, 1540

Was I not a king's fare in marriage,
Had I not plenty of every pleasant thing?
Merciful God, this is a strange reckoning;
Riches, honour, wealth, and ancestry,
Hath me forsaken[1]

It was down to Henry to prove that he had not had sex with Anne. This essentially began as a private matter concerning what had happened between the marital sheets, but, given the dynastic and national proportions that evolved from his challenge to Catherine of Aragon's virginity, the king was taking no chances. He roped his court into securing the result he wanted. Anne's marriage had to be annulled in order for him to make Catherine Howard his wife and, as it always had, his court obligingly rose to the challenge. According to the preparations drawn up by Bishop Gardiner, as much proof must be prepared in advance 'to declare the king's misliking, his Grace's dissent and abstinence *a carnali copula* and also her confession thereof of it'.[2] As they had in 1536, Henry's commissioners went in search of the details of his love life, or, in this case, the lack of it.

The most powerful evidence came from Henry's doctor. That July, William Butts testified that it had been the king's decision not to attempt consummation on the night of the wedding. There may have been a valid religious reason for this as, after having been delayed, the ceremony eventually took place on Epiphany, a major day of observation in the Catholic calendar, on which abstinence of all kinds was expected. It was also believed that children conceived on such dates would be less healthy, so the delay is understandable. Henry's comment to Cromwell on the following morning, that 'his nature hath abhorred her',[3] could be taken to refer to his inability to sleep with Anne, a metaphor for erectile dysfunction or simply a comment on the dislike that had been borne out of closer physical proximity, not necessarily of a sexual nature. Dr Butts reported that Henry attempted to consummate the match on the third and fourth night, on 8 and 9 January, but was unsuccessful. He claimed 'his heart would never consent to meddle with her carnally'.[4] He continued to lie with her every other night after this for short periods, but after he had 'felt' her 'breasts and belly' and believed them to indicate that she was not a virgin ('when I felt them, strake me so to the heart that I had neither will nor courage to prove the rest ... if she had brought her maidenhead with her') he 'never took any from her by true carnal copulation'. He told his doctor that 'he found her body disordered and indisposed to provoke any lust in him'.[5]

Setting Henry's case aside, it seems highly unlikely that Anne was not a virgin. Her sheltered upbringing and character, along with her reputed ignorance, suggest that she was, indeed, as pure as the day she had been born. Her status on the international marital market would have been damaged beyond repair if there had been even the slightest rumour of a previous physical relationship; the legal bond of her pre-contract proved problematic enough without any actual suitors complicating her reputation. Virginity was thought to be physically manifest in several ways, in the shape and firmness of the breasts, the smooth belly and clear urine. Henry's concerns over Anne's pre-contract led him to perceive her body in this context, reading it as a sign that she was legally contracted to another man, creating a psychological problem, a barrier or inhibition that would not allow him to consummate the match. As he admitted to Dr Butts, he had experienced emissions of seed (wet dreams) twice nightly during the marriage, which he claimed proved that he was capable of sleeping with a woman, just not this woman. Henry was keen for it to be known that he was a 'man like any other', particularly with an impending marriage to a young wife and the comments reputedly levelled at his sexual prowess by Anne Boleyn.

Night after night, Anne awaited her husband. She lay on the marital bed with its oak head, which depicted a pregnant woman, awaiting the time that she would become a mother. Just how far was she aware of what was expected of a married woman and how far the marriage had fallen short? She is usually depicted as a complete innocent, naïve to the ways of the world to such an extent that she was completely unaware of the sexual act and the means of becoming pregnant. However, the evidence suggests she may not have been as sheltered as this. As early as January, by his own later admission, Anne was seeking advice from Cromwell regarding the failure of her marriage. He, in turn, passed the task on to the Earl of Rutland, a difficult and delicate task in which he probably failed. Anne also still had her own Flemish women with her, including Mother Lowe, to whom she could have turned for advice. It would also be within her mother's remit to inform her of what to expect upon her departure for England. Sex and childbirth formed the subject of bawdy marital jokes, songs and sayings at the time; with privacy being elusive even for royalty, the conception and arrival of children was a far more public occurrence, being overheard at night through walls and closed doors. Sex was no great Tudor secret.

Then there is the standard of Anne's spoken English. In July, three of Anne's ladies – Jane, Viscountess Rochford; Eleanor, Countess of Rutland; and Catherine, widow of Sir Piers Edgecombe – testified that Anne had no knowledge of sex at all. When they asked her if she was pregnant, Anne apparently said,

> How can I be a maid ... and sleep every night with the king? ...
> When he comes to bed he kisses me, and takes me by the hand, and
> bids me, good night sweet heart; and in the morning kisses me, and
> bids me farewell darling. Is this not enough?[6]

But did she really utter these words, in exactly this way? Rutland required an interpreter to speak to Anne that same month, as neither could understand each other, so it seems very unlikely she was able to formulate such sentences to her waiting women. No interpreter is mentioned in their deposition. What seems most likely is that these three women willingly contributed the evidence Henry required, either by inventing this conversation or by signing a statement they knew not to be true but believed to accurately reflect the nature of the marriage. They may have created a version of what they believed Anne would have said if they questioned her under such circumstances. It would have been designed to expose her ignorance and thus prove that the marriage had been unconsummated and could, therefore, be annulled. Her virginity needed to be established beyond doubt to prevent her from being examined verbally or physically, as was frequently the case in annulments. Anne herself would never have seen this piece of evidence. She would never be able to challenge it in person. For whatever reason, Henry was unable to have sex with Anne. She probably knew it.

Next, Henry's privy gentlemen were questioned. Many of their statements echoed those of the king, even repeating his exact words. Wriothesley stated that 'eight days after the marriage, the Earl of Essex told him that "the queen was then a maid for the king's highness", who had no affection for her. He added that, a little before Easter, the king declared to him that the marriage had not been consummated.' Sir Thomas Heneage said that 'ever since the king saw the queen he had never liked her; and said as often as he went to bed to her, he mistrusted the queen's virginity, by reason of the looseness of her breasts and other tokens; and the marriage had never been consummated'.[7] Henry had made a similar confession to Sir Anthony Denny, 'as [his] confidential servant, that he could not induce himself to have affection for her, for she was not as reported and had her breasts so slack and other parts of her body in such sort, that he suspected her virginity, and that he could never consummate the marriage ... he lamented the state of princes to be far worse than that of poor men who could choose for themselves'. From his prison cell, Cromwell stated that 'after Candlemas and before Shrovetide, [Henry] once or twice said that he had never known her carnally, although he had lain nightly or every second night by her'.[8] By Easter and in Whitsun week, the king 'lamented his fate to Cromwell, that he should never have any more children if he so continued, declaring that before God he thought she was not his lawful wife'.[9]

Henry's instant dislike of Anne was easy enough to establish, as he had hardly kept it a secret from his servants and councillors. Charles Brandon, Duke of Suffolk, agreed that 'he saw that the king liked not the queens person' and Wriothesley admitted her had been 'very sorry to perceive the king, upon sight of her, so to mislike her person'.[10] Lord Russell had noticed that Henry was 'sore troubled' and 'amazed and abashed' in Rochester. He reported that the king had told him 'I promise you I see no such thing in her as hath been showed unto me of her, and am ashamed that men hath so praised her as they have done, and I like her not'.[11] Sir Anthony Browne added that Henry was 'dismayed', with such a 'discontent and misliking' of Anne that he did not stop to 'speak with her twenty words'. He had not given Anne the furs he had brought as a gift, but sent them via Browne the following day, 'with a cold message'.[12] His wife, Lady Browne, who had since died in childbed, had commented in January that 'she saw in the queen such fashion and manner of bringing up so gross that in her judgment the king should never heartily love her'. Henry himself added that when he saw her in Rochester 'he liked her so ill he was sorry she had come and he considered if it were possible to break off'.[13]

Cromwell was examined in his room in the Tower, fully cooperating, 'with ... heavy heart and trembling hand',[14] in the hope that it might yet save his neck. Following the impromptu meeting at Rochester, Henry had confessed he liked her 'nothing so well as she was spoken of, and that if [he] had known so much before, she should not have comen hither'.[15] He had solicited Henry's opinion again on the day he brought Anne back to Greenwich, 3 January, but the king had replied that 'she is nothing fair; the personage is well and seemly, but nothing else', adding that 'if it were not that she is come so far into England, and for fear of making a ruffle in the world and driving her brother into th' Emperor and the French king's hands, now being together, I would never have her; but now it is too far gone, wherefore I am sorry'.[16] On the eve of the wedding, Cromwell reported, the king had described the imminent nuptials as 'putting his head into the yoke'. Suffolk added that before the marriage, Henry 'constantly affirmed that he would do nothing in the matter of the marriage unless the precontract between the lady Anne of Cleves and the marquis of Lorraine were first cleared'.

Henry's examiners had the evidence they needed. On 6 July, Henry sent a written message to Anne at Richmond, informing her of the inquiry. According to Rutland, who understood her with the help of an interpreter, she took the news 'heavily' and did not respond to his encouragement to 'discharge her conscience' and 'rejoice and not ... be sorry'.[17] That afternoon, Henry sent a delegation of gentlemen to Richmond to explain the matter further and urge her to cooperate. More composed, Anne replied that she was 'content always with your majesty' but she was forbidden to send any messages to Henry. The case was heard at Westminster the following day. On 8 July, Anne summoned her advisor Carl Harst twice, to explain the situation further, and when he saw her the second time, late that night, she was 'sobbing so loudly and crying so violently it almost broke his heart'.[18] This belies the notion that Anne readily acquiesced to the annulment, although it may have owed more to the fear that she had jeopardised Cleves alliance than the loss of Henry himself. On 9 July, Parliament agreed that Henry and Anne had never been legally wed and that both were free to remarry.

Anne was now in a difficult situation. In a foreign country, far from home, she was no longer Henry's wife and queen and her status and future were uncertain. To return home as an unwanted bride only six months after the lengthy journey and elaborate ceremony of her arrival would be a terrible disgrace. She sent Harst to Henry to lodge her complaints but his lone voice could accomplish little against the king's decision, backed by his council, and her ambassador knew it. Returning to his mistress, he advised Anne to capitulate. On 11 July, she wrote to the king, accepting the verdict regarding their 'pretended matrimony', stating her 'worldly affection' for him and signing herself his 'sister and servant'. A relieved Henry responded with a generous settlement.

Anne would indeed become his sister by adoption, second only in status to his children and future wife, with extensive properties, a considerable annual income of £4,000, hangings, plate, furniture, jewels, pearls and the occasional invitation to court.[19] Henry wrote that 'when Parliament ends, we shall, in passing, see and speak with you, and you shall more largely see what a friend you and your friends have of us'. In the meantime, he required her to be 'quiet and merry'.[20] Faced with this solution instead of an ignominious return to Cleves, Anne returned her wedding ring with the message that 'it might be broken in pieces as a thing which she knew of no force or value'. She confessed to the 'integrity of her body' and wrote to her brother, Duke William, on 21 July, to reassure him that she had given her consent to the matter, 'wherein I had more respect [as beseemed me] to truth than to any worldly affection that might move me to the contrary, and did the rather condescend thereunto for that my body remaineth in the integrity which I brought into this realm'. She was 'well satisfied' and the English–Cleves alliance would 'not be impaired for this matter'. She declared her intention to live in England and signed herself as 'Anna, Duchess born of Cleves, Gulik, Geldre and Berge'.[21]

Writing to Francis I, Marillac reported on Anne's popularity: 'She is no longer to be called queen, but Lady Anne of Cleves; to the great regret of this people, who loved and esteemed her much as the sweetest, most gracious and kindest queen they ever had or would desire.' Henry's frequent visits across the Thames to Catherine Howard at Lambeth had also been noted: 'It is commonly said that this king will marry a lady of great beauty, daughter of Norfolk's deceased brother. If permitted to write what he hears, he would say this marriage has already taken place and is consummated; but as this is kept secret he dare not yet certify it as true.'[22] It was not true. Not yet.

Wages were paid to Anne's officers at the end of July, providing an insight into her household in this period of transition. Her chamberlain was Sir William Goring, who received £26 13s 4d, the same amount as was paid to her steward Jasper Horsey. Wymond Carew was her receiver, and Chomley her cofferer at £20 a head; her clerk controller Richard Tomewe got £13 6s 8d, as did her secretary Mathew; her physician Dr Cornelis received a large £46 13s 4d, as did four of her native Flemish servants, while four more got a slightly lower salary of £33 6s 8d. Two Dutchwomen in her employ, Katherine and Gertrude, received £10 each, her cook Schoulenburg and the butler Henry were given £5 while her footmen received £6 13s 4d.[23] No doubt the members of her staff were relieved to find the household was not to be disbanded following the annulment, and that their services were still required, albeit on a more modest scale.

Anne remained 'at the king's pleasure' at Richmond Palace, which now formed part of her settlement along with Bletchingley. It was at Richmond that Henry visited her on 6 August, to inform her in person that he had married her former maid-in-waiting, Catherine Howard.

53

Rose Without a Thorn, 1540–41

My husband doth sit like a Mome [Mummy] all the day
And at night in the bed he is cold as the clay
I would rather he would go and drink a pot or two
And come home and night and do what he should do.[1]

Henry and Catherine were married on 28 July at Oatlands Palace in Surrey. Like his wedding to Jane Seymour, which had also followed quickly upon the heels of the previous queen's removal, it was a quiet, secret affair, far removed from the elaborate ceremonials staged to mark Anne of Cleves' arrival. It seems probable that the marriage had already been consummated, with Henry keen to prove his vigour and manhood and Catherine able to draw on her sexual experience without shattering the illusion of her innocence. It is now impossible to know whether she explicitly claimed virginity, or put on a show of it, or whether this was entirely Henry's assumption. That night they shared the magnificent new 'pearl bed' bought from a Pierre Conyn, which was moved from Greenwich to Oatlands especially for the occasion.[2] This wedding night was clearly far more successful than the king's brief, disappointed handing of Anne of Cleves' breasts and belly. On that occasion, Henry had incorrectly believed his wife's body to be offering him the visual evidence that she was no virgin; with Catherine, he drew the wrong conclusions again. He believed himself to be his young, nubile wife's first and only lover.

On the same day that Henry and Catherine were married, Thomas Cromwell was beheaded on Tower Hill. His head was placed on a spike on London Bridge, along with those of other traitors. The fallout from such a death could be far reaching, impacting on an entire family's fortunes, so measures were necessary in order for the survivors to retain their position. Aware of this, Cromwell had written to the king from the Tower, beseeching him, on his knees, to be a good 'and gracious lord to my poor son, the good and virtu[ous lady his] wife, and their poor children'.[3] Three days after his death, Cromwell's daughter-in-law, Elizabeth, sister to the former Queen Jane, and wife to his son Gregory, wrote to Henry thanking him 'for the mercy he has shewn her poor husband and herself, which has much relieved the extreme indigence brought upon them by the heinous offences of her father-in-law'.[4] She had been 'unwilling to make any suit for fear of being troublesome, until the king is partly relieved from the pressure of his great affairs'. Elizabeth and Gregory, along with their surviving children, did receive the king's mercy, perhaps as a reflection of his new found marital happiness. Both would live long enough to see their nephew Edward on the throne, and Elizabeth would make a third marriage after Gregory's death from the sweating sickness in 1551.

Catherine made her first appearance as queen at Hampton Court on 8 August. Henry's infatuation with his new wife was immediately apparent to everyone, almost embarrassingly so, as he had never behaved like this towards any of his previous queens. It was a mark of the success of their physical relationship that he simply could not keep his hands off her, even in public. Marillac reported that he was 'so amorous of her that he cannot treat her well enough and caresses her more than he did the others', while the king's secretary, Ralph Morice, wrote that 'the king's affection was so marvellously set upon that gentlewoman as it was never known that he had the like to any woman'. As the new queen, Catherine's role was simply to please Henry in bed, to be cheerful and merry, to divert him from his illness and increasing old age and to appear on ceremonial occasions in the new clothes and jewels with which he showered her. There were plenty of precedents of girls in their teenage years marrying men of fifty, but few with such material and social advantages, such fine dresses, baubles and glittering trinkets as the new queen now enjoyed.

There is little doubt that the marriage was a dazzling and unexpected career move for Catherine, but this is not to suggest she was any more calculated or cynical than any other woman of her generation. She may not have been in love with Henry but she would certainly have been in awe of him; of his status, his physical person and the whole theatre of royalty, of which he was the heart. The kind of love a subject might feel for a king, of respect, admiration and devotion, was prized more highly in the marital stakes than romantic attachment; in serving and pleasing Henry, a doting older husband, Catherine had fallen on her feet. Her relationship with Dereham may have been a love match but, along with her contemporaries, she had hoped to attract a wealthy and powerful husband and her own romantic feelings were not necessarily relevant. She cannot have anticipated just how successful she would be at this. As Marillac reported, 'the new queen has completely acquired the king's grace'.

The inevitable rumours surfaced that Catherine was pregnant, that in fact she had been expecting a child before the marriage, which spurred the king to divorce Anne of Cleves and make her his wife. Once Catherine had submitted to his advances and allowed him to make love to her, he could not risk the legitimacy of any child she may bear. No doubt the speed of his remarriage ignited debate but it is also possible that Catherine, or her supporters, may have encouraged him in the belief that she would soon provide him with a Duke of York. Even before their marriage, on 21 July, Marillac reported gossip that the 'sudden settlement of so important an affair' was due to the fact that 'this king has already consummated marriage with this last lady ... and it is feared she is already enceinte'.[5] Manuel Cyrne also believed the pregnancy story and repeated it to John III of Portugal: 'Some say that there was a previous contract with the Duke of Lorraine, some that the king would marry an English lady, niece of the Duke of Norfolk, daughter of his brother, and that she is already with child ... there must be some other secret reason.'[6] Rumours reached Vatican in mid-August that Catherine was expecting a child, which had necessitated Henry's repudiation of the 'patient' Anne of Cleves. On 17 August, Philip Melanchthon urged, 'Let us cease to sing the praises of the English Nero. I know not whether you have heard of his cruelty to the queen.'[7] The circumstances of Henry's fifth marriage cemented his international reputation as a cruel husband. Absorbed in his newfound love, though, Henry really could not have cared less.

In September, Marillac visited the court at Grafton, where Henry was staying 'with a small company' for hunting and 'banquets being given to the new queen'.[8] He saw Catherine there for the first time, describing her as 'rather graceful than beautiful' and of short stature, dressed in the French style, along with her ladies.[9] Henry lavished wedding gifts on his new bride, including jewels from the royal coffer that had previously adorned his other wives, among them a pendant of gold set with a diamond, ruby and pearl; a square necklace of clustered rubies and pearls; and the gold trimming for a French hood adorned with diamonds.

Catherine's household featured many familiar names, those of women who had now served several queens, who had watched them rise and fall and sometimes participated in the process. Some, like Eleanor, Countess Rutland; Jane, Viscountess Parker; and Catherine, Lady Edgecumbe, had served the king as witnesses in his marital affairs; others were his relatives by blood or marriage, such as Margaret, Lady Douglas; Mary, Lady Howard; Elizabeth Seymour, Lady Cromwell; and Agnes Tilney, step-grandmother to both Catherine and her cousin Anne Boleyn. A few on the list may have been the king's lover, including Jane Ashley and Anne Bassett, or related to his lovers, like Margaret Arundel and Catherine Skipwith. Soon, though, two new arrivals among her household created a link with her past. Katherine Tilney and Alice Restwold had been lodged in the maiden's chamber with Catherine at Lambeth, and when they became her maids-in-waiting they brought their memories of her nightly antics with Dereham dangerously close. There was also Joan Bulmer from Lambeth, who asked Catherine to give her a place so she could share in her 'great destiny'. This could be read as a thinly veiled attempt to blackmail the new queen to share her success with those who knew her secrets.

Catherine continued to entice and captivate her husband. Always taking a keen interest in medicine and cures for various bodily ailments, Henry approached his fiftieth birthday with a newfound enthusiasm for life, no doubt continuing to ask the advice of Dr Butts when it came to his ability to perform in the bedroom. He was no longer the chivalric hero of his youthful affairs and, wary of the old literary clichés about old men unable to keep up with their young wives, he would have sought to sustain their love life in whatever ways he could. Contemporary medical texts recommended various herbal treatments for the penis, including the application of poultices made from boiled olive leaves with alum and honey, bathing in myrrh, saffron, oak galls and rose leaves and sometimes binding the member up to the stomach. In total, the surviving records of Henry's doctors show over two hundred different prescriptions for his various afflictions, to which total Henry also contributed his own remedies of plasters and ointments. That December, under the guidance of Dr Boorde, he began a new regime designed to assist in weight loss that involved rising at dawn and riding for two hours. As Lydgate's poem 'The Dietary' advised, moderation in work, sleep, habits and food was essential:

> Suffer no surfeit in thy house at nyght;
> Beware of rere-sopers and of grete excese
> And be wele wary of candyll lyght,
> Of sloth on morow and of idelnes,
> The whych of all vices is chief, as I gesse.[10]

Henry initially felt better, but the pain in his legs flared up the following March and he was prescribed rhubarb and advised to keep away from his young wife's bed. With Catherine left to her own devices, wondering exactly what was happening and believing the rumours that Henry might divorce her for childlessness, it was not a recommendation that would help the royal marriage. Marillac reported in April that 'this queen is thought to be with child, which would be a very great joy to this king', and that it was likely that her coronation would take place at Whitsuntide, but neither of these two stories proved to be true.

Anne of Cleves had made a smooth transition to her position as the king's sister. On 6 August, when Henry had visited her at Richmond, Marillac was dismissive of rumours that there was a chance that the pair might be reconciled. Even though they dined together 'so merrily', the change in their relationship and Anne's status was marked: 'She did not sup with him as she did when she was queen, but at another table adjoining his, as other ladies who are not of the blood do when he eats in company.' Nine days later he related that Anne was 'as joyous as ever, and wears new dresses every day; which argues either prudent dissimulation or stupid forgetfulness of what should so closely touch her heart', and on 3 September she was 'far from appearing disconsolate' but was 'unusually joyous and takes all the recreation she can in diversity of dress and pastime'.[11] Bearing in mind the invitation extended to Anne to visit court on occasion, she sent Henry a New Year gift of two horses in violet velvet and received gifts back from him. On 3 January, Anne travelled from Richmond to Hampton Court and, according to Chapuys, 'presented herself'.[12]

Anne was conveyed to the queen's lodgings, where she insisted on addressing her successor on her knees. Catherine 'showed her the utmost kindness' and Henry, entering, 'embraced and kissed her'. Chapuys continues, 'She occupied a seat near the bottom of the table at supper, but after the king had retired the queen and Lady Anne danced together and next day all three dined together. At this time the king sent his queen a present of a ring and two small dogs, which she passed over to Lady Anne.' The ex-queen then returned to Richmond. Expenses from that month show rewards being given to Catherine's minstrels Andrew Newman, William More and Thomas Evans, who received 30s as well as the 13s 4d paid to Mr Berde, the queen's gentleman usher. A payment of £4 was made to six players of the king's viols – Vincent and Alex da Venitia, Ambroso da Milano, Albertus da Venitia, Ivam Maria de Cramona [*sic*] and Anth. de Romano – and other rewards were given to riders, gentlemen of chapel, servants, ushers, clockmakers, coffer makers, players, bowyers, armourers, messengers and those who brought gifts to the king. Two men who brought pheasants received 20s and the same amount went to a man who gave the king perfumed gloves. Payment of 6s 8d was made to George Aynbury for bringing ambergris, John Godsalve for a gold pomander, Cornelius Smith for an iron casket and Anthony Tote for a table of the story of King Alexander. A goldsmith called Bollter who gave a purse garnished with gold and pearl was paid 20s, a woman who gave a 'book of wax' was given 5s, 64s was divided between poor men and women who brought capons, hens, eggs, books of wax 'and other trifles' and 20s went to the king's 'launder', who gave him handkerchiefs. Henry and Catherine remained at Hampton Court for most of January, making offerings there on all the Sundays of the month. At Candlemas they watched a play in the king's chamber that was enacted upon a stage or scaffold.[13]

On 19 March, Catherine was welcomed into London with a formal river pageant. As Chapuys related, 'the king lately took his queen to Greenwich, and as it was the first time since her marriage that she had passed through London by the Thames, the people gave her a splendid reception, and the Tower guns saluted her'. He then went on to add that 'from this triumphal march she took occasion to ask the release of Wyatt'. Here Catherine was interceding on behalf of the poet, who had been imprisoned earlier that year on a charge of treason, liaising with the exiled Yorkist Richard Pole. Henry granted her request, releasing the poet on the condition that he should return to his estranged wife of fifteen years. Wyatt and Elizabeth Brooke had been married as teenagers but he had left her on account of her adultery and was living with a mistress, Elizabeth Darrell. It was a harsh condition for Wyatt, especially considering the later rumours that his wife might become Henry's sixth wife. Did Catherine take pity on his plight, or was she urged to do so by her family, particularly Wyatt's fellow poet the Earl of Surrey? Whatever her motivation, the prisoner was released and allowed to return home to Allingham, where his pregnant mistress was living. Wyatt did not enjoy his freedom for long, though, dying at the age of thirty-nine in October 1542.

Another prisoner in the Tower was to be less fortunate. Margaret Pole, Henry's mother's cousin, had long been a feature of his court. The daughter of George, Duke of Clarence, she had served Catherine of Aragon from the days of her marriage to Arthur, being reappointed to the queen's service in 1509. As Henry's increasing irritation with Margaret's sons, the exiled Pole brothers, failed to secure their capture, he had resorted to imprisoning their mother in November 1538. Margaret had been a familiar face to Henry all his life; a wife, mother, countess and paragon of virtue and faith who had attempted to persuade her sons to desist from their papist 'follies'. It was not enough. Along with her son Henry and the king's cousin Exeter, also a bastion of the royal court from the start, Margaret was attainted and sentenced to death. She was executed on 27 May, with the inept axeman needing to strike ten blows in order to sever her head. It was a sign of the darker direction the king was taking in the later 1530s, which claimed other former friends, family and servants such as Sir Nicholas Carew, Edward Neville and Lord Lisle as its victims.

Early in May, Chapuys related that Catherine was the instigator of a visit he and Henry made to Prince Edward, then aged two and a half, at Waltham Holy Cross: 'The king and queen went a week ago to visit the prince at the request of the princess, but chiefly at the intercession of the queen herself'.[14] Catherine's relations with Henry's elder daughter, Princess Mary, were less cordial. With Mary several years older than her stepmother, Catherine did not feel the princess had treated her with due respect and threatened to reduce her number of maids until Mary 'found means to conciliate her' and kept her ladies with her. A few weeks later, when Henry granted his daughter permission to live at court full time, Catherine 'countenanced it with good grace'.[15] The following month, the court departed for a long progress into the north, taking a wealth of travelling tents and equipment to accommodate the vast panoply of royalty as Henry prepared to visit cities further from home than he had travelled before. By the time they rode away from the capital, Queen Catherine had fallen deeply in love. Unfortunately, it was not with her husband.

54

An Old Fool, 1541–42

What Monster is this? I never heard none such
For look how much more I have made her too much,
And so far at least she hath made me too little.[1]

It was during the spring of 1541, if not before, that Catherine found herself drawn to a handsome young man in the king's privy chamber. That March, when Henry visited Dover and left her behind at Greenwich, she sought the company of her distant cousin Thomas Culpeper, reputed to be a very handsome man and still unmarried even though he was probably in his mid- to late twenties. She may initially have solicited his advice about the king, or whiled away the time in conversation and dancing, but the innocent friendship quickly developed into a dangerous romantic attachment. In her loneliness, the queen may have desired the flattering attentions of a male friend; perhaps the pair simply indulged in some harmless flirtation, or maybe she thought she could pursue her own personal pleasure as well as keeping the king satisfied. There is even a chance that Catherine hoped to fall pregnant by the young man, in the light of Henry's disappointment at her failure to conceive. All these have been suggested as reasons for Catherine embarking on an illicit liaison that would eventually cost her her head. Yet history may have judged the young queen too harshly; no actual evidence survives to prove that she and Culpeper actually committed adultery and treason by sleeping together.

Culpeper may have been attractive, but he was hardly the romantic hero of romantic fiction. He was born around 1515 at the family seat of Bedgebury Manor, near Goudhurst in south-west Kent, and was a distant cousin of Catherine's mother, Jocasta Culpeper. He started his court life as a page, then became a groom and finally had progressed to being a Gentleman of the Privy Chamber, tending to Henry's most intimate needs, including the treatment of his bad legs. Yet Culpeper had a dark side. A man of the same name had previously been pardoned after raping the wife of a park keeper and killing a villager who had attempted to come to her aid. One account, written by a London merchant in 1541, describes the rape as taking place in a thicket while 'three or four of his most profligate attendants were holding her at his bidding'.[2] Whether this was Thomas, or his elder brother who bore the same name and was previously involved in a knife brawl, is still being debated by historians although the general consensus errs on the side of the younger man's guilt. If Catherine's Culpeper had been permitted by the king's favour to escape justice for two such serious crimes, he may have thought himself exempt from the dangers incurred by dallying with his wife.

Much has been made by historians of the surviving letter Catherine wrote to Culpeper, the composition of which has been placed both before the progress, as early as April 1541, and during it, in the summer or early autumn. It begins conventionally enough – 'Master Culpeper, I heartily recommend me unto you, praying you to send me word how that you do' – but develops into something more personal, as the queen has taken considerable 'pain ... in writing to you' and had 'heard that you were sick and never longed so much for anything as to see you and speak with you, the which I trust shall be shortly now'. She invited him to visit when Jane, Viscountess Rochford, was in attendance, as 'then I shall best leisure to be at your commandment ... it makes my heart die to think I cannot always be in your company' and added that 'my trust is always in you that you will be as you have promised me'.[3] She signed the letter 'yours as long as life endures'. Exactly what the nature of this promise was remains unclear, but Catherine's attachment to Culpeper cannot be doubted. What, though, were his motives, knowing the danger he must have been in, only four years since the Boleyn scandal? Did he genuinely fall for Catherine, or allow himself to be seduced, as he later suggested? Or was the affair a cynical move on his part, hoping to gain influence over her in the event of the king's incapacity or death?

The strain was already showing in the royal marriage before they left London, with Catherine shutting herself away in her royal chambers instead of dancing and amusing herself. Henry was reported to be avoiding her company, perhaps through displeasure at her failure to conceive after a year of marriage, perhaps as his resurfacing ill-health emphasised their age gap. That February, he had started walking with a stick. Yet the journey was designed to present a show of strength and majesty to the rebellious north. Whatever may have been happening in their bedroom, or not, Henry wanted his wife beside him, dressed in her finery, as a figurehead of his power and potency. On 1 July they were at Enfield, moving on three days later to St Albans, then Dunstable on 8 July and Ampthill on 9 July. The party had moved on to Grafton Regis by 15 July, where Catherine was reported to be ill and kept to her rooms. Given the details that later came out, this may have been a cover story to allow her to meet with Culpeper in secret.

The next stop was at Collyweston House, which had been a possession of Henry's grandmother, Margaret Beaufort, and during this time was reputed to have a great walnut tree in the outer courtyard. From there the party travelled to Grimsthorpe on 7 August, where they were hosted by Charles and Catherine Brandon, Duke and Duchess of Suffolk, who had prepared for their arrival by ordering provisions from the Earl of Shrewsbury a month before: 'Desires the Earl to send him a fat stag by the 5th Aug, at which time the king intends to visit him at Grymsthorpe. Grymsthorpe, 3 July.'[4]

On 10 August, the royal party arrived at Temple Brewer, seven miles outside the city, where tents had been erected for Henry and Catherine to replace their crimson and green velvet clothing with cloth of silver and gold. An account of their arrival lists the order of precedence as they rode into the city:

> The heralds put on their coats, the gentlemen pensioners and train rode according to the ancient order, then came lord Hastings bearing the sword, then the king, then his horse led by the Master of the Horse, then the children of honour, each after other on great coursers, then the earl of Rutland, queen's chamberlain, then the queen, then her horse of estate, then all the ladies, then the Captain of the Guard and the Guard, then the commoners.[5]

They were welcomed by the mayor and other city dignitaries to the ringing of church bells before processing to the cathedral, where stools, carpet and cushions of gold had been set out for them. Doused in incense, they heard Mass before retiring to their lodgings. It was here that Catherine arranged a secret meeting with Culpeper, using a secret door that led to a set of backstairs giving direct access to her bedchamber. Exactly what happened when the two were together until the early hours of the morning remains unclear.

From there, the progress moved to Gainsborough on 12 August and Hatfield Chase, where they rested for a while in a village of splendid tents and enjoyed hunting and feasting. Here Catherine was observed by her women looking out of a window to watch Culpeper, with such an expression on her face that it remained in their minds. The pair enjoyed more illicit meetings at Pontefract Castle, from 23 August, where Henry sent his servant Denny to Catherine and found her bedroom door bolted. That September they arrived in York, hoping that King James of Scotland would be able to meet them, although they waited in vain. In the meantime, a thousand men worked night and day to complete the conversion of the dissolved abbey of St

Mary's into a royal palace, sparking rumours that Catherine was to be crowned there. No coronation took place. By the beginning of October they had arrived in Hull, and after a sojourn there began the long journey south. It was at Ampthill, in Bedfordshire, that the king suffered an attack of malaria which exacerbated the ulcers in his legs, forcing him to stay in bed. Once he had recovered, as was often his pattern, Henry showered his wife with gifts, presenting her with a gold brooch set with diamonds and rubies. On 29 October they arrived back at Hampton Court, where Henry gave 'most humble and hearty thanks' for his good life with Catherine, which he 'trusted to lead' in the future. The next day, the storm broke.

Catherine had previously admitted some of her old friends to her household, including Francis Dereham himself, who was appointed secretary at Hampton Court in August 1541, perhaps in order to buy his silence over his past relationship with the queen. Dereham himself proved to be something of a loose cannon, clearly harbouring resentment over the end of his relationship with Catherine. He courted trouble, getting into an argument with one of Catherine's gentleman ushers, Mr Johns, when he breached court etiquette by lingering over a meal in a way that was only permitted to senior members of the household. When Johns posed the question of whether Dereham was a member of the council, to highlight this inappropriateness, Dereham made a dismissive and foolish response: 'I was of the queen's council before he knew her and shall be when she hath forgotten him.' With the intimate connotations of a man and woman 'keeping council', it was a reply that could only set tongues wagging.

Yet it was not Dereham who leaked Catherine's secret. He may have had a loose tongue, but it was not in his interests to bite the hand that was feeding him and incur the wrath of the king and queen. He was shrewd enough to know it would mark the end of his career, although he could not have predicted that it would also cost him his life. Another of the witnesses from the maiden's chamber now returned to haunt her. Mary Hall, *née* Lascelles, either applied to join Catherine's court and was rejected or refused to apply on the grounds of the queen's former 'light behaviour', both in living and condition. On hearing this, her brother John, a religious reformer and sewer in the king's privy chamber, reported her account of the queen's past behaviour to Cranmer in the early autumn. A later Protestant martyr, Lascelles may have been motivated by a desire to strike against the Catholic Howards, but his information was true enough. Cranmer knew that to withhold such details could be fatal, so he was forced to act. On 2 November, as Henry went to attend Mass in his private closet, he found a letter on his seat. Knowing the affection in which the king held his young wife, it was a wise move on Cranmer's part to lay down all the evidence against the queen in writing, to allow Henry to read it as his leisure and defuse the inevitable dramatic scene that would arise. At first the king refused to believe the report, but he nevertheless ordered an investigation into Catherine's behaviour prior to her marriage. It was this process, over the first two weeks of November, which led to the uncovering of her relationship with Culpeper.

The evidence was damning. On 5 November, Mary Hall related Henry Manox's words that Catherine had promised him her maidenhead and his boast that 'I have had her by the cunt and I know it among a hundred'.[6] Hauled in for questioning, Manox admitted on the same day that he had asked Catherine, 'Let me feel your secret and then I shall think indeed that you do love me.' To this Catherine replied that she was content 'so as you will desire no more but that'.[7] As a result, in the darkness of the duchess's chapel at Horsham, he had 'felt more than was convenient'. Dereham was also called in for questioning that day, admitting that he had lain 'in bed by her in his doublet and hosen divers times and six or seven times in naked bed with her'. Mary Hall added she had seen them 'hang by their [lips] together [as if] they were two sparrows'. Another witness, Margaret Benet, had seen them through a hole in a door, when Dereham lifted Catherine's clothes 'above her navel so that [she, Margaret] might well discern her body' and heard him claim that 'although he used the company of women ... yet he would get no child except he listed'.[8] More servants came out of the woodwork: an Andrew Maunsay described Dereham lying in bed with Catherine, which had also been witnessed by a laundress named Bess.[9]

On the night of 6 November, Henry left Hampton Court for Whitehall. There, in a council meeting that ran from midnight until the early hours, Henry broke down in tears, lamenting his 'ill-luck in meeting with such ill-conditioned wives' and calling for a sword so that he might kill her himself, so 'that wicked woman [would have] never such delight in her incontinency as she should have torture in her death'.[10] Left behind at Hampton Court, Catherine would never see him again.

The queen must have sensed something was wrong. For Henry to depart without a word of explanation was ominous enough and she kept to her chambers, telling her musicians there is 'no more time to dance'.[11] She did not have to wait long. On the evening of the following day, a delegation of the council confronted her with their findings, which she initially denied. At a meeting with Cranmer later than night, however, she admitted her guilt and made a full confession, tearful and distraught, 'in such lamentation and heaviness as I never saw no creature, so that it would have pitied any man's heart to have looked upon her'. She explained her misconduct in a way that sounds quite plausible and rings of truth: she had been 'blinded with desire of worldly glory' so that she had not considered 'how great a fault it was to conceal my former faults from your majesty'. On hearing this, Henry was inclined to be merciful. She had sinned before their marriage and her greatest fault had been not to admit this to him; a pre-contract with Dereham would allow her marriage to the king to be judged invalid. She was taken to Syon House, where she would await developments, 'and there lodged moderately as her life hath deserved', wearing dresses 'without stone or pearl'.[12] But then, on 11 November, under torture, Dereham admitted that he had been succeeded in the queen's affections by Thomas Culpeper.

This was treason. Under questioning, Catherine admitted that she had met with Culpeper in secret on three occasions at Lincoln, Pontefract and York, but laid the blame for it at his door and that of Jane Rochford, who had been their confidant and helped arrange their trysts. She categorically denied sleeping with him: 'as for the act ... she denieth upon her oath, or touching any bare part of her but her hand'. Yet the evidence seemed conclusive. Her waiting woman, Katherine Tilney, also from Horsham and Lambeth, was questioned on 13 November about the queen's movements at Lincoln, and stated that Catherine

> went two nights to lady Rochford's chamber, which was up a little pair of stairs by the queen's chamber. [She] and her fellow Marget went with her, but were sent back. Marget went up again eftsoons, and examinate went to bed with Friswyde. When Marget came to bed, about 2 o'clock, examinate said, 'Jesus, is not the queen abed yet?' She replied, 'Yes, even now.' The second night the queen sent the rest to bed ... but she was in a little place with Lady Rochford's woman and could not tell who came into Lady Rochford's chamber.[13]

Another of the queen's ladies, Margaret Morton confessed that 'she never mistrusted the queen until at Hatfeld she saw her look out of her chamber window on Mr Culpeper after such sort that she thought there was love between them. There the queen gave order that neither Mrs Lofkyng "nor no nother" should come into her bedchamber unless called'. Mrs Morton had also been asked to carry 'a sealed letter ... to my lady of Rochford', who prayed her to keep it a secret.[14] Jane Rochford must have been terrified as the story was uncovered, only four years after the adultery charges that had led to the deaths of her husband and sister-in-law. She was quick to cooperate and place the blame on Catherine, in the hope that it would save her, as it had done in 1536. Although quick to claim 'she heard or saw nothing' on some occasions, she was so deeply implicated that she had to confess that Catherine had asked for Culpeper daily and that she had witnessed him pick the lock to her chamber in Lincoln. She added that, in her opinion, 'Culpeper has known the queen carnally'.[15] But had he?

Through the ensuing scramble to pass the blame, both Catherine and Culpeper insisted they had not slept together. It may have been out of self-preservation, but both stated they were guilty of the desire to fornicate; they 'intended to do ill', although they had stopped short of the act. Culpeper admitted to secret meetings and receiving gifts from the queen, depicting the relationship as taking place at her insti-gation. She had given him gifts, with the instruction to conceal them under his cloak, sent him fish dinners when he was ill, and they had talked for several hours in her stool room at Lincoln. He related how she had said to him that 'if I had tarried still in the maidens' chamber I would have tried you'[16] but he had kissed her hand and told her 'he would presume no further'. It cannot be conclusively proven that they did have sex, which both would have known was an act of treason bearing the death penalty; to cross that line would have been an act of incredible folly. The only other person able to verify this was Jane Rochford, whose accusation stands alone regarding their adultery. Culpeper was sent to the Tower on 12 November and the inventories of his goods made in the following days were a powerful statement of his fate. Dead men did not need velvet caps, bedsteads and harnesses. Along with Francis Dereham, he was tried at the Guildhall for treason on 1 December and condemned to death. One of the concluding state-ments left little doubt as to the belief of the council, and king, that he and Catherine were guilty of adultery as charged:

Also the said queen, not satisfied with her vicious life aforesaid, on the 29 Aug. 33 Hen. VIII., at Pomfret, and at other times and places before and after, with Thos. Culpeper, late of London, one of the gentlemen of the king's privy chamber, falsely and traitor-ously held illicit meeting and conference to incite the said Culpeper to have carnal intercourse with her; and insinuated to him that she loved him above the king and all others. Similarly the said Culpeper incited the queen. And the better and more secretly to pursue their carnal life they retained Jane lady Rochford, late wife of Sir Geo. Boleyn late lord Rochford, as a go-between to contrive meetings in the queen's stole chamber and other suspect places; and so the said Jane falsely and traitorously aided and abetted them.[17]

On 4 December, two of Catherine's ladies, Jane Rattsey and Catherine Bassett, sister to Anne, were summoned to the king's council for gossip. Their idle questions, asking if 'God [is] working to make Anne of Cleves queen again' and 'what a man is the king! How many wives will he have', saw them committed to jail. Nine days later, Dereham suffered the full traitor's death of hanging, quartering and disembowelling at Tyburn, while Culpeper was beheaded. Afterwards, their heads were placed on spikes on London Bridge as a macabre and powerful deterrent.

The weeks passed. Catherine waited at Syon as Christmas was succeeded by New Year. All may have seemed quiet in the seclusion of the old abbey but the king's council were working furiously to pass the legislation required to allow her downfall. In late January, an Act of Attainder made it treason for a woman to become the king's wife without 'plain declaration before of her unchaste life' and confirming that adultery, to facilitate adultery, or the failure to admit adultery, was treason. Before this, Catherine had hoped she might still gain Henry's forgiveness; Chapuys described her 'making good cheer, fatter and more beautiful than ever, taking great care to be well apparelled and more imperious and troublesome to serve than even when she was with the king'.[18] Yet, the new Act made her death inevitable. Her accomplices had died in December and Catherine's death had been delayed in order for the legal process to take its due course, although it moved considerably slower than it had for Anne Boleyn. It is entirely possible that Henry was waiting to be completely sure that she was not pregnant. Even if the child had not been his, it was standard practise in Tudor law to establish that a condemned woman was not expecting, usually by examination carried out by a panel of matrons. Catherine was not pregnant; either by Culpeper or the king.

On 10 February, Catherine was conveyed from Syon House to the Tower 'with some resistance', dressed in black velvet. Two days later, she was informed that she would die the following morning, and 'wept, cried and tormented herself miserably without ceasing',[19] before requesting that the block be sent to her, in order to place 'her head on it by way of experiment'.[20] Catherine and Jane Rochford were executed one after the other, early in the morning on 13 February, on the same spot where Anne Boleyn had died. Their bodies joined hers in the Tower's chapel of St Peter ad Vincula.

PART NINE
Catherine Parr

55

The Learned Widow, 1542–43

When Summer took in hand the winter to assail,
With force of might, and virtue great, his stormy blasts to quail:
And when he clothed fair the earth about with green,
And every tree new garmented, that pleasure was to seen:
Mine heart gan new revive, and changed blood did stir,
Me to withdraw my winter woes, that kept within the dore.[1]

As early as the day of Catherine Howard's arrest, rumours were flying regarding the identity of Henry's next wife. According to Marillac, court gossip favoured his return to Anne of Cleves 'who has conducted herself wisely in her affliction, and is more beautiful than she was'[2] and had been invited to Greenwich at New Year, where she presented the king with pieces of crimson cloth and received a gift of glass pots and flagons in return. Having played the waiting game, accepting Henry's repudiation of her and prostrating herself before Catherine Howard, Anne may have believed herself to be in with a chance of being restored to the king's favour. Her ambassador, Harst, attempted to speak to Brandon and Cranmer regarding a remarriage and received a number of letters from German Princes in support, which he hesitated to show to Henry on account of the king's continuing grief. Arrangements were also well underway for the marriage of Anne's erstwhile fiancé to Christina of Milan, which removed the impediment on which the English match had floundered. A tract published in Europe in late 1541 might have contributed to her false hopes.

The Remonstrance of Anne of Cleves was printed by John of Luxembourg, Abbot of Ivry. It depicted Anne as overwhelmed with sorrow, taking the form of a direct appeal from her to Henry, lamenting that 'wives are given to men to obey them ... if then the king chooses to leave you and take another, ought you to go contrary to his will?' All the clothes and jewels, properties and lands she had received at his hands had 'been contaminated and defiled by the bad treatment, the wrong and the injury, exhibited by him to her'. This fictional 'Anne' continued 'if it be said that she is not so personally attractive in the king's eyes as he desired to find her, let it be replied that she did not seek the king, but he sought her' and by 'becoming entirely conformed to his desires ... she should be far more agreeable to him than any of those whose company he might [with scandal and sin] desire to use'.³ The French ambassador, William Paget, implored Francis I to suppress the tract, but without success. It was an embarrassment but it did nothing to advance Anne's case, if she was even aware of its existence. Henry continued to treat her as his sister; that March, when she lay ill at Richmond with 'tertian fever', he sent his doctors there to tend her.

On 29 January, two weeks before Catherine Howard was executed, Henry started to emerge from the depressive pall that had weighed him down since her arrest. Chapuys related that 'until then this king had never, since he detected the queen's conduct, shown joy; as he has done since, hosting a supper and banquet for over fifty ladies, twenty-six of whom sat at his table, with another thirty-five adjoining it'.⁴ According to Chapuys, he 'showed most favour and affection' to Elizabeth Brooke, the estranged wife of Thomas Wyatt, 'a beautiful girl, with wit enough, if she tried, to do as badly as the others'.⁵ Born in 1503, the daughter of Lord Cobham, Elizabeth, was then approaching forty and had produced one legitimate son. She would remarry after Wyatt's death that year but some have speculated that her age meant that Chapuys had confused her identity with that of her niece, who bore the same name and was then aged sixteen. Both women are likely candidates for the king's attention. Wyatt's wife was probably older than Henry hoped for in a wife, if he was still clinging to the possibility of fathering a Duke of York, but after Catherine Howard he may have decided not to set his sights on a young girl. His next wife would be a more mature woman, twice widowed. At the banquet of 29 January, he may have been simply seeking pleasant company, without intention of marriage, so this does not rule the elder Elizabeth Brooke out. Her niece, born in 1526, had been a maid to Catherine Howard and would soon cause a scandal at court by living in open adultery with William Parr, soon to become Henry's brother-in-law. Chapuys also identified two other possible candidates for Henry's hand, 'a daughter of the wife of Monsieur Lisle, formerly deputy of Calais, by her first marriage',⁶ which must have been Anne Bassett, and a mysterious daughter of 'Madame Albart, niece of the Grand Esquire, Mr Anthony Brown'. However, the woman Henry would choose as his next wife still had a husband; it would be a full year before the king remarried.

Catherine Parr was probably born in 1512, to Sir Thomas Parr, a descendant of Edward III and Maud Green, a cousin of Edward IV's wife, Elizabeth Wydeville. She probably arrived at the new family home in Blackfriars, which had been recently granted to the Parrs by Henry VIII, for their services to the Crown. Maud was a lady-in-waiting to Catherine of Aragon, so it was convenient for the family to be raised close to the court, as well as in their other main property of Rye House, Hertfordshire. Her education included the traditional regime of womanly accomplishments, but she was also able to speak French and Italian and, as her later writing and pursuits proved, she was clearly the possessor of a formidable curiosity and not little intelligence. More than that, she was pious, virtuous and an honest woman of good fame. Yet her fate was intended to be that of most women of her class. Catherine was married at the age of seventeen to Sir Edward Burgh, or Borough, sometimes confused with his grandfather of the same name. Her father-in-law, Thomas, had been appointed Anne Boleyn's chamberlain and carried her coronation train in May 1533 but received a severe warning after he had seized Catherine of Aragon's barge and violently ripped off her coat of arms. What Catherine thought of Anne is unrecorded, although her childhood connection to Princess Mary and her mother might suggest where her sympathies lay. The young couple lived first at Gainsborough Old Hall and then, in 1530, after a visit from her mother, set up home at Kirton-in-Lindsey. There were no recorded surviving children from the marriage on Edward's death three years later.

A year later, Catherine remarried. Her new husband was John Neville, Lord Latimer, a widower of the old faith with two children, who lived a quiet life away from court after having served in Henry's 1513 French campaign. The bride was then twenty-one, the groom forty-three. Their married life was mostly spent at Snape Castle in Yorkshire, a sprawling residence with solid square turrets built of yellow-grey stone. It was a good career move for Catherine, taking her up a social step and providing her with a good home and public standing, although her husband's unfortunate involvement with the Pilgrimage of Grace, the northern Catholic rebellions of 1536–37, made the future of the Latimers less certain. It was unclear to Henry exactly what role Latimer had played in the uprising, whether he was a supporter of the rebels or forced by necessity to negotiate with them to ensure the safety of his family at Snape, but, with family assistance, Latimer was given the benefit of the doubt, although his reputation never recovered. The exact date of his death is unclear; it may have been as early as December 1542 or as late as March 1543, when his will was proved. It is likely to have been closer to the former as, in early February, Catherine was already at court, to visit her siblings and perhaps to renew her friendship with Princess Mary, whom she had known as a child. She may also have been hoping to make a new marriage, to the man who had already captured her heart: Prince Edward's handsome uncle Thomas Seymour.

Catherine was left a wealthy woman. Having gone through two marriages of duty, and with both her parents dead, she was now ready to embrace the chance to take a husband of her own choosing. The marriage of Jane Seymour had catapulted her brothers into prominence as uncles of a future king. Thomas was a dashing, handsome figure, described as 'hardy, wise and liberal ... fierce in courage, courtly in fashion, in personage stately, in voice magnificent, but somewhat empty of matter'. He also had an air of danger about him, and in September 1540 the Privy Council had bound him and Edward Rogers to keep the peace towards each other, at a penalty of £1,000 each.[7] Like many of his noble contemporaries, Seymour had benefited from Henry's policy of dissolving the monasteries. In June 1541 he had been granted lands that belonged to the late monastery of Cirencester, and the following month he gained the manor attached to that at Amesbury, receiving further land in Berkshire and Westmorland before the end of the year.[8] Described as Henry's 'trusty and well-beloved servant ... knight, one of the gentlemen of his grace's privy chamber', Seymour had been ambassador to Vienna for eight months by the end of 1542. He wrote to Henry from Nuremburg on 29 December, where he was considering the possibility of hiring mercenaries to fight for the king, although he 'hoped to return to England shortly'.[9] He was back at court in the early spring, at which point Catherine hoped he would make her his wife. However, the emergence of a more significant suitor would delay this love match for another four years.

Catherine was a good catch. At almost thirty-one, she was experienced and wise, without being too old that her childbearing years were over. According to John Foxe, she possessed 'rare gifts of nature, as singular beauty, favour and a comely personage; things wherein the king was delighted', as well as the 'virtues of her mind'. Her appearance was 'lively' and 'pleasing' and her 'cheerful countenance', as painted by William Scrots, shows a round, open face with brown or auburn hair and the fashionable pale skin. A second image, a miniature by Lucas Horenbout, depicts her with a slimmer face and lighter hair. In spite of the religious leanings of her second husband, the identification of her mother with the Aragon faction and her friendship with the Catholic Mary, she was passionately interested in religious reform, bordering on Protestantism, and welcomed Hugh Latimer and Miles Coverdale at her house. The iconoclast Latimer had been preaching in favour of an English translation of the Bible since the late 1520s and had recently suffered imprisonment for opposing Henry's Six Articles; later he would suffer a martyr's death by burning at the stake. Coverdale was responsible for translating and publishing a 1535 version of the Bible, building on the work of the martyred William Tyndale, although Henry had welcomed this, ordering a copy of Coverdale's work to be placed in every church. He would become Catherine's chaplain and almoner in the years ahead. Catherine was well aware of the dangers of her faith; that July, just after her wedding, four men were burned at Windsor for preaching and holding heretical beliefs.

By January 1543, according to Chapuys, there were rumours that Henry was considering remarriage. He hosted a great feast and summoned Princess Mary and her ladies to court, in order to act as host: 'This came very apropos for the Princess, who, in default of a queen, was called to court triumphantly, accompanied by many ladies ... Many think that before the end of these feasts the king might think of marrying again, but hitherto there is no appearance of it.' Henry's interest in Catherine may have predated Lord Latimer's death and he had probably known her all her life, seeing her grow up around the court. In February, the king paid a tailor's bill for Catherine and her stepdaughter, for 'numerous items' of cotton, linen, buckram, hoods and sleeves, Italian, Venetian, French and Dutch gowns, totalling over £8.[10] As with his other wives, one of the first signs was the preferment of her relatives; that March, Catherine's brother William became a member of the Privy Council and was elected to Knight of the Garter in April. He also granted William a divorce, on 17 April, after his wife, Anne Bourchier, was accused of adultery. By this point she must have become aware of his interest, and she struggled to reconcile what she later came to consider to be God's will with the brief hope she had glimpsed of personal happiness. Henry needed to ensure his rival, Seymour, was out of the way. Nothing was more effective than putting a large distance between him and Catherine, so in April Thomas received his instructions for a new embassy to Flanders. He left in May. By this point, Henry had probably already proposed to Catherine.

While the king awaited her reply, news arrived at court of the death of one of his previous loves. Following the scandal of 1536, Mary Boleyn had lived in quiet obscurity with her second husband, William Stafford, at Rochford Hall, Essex. She had lost both her parents too, with Elizabeth Howard dying in 1538 and Sir Thomas Boleyn the following year, from whom she inherited some more property in the area. Mary was fortunate in her quiet life; she had married Stafford for love, stating in the 1530s that she would rather 'beg [her] bread' with him than be 'the greatest queen in Christendom'. She may have borne him a couple of children, in addition to seeing the careers of her son and daughter by William Carey develop, and there are no records of her returning to court. Mary's final years are as elusive as her first; she had briefly enjoyed the limelight of Henry's affection, then witnessed the meteoric rise and fall of her siblings, before retreating into what appears to have been domestic harmony. When she died in June 1543, she was the king's last link with the glittering, dangerous world of a decade ago.

Yet Henry was keen to plunge into married life again. In reality, Catherine had little choice but to accept his offer and the necessary licence was issued by Cranmer on 10 July. Two days later, Catherine and Henry were married in the queen's closet and Hampton Court by Bishop Gardiner, 'in the presence of noble and gentle persons' but 'privately and without ceremony'.[11] After feasting, the wedding night was spent in the palace, with Catherine, already experienced in the ways of one ageing husband, awaiting the arrival of a king whose physical dimensions must have restricted his movements and ability to perform. It was also a time of unease, with plague breaking out in the capital, causing a proclamation to be issued three days later to 'prevent Londoners from entering the gates of any house wherein the king or queen lie, and forbidding servants of the court to go to London and return to court again'.[12] Perhaps it was this that prompted Henry and Catherine to depart for Oatlands later that month. From there, Catherine wrote to her brother describing the marriage as 'the greatest joy and comfort that could happen' to her. He replied that it 'revived my troubled spirit and turned all my care into solace and rejoicing'.[13] From Oatlands, the newly weds set off on a summer progress through the Home Counties.

Catherine's household included her close friend Catherine, Duchess of Suffolk, and her cousin Maud, along with many ladies who had formerly served Henry's previous wives: Mary, Countess of Arundel; Joan, Lady Denny; Lady Margaret Douglas; Jane Dudley, Lady Lisle; Anne Bassett; Jane, Lady Wriothesley; and Mary Wotton, Lady Carew. There was also Thomas Seymour's sister-in-law, Anne Stanhope, Lady Hertford, who must have served as a reminder of Thomas and, possibly, a source of information about him during his absence. A Francis Goldsmith, writing to thank Catherine for giving him a place as chaplain in her household, lavished her with praise: 'God has so formed her mind for pious studies, that she considers everything of small value compared to Christ. Her rare goodness has made every day like Sunday, a thing hitherto unheard of, especially in a royal palace. Her piety cherishes the religion long since introduced, not without great labour, to the palace.'[14] The new queen appears to have been very popular, even among those who might resent her new position. Catherine had maintained good relationships with her Latimer stepchildren and now responded with warmth to Henry's three offspring, assisted by the fact of her longstanding friendship with Mary. While they were away in August, she persuaded Henry to detour on their way to Ampthill to visit his children at Ashridge in Hertfordshire. The only sour note was sounded by Anne of Cleves, disappointed that Henry had married a woman she believed to be 'not nearly as beautiful as she'.[15]

An inventory of 1547 gives a glimpse into Catherine's opulent world at Hampton Court. Along with a withdrawing chamber for the queen it lists the king's bedchamber, which led to the queen's gallery and on to her bedchamber, from which three more privy chambers were accessible for her use.[16] In addition to her ladies, her household included George Day, Bishop of Chichester, as almoner and humanist scholar Sir Anthony Cope as her vice-chamberlain, along with her master of the horse, secretary, chaplains, physicians, apothecary, clerk of the closet and her learned council, which contained lawyers and clerks. There were fifty-one men in her immediate service, including ushers, grooms, pagers, sewers, waiters and yeomen, as well as her own messengers, goldsmith, tailor and those who cared her for animals.[17] In addition to this, she had another set of servants for the kitchen and service of meals, which mirrored that of the king, as well as her laundresses and the menial staff who lit fires and lamps, swept the floors and carried wood or water. She also had her own jester, a woman named 'Jane the Fool'.

Catherine has often been cast as the nurse of Henry's twilight years, through his terrible afflictions with his ulcerated legs. This is far from the truth. Henry possessed sufficient nurses to tend to his health, which would have been unseemly for a woman of Catherine's status. Instead, he wanted her to be an ornament to his court, to divert him with pleasure, to which end he happily indulged her passions for dancing and music, clothes and flowers. Daily payments were made for flowers and perfumes for her rooms and she kept a group of Italian viol players. She was also reputed to bathe in milk[18] to soften her skin and some medical manuals of the time do recommend this, along with the use of flowers and herbs, perhaps in the new bathrooms Henry had installed at the Tower and Whitehall in the 1540s. Henry showered her with gifts: a pet spaniel named Rig who wore a collar of crimson velvet and gold, a parrot that was fed on hemp seeds, diamond brooches, tablets with bejewelled initials and ostrich feathers and portraits of himself painted on gold.

The new queen inherited her predecessor's wardrobe, which was customised to fit her by the royal tailor John Scut, who had served all Henry's wives. The process must have required some additional material, perhaps panels and fringes to lengthen skirts, as Catherine Howard was reputed to be very short while Catherine Parr's coffin would measure five feet and ten inches in length. She also commissioned new clothes, sending for silks to Antwerp, and was noted by the Duke of Najera for her elegance and opulence, dressed in a robe of cloth of gold over a brocade kirtle, sleeves lined with crimson satin, a two-yard-long train, a gold girdle adorned with pendants, diamonds in her headdress and more on the jewel she wore. He also noted the two crosses around her neck.[19] Catherine may have been pious, intelligent and devout but she was also something of a sensualist.

56

More than an Ornament, 1544–45

Too dearly had I bought my green and youthful years,
If in mine age I could not find when craft for love appears.[1]

Catherine's experiences of Henry as a lover, at the age of fifty-five, with ulcerated legs and a waist of fifty-three inches, were vastly different from those of his first two wives. The bedrooms that he shared with his last wife, at Greenwich, Hampton Court or Oatlands, Woodstock, Nonsuch or Whitehall, were gorgeously hung with tapestries and furnishings like those listed among the 1536 effects of Catherine of Aragon. The ageing king may have reclined on blue velvet bedsheets embroidered with roses and fringed with red silk, shielded by bed curtains of Turkish gold damask fringed with purple silk and gold tissue. Over his head in its nightcap were stretched canopies like that which combined yellow cloth of gold with green and blue velvet embroidered with crowned roses and lined with purple sarsenet, fringed with green silk and Venetian gold. To either side, on top of the sheets of fine Holland cloth and crimson counterpane, were scattered cushions of red and gold tissue or embroidered green damask, some of them more than a yard long. However, with his doublets now large enough for three men to fit inside and his weeping sores necessitating a brand-new pair of hose almost every day, Henry's love life in his twilight years must have been a more sedate affair.

Catherine had promised to be 'bonaire and buxom' in her wedding vows and no doubt she made an effort to please her husband, as Henry's contentment with the marriage suggests. Although it can hardly have been satisfying for her, she considered it in the way of a calling, perhaps seeing herself in a position to become an advocate of the new faith, and keeping the king happy in bed was all part of that plan. The sentiments of Henry Howard, Earl of Surrey, poet and courtier, may express something of the ageing king as lover, as the words of his friend Thomas Wyatt had done so in Henry's youth:

> Thus thoughtful as I lay, I saw my wither'd skin,
> How it doth shew my dented chews, the flesh was worn so thin.
> And eke my toothless chaps, the gates of my right way,
> That opes and shuts as I do speak, do thus unto me say:
> 'Thy white and hoarish airs, the messengers of age,
> That shew, like lines of true belief, that this life doth assuage;
> Bid thee lay hand, and feel them hanging on thy chin;
> The which do write two ages past, the third now coming in.
> Hang up therefore the bit of thy young wanton time:
> And thou that therein beaten art, the happiest life define.'

Increasingly, Henry suffered from the impotence and frustration that he claimed had been instigated by his physical dislike of Anne of Cleves. Yet now, two wives later, there was no disguising his inability to perform as he had in his youth, which must have required delicate handling, both metaphorical and literal, from Catherine. No doubt she had to pay as much attention to the king's sense of pride as his decaying body. Surrey wrote,

> The rich old man that sees his end draw on so sore,
> How he would be a boy again, to live so much the more.

And his contemporary Thomas, Lord Vaux, added,

> My lusts they do me leave,
> My fancies all be fled,
> And tract of time begins to weave
> Grey hairs upon my head.

Yet Henry was to have one last Indian summer. He might have been incapable of making love to the last Catherine with the vigour he had expended on the first, but he would certainly attempt to recapture something of the glory of his youth in another respect. He would invade France.

Relations between England and the Auld Alliance, of Scotland and France, had been deteriorating for some time. After James V had failed to meet Henry in York on his summer progress of 1541, hostilities over religious change deepened and an English army had achieved a resounding victory at Solway Moss in November 1542. Two weeks later, James died of a fever – or reputedly heartbreak at the shame – leaving a six-day-old daughter, Mary, to inherit his kingdom. With the Scots in submission, Henry concluded a secret alliance with the Emperor and turned all £650,000 worth of his military force against his old friend and adversary Francis I. Better still, in spite of the agony in his legs and his frequent inability to walk, he would lead the army in person, clad in his giant-sized newly made armour. That February, when his ulcers had flared up again, leaving him bedridden in a fever, Catherine requested that her bed be moved into a closet leading off his bedchamber, ordered plaster and sponges, comfits and pastilles from her apothecary and was glimpsed sitting with his bad leg in her lap.[2] Henry's doctors urged him not to travel to France in person but to deputise the role, as he had done in Scotland. It seemed impossible to think of a man who could barely stand leading an army across the channel. Nothing would change the king's mind, though.

On 7 July, Henry appointed Catherine as regent in his absence, stipulated that his process of government would pass to her and that 'a commission for this be delivered to her before his departure'. She was to be assisted by Cranmer as Archbishop of Canterbury; Lord Chancellor Wriothesley; Edward Seymour, Earl of Hertford; Stephen Gardiner, Bishop of Winchester; and secretary Sir William Petre, who were to report to her once a month on 'the state of the country'. Catherine was also granted the manors of Chelsea, Hanworth and Mortlake. It marked the height of her influence. At the end of the month, she accompanied Henry to the wedding of his niece Lady Margaret Douglas to the Earl of Lennox, which took place in the chapel royal of St James' Palace. His health had significantly improved by the arrival of the campaign, to the extent that Edward Seymour commented that he was in 'as good health as I have seen his Grace at any time this seven year'.[3]

Henry was in France from 14 July until 30 September, laying siege to Boulogne, which finally fell to him after almost two months. In his absence, Catherine played the role of the 'humble, obedient loving wife and servant', writing soon after his departure that 'the want of your presence, so much beloved and desired by me, makes me that I cannot quietly enjoy anything until I hear from your Majesty' and that 'love and affection compels me to desire your presence'. Yet she combined this with the strength and steel required to oversee the running of the country, from dealing with Scottish prisoners to equipping the French campaign. Only 25 July she was at Hampton Court, where she wrote to Henry to inform him that a further £40,000 was being advanced to him by the council and that 4,000 men were ready to be sent as reinforcements at an hour's notice.[4] A week later, she wrote again from the palace with news from the Lieutenant of the North and enclosing other letters of business, concluding with her usual reassurance that the children were all in good health. They had all spent a brief spell together at Enfield and Oakham Castle, to exchange the dangerously pestilent air of the capital for that of the countryside. Catherine was back at Greenwich on 6 August and reported that rumours were circulating that the French had landed on the English coast, knowing that 'such vain rumours fly fast, and this may have reached the king'[5] and on 9 September she was at Westminster to issue proclamations to deal with deserters: 'for the examination of persons returning from the king's army in France and punishing of such as have insufficient passports to do so' and for the containment of a fresh outbreak of the plague.[6]

Henry left Calais disappointed, knowing his victory was a pyrrhic one, with the Emperor and Francis immediately reconciling. He crossed the channel in a despondency that would last into the autumn, anticipating French retaliation. It came in the summer of 1545, when a fleet of Francis's galleys burned Brighton on the Sussex coast, then a small fishing village, before moving west and sinking the *Mary Rose*. A month later, his troops in Portsmouth were mutinous as John Dudley, now Lord Lisle, wrote: 'The army cannot return to the sea for lack of victual and men, for the men had rather be hanged than go forth again. The common people grudge that their king has been at great charge and nothing done.'[7] While he was digesting this information, Henry received word that his oldest and closest friend, and one-time brother-in-law, Charles Brandon, Duke of Suffolk, had died. It was a shattering loss of a man who had been present in the king's life since his early childhood and a reminder that his own days were numbered. The mood at court that autumn must have been a sombre one, especially as it had been a terrible year for Henry's health.

That December, Henry delivered an uncharacteristically 'eloquent oration'[8] in Parliament, in which he extolled them to live more charitably and 'set forth God's word by true preaching and good example'. He was 'sorry to hear "how unreverently that most precious jewel, the Word of God, is disputed, rhymed, sung and jangled in every alehouse and tavern", and that the readers of it follow it so faintly and coldly. I am sure there never was less virtuous or godly living, nor God himself ever, among Christians, less reverenced.'[9] The word of the Bible had always held symbolic power for Henry; it had provided him with the justification and means to annul his first marriage and break from Rome. Now, it would return to threaten the life of his 'obedient, loving wife and servant', Catherine Parr.

57

Queen in Danger, 1546

When youth had led me half the race
That Cupid's scourge had made me run;
I looked back to mete the place
From whence my weary course begun.[1]

Catherine's role during 1545–46 had combined compassion and sympathy with erudite reformist scholarship. In the spring of 1545, Henry had suffered a terrible fever which had spread to his legs and kept him in his rooms for several weeks, attended by his doctors and apothecaries. The pain returned again the following year, forcing him back to bed again at regular intervals. His legs caused him pain in March, and that July he fell ill with colic. During this time, while her husband was unavailable, Catherine relied on the company of her ladies, but the nature of her household was very different from that of Catherine of Aragon or Anne Boleyn. The new queen enjoyed dancing and poetry as much as her predecessors but she was also fomenting something of a hotbed of radical reform.

Catherine had established a circle of women at court who shared her Protestant leanings, including her sister Anne Parr; Anne, Countess of Sussex; Catherine, Duchess of Suffolk; Anne Stanhope, Lady Hertford; and Lady Denny. Her passion for humanist teaching and reforms extended into her relationship with her stepchildren, as she encouraged Mary and Elizabeth to undertake English translations of Erasmus' *Paraphrase of the Gospel of St John* and Marguerite of Navarre's *The Mirror of the Sinful Soul* respectively. She was also an accomplished writer, publishing the popular *Prayers Stirring the Mind unto Heavenly Meditations* in 1545, which Elizabeth would translate into Latin, French and Italian, bound in crimson silk, for her stepmother's Christmas present that year. However, Catherine clearly held back some of her more extreme views from her husband, waiting until after his death to publish her second book, *Lamentations of a Sinner*, which, although it presented Henry as an English Moses, leading his people to the light, it also argued in favour of consubstantiation, instead of transubstantiation, that the bread and wine of Mass was only a metaphor for the body and blood of Christ, rather than becoming the real thing. It was such views as this that aroused the animosity of Wriothesley and Bishop Gardiner, who wanted Henry to halt the process of reform. In the spring of 1546, the emergence of an unusual woman named Anne Askew provided them with an opportunity to pose a challenge to the queen.

Anne's early life in Lincolnshire had appeared to be fairly conventional until her husband had ejected her from their home for holding Protestant beliefs. She travelled to London and began preaching, which led to her first brief arrest in 1545, after which she came to the attention of the queen. In May 1546 she was arrested again and taken to the Tower, where she was tortured on the rack by Wriothesley and Sir Richard Rich, who demanded that she implicate other highborn women who shared her religious convictions. Anne, though, refused. Foxe's *Book of Martyrs* has her relate,

> Then came Rich and one of the council, charging me upon my obedience, to show unto them, if I knew any man or woman of my sect. My answer was, that I knew none. Then they asked me of my Lady of Suffolk, my Lady of Sussex, my Lady of Hertford, my Lady Denny, and my Lady Fitzwilliam. To whom I answered, if I should pronounce anything against them, that I were not able to prove it. Then said they unto me, that the king was informed that I could name, if I would, a great number of my sect. I answered, that the king was as well deceived in that behalf, as dissembled with in other matters.[2]

Awaiting news, Henry sanctioned a search at court for banned books, focusing particularly on the chambers of the queen's ladies, which led to the hasty changing of locks and concealment of those texts that could be considered heretical. The investigators went away empty handed. However, they had not given up.

Catherine's position had also been unwittingly weakened by her closest friend, Catherine, Duchess of Suffolk. Following Brandon's death, court rumour suggested that Henry was considering setting aside his queen and taking a seventh wife. In February 1546, the new Imperial ambassador, Francois van der Delft, wrote to the Emperor that 'there are rumours of a new queen. Some attribute it to the sterility of the present queen, while others say that there will be no change during the present war. Madame Suffolk is much talked about and is in great favour; but the king shows no alteration in his behaviour to the queen, although she is said to be annoyed by the rumour.'[3] Catherine had set aside her own hopes for happiness to enter into a marriage with an ageing, difficult and unpredictable man, to whom she had been nothing less than devoted, charming and gracious. No wonder she was annoyed.

Catherine Willoughby was the daughter of Maria de Salinas, one of Catherine of Aragon's original waiting women who had been in her retinue since 1501. After fifteen years in England, Maria married William, Baron Willoughby de Eresby, and Henry VIII granted them Grimsthorpe Castle in Lincolnshire, although Maria was still often at court in the service of the queen. In March 1519 Maria was at Parham Old Hall, in Suffolk, where she delivered her only daughter, who was probably named in honour of Maria's mistress; two sons were also born to the marriage but died as infants. After the death of her father, the wardship of the seven-year-old Catherine Willoughby was granted by the king to Charles Brandon, Duke of Suffolk, and for five years the girl lived with him and his wife, Mary Tudor. She was betrothed to their second son, Henry Brandon, who was a few years her junior. However, Catherine Willoughby had attracted the attention of an older man. Just weeks after the death of Mary Tudor in 1533, Catherine's engagement to young Henry was broken when she became the wife of his father, Brandon, becoming Duchess of Suffolk. She was fourteen and he was in his late forties but it appears to have been a successful match, with Catherine bearing two sons and quickly adapting to take part in court life and developing a reputation for being clever, attractive and witty, as well as a proponent of the reformed faith. When the marks of Henry's favour towards the duchess were commented on by the court, the two women may have discussed the matter. Perhaps there was some substance to the report, although, as van der Delft admitted, there was no change in Henry's behaviour towards his wife. It may have been that he had considered her as a replacement if the queen proved to be a heretic or, alternatively, he was showing her favour as the widow of his old friend.

As a result of Anne Askew's interrogation, something changed. In early July, Gardiner managed to persuade Henry to sign a warrant for Catherine's arrest. After she contradicted the king in debate, which irritated the unwell king, he snapped to the bishop that 'a good hearing it is when women become such clerks and a thing much to my comfort to come in my old days to be taught by a woman'.[4] By accident or design, a copy of the warrant was left in a place where Catherine could find it and, suddenly understanding the extent of the danger she was in, she hurried to explain herself to the king, claiming she was only contradicting him in order to learn from him through debate and take his mind off his pain, and 'your majesty [has] very much mistaken me, for I have always held it preposterous for a woman to instruct her lord'.[5] No doubt she was terrified, picturing herself suffering the same fate as Henry's previous wives or even that of Askew herself. Her clever and quick response showed the extent to which Catherine understood her husband and just how capable she was. She had been lucky, though, that the tipoff, possibly from Henry's doctor, had allowed her to pre-empt the strike before Henry had decisively moved on and refused to hear or see her, as he had done in the cases of Catherine of Aragon, Anne Boleyn, Catherine Howard and, briefly, even Anne of Cleves, physically removing himself from their presence. Catherine understood that Henry's objection was less to her religious views than the fact that she had dared to publicly oppose him and her deft submission brought an instant reconciliation. Foxe related that he took his wife on his knee and reassured her of his love, before ordering 'all manner of jewels, pearls and precious stones ... skins and sable furs ... for our dearest wife, the queen'.[6]

Catherine had talked her way out of her arrest, probably saving her own life. However, Henry had forgotten to call off his henchmen. The following afternoon, while they sat in the privy gardens, Wriothesley appeared with an armed guard of forty men and Catherine had a glimpse of what her fate would have been. His mood rapidly changing, the king berated him and ordered him to leave. As Catherine attempted to comfort her husband, in the full knowledge of what she had witnessed, Henry told her, 'You little know how evil he deserves this grace at your hands.' Catherine might have privately mused that the sentiment was equally applicable to him.[7] Anne Askew was burned at the stake at Smithfield on 16 July, having been carried there in a chair as the extent of her torture made her incapable of walking. In a twist of irony, she shared her fate with John Lascelles, whose evidence had led to the downfall of Catherine Howard.

The late summer and early autumn were a period of quiet happiness for Catherine and Henry. A peace treaty was signed with the French, and on St Bartholomew's Day, 24 August, the king appeared with the Admiral of France, for which occasion many costly banquet houses were built, with great masques and hunts being held for their pleasure and the visitors being lodged in tents made of cloth of gold.[8] Catherine loved to dance, but the king who had once relished appearing in disguise could only sit and watch. That year, Henry found it increasingly difficult to walk on his swollen legs and spent more time shut away in his rooms. The eight-year-old Prince Edward had taken his place to formally welcome the French at Hounslow, before they had arrived at Hampton Court. That summer, a short progress had taken Henry and Catherine to Oatlands, where a ramp was installed to allow him to mount his horse, and he was able to hunt also at Chobham that August, but the effort exhausted him, so the plan to visit Guildford was abandoned and the royal party returned to Windsor. Van der Delft related that Henry's physicians had been in despair, giving up all hope for his recovery, and that he was in 'great danger'. Two 'trams' or moveable chairs were built, 'for the king's majesty to sit in, to be carried to and fro', and that October Van der Delft described Henry as 'passing in his chair'. Hall related that Henry required 'an engine' to help him climb and descend stair-cases and the Duke of Norfolk confirmed that a device was installed for him on the stairs.[9] The bill for the king's medicines jumped up from £5 in August to £25 in December. In November, Henry moved to Whitehall and undertook as series of medicinal baths, combining herbs, spices and salts believed to have a soothing effect. His rooms were freshly perfumed, to obscure the smell of his rotten leg and the evil vapours of disease, and several pairs of velvet slippers were made for the comfort of his swollen feet.

Having watched her second husband weaken and die, Catherine must have recognised the signs. However, what followed must still have come as a surprise. On Christmas Eve, she, Princess Mary and Princess Elizabeth were ordered to leave Whitehall and spend Christmas at Greenwich. It was a significant step, designed to distance his wife and daughters from him during the final weeks of terrible suffering. Henry had always retreated from his women while in pain, but on this occasion Catherine was left in the role of stepmother instead of comforter. She sent a gift of a double portrait of Henry and Edward to the prince, who was passing the season at Ashridge. On the first day of 1547, fever stuck Henry again and Catherine may have heard the rumours that he was dead, although she would not have dared believe them until official confirmation arrived. The king rallied, yet again, but his strength was completely gone and his body was 'wasted'. Van der Delft reported that 'the king is so unwell that considering his age and corpulence, fears are entertained that he will be unable to survive further attacks'.[10]

News also arrived at court that year of the death of another of the figures from Henry's past: the vivacious young teenager Elizabeth Carew, who had captured both the king's attention and that of Charles Brandon, had lived out her widowhood quietly after the execution of her husband Sir Nicholas in 1538. Her close friend Anne Hastings, with whom the king had dallied in 1510, causing his first argument with Catherine of Aragon, had passed away in 1544. Their deaths marked a greater severance with the king's youth. In 1546, the beautiful Mary Shelton, once considered as a potential bride for Henry, married her cousin Sir Anthony Heveningham and would go on to bear him a number of children.

Catherine would not see her husband again. On 10 January 1547, she left Greenwich for Westminster but was not permitted to see the king, who was prostrate in bed by this point. The next two weeks were spent waiting. She did not know it, but in his final days Henry made provision for her future, allowing her a generous annual allowance of £7,000 and stipulating that she should be afforded the treatment due to a queen, although she was not to be appointed to act as regent for the young king to be, the nine-year-old Edward. Henry died at two o'clock on the morning of 28 January. It was kept secret for two days, but the news would have been broken to Catherine soon after the public announcement on 30 January. She must have experienced a mixture of loss and relief, as she dressed herself in the now familiar widow's weeds and headed for her manor house at Chelsea. The king's life was over, but that of his final wife could finally begin.

58

The Survivors, 1547

They set thee up, they took thee down,
They served thee with humility.[1]

Contrary to the popular rhyme, 'divorced, beheaded, died, divorced, beheaded, survived', Henry VIII was outlived by two of his wives. After the king's death, Catherine Parr wrote to Thomas Seymour that

'I would not have you think that this mine honest goodwill towards you to proceed of any sudden motion of passion; for, as truly as God is God, my mind was fully bent, the other time I was at liberty, to marry you before any man I know'. They probably reached some private arrangement within weeks of Henry's death, but as she was his widow, the couple believed the council would not wish to see her married so soon. Yet Catherine and Thomas could not wait to be together. She was thirty-five, an advanced age for any potential childbearing, and deeply in love; he was approaching forty and knew a good match when he saw one. They were wed in secret that May.

However, it would appear that Catherine was not her husband's first choice. Back in February, in the days following the coronation of the young Edward VI, Seymour had investigated the possibility of marrying the thirteen-year-old Princess Elizabeth, writing to her in a way that made his intention plain:

> I have so much respect for you my princess, that I dare not tell you of the fire which consumes me, and the impatience with which I yearn to show you my devotion. If it is my good fortune to inspire in you feelings of kindness, and you will consent to a marriage you may assure yourself of having made the happiness of a man who will adore you till death.[2]

If Catherine was unaware of the extent of her husband's interest in her stepdaughter, she could no longer remain in ignorance after she and Seymour set up house in Chelsea. The dowager queen had been denied the regency of Edward and damaged her relations with Mary after remarrying so soon but she still maintained a warm connection with Elizabeth, whom she invited to live with them. Seymour's attentions to the young girl soon strayed into the inappropriate, when he would come into her bedchamber early in the morning before she had risen and 'strike her on the back or buttocks familiarly'. If she was still in bed, 'he would put open the curtains and make as though he would come at her and one morning he strove to have kissed her in bed'. On another occasion, they 'romped in the garden' and he cut Elizabeth's gown 'into a hundred pieces', even getting Catherine to hold the girl while he did it. This was a very uncomfortable situation. Gradually, Catherine recognised the nature of the relationship and, in the summer of 1548, she arranged for Elizabeth to leave. By this point, Catherine was also pregnant.

The next few months proved difficult. Catherine appears to have had a difficult pregnancy, and she was angry and hurt after being snubbed at court and by her brother-in-law's refusal to return her jewels, which had been taken in Henry's last days and remained in the Tower. In mid-June Seymour moved her to Sudeley Castle, where she went into labour six weeks later. Catherine gave birth to a daughter, named Mary, on 30 August; the birth had been a success, but within a few days Catherine descended into a fever. She died on 5 September 1548 and her daughter was given over to the care of Catherine, Duchess of Suffolk, although she appears not to have survived infancy. Seymour went to the block in March 1549, accused of treasonous activities including the wooing of Princess Elizabeth.

Her tomb in the chapel at Sudeley Castle is inscribed with the words of her chaplain, Dr Parkhurst:

> In this new tomb, the royal Kath'rine lies
> Flower of her sex, renowned, great and wise.
> A wife by every nuptial virtue known
> A faithful partner once of Henry's throne.
> To Seymour next her plighted hand she yields
> (Seymour who Neptune's trident justly wields.)
> From him a beauteous daughter blessed her arms
> An infant copy of her parents' charms
> When now seven days this tender flower had bloom'd
> Heaven in its wrath the mother's soul resumed.
> Great Kath'rine's merit in our grief appears
> While fair Britannia dews her cheek with tears,
> Our loyal breast with rising sighs are torn
> With saints she triumphs, we with mortals mourn.

That only left Anne of Cleves. After the death of Henry, Anne had moved from Richmond to Bletchley and then on to Penshurst Place in Kent, close to her other property, the former Boleyn home Hever Castle. She was an occasional presence at the court and, after the death of Prince Edward in 1553, attended the coronation of his sister, Princess Mary. For some reason, Anne was implicated in a rebellion of 1554 against Mary's Spanish marriage and Catholic leanings, which was organised by the son of Thomas Wyatt. Princess Elizabeth was also implicated in this, although it is most likely that the rebels simply rose in her name, but according to the Imperial ambassador her closeness to Anne was enough to turn Queen Mary against her former stepmother. She never remarried, although she could have, even being suggested by King Edward as a potential bride for Thomas Seymour in 1547. Anne lived out the remainder of her life quietly and died in Catherine Parr's old home at Chelsea, on 16 July 1557, at the age of forty-one.

In her will, Anne left bequeaths to the gentlewomen of her privy chamber 'for their great pains taken with us', around £40 each, to enable them to marry. She left 40s to Mother Lovell 'for her attendance upon us in this time of this our sickness' and 20s to every child in her household. To her brother, she sent a gold ring set with a diamond in the shape of a heart and to his wife, a black enamelled ring bearing a great ruby. She left a gold ring with a table diamond to Catherine, Duchess of Suffolk, and another engraved with the letters H and J, for Henry and Jane Seymour, to Mary, Countess of Arundel. She remembered her physician, surgeon, servants, courtiers, chaplains, her old laundress and friends, as well as the alms-children and poor of her parishes.[3] Anne was the only one of Henry's wives to be buried in Westminster Abbey.

Only a handful of the women associated with Henry would outlive him. Mary Shelton lived long enough to see the succession of Queen Elizabeth in November 1558, who welcomed Mary's daughter Abigail into her household. Having been widowed the previous year, she remarried to a Philip Appleyard and died in 1571. Her sister Margaret, with whom she had sometimes been confused, and who captivated Sir Henry Norris, may well also have been the mistress of the king. She married Sir Thomas Wodehouse and had a large family, but lost her husband and one of her sons at the Battle of Musselborough, in September 1547. Evidence suggests she survived into the reign of Elizabeth, but the exact date of her death is unknown.

Anne Bassett, whose name had been coupled with Henry's several times during the late 1530s and early 1540s, attended his funeral in 1547. Along with her sister Catherine, she received an allowance of cloth for mourning clothes, suggesting they were among the many mourners who took part in the procession to St George's Chapel, Windsor three weeks after his death. Anne went on to become a maid of honour to Queen Mary in 1553. The following year, she married Sir Walter Hungerford of Farley, a man renowned for his athletic ability but tainted by scandal, following the execution of his father for offenses committed under the first sodomy law of 1533. Anne bore her husband two children but may have died in childbirth or a complication arising afterwards, as Walter remarried less than four years later, in May 1558. Catherine Bassett married Sir Henry Ashley on 8 December 1547, who was knighted at the coronation of Mary I. She bore a son, Henry, who served Queen Elizabeth but died at some unknown point before her husband's death in 1588.

Catherine, the widowed Duchess of Suffolk, whom Henry may have considered marrying in 1546, suffered a terrible tragedy in 1551, when both her young sons died of the sweating sickness within hours of each other. Two years later, she remarried to Richard Bertie, her usher and master of the horse, in what appears to have been a love match. Continuing to advocate the reformed faith, the Berties fled into exile during the reign of the Catholic Mary, living at Wesel, in Germany, then in Polish Lithuania. During their absence, Catherine bore a son, Peregrine Bertie, in October 1555, but the family only felt safe to return to England in 1558, after Mary's death. Catherine died in 1580.

Henry VIII's body, so intimately known to these women, was laid to rest beside that of Jane Seymour, under the choir in St George's Chapel, Windsor. In transit, his coffin had rested at Syon Abbey, the last home of Catherine Howard, where fluids from his corpse leaked and were reputed to have been licked away by stray dogs. When the vault was opened in 1813, his coffin was considerably damaged, perhaps as a result of the introduction of later inmates or, as Victorian historian A. Y. Nutt suggested, due to the 'action of internal forces outward'. The magnificent tomb the king had planned was described by John Speed in the seventeenth century as featuring life-sized statues of Henry and Queen Jane, along with statue of Henry on horseback, amid an assembly of 130 biblical figures in brass gilt, set among marble pillars and gilded bronze angels. The tomb was never built and today Henry lies under a simple floor slab, far less ceremonious than the modest tomb he had allowed Catherine of Aragon.

Notes

Introduction: The Six Wives and Many Mistresses?
1. Sir Thomas More.

1 A Maid from Spain, 1485–1500
1. Anon., *The Receyt of the Ladie Kateryn* in Astle, Thomas, Grose, Francis *et al.* (eds), *The Antiquarian Repertory: a miscellaneous assemblage of topography, history, biography, customs and manners intended to illustrate and preserve several valuable remains of old times.* (London: E. Jeffery, 1807).
2. Williams, Patrick, *Katharine of Aragon* (Amberley, 2013).
3. Cowans, Jon (ed.), *Early Modern Spain: A Documentary History* (University of Pennsylvania, 2003).
4. *Ibid.*
5. *Ibid.*
6. Tremlett, Giles, *Catherine of Aragon: Henry's Spanish Queen* (Faber and Faber, 2010).
7. *Ibid.*
8. CSP Spain 5 Nov. 1485.
9. CSP Spain 30 April 1488.
10. CSP Spain 6 July 1488.
11. Course Material, 'England in the Time of Richard III' (University of Leicester, 2013).
12. Rubin, Nancy, *Isabella of Castile, the First Renaissance Queen* (St Martin's Press, 1991).
13. *Ibid.*
14. CSP Spain March 1499.
15. *Ibid.*
16. CSP Spain May 1499.
17. *Ibid.*
18. CSP Spain Oct. 1499.

2 A Royal Welcome, 1501
1. Dunbar, from 'The Thistle and the Rose' with my substitution of 'England' for 'Scotland.'
2. *Ibid.*
3. *Ibid.*
4. Starkey, David, *Six Wives: The Queens of Henry VIII* (Vintage, 2004).
5. Erickson, Carolly, *Great Harry: The Extravagant Life of Henry VIII* (Robson Books, 2004 edn).
6. Receyt.
7. *Ibid.*
8. Nichols, John Gough, *London Pageants 1: An Account of Sixty Royal Processions and Entertainments in the City of London* (J. B. Nichols and Son, 1831).
9. *Ibid.*
10. *Ibid.*
11. *Ibid.*
12. Rubin.
13. CSP Spain June 1505.

3 Marrying Arthur, 1501
1. Udall, Nicholas, from *Ralph Roister Doister.*
2. Receyt.
3. *Ibid.*

4. Leland.
5. *Ibid.*
6. *Ibid.*
7. Receyt.
8. *Ibid.*
9. Hall.
10. Receyt.
11. *Ibid.*
12. *Ibid.*
13. Licence, Amy, *Elizabeth of York* (Amberley, 2013).
14. Tremlett.
15. CSP Spain Nov 1501.
16. *Ibid.*
17. *Ibid.*

4 Ludlow, 1502
1. Thomas, Lord Vaux.
2. Williams.
3. CSP Spain Supplement to Volume 1 1501.
4. *Ibid.*
18. Rubin.
5. CSP Spain Supp.
6. Norton, Elizabeth, *Bessie Blount* (Amberley, 2011).
7. CSP Spain Supp.
8. *Ibid.*
9. For the best description of the Ludlow household, see Gunn, Stephen and Monckton, Linda (eds), *Arthur Tudor, Prince of Wales, Life, Death and Commemoration* (Boydell Press, 2009).
10. Tremlett.
11. Receyt.
12. *Ibid.*
13. *Ibid.*
14. *Ibid.*

5 The Young Widow, 1502–03
1. Henry Howard, Earl of Surrey.
2. Cotton MS Vitellus Appendix xxvii f. 145.
3. Hutchinson, Robert, *The Rise of Henry VIII* (Weidenfeld and Nicolson, 2011).
4. CSP Spain May 1502.
5. *Ibid.*
6. *Ibid.*
7. *Ibid.*

6 Betrothal Games, 1503–05
1. Anon, 'Greensleeves'.
2. Tremlett.
3. Stow, John, *The Survey of London* (Everyman, 1912).
4. Vergil, Polydore, *Anglia Historia 1485–1537.*
5. CSP Spain April 1503.
6. *Ibid.*
7. CSP Spain June 1503.
8. *Ibid.*
9. Erickson.
10. CSP Spain June 1503.
11. Tremlett.
12. CSP Spain June 1505.
13. *Ibid.*
14. *Ibid.*

7 The Other Spanish Princess, 1506–07
1. From Skelton, John, 'Go, Piteous Heart'.
2. Matusiak.
3. *Ibid.*
4. CSP Spain Sept. 1505.
5. *Ibid.*
6. Wood, Mary Anne Everett (ed.), *Letters of Royal and Illustrious Ladies of Great Britain*, Volume 1 (London: Henry Colburn, 1846).
7. *Ibid.*
8. CSP Spain June 1505.
9. *Ibid.*
10. Matusiak.
11. CSP Spain 1507.
12. *Ibid.*
13. Hutchinson.
14. Tremlett.
15. Vergil.
16. Hutchinson.
17. BL Add MS 21, 404 fl. 9.
18. Tremlett.
19. CSP Spain March 1507.
20. *Ibid.*
21. CSP Spain Oct. 1506.
22. *Ibid.*
23. CSP Spain Oct. 1507.
24. CSP Spain April 1507.

8 Princess of Scandal, 1507–09
1. From Skelton, John 'The Bowge of Court'.

2. Fredericks.
3. Hutchinson.
4. Williams.
5. *Letters of Royal and Illustrious Ladies.*
6. CSP Spain Supplement to Volumes 1 and 2, Queen Katherine.
7. *Ibid.*
8. Tremlett.
9. CSP Spain Supplement, Queen Katherine.
10. Williams.
11. Mattingly, Garrett.
12. Tremlett.
13. *Ibid.*
14. CSPS Supp. QK.
15. *Ibid.*
16. CSP Spain March 1509.
14. CSPS Supp. QK.
17. *Ibid.*
18. CSP Spain March 1509.
19. Tremlett.
20. CSP Spain March 1509.
21. *Ibid.*
22. *Ibid.*
23. CSP Spain Supp. QK.
24. Erickson.

9 In Henry's Bed, June 1509
1. Gower, from *Confessio Amantis.*
2. Hutchinson.
3. *Ibid.*
4. Williams.
5. Starkey.
6. Williams.
7. Anglo.
8. *Ibid.*
9. *Archaeologia.*
10. Tannahill.
11. Niebrzydowski, Sue, *Bonoure and Buxom: A Study of Wives in Late Medieval Literature* (Peter Land, 2006).
12. Jones, P.
13. Dunbar.
14. SLP Henry VIII April 1533.

10 Coronation, 24 June 1509
1. 2 Kings, 11:12.
2. CSP Spain June 1509.

3. Hall.
4. Hutchinson.
5. SLP Henry VIII July 1509.
6. *Ibid.*
7. Hall.
8. More.
9. *Ibid.*
10. Hall.
11. *Ibid.*
12. *Ibid.*

11 Catherine's Court, 1509
1. Thomas More's coronation verses.
2. *Ibid.*
3. Skelton, John, *Speculum principis* (1501).
4. Williams.
5. More, © Yale University Press.
6. CSP Henry VIII July 1509.
7. *Ibid.*
8. CSP Spain July 1509.
9. Starkey.
10. CSP Spain Supplement 1510.
11. Niebrzydowski.
12. *Ibid.*
13. *Ibid.*
14. Anon., *Sidrak and Bokkus.*
15. Williams.

12 Pregnancy, 1509–10
1. Anon., *Sidrak and Bokkus.*
2. Licence, Amy, *In Bed with the Tudors* (Amberley, 2012).
3. *Sidrak and Bokkus.*
4. *Ibid.*
5. SLP Henry VIII 1509.
6. Hall.
7. SLP Henry VIII May 1509.

13 Anne, Lady Hastings, 1510
1. More.
2. Holinshed.
3. SLP Henry VIII May 1510.
4. *Ibid.*
5. Stow.
6. *Ibid.*
7. Fraser.
8. Norton, Elizabeth, *The Boleyn Women* (Amberley, 2013).
9. SLP Henry VIII March 1522.

14 The Baby Prince, 1510–11
1. *Sidrak and Bokkus.*
2. Thurley.
3. Fox.
4. Chamberlayne.
5. *Ibid.*
6. Hall.
7. *Ibid.*
8. Holinshed.
9. Niebrzydowski.

15 Regent, 1511–13
1. Williams, letter from Catherine to Henry.
2. CSP Spain November 1512.
3. SLP Henry VIII June 1513.
4. Hastead.
5. Starkey.
6. *Ibid.*
7. Starkey.
8. SLP Milan Sept. 1512.
9. *Ibid.*
10. Fox.
11. SLP Milan Sept. 1513.
12. *Ibid.*

16 Etiennette de la Baume, 1513
1. Wyatt.
2. SLP Milan Sept. 1513.
3. *Ibid.*
4. *Ibid.*
5. *Ibid.* Oct.
6. SLP Henry VIII Oct. 1513.
7. Hall.
8. *Ibid.*
9. SLP Henry VIII Aug. 1514.
10. *Ibid.*
11. *Ibid.*
12. *Ibid.*

17 Jane Popincourt, 1514
1. Heywood, *The Play of the Weather.*
2. CSP Venice Sept. 1514.
3. *Ibid.*
4. SLP Henry VIII Aug. 1514.
5. Jones.
6. Hall.
7. CSP Venice Aug. 1514.
8. Fraser.

18 Elizabeth Carew, 1514
1. Skelton, John, *Womanhood, Wanton Ye Want.*
2. Michell.
3. Weir.
4. Matusiak.
5. SLP Henry VIII Nov. 1514.
6. Matusiak.
7. Warnicke.
8. SLP Henry VIII Sept. 1537.
9. Erickson.

19 Labour and Loss, 1514–15
1. Caxton.
2. SLP Henry VIII Nov. 1515.
3. Hall.
4. SLP Dec. 1514.
5. Holinshed.
6. Kramer, Kyra, *Blood Will Tell: A Medical Explanation for the Tyranny of Henry VIII* (CreateSpace, 2012).
7. *Sidrak and Bokkus.*
8. *Ibid.*
9. *Ibid.*

20 Catching the King's Eye, 1514–15
1. Anon, *Guystarde and Sygysmonde* (1532).
2. Hall.
3. Possibly a misspelling of St Leger.
4. Hall.
5. Vives, *Education of a Christian Woman* (1524).
6. *Ibid.*
7. Heywood, *The Play of the Weather.*
8. *Ibid.*
9. SLP Henry VIII Oct. 1515.
10. SLP Henry VIII Dec. 1514.
11. SLP Henry VIII Jan. 1515.
12. *Ibid.*
13. Holinshed.
14. Hall.
15. *Ibid.*
16. *Ibid.*

21 Begetting a Boy, 1515–16
1. Anon.
2. Benedek.
3. *Ibid.*
4. Furdell.
5. *Ibid.*

6. *Ibid.*
7. CSP Spain Oct. 1515.
8. SLP Henry VIII Jan. 1516.
9. Guistinian.
10. Starkey.

22 The Quiet Queen, 1516–18
1. Skelton, John, *A Garland of Laurels.*
2. Cherbury.
3. Matusiak.
4. *Ibid.*
5. SLP Henry VIII April 1518.
6. Weir.
7. Hall.
8. *Ibid.*
9. *Ibid.*
10. Starkey.

23 The Illegitimate Son, 1519
1. Wyatt.
2. Perry.
3. Skelton.
4. Burke.

24 The Proud Aunt, 1520
1. Anon., 'Greensleeves'.
2. Tremlett.
3. SLP Venice 1520.
4. SLP Henry VIII May 1520.
5. Hall.
6. *Ibid.*
7. *Ibid.*
8. Fox.
9. SLP Henry VIII May 1520.
10. *Ibid.*
11. *Ibid.*
12. *Ibid.*
13. *Ibid.*

25 Field of Cloth of Gold, 1520
1. More.
2. Hall.
3. *Ibid.*
4. *Ibid.*
5. Rutland Papers.
6. Cotton MS Augustus III 18.
7. *Ibid.*
8. SLP Henry VIII June 1520.
9. Hall.
10. SLP Henry VIII June 1520.
11. *Ibid.*

12. Hall.
13. *Ibid.*
14. SLP Henry VIII June 1520.
15. Rutland.
16. *Ibid.*
17. SLP June 1520.
18. *Ibid.*
19. *Ibid.*
20. Rutland.
21. SLP Henry VIII June 1520.
22. June.

26 Mother of the Princess, 1520–22
1. More.
2. SLP Henry VIII Sept. 1520.
3. *Letters of Royal and Illustrious Ladies.*
4. SLP Henry VIII Jan. 1521.
5. Fox.
6. *Ibid.*
7. Hall.
8. *Ibid.*
9. More.

27 Kindness, 1520–22
1. *Castle of Perseverance.*
2. Hall.
3. *Ibid.*
4. Lingard.
5. Cattermole.
6. Lingard 2.
7. Emery.
8. Norton.
9. *Ibid.*
10. Perry.
11. Chaucer, *The Merchant's Tale.*
12. Norton.
13. Weir.
14. Norton.
15. http://www.webmd.com/sexual-conditions/tc/syphilis-what-increases-your-risk.

28 The King's Mistress, 1522–25
1. Wyatt.
2. Hall.
3. Thurley.
4. http://www.bbc.co.uk/dna/place-london/A49292760.
5. Thurley.
6. Weir.

7. Lydgate, John, *Dietary*.
8. The Bible.
9. SLP Venice June 1525.

29 The Other Boleyn Girl, 1513–22
1. Marguerite of Navarre, *Chansons* in Picker.
2. *Ibid*.
3. Ives.
4. Picker.
5. *Ibid*.
6. Warnicke.
7. Picker.
8. *Ibid*.
9. Denny.
10. *Ibid*.
11. *Ibid*.
12. Wilkinson.
13. Ridgway and Cherry.
14. Grueninger and Morris.
15. Norton.
16. SLP Henry VIII Feb. 1528.

30 Henry Percy's Fiancée, 1522–23
1. Wyatt.
2. Cavendish.
3. *Ibid*.
4. *Ibid*.
5. *Ibid*.
6. *Ibid*.
7. *Ibid*.
8. Norton.

31 Brunet, 1523–25
1. Wyatt.
2. Cavendish.
3. Shulman.
4. Cavendish.
5. Hall.
6. *Ibid*.
7. *Ibid*.
8. *Ibid*.
9. *Ibid*.
10. *Ibid*.
11. *Ibid*.
12. *Ibid*.
13. *Ibid*.
14. *Ibid*.
15. *Ibid*.
16. *Ibid*.

17. *Ibid*.
18. Skelton.
19. Cavendish.

32 A Vanishing World, 1525–26
1. Skelton.
2. Hall.
3. Vives.
4. *Ibid*.
5. Letter of Henry VIII to Anne Boleyn, reproduced in Norton.
6. *Ibid*.
7. *Ibid*.

33 Love Letters, 1526–27
1. SLP Henry VIII.
2. *Ibid*.
3. *Ibid*.
4. *Ibid*.
5. SLP Spain 1527.
6. *Spanish Chronicle*.
7. Letters of Henry VIII to Anne Boleyn, from Norton.

34 Anticipation, 1527
1. Wyatt.
2. Hall.
3. *Ibid*.
4. SLP Henry VIII Sep 1527.
5. *Ibid*.
6. CSP Spain March 1527.
7. *Ibid*.
8. CSP Spain March 1527.
9. *Ibid*.

35 The King's Darling, 1527–28
1. Mendoza in SLP.
2. *Ibid*.
3. *Ibid*.
4. *Ibid*.
5. SLP Spain 1527.
6. *Spanish Chronicle*.
7. Letters in Norton.
8. SLP Henry VIII 1527.
9. Vives.
10. Tremlett.
11. SLP Henry VIII Nov. 1527.
12. *Ibid*.
13. *Ibid*.

36 Ménage à Trois, 1527–28
1. Dante.
2. Norton.
3. *Ibid.*
4. *Ibid.*
5. SLP Miscellaneous 1531.
6. *Ibid.*
7. *Ibid.*
8. *Ibid.*
9. Grueninger and Morris.
10. SLP.
11. Fox.

37 The Blackfriars Trial, 1529
1. Cavendish.
2. *Ibid.*
3. *Ibid.*
4. *Ibid.*
5. *Ibid.*
6. *Ibid.*
7. SLP Henry VIII Oct. 1529.
8. *Ibid.*
9. *Ibid.*
10. SLP Henry VIII Dec. 1529.
11. SLP Henry VIII Oct. 1529.
12. SLP Henry VIII Nov./Dec. 1529.
13. *Ibid.*
14. CSP Spain 1529.
15. *Ibid.*
16. *Ibid.*
17. *Ibid.*

38 The Other Women, 1525–32
1. From a poem about George Boleyn.
2. SLP Henry VIII Aug. 1524.
3. Jones.
4. SLP Henry VIII Jan. 1547.
5. Ordinances.
6. Lingard, John, *A History of England from the First Invasion of the Romans to the Accession of Henry VIII*, Volume 6 (1819).
7. SLP Henry VIII Feb. 1531.
8. *Ibid.*
9. SLP Henry VIII Dec. 1530.
10. SLP Henry VIII Jan. 1531.

39 Rejected Queen, 1531–32
1. Grueninger and Morris.
2. SLP Henry VIII May 1531.
3. Grueninger and Morris.
4. *Ibid.*
5. Thurley.
6. SLP Henry VIII Nov. 1532.
7. *Ibid.*
8. *Ibid.*
9. SLP Henry VIII Nov. 1531.
10. Hall.
11. SLP Henry VIII Jan. 1532.
12. *Ibid.*
13. SLP Henry VIII May 1532.
14. SLP Henry VIII 1532.
15. Hall.

40 Calais, 1532
1. Anon., *Romance of Sir Tyramore*.
2. SLP Henry VIII Sept. 1532.
3. SLP Henry VIII June 1532.
4. *Ibid.*
5. *Ibid.*
6. *Ibid.*
7. *Ibid.*
8. Hall.
9. *Ibid.*

41 Rise of the Falcon, 1533
1. Udall.
2. Hall.
3. *Ibid.*
4. *Ibid.*
5. *Ibid.*
6. *Ibid.*
7. Thurley.
8. Williams.
9. Denny.
10. SLP Henry VIII Aug. 1533.

42 A Familiar Story, 1533–34
1. Ovid.
2. British History Online, Victoria County History, Cambridgeshire.
3. *Ibid.*

43 The Shelton Sisters, 1535
1. Udall.
2. SLP Henry VIII Dec. 1535.
3. *Ibid.*
4. Hall.
5. SLP Henry VIII Oct. 1535.
6. SLP Henry VIII Dec. 1535.
7. Devonshire MS.
8. *Ibid.*

44 Death of a Queen, January 1536
1. Anon., 'Greensleeves'.
2. SLP Henry VIII 1535.
3. *Ibid.*
4. Warnicke.
5. SLP Henry VIII Jan. 1536.
6. *Ibid.*
7. *Ibid.*
8. *Ibid.*
9. Denny.
10. Wilson.
11. Denny.

45 A Little Neck, May 1536
1. Wyatt.
2. SLP Henry VIII 1536.
3. *Spanish Chronicle.*
4. Weir.
5. Cavendish.
6. Norton.
7. SLP Vienna 1536.
8. Bernard, G. W., *Fatal Attractions* (Yale University Press, 2011).

46 Queen Jane, 1536–37
1. Anonymous Ballad.
2. Norton.
3. SLP Henry VIII 1536.
4. *Ibid.*
5. *Ibid.*
6. SLP May 1536.
7. *Ibid.*
8. SLP Henry VIII June 1536.
9. Lisle Letters.
10. SLP June 1536.
11. *Ibid.*
12. CSP Spain June 1536.
13. SLP 1536.
14. SLP June 1536.
15. SLP Miscellaneous 1536.

47 A Prince at Last, 1537
1. SLP Henry VIII Jan. 1541.
2. SLP Sept. 1536.
3. SLP Oct. 1536.
4. SLP Jan. 1537.
5. Lisle Letters.
6. *Ibid.*
7. *Ibid.*
8. *Ibid.*
9. SLP July 1537.

10. SLP Sep 1537.
11. *Ibid.*
12. SLP Oct. 1537.
13. *Ibid.*
14. *Ibid.*
15. *Ibid.*
16. *Ibid.*
17. *Ibid.*
18. *Ibid.*
19. SLP Oct. 1537.
20. *Ibid.*
21. *Ibid.*
22. *Ibid.*
23. *Ibid.*
24. *Ibid.*

48 Vacancy in the Bed, 1537–39
1. Wyatt.
2. SLP Henry VIII Oct. 1537.
3. Fraser.
4. SLP 1537.
5. Erickson.
6. SLP Nov. 1537.
7. SLP Dec. 1537.
8. Warnicke.
9. *Ibid.*
10. SLP 1537.
11. *Ibid.*
12. *Ibid.*
13. SLP Jan. 1538.
14. SLP 1538.
15. Lisle Letters.
16. *Ibid.*
17. *Ibid.*
18. SLP Dec. 1537.
19. SLP June 1539.
20. Lisle.
21. SLP Jan. 1538.
22. SLP April 1539.
23. Erickson.
24. Surrey.
25. SLP Jan. 1539.
26. SLP July 1539.
27. SLP July 1539.
28. Lisle Letters.
29. SLP June 1539.
30. SLP 1539.

49 I Like Her Not, 1539–40
1. Heywood.

2. SLP 1539.
3. *Ibid.*
4. Hall.
5. SLP Dec. 1539.
6. *Ibid.*
7. Fraser.
8. *Ibid.*
9. *Ibid.*
10. *Ibid.*
11. SLP Dec. 1539.
12. *Ibid.*
13. SLP 1539.
14. Hall.
15. SLP Dec. 1539.
16. Hall.

50 The Unwanted Bride, 1540
1. Chaucer.
2. Hall.
3. SLP Henry VIII Jan. 1540.
4. Hall.
5. *Ibid.*
6. SLP Jan. 1540.
7. Hall.
8. *Ibid.*
9. *Ibid.*
10. Fraser.
11. Hall.
12. *Ibid.*
13. *Ibid.*

51 The King's Infatuation, 1540
1. Surrey.
2. Hall.
3. SLP Henry VIII Jan. 1540.
4. *Ibid.*
5. *Ibid.*
6. *Ibid.*
7. SLP Feb. 1540.
8. SLP April 1540.
9. SLP 1539.
10. Lacey Baldwin-Smith.
11. *Ibid.*
12. Hart.
13. Starkey.
14. *Ibid.*
15. *Ibid.*
16. Starkey.
17. *Ibid.*
18. *Ibid.*

52 The King's Sister, 1540
1. More.
2. SLP Henry VIII July 1540.
3. *Ibid.*
4. *Ibid.*
5. Furdell.
6. Warnicke.
7. SLP July 1540.
8. *Ibid.*
9. *Ibid.*
10. *Ibid.*
11. *Ibid.*
12. *Ibid.*
13. *Ibid.*
14. *Ibid.*
15. *Ibid.*
16. *Ibid.*
17. *Ibid.*
18. Warnicke.
19. SLP July 1540.
20. *Ibid.*
21. *Ibid.*
22. *Ibid.*
23. *Ibid.*

53 Rose Without a Thorn, 1540–41
1. Anon., *Wives in the Tavern.*
2. SLP Henry VIII May 1540.
3. SLP July 1540.
4. *Ibid.*
5. SLP July 1540.
6. *Ibid.*
7. SLP Aug. 1540.
8. SLP Sept. 1540.
9. *Ibid.*
10. Lydgate, *Dietary.*
11. SLP 1540.
12. *Ibid.*
13. SLP Jan. 1541.
14. SLP May 1541.
15. *Ibid.*

54 An Old Fool, 1541–42
1. Heywood.
2. Robinson.
3. SLP Henry VIII April 1541.
4. SLP July 1541.
5. SLP August 1541.
6. Starkey.
7. *Ibid.*

8. SLP November 1541.
9. *Ibid.*
10. Hutchinson.
11. SLP Nov. 1541.
12. SLP Nov. 1541.
13. *Ibid.*
14. *Ibid.*
15. *Ibid.*
16. *Ibid.*
17. *Ibid.*
18. *Ibid.*
19. SLP Feb. 1542.
20. *Ibid.*

55 The Learned Widow, 1542–43
1. Surrey.
2. SLP Henry VIII Nov. 1541.
3. *The Remonstrance of Anne of Cleves.*
4. SLP Jan. 1542.
5. *Ibid.*
6. *Ibid.*
7. SLP Sept. 1540.
8. SLP June 1541.
9. SLP Dec. 1542.
10. SLP Feb. 1543.
11. Hall.
12. SLP July 1543.
13. Hamilton.
14. SLP 1543.
15. *Ibid.*

16. Hamilton.
17. *Ibid.*
18. Porter.
19. Fraser.

56 More than an Ornament, 1544–45
1. Surrey.
2. Weir.
3. *Ibid.*
4. SLP July 1544.
5. SLP Aug. 1544.
6. SLP Sep. 1544.
7. SLP Aug. 1545.
8. Hall.
9. SLP Dec. 1545.

57 Queen in Danger, 1546
1. Surrey.
2. Foxe.
3. SLP Feb. 1546.
4. Hutchinson.
5. Foxe.
6. *Ibid.*
7. *Ibid.*
8. Hall.
9. Weir.
10. SLP Jan. 1547.

58 The Survivors, 1547
1. Anon., 'Greensleeves'.
2. SLP Feb. 1547.
3. *Excerpta Historica.*

Bibliography

Ackroyd, Peter, *Tudors* (Pan Macmillan, 2012)

Anglo, Sydney, *Images of Tudor Kingship* (Seaby, 1992)

Anon., 'The Reputation of Dr De Puebla', *English Historical Review*, LV (CCLXVII) 27–46 (1940)

Anon., 'The Receyt of the Ladie Kateryn' in Astle, Thomas and Grose, Francis *et al.* (eds), *The Antiquarian Repertory: a miscellaneous assemblage of topography, history, biography, customs and manners intended to illustrate and preserve several valuable remains of old times* (London: E. Jeffery, 1807)

Benedek, Thomas G., 'Beliefs about Human Sexuality Function in the Middle Ages and Renaissance' in Radcliff-Umstead, Douglas (ed.), *Human Sexuality in the Middle Ages and Renaissance* (Pittsburgh, 1978)

Bentley, Samuel, *Exerpta Historica* (London: Richard Bentley, 1833)

Bernard, G. W., *Fatal Attractions* (Yale University Press, 2011)

Bordo, Susan, *The Creation of Anne Boleyn* (Houghton Mifflin, 2013)

Brooke, in 'Archaeologia: Or Miscellaeneous Tracts relating to Antiquity', *The Society of Antiquaries of London*, IV (1777)

Burke, Hubert S., *Historical Portrait of the Tudor Dynasty* (1883)

Cattermole, Philip H., *John Lingard, The Historian as Apologist* (Troubador, 2013)

Chamberlayne, Joanna, L., 'Medieval Queens 1445–1503' (University of York: Unpublished doctoral thesis, 1999)

Chapman, Hester W., *Anne Boleyn* (Jonathan Cape, 1974)

Cowans, Jon (ed.), *Early Modern Spain: A Documentary History* (University of Pennsylvania, 2003).

Cressy, David, *Birth, Marriage and Death: Ritual, Religion and the Life-Cycle in Tudor and Stuart England* (Oxford University Press, 1997)

Cressy, David, *Travesties and Transgression in Tudor and Stuart England* (Oxford University Press, 2000)

CSP Milan

CSP Spain

CSP Venice

Denny, Joanna, *Anne Boleyn* (Portrait, 2004)

Denny, Joanna, *Katherine Howard, A Tudor Conspiracy* (Piatkus, 2007)

Eccles, Audrey, *Obstetrics and Gynaecology in Tudor and Stuart England* (Croom Helm, 1982)

Emery, Anthony, *Greater Medieval Houses of England and Wales 1300–1500 Volume 2, East Anglia, Central England and Wales* (Cambridge University Press, 2000)

Carolly, *Great Harry: The Extravagant Life of Henry VIII* (Robson Books,
  ...dn)

...hristopher (ed.), *The Private Lives of the Tudor Monarchs* (London Folio
  Society, 1974)

Fletcher, Catherine, *The Divorce of Henry VIII: The Untold Story* (Vintage, 2013)

Fox, Julia, *Jane Boleyn: The Infamous Lady Rochford* (Phoenix, 2007)

Fox, Julia, *Sister Queens: Katherine of Aragon and Juana, Queen of Castile*
  (Weidenfeld and Nicolson, 2011)

Foxe, John, *Foxe's Book of Martyrs*

Fraser, Antonia, *The Six Wives of Henry VIII* (Weidenfeld and Nicolson, 1992)

Fredericks, Randi, *Fasting: An Exceptional Human Experience* (Author House,
  2012)

Furdell, Elizabeth Lane, *The Royal Doctors 1485–1714: Medical Personnel at the
  Tudor and Stuart Court.*

Gransden, K. W., *Tudor Verse Satire* (The Athlone Press, 1970)

Gunn, Stephen, and Monckton, Linda (eds), *Arthur Tudor, Prince of Wales, Life,
  Death and Commemoration* (Boydell Press, 2009)

Hall-King, Evelyn, *Passionate Lives* (Piatkus, 1985)

Hamilton, Dakota L., *The Household of Queen Katherine Parr* (Somerville College,
  Oxford University: unpublished thesis, 1992)

Hart, Kelly, *The Mistresses of Henry VIII* (The History Press, 2009)

Hastead, Edward, *The History and Topographical Survey of the County of Kent,*
  Volume 12 (BHO 1801)

Hayward, Maria, *Treasured Possessions: The Material World of Henry VIII*
  (Southampton University: Unpublished essay)

Hutchinson, Robert, *The Last Days of Henry VIII* (Phoenix, 2005)

Hutchinson, Robert, *The Rise of Henry VIII* (Weidenfeld and Nicolson, 2011)

Ives, Eric, *The Life and Death of Anne Boleyn, The Most Happy* (Wiley-Blackwell,
  2005)

Jones, Philippa, *The Other Tudors: Henry VIII's Mistresses and Bastards* (New
  Holland, 2009)

Kramer, Kyra, *Blood Will Tell: A Medical Explanation for the Tyranny of Henry VIII*
  (CreateSpace, 2012)

Licence, A. L., *In Bed with the Tudors* (Amberley, 2012)

Lingard, John, *A History of England from the First Invasion of the Romans to the
  Accession of Henry VIII*, Volume 6 (1819)

Lingard, John, *A Vindication of Certain Passages in the Fourth and Fifth Volumes of
  the History of England* (London: J. Mawman, 1826).

Makowski, Elizabeth M., *The Conjugal Debt and Medieval Canon Law* from
  Various, *Equally in God's Image: Women in the Middle Ages* (Peter Lang, 1990)

Michell, Ronald, *The Carews of Beddington* (Sutton, 1981)

Morris, Sarah and Grueninger, Natalie, *In the Footsteps of Anne Boleyn* (Amberley,
  2013)

Murphy, A. Beverley, *Bastard Prince: Henry VIII's Lost Son* (The History Press,
  2001)

Niebrzydowski, Sue, *Bonoure and Buxom: A Study of Wives in Late Medieval
  Literature* (Peter Land, 2006)

Nichols, John Gough, *London Pageants 1: An Account of Sixty Royal Processions
  and Entertainments in the city of London* (J. B. Nichols and Son, 1831)

Nichols, Robert E. Jnr, 'Procreation, Pregnancy and Parturition: Extracts from a
  Middle English Metrical' in *Medical History Journal*, 11(2) (April, 1967)

Norton, Elizabeth *Anne Boleyn in Her Own Words and the Words of Those Who Knew Her* (Amberley, 2011)

Norton, Elizabeth, *Anne of Cleves, Henry VIII's Discarded Bride* (Amberley, 2010)

Norton, Elizabeth, *Bessie Blount* (Amberley, 2011)

Norton, Elizabeth, *Catherine Parr* (Amberley, 2011)

Norton, Elizabeth, *Jane Seymour, Henry VIII's True Love* (Amberley, 2010)

Norton, Elizabeth, *The Boleyn Women* (Amberley, 2013)

Page, William (ed.), *A History of the County of Kent*, Volume 2 (Victoria County History Series, 1926)

Palmer, M. D., *Henry VIII* (Longman, 1971)

Picker, Martin, *The Chanson Albums of Marguerite of Austria* (University of California, 1965)

Porter, Linda, *Katherine the Queen* (Pan Macmillan, 2010)

Ridgway, Claire and Cherry, Clare, *George Boleyn: Tudor Poet, Courtier and Diplomat* (MadeGlobal, 2014)

Robinson, H. (ed.), *Original Letters Relative to the English Reformation* (Cambridge, 1846–47)

Rowse, A. L., *Court and Country: Studies in Tudor Social History* (Harvester, 1987)

SLP Henry VII 1485–1509

SLP Henry VIII 1509–1547

Shulman, Nicola, *Graven with Diamonds* (Short Books, 2011)

Smith, Lacey Baldwin, *Anne Boleyn: The Queen of Controversy* (Amberley, 2013)

Smith, Lacey Baldwin, *Henry VIII: The Mask of Royalty* (Jonathan Cape, 1971)

Spanish Chronicle

Starkey, David, *Henry: The Prince Who Would Turn into a Tyrant* (Harper Collins, 2009)

Starkey, David, *Six Wives: The Queens of Henry VIII* (Vintage, 2004)

Stow, John, *The Survey of London* (Everyman, 1912)

Stuart, Nancy Rubin, *Isabella of Castile, the First Renaissance Queen* (St Martin's Press, 1991)

Tannahill, Reay, *Sex in History* (Hamish Hamilton, 1980)

Tremlett, Giles, *Catherine of Aragon: Henry's Spanish Queen* (Faber and Faber, 2010)

Vergil, Polydore, *Anglia Historia 1485–1537*

Warnicke, Retha M., *The Rise and Fall of Anne Boleyn* (Cambridge University Press, 1989)

Warnicke, Retha M., *The Marrying of Anne of Cleves: Royal Protocol in Tudor England* (Cambridge University Press, 2000)

Weir, Alison, *Henry VIII: King and Court* (Jonathan Cape, 2001)

Weir, Alison, *Mary Boleyn: The Great and Infamous Whore* (Jonathan Cape, 2011)

Wilkinson, Josephine, *Anne Boleyn: The Young Queen to Be* (Amberley, 2009)

Williams, Neville, *Henry VIII and his Court* (Weidenfeld and Nicolson, 1971)

Williams, Patrick, *Katharine of Aragon* (Amberley, 2013)

Wilson, Derek, *In the Lion's Court Power, Ambition and Sudden Death in the Reign of Henry VIII* (Pimlico, 2002)

Wood, Mary Anne Everett, *Letters of Royal and Illustrious Ladies of Great Britain* (London: Henry Colburn, 1846)

Acknowledgements

Thanks go to the team at Amberley, particularly Jonathan and Nicola for their continuing support and promotion. I have also been particularly lucky to have made some wonderfully helpful and knowledgeable friends online who have generously shared their thoughts and time with me, in particular the members of my Edward IV discussion group. Thanks also to all my family, to my husband Tom for his love and support; also the Hunts, for Sue's generosity and John's local knowledge and continual supply of interesting and unusual books. Most of all, this book is for my mother for her invaluable proofreading skills and for my father for his empathy and enthusiasm. This is the result of the books they read me, the museums they took me to as a child and the love and imagination with which they encouraged me.

List of Illustrations

1. Steve Cadman
2. Jonathan Reeve JRCD2b20p769 15501600
3. Jonathan Reeve JR962b20p895 15001600
4. Courtesy of Ripon Cathedral
5. Elizabeth Norton
6. Elizabeth Norton
7. Elizabeth Norton
8. Amy Licence
9. Elizabeth Norton
10. Courtesy of Hever Castle
11. Grueninger and Morris
12. Courtesy of Ripon Cathedral
13. Amy Licence
14. Grueninger and Morris
15. Elizabeth Norton
16. Courtesy of Ripon Cathedral
17. George Groutas
18. Elizabeth Norton
19. Stephen Porter
20. Elizabeth Norton
21. Elizabeth Norton
22. Stephen Porter
23. Elizabeth Norton
24. Jonathan Reeve JRpc219 15001550
25. Paul Fairbrass
26. Amy Licence
27. Elizabeth Norton
28. Paul Fairbrass
29. Elizabeth Norton
30. Jonathan Reeve JR998b66fp56 15001600
31. Elizabeth Norton

Index

Kings & Queens of England from Amberley Publishing

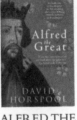

THOMAS CROMWELL
David Loades

'Fresh, fair, lucid and a pleasure to read'.
HILARY MANTEL

£25.99   978-1-4456-1538-7   352 pages HB 27 illus, 20 col

INSIDE THE TUDOR COURT
Lauren Mackay

'A superb, sound, engagingly written & much needed study...
highly recommended '
ALISON WEIR

£20.00   978-1-4456-0957-7   288 pages HB

ALFRED THE GREAT
David Horspool

'If you have time to read just one book about the great man, you
should make it this one'
THE DAILY TELEGRAPH

£9.99   978-1-4456-3936-9   272 pages PB 40 illus, 30 col

THE PRINCES IN THE TOWER
Josephine Wilkinson

'Wilkinson investigates the prime suspects, asks wether they might have
survived and presents her own theory about what really happened to them'
ALL ABOUT HISTORY

£18.99   978-1-4456-1974-3   192 pages HB

QUEEN VICTORIA & THE STALKER
Jan Bondeson

'The amazing story of the first celebrity stalker' **THE SUN**

£12.99   978-1-4456-0697-2   224 pages PB 47 illus

RICHARD III
Terry Breverton

£16.99   978-1-4456-2105-0   200 pages HB 20 col illus

CATHERINE HOWARD
Lacey Baldwin Smith

'Beautifully written'
SUZANNAH LIPSCOMB, BBC HISTORY MAGAZINE

£9.99   978-1-84868-321-5   288 pages PB 25 col illus

JANE SEYMOUR
David Loades

£20.00   978-1-4456-1157-0   192 pages HB 40 illus, 20 col

RICHARD III
Amy Licence

£9.99 978-1-4456-2175-3

96 pages PB 75 col illus

THE KINGS AND QUEENS OF ENGLAND
Robert J. Parker

£9.99 978-1-4456-1497-7

128 pages PB 80 illus

ANNE OF CLEVES
Elizabeth Norton

£9.99 978-1-4456-0183-0

224 pages PB 57 illus, 27 col

RICHARD III
Peter Rex

£12.99 978-1-4456-0476-1

256 pages PB 30 col illus

Also available as ebooks
Available from all good bookshops or to order direct
Please call **01453-847-800 www.amberley-books.com**